Assessing Risk Assessment

Christian Hugo Hoffmann

Assessing Risk Assessment

Towards Alternative Risk Measures for Complex Financial Systems

Springer Gabler

Christian Hugo Hoffmann
Kreuzlingen, Switzerland

Dissertation der Universität St. Gallen, 2017

Die Universität St. Gallen, Hochschule für Wirtschafts-, Rechts- und Sozialwissenschaften sowie internationale Beziehungen (HSG), gestattet hiermit die Drucklegung der vorliegenden Dissertation, ohne damit zu den darin angesprochenen Anschauungen Stellung zu nehmen.

OnlinePlus material to this book is available on
http://www.springer.com/978-3-658-20032-9

ISBN 978-3-658-20031-2 ISBN 978-3-658-20032-9 (eBook)
https://doi.org/10.1007/978-3-658-20032-9

Library of Congress Control Number: 2017957211

Springer Gabler

Printed on acid-free paper

This Springer Gabler imprint is published by Springer Nature
The registered company is Springer Fachmedien Wiesbaden GmbH
The registered company address is: Abraham-Lincoln-Str. 46, 65189 Wiesbaden, Germany

Table of Contents

To access the book's appendix, please visit www.springer.com and search for the author's name. URL: http://www.springer.com/978-3-658-20032-9

[illegible]

List of Tables and Figures

Abstract

Traditional and much of modern risk assessment and management is old fashioned, unrealistic and trapped in a dogmatic slumber. It generates its own risks, evoked by an improper notion of risk which lacks a systemic viewpoint. A culture dominates theory (economics and finance) and practice (financial institutions) where risk modeling is no longer a *functional* tool but has become an end in itself. It is high time to put an end to the cult of conventional probabilistic risk modeling which is not able to cope with the kind of low-probability, high-impact events that characterize systemic risk, in particular.

In this dissertation, our aim is threefold. Our first result is a negative one: We argue – from a complexity and systems science perspective – that modern financial systems are dynamically and organizationally complex which requires explanatory models for an effective and successful approach to the management of systemic risks. Yet, risk evaluations based on statistical calculations are not sufficiently explanatory. Even worse for the mainstream, this study undermines the citadel of risk assessment and management, arguing that *probability theory is not an adequate foundation for modeling systemic and extreme risk (in a banking context)*.

Secondly, we present a kind of risk model on the constructive side which is novel on two accounts. Firstly, in contrast to standard risk modeling approaches used by banks, our proposal focuses on the knowledge dimension (banks' assets and liabilities are known) rather than the speculation dimension (unknown minimum or expected losses). Furthermore, in contrast to risk models aimed at regulators who analyze systemic risk in order to preserve financial stability, our objective is not to model the financial system and its changes, but market participants' own positions and their propensity to react to outside changes. Our plea for symbolic and logic-based risk modeling is illustrated with the example of a certain credit crisis (Long-Term Capital Management) which we regard as a systemic risk event in terms of its high rareness and its serious or extreme consequences. In this context, our approach is based on the following key ideas: We formally represent extreme and systemic risks that financial institutions are exposed to by measuring risks of their financial products and instruments (derivatives such as options, swaps, futures, etc.) which we describe in a programming language for financial contracts. This vocabulary is based on a small set of primitive or atomic contracts that are expressive enough to reconstruct many of them through composition. Programs in this language are then interpreted as uncertain sequences of transactions, which can be grounded in a number of different formal models of uncertainty. While domain-specific languages have been well-researched within functional programming, as have uncertainty models within formal epistemology, the potential of a combination of the two for a novel approach to risk management has not been realized so far. Our work seeks to close this important gap and to expand the toolset for assessing extreme and systemic financial risks effectively.

The thesis is thirdly closed by a synthetical reflection on methods by elaborating on the meaning of decision-making competency in a risk management context in banking. By choosing this poly-dimensional approach, its purpose is, finally, to not only systematically explore shortcomings of financial institutions' risk management approaches, but also to point out how they might be overcome. In the end, this thesis intends to contribute to the development of a more stable and humane financial economy by means of a truly effective or an effectively effective, rather than an efficiency-seeking but eventually ineffective, risk management approach for banks.

Zusammenfassung

Traditionelle und ein Grossteil moderner Risikobewertungs- und -managementansätze sind altmodisch, unrealistisch und auf einen dogmatischen Schlummer ihrer Urheber zurückzuführen. Klassische Risikomessungsinstrumente bergen ihre eigenen Risiken, die von einer unzureichenden, weil nicht-systemischen Konzeptionalisierung von Risiko herrühren. Eine Kultur, wo Risikomodellierung nicht länger zweckmässig ist, sondern sich zu einem Selbstzweck entwickelt hat, dominiert Theorie (Economics and Finance) wie Praxis (Finanzinstitute). Es gebietet sich deshalb, dem Kult der konventionellen probabilistischen Risikomodellierung ein Ende zu setzen, da sie insbesondere nicht in der Lage ist, (sehr) geringe Wahrscheinlichkeiten und Extremverluste, die wiederum systemische Risiken im Finanzsektor charakterisieren, akkurat zu erfassen.

Das Anliegen dieser Dissertation ist ein dreifaches. Unser erstes negatives Forschungsergebnis lautet, dass klassische Risikobewertungen, die auf statistischen Berechnungen basieren, nicht ausreichend erklärend (sondern primär deskriptiv) sind, wohingegen dynamische und organisierte Komplexität, die auf moderne Finanzsysteme und Risikomanagement in diesem Zusammenhang zutrifft, erklärende (Risiko-)Modelle erfordert. In einem fundamentalen Sinne übt diese Arbeit ferner die begriffliche Kritik am Zeitgeist, dass die Kolmogorovsche (Pascalsche) Wahrscheinlichkeitstheorie für die Modellierung von systemischen und extremen Risiken (im Bankenkontext) keine adäquate Grundlage stiftet.

Zum anderen entwerfen wir eine neuartige Risikomodellierungsweise auf der konstruktiven Seite, die erstens im Gegensatz zu den Standardansätzen von Banken das betont, was uns Modellierern bekannt ist (etwa Aktiva und Passiva der Banken) und nicht kaum begründeter Spekulation frönt (etwa durch die Berechnung von minimalen oder erwarteten Verlusten). Zweitens in Abgrenzung zu etablierten Systemrisikomodellen, womit Regulatoren auf die Bewahrung der Finanzstabilität zielen, geht es uns nicht um die dynamische Beschreibung des Finanzsystems per se, sondern um die Modellierung der Positionen (im Portfolio) der Marktteilnehmer sowie ihre Propensität auf Systemveränderungen zu reagieren. Unser Plädoyer für symbolische und logikbasierte Risikomodellierung wird am Beispiel der Kreditkrise von Long-Term Capital Management illustriert. Wir bauen dabei auf die folgenden drei Grundideen: Zunächst operationalisieren wir die Messung von Extrem- und Systemrisiken für Finanzinstitute, indem wir Risiken ihrer Finanzprodukte und -instrumente (Derivate wie Optionen, Swaps, Futures, etc.) fokussieren, und diese mithilfe einer Zerlegung in atomare Finanzkontrakte in einer Programmiersprache abbilden. Programme in dieser Sprache werden dann als sogenannte unsichere Sequenzen von Transaktionen interpretiert, die in einer Reihe von verschiedenen formalen Modellen zur Repräsentation von Ungewissheit gründen können. Während domänenspezifische Sprachen Forschungsgegenstand der Funktionalen Programmierung bilden, und Modelle zur Messung von Ungewissheit im Rahmen der formalen Epistemologie erforscht werden, wurde das Potenzial, das aus ihrer Kombination resultiert, noch nicht geborgen respektive für quantitatives Risikomanagement fruchtbar gemacht. Die vorliegende Dissertation ist bemüht, diese eklatante Lücke zu schliessen und das Toolset für die effektive Evaluierung von extremen und systemischen finanziellen Risiken zu erweitern.

Eine Methodenreflexion sowie eine synthetische Betrachtung von Risikomessung im grösseren Gefüge von Risikomanagement schliesst die Arbeit im vierten Teil ab. Unter diesem Titel erörtern wir die Frage nach der Bedeutung von Entscheidungskompetenz in einem Risikomanagementkontext. Am Ende des Tages hoffen wir durch die Skizzierung eines effektiv effektiven, anstatt eines nach Effizienz trachtendem, aber schlussendlich unwirksamen Risikomanagementvorschlags für Banken einen Beitrag zur nachhaltigen Entwicklung einer stabileren und humanen Finanzwirtschaft erbracht zu haben.

Introduction

For it is your business, when the wall next door catches fire.
(Horace 65–8 BC, Epistles)

Ignorance is preferable to error
And he is less remote from the truth who believes nothing
Than he who believes what is wrong.
(Thomas Jefferson, 1781)

It is soberly true that science has, to date,
succeeded in solving a bewildering number of relatively easy problems,
whereas the hard problems, and the ones
which perhaps promise most for man's future, lie ahead.
(Warren Weaver, 1948)

Le serment d'Hippocrate demande au médecin de ne pas causer de tort.
En finance, je pense que les modèles conventionnels
et leurs «corrections» les plus récentes violent ce serment. [...]
Dans un monde toujours plus complexe, les scientifiques ont besoin
des deux outils: des images aussi bien que des nombres [...].
(Benoît Mandelbrot, 2005)

The recent global financial crisis of 2007-09[1] had many intertwined and mutually reinforcing causes (Detken & Nymand-Andersen, 2013: 749). The Financial Crisis Inquiry Commission (FCIC) identified "dramatic failures of corporate

1 "It is generally agreed that the subprime-originated US financial crisis started in 2007, but debates are still active about when it ended – or will end" (Choi & Douady, 2013: 454). We assume here that the crisis ended sometime in 2009, "but its impact lingered long enough to look as if the crisis had still continued" (ibid.).
A financial crisis is said to be an event, for example, in which a panic (or fear of panic) affects the functioning of the financial system (Geithner & Metrick, 2015). Financial markets fail to function; it is supposed that serious changes in the value of financial institutions' assets occur, that "liquidity dries up" because of a "loss of confidence", to the extent that the sustainability of the financial system is in danger. Technically, a financial crisis is different from and more fatal than a market crash or a banking crisis. Cf. also Gorton & Metrick, 2009; Abberger & Nierhaus, 2008; Bernanke & James, 1991: Table 7; Kindleberger, 1978. Other ways of understanding exist.
In successive sections, we do not always pay careful attention to the differences between collapses, crises, crashes, shocks, turmoils, panics, etc.

governance and risk management at many systemically important firms" as one of the key causes of the crisis (FCIC, 2011: xviii; cf. also Sullivan, 2009). Among others, the crisis has demonstrated the need to rethink the conceptual approach to risk, risk assessment and management.[2]

To put it radically, our enduring obsession with outdated concepts, in both academia and the economic practice, is partly culpable for the disaster. Financial risk management has been, and still is, in a state of confusion. For decades, banks' risk management experts have employed analytical instruments, designed in the 'ivory tower'of Economics and Finance, such as statistical risk measures (e.g., Value at Risk) and qualitative risk analysis tools (e.g., stress testing) for dealing with risk and uncertainty.[3] For instance, as declared by some banks themselves (e.g., UBS, 2008; Swiss Federal Banking Commission, 2008), risk management and risk control practice, on the one hand, has put excessive confidence in received quantitative methods of analysis, stress tests and estimates of value at risk using statistical models. On the other hand, according to Hellwig (2008: 52) and others (cf. also Duffie, 2007; Stulz, 2009; Daníelsson et al., 2001), the reliability of a quantitative risk model is very limited. Admittedly, statistical instruments and inference have also been used in other contexts, i.e., in other business units (e.g., Stulz, 1996: 16) or industries and, undeniably, with often high success rates – e.g., insurance companies base their entire business model successfully on the ground of statistics, diagnosis and prognosis (see also Chapter 6.1.2.). Therefore, the current study is positioned, not in the context of 'regular' market swings nor the insurance industry, but in the context of (the assessment of) extreme, tail and systemic risks in modern financial systems (banking in particular) while we are inclined to not exclude that it might also add to a broader discussion (see Chapter 22). There are several more reasons, apart from the lessons drawn from the recent global financial crisis, for examining risk concepts, risk assessment and management approaches in the financial sector; among them are the following:

---

2 Note, however, that risk management failures such as the demise of Lehman Brothers can also have other sufficient causes, which are rather practical than theoretical or conceptual (Wiggins & Metrick, 2014; see below).

3 "Risk" and "uncertainty" are sometimes used synonymously (Gronemeyer, 2014: 86). It is a central objective of this dissertation to establish clarity on the relevant concepts in the realm of (financial) risk management (such as "risk" and "uncertainty"). See Chapter 4.

1) *A paradigm from a complexity/systems lens*: Modern financial systems are more interconnected and complex than many other economic systems (Bookstaber et al., 2015: 152; see Chapter 6.3.).
2) *Global importance*: The financial industry, in general, has a fundamental and essential function within the economy; namely, primarily, of channeling funds from those with surplus funds to those with shortages of funds (Saunders & Cornett, 2010: 4-10).[4] "Banking really is at the nexus of the real economy" (Braswell & Mark, 2014: 268; cf. also French et al., 2010: 86).
3) *Special status*: Whereas in organizations of other industries risk management usually focuses on the negative – threats and failures rather than opportunities and successes (Kaplan & Mikes, 2012: 50) –, risk management plays a decisively different, namely a broader and more central and sophisticated role in financial institutions: In the financial universe, risk and return are two sides of the same coin. Absorbing, repackaging and passing on risks to others (with different levels of intensity, to be sure) is the core of their business model (Bessis, 2010: 38).[5] Accordingly, the effective management of risks is central to a financial institution's performance (Saunders & Cornett, 2010: 182).
4) *Expertise*: Financial institutions and intermediaries have been regarded as the world's processors of risk par excellence, as leaders in the use of risk assessment and management techniques (Pergler & Freeman, 2008: 13; Mehta et al., 2012). Yet, numerous examples, including the fact that these same institutions have also been the worst hit by the financial and economic crisis that erupted in 2008, seem to highlight shortcomings in their methodologies and presage that too much emphasis has been placed on the deceptively precise outputs of statistical

4 Standard references and textbooks on banking refer to what is called "*maturity transformation*" as a core function that banks perform for the economy (Admati & Hellwig, 2013: 51; Mishkin, 2007: 223; Gurley & Shaw, 1960). For a critical reply, cf., e.g., Hellwig (1994, 1995, 1998).

5 Cf. also the following quotes: "In contrast to industrial corporations, the primary function of financial institutions is to manage risk to make money" (Philippe Jorion, Professor of Finance, University of California) and "Banking is not about money, banking is about taking risk!" (Charles S. Sanford, Jr., Former Chairman Bankers Trust). These quotes are taken from Stegemann, 2013: 16. Risk has always been traded in financial markets. "What is new is the development of markets that deal only with risk, which have learned to standardize risk enough to be able to exchange it and give it a price" (Esposito, 2011: 107).

> measures and probabilistic models – "the hubris of spurious precision" (Rebonato, 2007: xi).[6] Financial institutions have not managed to act as the specialists in risk measurement/management they are supposed to be (Saunders & Cornett, 2010: 18).

All things considered, attention to risk assessment and management in the financial industry is thus required now more than ever. But what kind(s) of risk, it may fairly be asked, should be looked at and from whose perspective (e.g., states, regulators, banks, individuals)? While financial institutions (banks, for short) usually classify uncertainties into risk categories, there is, in the wake of the global financial crisis that began in 2007, increasing recognition of the need to address risk at the systemic level (Bookstaber et al., 2015; Haldane & May, 2011: 351). Therefore, we look at systemic, and more broadly (see 4.2.), extreme risks, but not from bank practitioners', but from a system theorist's point of view and canvass the impact of our findings for primarily the risk management literature as well as, secondarily, banks (not states or regulators that are also interested in, and affected by, systemic risks). In other words, our target audience are risk experts and professionals in academia and practice as well as complexity explorers (which subsumes not only scholars) keen to understand and design risk management systems.

In successive chapters, we show why the tenets, on which the citadel of modern risk assessment and management rests, are false, offering in their place an alternative viewpoint for dealing with the kind of low-probability, high-impact events (e.g., the crisis which crescendoed in 2008, the collapse of Barings Bank or the Asian crisis) that characterize extreme and systemic risk.

The overall *research hypothesis* of this dissertation is the following:

> "Conventional probabilistic risk models used by banks are *not* effective for dealing with extreme and systemic risks, while certain non-probabilistic, structural risk models are suitable tools."

Most risk professionals know from experience how inaccurate stochastic risk modeling can be. On this point, there is probably a large consensus. Our thesis –

6 We regard "statistical measures/models" and "probabilistic measures/models" as mutually interchangeable in this piece of work, which does not imply that there is no difference between probability theories and statistics. But this difference can be neglected if mathematical statistics is understood as applied probability theory (Weaver, 1967: 154). See also Chapter 7.2.

on which agreement may be less general – is this: Firstly, the problem is far more fundamental than you might think and perhaps even insurmountable and, therefore, the way to solve this problem is not to look for better probabilistic risk models by perfecting techniques. Secondly, the better approach, this author believes, is to accept barely measurable *deep* (see Chapter 6.1.4. and Appendix A) uncertainty at face value, focus on what drives risks instead, the system and its structure, try to understand it, and make it part of our reasoning.

Effectively Ineffective: How Efficiency Seeking misses the point

It is an old and hotly debated question concerning financial systems whether or not they work *efficiently*. The Nobel Prize in economics in 2013 was awarded jointly to Eugene Fama, who believes in efficient markets (where prices reflect all relevant information)[7], Robert Shiller, the father of behavioral economics and a vehement critic of Fama's efficient-market hypothesis, and Lars Hansen, who developed tests of market efficiency (Pedersen, 2015). Financial systems' *effectivity*, i.e., their ability to actually perform their intended functions, by contrast, receives much less attention and is, rather, taken for granted.[8]

Concomitantly, risk managers[9] and modelers in the financial world become so absorbed that they tend to forget to pose the right questions; uncircumventable if we do not want to be left trapped in our conceptual errors (Bernstein, 1996b: 336). Research in financial risk management, advancing, for example, from one conventional risk measure like Value at Risk to another conventional risk measure like Expected Shortfall (see 2.2.3.; Acerbi & Tasche, 2001) without challeng-

7 Put differently, "the market price always equals the fundamental value and, as soon as news comes out, prices immediately react to fully reflect the new information. If markets are fully efficient, there is no point in active investing because the prices already reflect as much information as you could hope to collect. But without active investors, who would make the market efficient in the first place?" (Pedersen, 2015: 3).

8 Doubt might be legitimate as "the financial system is self-organized. Individual financial entities generally have risk-management procedures and controls to preserve their own stability, but the system as a whole was never engineered for safety and stability." (Bookstaber et al., 2015: 148).

9 Given the central significance of risk for banks, it is not trivial to say which persons or job titles are included by "risk managers in banks". Here, a broad meaning of the term is chosen because not only the risk experts in the risk management department of a bank, but also traders, senior or general managers, managing directors (including, in some firms, a chief risk officer) and others need to manage (systemic) risks (Rossi, 2014: 76) – firms typically claim that the management of risk is everyone's task (which is, of course, difficult to achieve in practice). We might also personify the bank as a whole and speak of the bank as a risk manager.

ing the fundamentals, is in this sense obsessed with aspiration for efficiency. In particular, every financial turmoil is a crisis of confidence; confidence on which, after all, financial systems are built. Risk managers lose confidence in their models as 'extraordinary' losses are realized in the banking community, the magnitude of which defies estimates from most standard risk models (Thiagarajan et al., 2015: 113). The market events make risk managers painfully aware of the need to measure risks more reliably. Yet, after some "fancier econometric footwork" (Lucas, 1976) has been undertaken (i.e., efficiency seeking), the next turmoil happens, and the same reaction sets in again. In this sense, orthodox risk modeling actually turns out to be ineffective and, thus, it can be called *entirely ineffective* or, synonymously, *effectively ineffective*[10] – with the duplicate attribute signaling that the effectiveness of risk management is generally not questioned. Since efficiency presupposes effectivity, efficiency-seeking approaches that ultimately prove to be ineffective miss the point. Under the circumstances of their application, the cycle of financial turmoil followed by intensified risk modeling ambitions followed by financial turmoil does not seem to stop or to produce any relief. To us, this signifies that it is not some performance properties of the models, that need to be changed, but the complete models themselves, which facilitates true, effective effectiveness.

This dissertation is, therefore, purely conceptual, theoretical, and aims at contributing to a *truly effective* approach towards managing extreme and systemic risks within modern financial systems. At the end, truly effective risk management is tantamount to well-informed decision-making where the risks are known and understood by the decision-makers (Part IV). It calls for, or is at least fostered by, effectively effective risk modeling which subverts the fundamentals and expands the realm of known risks (Part III). As Peter Drucker said, the greatest danger in times of turbulence is not the turbulence; it is to act with yesterday's patterns of thinking.

The interesting aspect in the turbulent environment of our time is less the often praised '*optimization*', '*efficiency*' ("doing things right") of a certain unquestioned approach (Churchman, 1968: chapter 2) – optimization simply engenders vulnerability of banks to changes in the environment (Taleb et al., 2009: 80) –, but the primary determination of (a) *robust*, *reliable* and *effective* ("doing

10 However, "effectively ineffective" is not synonymous with "ineffectively effective" because the latter term just does not make much sense.

the right things")[11] path(s) for addressing an issue like evaluating systemic risks within dynamically complex financial systems. For most of the great real problems, where mathematical methods are useful and come into play, they fall far short of being able to find the 'best' solution (Forrester, 1975: 47). The misleading objective of trying only for an optimum or efficient solution "often results in simplifying the problem until it is devoid of practical interest" (ibid.).[12] If then the optimum or efficient solution to the problem on the paper is transferred to the real-world problem, real damage can occur as the former is relatively simple while the latter is complex, which necessitates essentially different mathematical treatments (see Chapter 6).

Much of finance theory and risk management approaches are predicated on the notion that risks in the financial system can be captured precisely in probability terms and that "highly probable outcomes occur near the center of a normal distribution and tail events are rare" (Thiagarajan et al., 2015: 115). Yet, this focus and restriction on more or less well probabilistically quantifiable risks comes at a cost: the undervaluation of (at least) extreme risks (Bhansali & Wise, 2001).[13] But instead of simply locating extreme risk management to lie 'outside the efficient frontier', the quest for an effectively effective risk management approach is launched in order to get a better grasp on just how exposed banks' positions are to sudden high-impact, low-probability changes in the environment they operate in. It is indeed insights into how sensitive the firms' financial positions are "to a wide variety of external circumstances that lie at the heart of effective management of risk" (Braswell & Mark, 2014: 188).

Theoretically speaking, progress in risk assessment and management can be achieved by adopting a perspective of complexity and systems science because "[e]ffective decision making and learning in a world of growing *dynamic complexity* [see Chapter 2.1., Appendix A] requires us to become systems thinkers" (Sterman, 2000: vii); while on the practical side, the insights gained will caution

---

11 Peter Drucker reminds us that effectiveness relates to getting the right things done and that effectiveness must be learned (Drucker, 2006).

12 "The lack of utility does not, however, detract from the elegance of the analysis as an exercise in mathematical logic [i.e., a brain-teaser, C.H.]" (ibid.).

13 That low-probability events, for instance, immediately prior to the recent financial crisis, have been and still are actually underweighted (Bhansali, 2014: 161) does not necessarily contradict behavioral economics (e.g., Kahneman & Tversky's prospect theory) which purports that people generally tend to overweight the probability of rare events and underweight the probability of more common events.

professionals and leaders of financial firms against succumbing to the traps of optimization and complexity, while improving their managerial effectiveness.

Von Bertalanffy (1968/2013: xvii) observes that the systems movement has penetrated and epitomizes a novel "paradigm" in scientific thinking (to use Thomas Kuhn's expression)[14]. Likewise, time has now come to alter the *modus operandi* of risk management itself. To put it in a nutshell, we will draw on the thriving paradigm of systems thinking to inject momentum into a Kuhnian paradigm shift in (the literature on) risk management in banking. Starting from a complexity and systems scientific angle, this study attempts to pave the way for a scientific revolution in risk management and finance as well as to provide a rationale for a shift from mainly efficiency seeking and data-driven to effectivity reaching and explanatory risk modeling. From there, the ground of real risk modeling (on the object level in contrast to critical and systems thinking *on* risk modeling on a meta level) is entered and a disruptive approach for dealing with extreme and systemic risks is both described and discussed (Part III).

The Purpose of this Thesis, its Scope and an Outline

Hence, the purpose of this study is, on the one hand, to systematically explore and expound the principal shortcomings of banks' conventional risk management approaches and, on the other hand, to provide a proposal for overcoming them by presenting an entirely effective approach towards managing extreme and systemic risks. First and foremost, the thesis intends to add to theory-building and to the literature of critical finance as well as on extreme risk assessment, in particular.

Theory building, in principle, "is more than an exercise in academic abstractions, but rather an activity fundamental to the survival of societies, organizations and even individuals" (Schwaninger & Grösser, 2008: 448; cf. also Schwaninger & Hamann, 2005). Theory building, as conceived of here and guided by meticulous observation of and reflection on what is going on in the real

14 In the sense of Kuhn (1970), "[p]aradigms are self-consistent communities of like-minded scientists, sharing a worldview encompassing not only a body of theory and evidence but also methods of inquiry, standards of proof, textbook examples, and heroes" (Sterman, 2000: 849). "Eventually comes a period when the ruling paradigm cannot solve certain problems, and scientists start questioning the paradigm's fundamental assumptions. When enough scientists become convinced that it is impossible to solve the anomalies accumulating within the framework of the ruling paradigm, and only if an alternative paradigm is available, then a scientific revolution takes place." (Barlas & Carpenter, 1990: 156).

world, consists of generating, complementing and formalizing *theory*[15] in order to orientate action.

Along these lines, this thesis pursues several specific key objectives:

- In theoretical terms, it will facilitate the integration of economic (Finance), and system- / complexity-theoretical variables and constructs into the study and analysis of systemic and extreme financial risk and risk management in banking. Issues of risk cut across traditional disciplinary boundaries. In this light, a systems perspective is adequate to investigate financial systems (Hoffmann & Grösser, 2014) and to explain the inappropriateness of risk models used by banks (Hoffmann, 2016).
- The main objective in *Part I* of the dissertation, dealing primarily with the model level (i.e., with how a system and its components are represented), is to define and locate risk and systemic risk, respectively, in order to clarify the meaning and extension of these terms.[16] In this way, we provide a sound starting point for demonstrating, on the one hand, the relevance of systemic risk for banks and for disclosing, on the other hand, *conceptual* weaknesses of standard quantitative risk assessment/management approaches in the light of dynamic and organized complexity which characterizes modern financial systems. In other words, if we take complexity in financial systems seriously and at face value, we must stop operating with probability distributions, which are, after all, central to conventional risk measures or models (because the latter are derived from *return* or *loss distributions*[17], which are ultimately derived from random variables). Finally, we will gain important insights on the notion of complexity and its connection to randomness and risk on the way.

15 It suffices to conceive of a *theory* as "a structured, explanatory, abstract and coherent set of interconnected statements about a reality" (Schwaninger & Grösser, 2008: 448); or to follow Davis et al. (2007: 481) in defining theory as "consisting of constructs linked together by propositions that have an underlying, coherent logic and related assumptions".

16 This clarification is already an important contribution to the relevant literature, see the section "Methodology".

17 In Chapter 4.1., we state that it makes sense in the context of risk management in banking to primarily associate risks with adverse, negative or undesirable events. As a consequence, if probability distributions are focused, the focus lies rather on loss distributions (less on return distributions). Working directly with the return distribution (not the loss distribution), however, is often more convenient (McNeil et al., 2005).

- *Part II*, a transition from the model to the decision level, briefly reviews and evaluates scenario analysis as well as stress testing for mainly two reasons: it forms an indispensable stepping stone to pave the way for Part III; and given the negative result from Part I, qualitative approaches could be considered suitable for filling the yawning gap. This point has indeed been made firmly by an emerging and flourishing critical finance society. However, despite the possible inclusion of systems thinking in scenario and stress test analysis to some extent, we argue that those qualitative risk analysis instruments are rather rendered obsolete too by the problems of induction and complexity, familiar from Part I. Therefore, lessons for rethinking the approach to assessing extreme and systemic risks are derived before a constructive counterproposal is presented and discussed.
- In *Part III*, we concoct several ideas for an enhanced conceptual approach towards responding to systemic and extreme risks in the financial system. In a nutshell, we are measuring risks of banks' financial instruments and transactions, which we describe in a programming language for financial contracts. The output in this language is interpreted as a set of scenarios of transactions, which can be grounded in a number of different formal models of uncertainty. As a first step in this direction, our goal is to not only introduce the indispensable theoretical underpinnings of such a formalism, but also install a novel type of risk measure based chiefly on ranking theory as well as on an algebraic description of financial products, making no assumptions about the probabilities of external events. This Third Way describes precise models of what is known (one's own assets and liabilities) rather than spuriously precise models of what is not known (the future behavior of the financial system). It will be illustrated and tested by the case of the fall of the hedge fund Long-Term Capital Management, LTCM. Moreover, the new models can be regarded as constituting an exact, explanatory scenario planning method from complexity principles. Managerial implications will be drawn.
- Finally, the main purpose of *Part IV* is to adopt a critical and global perspective on a meta level by further exploring the meaning of *effective* risk management with recourse to the results from the previous

parts of the study and by taking into account that risk management has a decision-guiding purpose and ultimately comes down to making good decisions. In line with the novel proposal in Part III, a case for well-informed decision-making is made where the risks are known and understood by decision-makers. This reflection on methods not only concludes and closes the study, but also manifests a synthesis, essential for systems thinking (Appendix A), where we envision the focal object, risk measurement, as being part of the overall process of risk management in banking and beyond.

Thus, we consider primarily systemic risk and complexity in financial systems, risk assessment models and instruments used or usable in banks as *units of analysis*. More precisely, the units of analysis of this research project are found in the notions of systemic risk and dynamic or organized complexity as well as probabilistic risk modeling in Part I, in scenario and stress test analysis in Part II, and in formal logic-based risk modeling in Part III. Part IV, by contrast, has the function of a concluding paragraph only, which does, therefore, not launch another in-depth discussion.

Why look at tools at all? Instead of indulging in the credulous belief of simply regarding tools and risk management tools, in particular, as a *materialization of (economic) rationality*, many management theorists and others have started to think otherwise[18] and call attention to limitations and the functioning of tools or compare them to practices, institutions, human actors, etc.

Methodology

The financial fallout of 2007-09, one of this author's main drivers for grappling with some of the most compelling and complex problems of risk management, can be regarded as very special or even unique, a caesura in the history of financial combustions:[19] It is systemic in nature (Bessis, 2010: xi). "The interplay of partial crises [and crashes,[20] C.H.] (which were indeed known and not new)

18 Cf., e.g., the entries in the blog "Socializing finance": https://socfinance.wordpress.com/ (25/10/15).

19 By contrast, Reinhart & Rogoff (2013, 2009) foreground common features of financial fallouts throughout many centuries. Despite the regularities they identify from *one* point of view, the gobal crisis of 2007-09 can still be very special from another point of view.

20 E.g., the bursting of the US-American housing bubble; cf. Gorton & Metrick (2012) and Shiller (2005).

resulted in emergent properties of the system of global finance which nobody had intended or foreseen" (Willke et al., 2013: 23).[21] [22] The modern financial system "is self-organized; it did not develop as a carefully engineered system with proper consideration given to the stability and the management of its complex interactions" (Bookstaber et al., 2015: 161). "The financial system had changed in ways that nobody fully appreciated" (Krugman, 2009: 152), which has demonstrated how traditional ideas are not able to deal with complexity (Bar-Yam in Gershenson, 2008: 19). As academics, we have a moral obligation and a societal duty to ask ourselves: "What really went wrong?" (Das et al., 2013: 701).

This study suggests that a systems- and complexity-oriented framework is a useful paradigm for this challenge when the question is narrowed to theoretical issues of risk management failures – the topic of this thesis. Our intention is, however, neither to apply a specific systems theory to risks and risk management nor a recourse to concepts of complexity which is fraught with obstacles (Chapter 6). Rather, we perpetuate systems thinking (Appendix A) and principles to enrich notions of risk (which lack a systemic viewpoint), to comprehend and evaluate risk management instruments according to finance or in banking (from a systems theoretical lens), and to propose a precise, structure-oriented modeling approach (derived from complexity or systems principles). Especially in terms of systemic risks, it should be clear that "[w]ithout at least [...] some acquaintance with systems theory, it appears to be very improbable that the term *systemic risk* can be constructed and used except in a merely metaphorical way" (Willke et al., 2013: 18f.). "Systemic risk is a classic complex systems problem" (Thurner, 2012: 24; see Chapter 5.1.). As Willke et al. (2013: 19) underscore, the point of immersing in the subject of systemic risk is *not* that the system (whatever it may be) might crash or that it is in danger of collapsing due to an *external* shock. Systems thinking rather teaches that the *orthodox way of thinking and acting,*

21 Warning signs of the crisis were, for example, perceived by Shiller (2005) who warned of an asset bubble in the U.S. housing market or Rajan (2006) who presented research showing that recent financial innovations had increased risk in the banking sector.

22 There is bewildering dissent on the precise meaning of "emergence". Consider, e.g., the following definition: "Emergence occurs when a complex system exhibits properties that can't be predicted by considering its subcompo-nents in isolation" (Nitschke, 2009). An unpleasant consequence then would be that "calling a property 'emergent' is uncomfortably close to saying 'I wasn't clever enough to predict it', or worse" (ibid.) as predictability is subjective.

manifested in probability-based risk modeling and contributing to the regular operational mode of the system, as it is, can lead to the self-destruction of that system. This clarification of "systemic" has major implications for not only understanding a term (the level of language), but especially for revolutionizing risk modeling *practice*.

On the methodological side, most previous studies on systemic risk in financial systems have focused on the stability of systems as wholes (Cont et al., 2013: 330), either in stylized equilibrium settings (Allen & Gale, 2000; Freixas et al., 2000; Battiston et al., 2012) or in simulation studies of default cascades (Upper & Worms, 2004; Mistrulli, 2011; Nier et al., 2007). Yet, the subject of systemic risk in financial systems and its management in banking is still in its infancy if it is located in the realm of systems theories and complexity. This thesis' contributions to this subject are packaged in a range of *propositions*, which epitomize the central research results of this study. Overall, we develop specific propositions or theses which we are able to derive from our argumentation. While mathematics views propositions technically as theorems,[23] "proposition" is used here more loosely and informally, more in the sense of management research, where it can be broadly paraphrased as "a declarative sentence expressing a relationship" (Van de Ven, 2007: 117). Furthermore, this study remains silent on empirical work to test our propositions or corresponding hypotheses. We differentiate between fully fledged propositions and less developed, underdetermined conjectures. Our research statements are falsifiable and do not necessitate verification which is impossible in our realm (Chapter 19). They stand for themselves as a contribution to theory-building, extension as well as refinement and are available at one glance in *Appendix B*.

Both deduction and induction are components of the research process here, but deductive reasoning does take center stage. For example, the Central Argument of Part I in Chapter 7 is demonstrably complete. Or with regard to the introduction of our novel risk modeling approach in Part III, we first proceed deductively by postulating a number of formal laws and requirements before we concoct a mathematical model, which obeys the postulates. After the theoretical validation in the form of propositions, theorems etc. we draw on a case study

23 Strictly speaking, the terms are not completely synonymous (e.g., when "proposition" is reserved for theorems of no particular importance).

(LTCM) to show how our risk model can be applied specifically to a portfolio of financial products and how it is to be validated in this more practical context.

The nature of this dissertation is descriptive (e.g., what are the tools of risk management in banking), mainly explorative (e.g., in what sense and why are risk management tools not appropriate), but also prescriptive (e.g., how risks should be managed) and analytic (in terms of concepts and conceptual relationships). In contrast to empirical research (quantitative, qualitative, multi-paradigmatic), purely conceptual work is central for this research project (cf. Corley & Gioia, 2011). A primarily empirical approach towards the research topic is repudiated for at least six reasons:

1) Scholars are generally aligned around the idea that there is a major need for theory-building in management research[24] and beyond (Zikmund et al., 2013; Whetten, 1989; Dubin, 1978). A key strength of theory-building or conceptual approaches is that they are well suited "to challenge and extend existing knowledge" (Whetten, 1989: 491), and that logical reasoning predominates (*rigor*), enabling theorists to convince others that their *propositions* make sense.

More specifically:

2) This kind of reflective thinking or reasoning, in which one step leads in an orderly way to the next step, the whole consecutive process converging finally to a conclusion, reaches a particularly refined level of mathematics, serving in one form (probability theory, Part I) or another (non-classical logics, Part III) as a breeding ground for establishing risk models. Hence, conceptual work is absolutely essential for this dissertation when it is committed to making a contribution to formal risk modeling.
3) As we will see in successive chapters, it makes much sense (*relevance*) and it has been omitted by past studies (*innovativeness*) to shed light on banks' analytical risk management instruments by simultaneously adopting different theoretical perspectives (from systems and computer science, the philosophy of science). A valuable contribution to scien-

24 This thesis can be regarded as being embedded in the broad field of Management because managing and uncertainty [and, thus, risk and complexity; C.H.] are two sides of the same coin (Smith & Tombs, 2000: 7).

tific communities is reached by critically integrating results, insights, ideas from different streams of research which, by definition, characterizes conceptual work.

4) It would be beyond the scope of *one* single dissertation to conduct conceptual *and* empirical work to address the research questions presented below (Chapter 3 and 14).
5) A more *substantial* contribution can be made by means of theoretical research. On the one hand, many empirical studies do not bear fruits, they utilize maladaptive methods, and have a relatively limited impact on future research (The Economist, 2014; Taleb, 2012; Gibbert & Ruigrok, 2010; Gibbert et al., 2008; Gary et al., 2008). On the other hand, to establish clarity on relevant concepts (in the realm of financial risk management, for example) is already an important contribution to the pertinent literature since a problem cannot be solved if it cannot be defined – or, at least, it cannot be solved sustainably– "because confusion over the nature of the problem can obscure attempts to provide solutions" (Schwarcz, 2008: 197; cf. also Heinemann, 2014: 172).
6) To plausibilize the relevance of our work for practitioners as well (managerial implications), some secondary data is taken into account. Secondary sources include corporate reports like (UBS, 2008), reports by governmental bodies or investigation committees like the FCIC, empirical studies, and other specific material, e.g., McKinsey's working papers on risk.[25]

Given the complexity and large scope of the topic, slightly different methods will be needed for the realization of the research activities. In the following list (Table 1), a number of methods and rules are suggested and linked to the different parts of the thesis.

25 The rigor-relevance debate is a recurring theme in discussions concerning gaps between research and practice, which often turns into simplistic either/or arguments (Gulati, 2007; Lorsch, 2009). We believe that the notion of rigor versus relevance needs to be replaced with recognition that achieving direct relevance for the economic practice is dependent upon rigorous thought and action in the face of, and at the same time focused upon addressing, the complexity of practitioners' situations and perceptions.

Table 1: Methods and rules to realize the research objectives.

Part of the thesis	*Method*
Part I: Concepts, Model Level and Risk Assessment – The Risk of Ineffective Risk Management I: Limitations of Quantitative Risk Models in Banks	- Literature review - Logical reasoning: explication and analysis of concepts, characteristics of / relationships between concepts, concept extensions, deriving (also normative) conclusions - Causal loop diagrams (CLDs) - Single case study analysis (for illustration purposes only) - Knowledge integration and progress through critical discourse with scholars - Systematic, theoretical analysis of, and reflection on, the (quantitative) methods applied to risk management in banks
Part II: The Transition to the Decision Level, Risk Assessment and Management – The Risk of Ineffective Risk Management II: Overcoming Limitations of the Qualitative Risk Analysis Approach in favor of Logic-Based Risk Modeling	- Literature review - Comparative analysis - Evaluation - Logical reasoning - Systematic, theoretical analysis of, and reflection on, the (qualitative) methods applied to risk management in banks
Part III: In Search of a New Paradigm: The Third Way as a Road to Logic-Based Risk Modeling	- Logical and mathematical reasoning: axiomatization, derivation of theorems, developing a semantics of a formal language - Model interpretation - Knowledge integration - Risk *analysis* (model the risk of complex financial instruments as a combination of the risk of their underlyings) and risk *synthesis* (model the function of basal models in more encompassing risk models) - Single case study analysis (for illustration) - Model validation
Part IV: Meta level: Thinking about Thinking and Practices – What it Means to Reach Effective Risk Management Decisions	- Synthesis: Focus on the whole (risk management), not the part (risk measurement), and outlining the role or function of risk assessment in a larger context - "The art of reflection"

Outlook and Limitations

Together, the following chapters seek to show why, in what way extant risk management tools are *not* an adequate approach to deal with systemic and extreme risks (1-12) and how to manage them effectively and competently (13-22). Individually, the four parts are situated on different levels of analysis with relevance both to the dissertation's overall alignment and to related, yet distinct bodies of literature.

Given the ambitious and courageous goals set in this study, it is clear that its four parts (especially Part III) to some extent merely set out a program and delineate an agenda for future theoretical and empirical research. In other words, not all of the research questions stated in Chapter 3 and 14 can be answered comprehensively (see Chapter 22). But most importantly, a crucial challenge for this research endeavor is to find a good trade-off between highlighting the conceptual diversity of the topic and placing importance on adopting an integrative viewpoint, on the one hand, and strengthening the argumentation by providing a lucid understanding of the central concepts and by explaining in detail how the theoretical perspectives (of finance, critical finance, and complexity) can enrich both the concept of risk and risk management approaches in the financial industry, on the other hand. Therefore, in order to promote the feasibility of the project, we are explicitly reluctant to look at the following questions and aspects:[26]

- Since this study's focus is on risk management tools, it could, in principle, contribute to both theory (economics & finance), where they are developed, studied, validated, and practice (banking and real-world financial systems), where they are applied as decision support. However, even though some managerial implications will be presented, emphasis is predominantly placed on theoretical contributions for several reasons. For example, a practical issue: if it was planned to conduct empirical analyses to investigate the inappropriateness of risk management methods used by actual banks, field access would be a decisive success factor. Yet, it is very doubtful whether sufficient and sufficiently reliable data could be collected due to its confidential nature. On top of that, a theoretical and strategic thought: There is a myriad of sufficient causes for risk management failures in practice (which do not even require extreme events of happening) and the selection of a conceptual critique of probabilistic risk modeling, which leads to ineffective risk management, might not seem to be the most pressing problem for practitioners (Wiggins & Metrick, 2014; see also Chapter 17); whereas the consequences for academia are devastating: the critique demonstrates that the house of modern risk measurement research is

26 This list of questions that are excluded from analysis might be subject to changes (i.e., extensions or cutbacks) in the future (see Chapter 22).

not in danger of collapsing but has never been well-established since it lacks a theoretical foundation for extreme events. Yet, to stress the dual importance of our research we also speak of "risk management tools *used by banks*" – which is really uncontroversial (Wiggins & Metrick, 2014; Saunders & Cornett, 2010; Bessis, 2010; Pergler & Freeman, 2008; Stulz, 2002).

- The global financial crisis was a sharp reminder of the overriding importance of monitoring and tackling risks across the financial system as a whole (Brose & Flood, 2014: 6) and of the fact that systemic financial risk management is a critical task (Bookstaber et al., 2015: 148). However, we do not aim to provide a systematic analysis of the global financial crisis and its causes. The reference to it in the Introduction serves as one piece of motivation (among others) for studying extreme or systemic financial risks and techniques for their measurement, respectively. Surely, not only that risk management failures trace back to other roots than ineffective risk assessment (which we aspire to overcome here), but also many phenomena not related to risk management would deserve appreciation if we looked at the global financial crisis more closely: the shareholder value principle (Mayer, 2013: 37f.), leverage effects, political interests, (universal) banks' business models, etc.
- Theoretical approaches to decision-making under risk or uncertainty (Luce & Raiffa, 1957), including Bayesian epistemology or decision theory (Talbott, 2008), are not considered;[27] nor their strengths and weaknesses or the possible links to risk management.
- Risk management is not contextualized in financial mathematics, concrete asset or options pricing theories, etc. either; risk management/measurement (in the financial world) is investigated in itself.
- How can/should the term "dynamic complexity" be measured and operationalized?[28]

27 For example, in the "risk" case: Expected Utility Theory, Prospect Theory, etc.; in the (completely) "uncertain" case, many strategies have been proposed, including the Minimax strategy (von Neumann & Morgenstern, 1944; Wald, 1950), Savage's "Minimax of Regret" or "Horowitz's alpha".

28 That this question is of subordinate value follows from Proposition 3 in Chapter 6.

- What is the exact scope of a logic-based risk modeling approach? How does it work in practice? How should one interpret "probability" in the light of the plea for 'qualitative probabilities' which is offered?[29]
- Explanatory risk modeling in the guise of network analysis and agent based models is not discussed due to several reasons (see 2.3. and 2.4.).
- Neither the potential applicability of our ideas and research outputs to *regulatory* risk management contexts is examined, as opposed to *banks' internal* or in-house risk management purposes (to the extent that managerial implications are drawn); nor are the successive propositions going to be tested empirically (see also Chapter 22).
- Etc.

The task ahead is to review and evaluate quantitative risk assessment and management approaches in banking.

29 Details on this innovative risk modeling approach are expounded elsewhere; cf. Hoffmann & Müller, 2017; Müller & Hoffmann 2017a,b.

Part I:
Concepts, Model Level and Risk Assessment

The Risk of Ineffective Risk Management I: Limitations of Quantitative Risk Models in Banks

1. Introduction to Part I

Statistical thinking will one day be as necessary
for efficient citizenship as the ability to read and write.
(Herbert G. Wells, 1951)

Conventional quantitative risk management, characterized by probability-based risk assessment and designed for monitoring and addressing those risks in a way that ensures the firm bears only the risks its management and board want exposure to (Stulz, 2008: 58f.), produces its own risks, generated through an inadequate notion of risk which lacks a proper systemic viewpoint. A culture has emerged in theory (economics and finance) and practice (financial institutions) in which risk modeling is no longer a *functional* tool but has become an end in itself. In particular, a trend towards addressing risk in its extreme form (e.g., Taleb's black swans) by statistical extreme value methods (e.g., McKelvey, 2013: Vol. 5; Bernard et al., 2013; Das et al., 2013; Johansen & Sornette, 2010; Allen & Gale, 2009; Malevergne & Sornette, 2006) can be observed in the aftermath of the financial crisis which crescendoed in 2008 since failure to manage these risks has been witnessed to be extremely costly for the players (Thiagarajan et al., 2015: 113) and for society as a whole (Poledna & Thurner, 2016). Indeed, there are very few trends in the financial world that have proliferated as much as extreme risk management following the global financial crisis (Thiagarajan et al., 2015: 113). Yet, "in the face of crisis and criticism, proponents of 'counting' do not abandon their measurement efforts but, rather, intensify them" (Mikes, 2011: 227; cf. also Power, 2004a).

However, it is high time to acknowledge the quite reasonable ineffectiveness of stochastic methods for dealing with the kind of low-probability, high-impact events that characterize systemic and extreme risk. In this part of the dissertation, we show – from a complexity and systems science perspective – that theoretical quantitative risk assessment and management approaches, which are also used in practice (Mehta et al., 2012), suffer from conceptual weaknesses.

We argue that these caveats are not just minor issues that could be remedied with better models or distributions, but that they form part of a fundamental problem, namely that *probabilistic reasoning is not an adequate foundation for modeling systemic or extreme risk in a banking context.*

After consolidating the relevant literature where some foundational concepts of quantitative risk modeling are restated (Chapter 2) and developing guiding research questions (Chapter 3), we begin by briefly presenting and discussing notions of risk and systemic risk in the realm of banking (Chapter 4). We then argue and emphasize that (private) banks (and not only regulators) should take account of, and try to deal with, systemic risks in the sense which will be espoused in this survey. Moreover, we provide concrete systemic risk scenarios for banks by shedding light on the illustrative case of the rise and fall of Long-Term Capital Management (LTCM) (Chapter 5). Thirdly, in Chapter 6, we propose a specification and characterization of complexity by drawing on the concept of *organized complexity* which was coined by Weaver (1948). This step appears promising because he stipulated that phenomena of organized situations escape statistical or probabilistic approaches. On this basis, we attempt to show that the assessment of extreme and systemic risks can be classified as a case of organized complexity. Yet, this endeavor turns out to be doomed to failure since the (Weaverian) notion of (organized) complexity seems to elude a conceptual analysis and, therefore, remains somehow obfuscatory. A separate argument for deriving the ineffectiveness of conventional risk modeling is required and, indeed, propounded in Chapter 7. Before Part I is closed by detailing lessons learned and a path of inquiry for the remainder (Chapter 8), this Central Argument constitutes a good (and sufficient) reason for declining probability statistics for the modeling of extreme and systemic risks and goes far beyond of what the current state of research considers as obstacles to effective extreme and systemic risk management. Ultimately, statistical thinking is not only about efficient citizenship, but *good* statistical thinking also includes raising awareness for its limitations, and it deals with effectiveness in the first place.

2. Literature Synthesis, Theoretical Background and Research Focus

Another treatise on systemic risk is a risky venture for any author. There are simply so many of them. However, despite the amount of research undertaken in the area of systemic risk in the financial sector (e.g., Battiston et al., 2012; Billio et al., 2012; Blyth, 2010; Sornette, 2009; Gorton & Metrick, 2009; Huang et al., 2009a; Hellwig, 2008; Schwarcz, 2008; Taleb, 2007a; etc.), a holistic and, especially, a complexity/systems theories driven and logic-based perspective can be very fruitful for contributing to how to be better equipped for assessing and managing systemic risks more effectively in the future (Klimek et al., 2015; Thurner et al., 2010); a critical perspective on systemic and extreme risks in financial systems and quantitative risk models that lie within banks' scope. To start with, it ought to be acknowledged that systems theoretic notions are beginning to provide new insights on risk and resilience of banks (e.g., Battiston et al., 2016; Bonabeau, 2007: 64)[30]. Therefore, we immerse ourselves in reviewing notions of system, financial systems and complexity before the spotlight is turned to risk, systemic risk and risk modeling in the financial sector.

2.1. Complexity and Modern Financial Systems

There are many definitions of the fundamental term "system" (cf. e.g. Stacey, 2010: 122f. for an overview). Schwaninger (2011: 753) gives two examples: "A portion of the world sufficiently well-defined to be the subject of study; something characterized by a structure, for example, a social system (Anatol Rapoport). A system is a family of relationships between its members acting as a whole (In-

---

30 For example, Bonabeau (2007: 64) stresses that it is the context of complex systems where systemic risks arise. Literature has not yet sufficiently examined this relationship between complexity and systemic risks. Thus, it is picked up in this dissertation (Chapter 6).

ternational Society for the Systems Sciences)."[31] What is crucial to know about the concept of system is that it is a *formal* concept, which designates the form of many, in practice very different objects and phenomena. In particular, it applies not only to 'classical objects' (financial system vs. ecosystem vs. a car as a system, etc.), but also many other different things such as problems are termed systems (Gomez & Probst, 1997: 14f.; Ulrich & Probst, 1990: 109; Beer, 1959: 24 and see Weaver, 1948 in Chapter 6).[32] The demarcation between a system and its environment is highlighted by specifying a *boundary* of the system (Klir, 1991: 10f., 30).[33] The following Figure 1, adapted from Schwaninger (2005: 31), depicts the system as a whole with elements, subsystems, relationships and environment.

Banks are systems and they are embedded in (larger) financial systems (see also 6.3.). According to Cecchetti (2008: 2), a financial system is constituted of five parts, each of which plays a fundamental role in a country's economy. Those parts are money, financial instruments, financial markets (comprising credit, capital, and money markets), financial institutions, and central banks.[34] Gurusamy (2008: 3) defines a financial system similarly as a set of "interconnected financial institutions, markets, instruments, services, practices, and transactions"; cf. also Schinasi (2004: 6) and the simple toy models of the financial and real economy in Thurner & Poledna (2013: 2) and Rossi (2011: 70). Notwithstanding these and

31 It can be left open whether systems exist in the real world (Flood & Carson, 1993: 250). There exist several definitions of systems science. For example, Klir (1991: 6) defines it as "a science whose domain of inquiry consists of those properties of systems and associated problems that emanate from the general notion of systemhood". For more details, see Chapter 6.

32 "We have also come to realize that no problem ever exists in complete isolation. Every problem interacts with other problems and is therefore part of a set of interrelated problems, a *system of problems*." (Ackoff, 1974: 21).

33 This distinction is absolute in the theoretical construct of a *closed system*, i.e. where no relationships are found or made between elements of a system and things external to it (Flood & Carson, 1993: 8). Conversely, an *open system* exchanges material, information, and/or energy with its environment across a boundary (ibid.).

34 Simply put, money functions as a medium of exchange; a unit of account; a store of value; and, perhaps, a standard of deferred payment. Financial instruments are used to transfer resources from savers to investors and to transfer risk to those "who are best equipped to bear it" (Cecchetti, 2008: 2). Stocks, mortgages, and insurance policies are examples of financial instruments. The third part of a financial system, financial markets, allows participants to buy and sell financial instruments quickly and cheaply (ibid.). The New York Stock Exchange (NYSE) is an example of a financial market. Fourth, financial institutions (or banks, for short) provide a myriad of services, including access to the financial markets and collection of information about prospective borrowers to ensure that they are creditworthy etc. (ibid.). Finally, central banks like the ECB or the Fed manage a state's or a confederation's currency, money supply, and interest rates and monitor and stabilize the economy (ibid.).

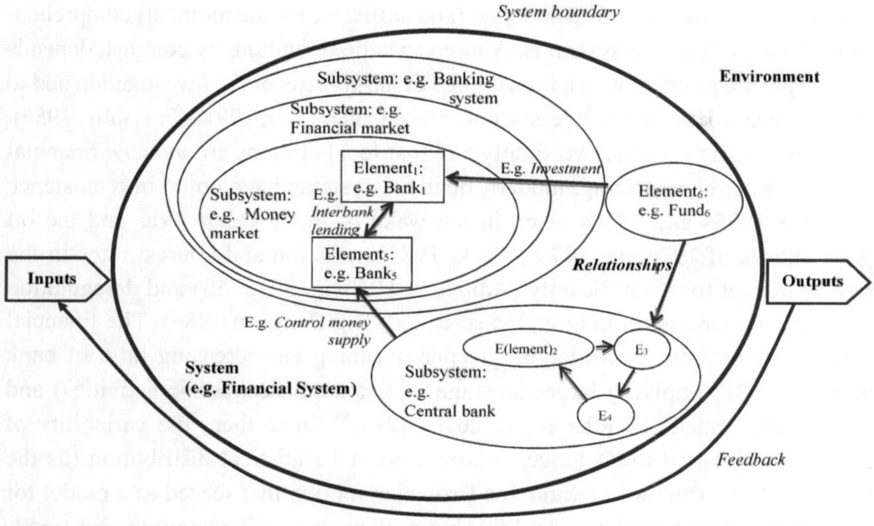

Figure 1: The systems view (After: Schwaninger, 2005).[35]
In addition to that, Appendix E gives an insight into the utter interconnectedness of financial systems by sketching the global banking network in 2007Q4 and 2008Q4.

other definitions, the fact should not be masqueraded that system boundaries are not absolute or fixed (Klir, 1991: 30), but rather each definition of the system boundaries is arbitrary to some extent and subject to the peculiar issue at hand (Ulrich & Probst, 1990: 50; Gomez, 1981: 40f.). Therefore, the concrete definitions by Cecchetti or

35 To receive some impression of the workings and dynamics of financial systems, we cite from the system description in Bookstaber et al. (2015: 150f.): "A bank/dealer acts as an intermediary between buyers and sellers of securities, and between lenders and borrowers of funding. Its clients are investors, such as asset management firms, hedge funds, and pension funds, as well as other bank/dealers. There are specific business units within the bank/dealer that process funding and securities to create products for these clients. The bank/dealer's network, with its connections to other financial entities and among its business units, is complex. For the sake of simplicity, […], we now consider a simplified version of the reality and focus only on two types of bank/dealer activities […]: 1. Funding and securities lending: The bank/dealer goes to sources of funding such as money market funds through the repo [repurchase agreement, C.H.] market [a part of the money market, C.H.], and to security lenders such as pension funds and asset management firms through their custodian banks. 2. Providing liquidity as a market maker: The bank/dealer goes to the asset markets, to institutions that hold assets, and to other market makers to acquire positions in the securities that the clients demand. This function also includes securitization taking securities and restructuring them (see also the glossary at the end, Appendix A). This involves liquidity and risk transformations." The function of the central bank is it to manage, for example, the money supply for banks and in the economy, e.g. by setting interest rates.

Gurusamy etc. just allow to gain a first (and sufficient for the moment) comprehension of what a financial system is. A more specific definition, by contrast, depends on the specific problem which is examined or the *purpose* of the investigation and to provide such a definition is at least a non-trivial matter (Klir, 1991: 47; Ashby, 1956).

On specific grounds, we simply add that focal systems are *modern* financial systems. Roughly speaking, modern financial systems have come into existence since the 1970s and 1980s when in the wake of the Vietnam War and the oil price shocks of 1974 and 1979 (Wack, 1985), inflation and interest rates in the money market rose significantly (Admati & Hellwig, 2013: 53) and deregulation of financial markets set in (e.g., the so-called 'Big Bang' in 1986). The financial system has become "considerably deeper (meaning an increasing ratio of bank assets-to-GDP, implying larger leverage of finance on economic activities) and more concentrated" (Willke et al., 2013: 12f.).[36] Since then, the variability of markets has started to no longer follow a normal statistical distribution (as the movement of particles in a fluid, the Brownian motion that served as a model for options pricing techniques; see 2.5.), but now shows *wild variations* and trends with the possibility of much wider and much more frequent fluctuations (Wack, 1985a: 73; Esposito, 2011: 149). As we will see below, these reports could be illuminated by exploring a system's property of complexity (Chapter 6).

On general grounds, it is safe to say (see 6.3.) that financial systems are *dynamic* wholes (Ulrich & Probst, 1990: 30), i.e., they are able to assume different states or to change over time, and that they are *open* (Katz & Kahn, 1969), i.e., in exchange of matter, energy and information with its environment, presenting import and export, building-up and breaking-down of its material components.[37] In contrast to a simple dynamic and open system, in contrast to what von Foerster (2003, 1985) baptizes 'a trivial machine', which constantly converts a certain input to a predictable output, systems of interest here do not exhibit a

---

36 Furthermore, "there are good arguments to distinguish between a Bretton-Woods era of mostly national financial systems and a post-Bretton-Woods [modern] era (starting in the 1970s, accelerating in the Reagan-Thatcher era of the 1980s, and coming into bloom in the 1990s) of a mostly globalized financial system" (ibid.: 33). Specifying the demarcation between the eras could go on: the globally pervasive emergence of a shadow banking system, the equally pervasive use of highly sophisticated financial instruments such as CDOs (collateralized debt obligations), currency debt swaps, or auction rate preferred securities, etc. are all peculiar to modern financial systems. For more details on their characterization, cf. Willke et al., 2013; Rossi, 2011; Neave, 2010; Minsky, 1986/2008.

37 As can be seen in Figure 1, the system influences its environment ("outputs"), but the environment also affects the system (via "feedback").

certain transformation function where the same input steadily leads to the same output (which would make the system's behavior extremely predictable).[38] Financial systems are non-trivial in the sense that a certain input is not always transformed into the same output by the system because the system possesses its own internal dynamics (eigendynamics), the transformation function is not unvarying (Ulrich & Probst, 1990: 60). Overall, this variability in different dimensions alludes to a third general property of financial systems: *complexity*.

In the aftermath of the recent crisis of 2007-09, financial systems have been characterized as consisting of occasional periods of severe market stress (Litzenberger & Modest, 2010), they have been labeled as "non-robust and non-deterministic" (Fouque & Langsam, 2013), as "chaotic" (Mandelbrot & Taleb, 2010; Hsieh, 1991), "turbulent" (Allen & Gale, 2009) and "vulnerable to failure that can pull down the entire system" (Helbing, 2013; Admati & Hellwig, 2013). Here, the objective is not simply to add another label to this list, but to provide a systematic analysis of the *complexity* of modern financial systems (Neave, 2010) that will steer the whole reasoning in the course of this study.

In the last 30 years there has been a tremendous amount of interest in "complex systems" of various kinds (Edmonds, 1999; Gell-Mann, 1994; Klir, 1991: 113f.).[39] A standard definition of "complexity" is that "[...] complexity consists in a large number of distinct (potential or actual) states or modes of behavior" of a system (Schwaninger, 2009: 12). Yet, there might not be a single good definition and there are certainly many different ways in which the term "complexity" is used. Seth Lloyd even once said that "the main feature of complexity is that it resists all attempts to define it" (Lloyd in Gershenson, 2008: 87; cf. also Cilliers in Gershenson, 2008: 28f.). Additionally, "complexity is given a somewhat subjective connotation since it is related to the ability to understand or cope with the thing under consideration" (Klir, 1985: 131). Further, there is not (yet) a single science of complexity, but rather several different theoretical perspectives on complexity (Mitchell, 2009: 95). For example, the physicists Jim Crutchfield and Karl Young shaped the term "*statistical complexity*", which measures the minimum amount of information about the past behavior of a system that is needed to optimally predict

38 To produce such a deterministic and predictable behavior is exactly what we aspire to as far as the construction of technical facilities is concerned (e.g., a punching machine).

39 Etymologically, complexity comes from the Latin term "*plexus*", which means "interwoven" whereas the similar English word "complicated" uses the Latin "*plic(āre)*" which means "to fold".

the statistical behavior of the system in the future. Simon (1962), by contrast, proposes that the complexity of a system can be characterized in terms of its degree of hierarchy: the complex system being composed of subsystems that, in turn, have their own subsystems, and so on. Lloyd (2001) even compiles 45 definitions of complexity; Philip W. Anderson, at the other end, thinks that it is a mistake to try to define complexity at all (cf. also Mitchell, 2009: Chapter 7; Gershenson, 2008; and Edmonds, 1999: Appendix 1 for an overview). This is but a small selection of academic treatises where "complexity" pops up, but it is sufficient to get the picture: work on this topic is still far from establishing clarity and consensus.

Helbing (2010: 3) distinguishes three different types of complexity out of which the first two mentioned are relevant in this context of risk management in banking (cf. also Ulrich & Probst, 1990: 57ff.).[40]

1) **Structural complexity or complicatedness** refers to systems that have many (moving) parts, but they operate in patterned ways (Sargut & Mc Grath, 2011: 70). A complicated system can be meaningfully analyzed and integrated, i.e., it can be taken apart into its components and reassembled from those components, which means crucially that it can be described by a mathematical system founded on *linearity* (Byrne & Callaghan, 2014: 4; Zadeh & Desoer, 1979: 132f.). Structural complexity or complicatedness applies, for example, to a car, which is a designed and complicated system made up of many parts. But these parts are constructed in a way that let them behave in a predictable and deterministic way, i.e. according to fixed rules. Therefore, a car is relatively easy to control (Helbing, 2010: 3). In other words, a complicated system is folded (Latin "*plic*") and consequently conceals its internal structure. Nevertheless, given enough time, we can discover how it works (Rzevski & Skobelev, 2014: 5).
2) Instead of the previous 'analytical' or 'reductionist' approach, characterized by "decomposing a system in components, such that the detailed understanding of each component was believed to bring understanding in

40 Apart from structural complexity and dynamic complexity, Helbing (2010) introduces the term "algorithmic complexity", pioneered by Andrei Kolmogorov, Ray Solomonov and Gregory Chaitin, which quantitatively measures the amount of resources (such as time and storage) needed by an algorithm or a computer to solve certain problems requiring significant resources. This notion of complexity is traditionally prevalent in theoretical computer science (see Appendix C), but less interesting for applications to risk management. Because, for example, Nicolis (in Gershenson, 2008: 107) states that algorithmic complexity is a static, equilibrium like concept.

the functioning of the whole" (Sornette, 2009: 1), **dynamic complexity** demands that one tries to comprehend the interconnections and relationships, i.e., "the whole picture as well as the component parts" (ibid.); this in turn includes analysis as well as synthesis (so-called 'systems thinking' is circular, Schwaninger, 2005: 32, 37; Morin, 2008; Suppes, 1983). Dynamic complexity can arise even in simple systems[41] (Pina & Rego, 2010: 92f.; Gribbin, 2005: 97) in terms of a low number of variables or components in a system (low levels of *combinatorial* or *detail* complexity; Morecroft, 2007: 21; Sterman, 2000)[42]; but, ceteris paribus, the more complex the system in the structural or combinatorial sense, the more it is dynamically complex. The latter primarily results from the interactions among the agents of a system *over time* (Morecroft, 2007: 21; Sterman, 2000: 21). It may be illustrated by freeway traffic where "the interaction of many independent driver-vehicle units with a largely autonomous behaviour can cause the self-organisation of different kinds of traffic jams, the occurrence of which is hard to predict" (Helbing, 2010: 3).[43]

41 If a system contains few interactions and if its behavior is extremely predictable, it is called a simple system – e.g., switching a light on and off: The same action produces the same result under normal conditions (Sargut & McGrath, 2011: 70). On more philosophical grounds, Rosen (1987: 324) calls a system "simple" if it is one in which "Aristotelian causal categories can be independently segregated from one another". Other forms of distinction exist and the one proposed by Weaver (1948) is particularly interesting. See Chapter 6.

42 Sterman (2000: 21) and Senge (2006: 71f.) who use this term do not further explicate the concept of *combinatorial* (Sterman) or *detail* (Senge) complexity.

43 At first glance, it might be objected that it would be illegitimate or overstating the case to draw a *qualitative* distinction between structural and dynamic complexity: If a 'combinatorially complex' situation is understood as one where you have to expect a large amount of possible outcome states (whose individual probabilities may be difficult to determine because they depend on a large number of aspects or variables), then taking additionally into account the interaction between agents over time just seems to multiply the number of possible outcome states. Indeed, it is hard to see why a 'purely combinatorially complex' system, able to assume many different states because of high numbers of components in a system and/or combinations, cannot be as complex as a dynamically complex system in finite time (i.e., in terms of the degree of complexity or variety) whose agents or system elements interact heavily, but are only few in number. Therefore, for the sake of the argument, interaction over time by itself seems simply to be one among other factors affecting/increasing the overall complexity.
While this objection might be valid to some complexity or systems researchers, because they do not sufficiently explain the difference between different notions of complexity (e.g., Sterman, 2000; Senge, 2006; Grösser, 2013), it should and will be elaborated on the special features of systems as *dynamically and organized* complex, which require, for example, specific modeling approaches, pointing, in turn, to a qualitative distinction between dynamic and other forms of complexity.

This dissertation focuses mainly on dynamic complexity because social systems, including financial systems,[44] are dynamic (i.e., *dynamic* wholes, Ulrich & Probst, 1990: 30), and "it is not so much discrete states which are of interest, but rather dynamic patterns or modes of behavior" (Schwaninger, 2009: 12; cf. also Peters & Gell-Mann, 2016). How, then, can we frame dynamic complexity? Naturally, one could simply introduce the term "*dynamic* complexity" by building on the general definition by Schwaninger (2009: 12): "A system is dynamically complex if, and only if, it is able to assume many different states or to produce many different behavior patterns *over time*." (Cf. also Ulrich & Probst, 1990: 58). This is a plausible, general definition, outlining complexity as a global characteristic or property of a system and which is intended to have different interpretations in different contexts; but at the end of the day, it might not be sufficiently enlightening or apt for application to real-world systems (Hoffmann, 2016).

A first step towards a concept clarification and refinement, which is very relevant for our purposes where ultimately doubt should be casted on the trustworthiness of statistical risk model results, was undertaken by Weaver (1948). His approach is outlined and extended in Chapter 6. For now, the previous findings from the literature are summarized in Figure 2.

2.2. Risk and Risk Management in the Financial World

Risk is absolutely central to modern finance (Lee et al., 2010; Saunders & Cornett, 2010; Allen & Gale, 2009). It is often captured by the concept of volatility and its cognates like variance and standard deviation (Markowitz, 1952; Rothschild & Stiglitz, 1970: 226; but also more recently: Goldstein & Taleb, 2007; Adrian, 2007: 3; Cecchetti, 2008: 97f.; Esposito, 2014: 22; Thiagarajan et al., 2015: 113).[45]

44 Social systems "may be groups, organizations, societies or functional subsystems of society such as an economy, a legal or a financial system" (Willke et al., 2013: 19). In modern financial systems, in particular, periods of stability (or of tranquility) are only transitory (Minsky, 1986/2008: ix). "The difficult part of understanding social systems is that they develop properties beyond the mere interaction of people [see below, Chapter 6]." (Willke et al., 2013: 19).

45 Compared to the variance, the standard deviation is more useful because it is measured in the same unit as the payoffs: monetary units. (Variance is measured in value terms (Swiss francs, say) squared.) Volatility or the standard deviation of returns measured in percentage terms are usually provided on an annual basis. Volatility is a critical variable in risk as it measures the magnitude of deviations from the mean of a market variable. The simplest definition of the volatility of random variables is the standard deviation.

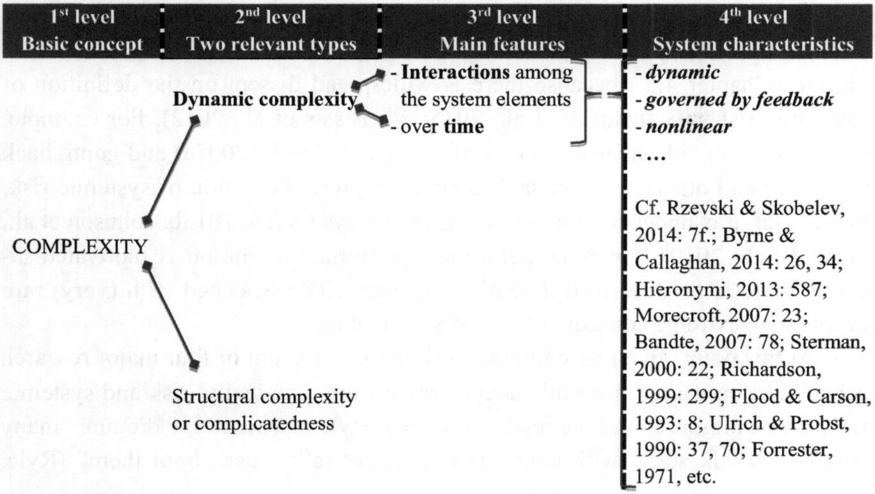

Figure 2: The disassembly of complexity I (with ◆—◆ for illustration's sake only).

Yet, this interpretation is not unproblematic. For example, the "*volatility paradox*" that characterized the mid-2000s – low market volatility as risks were building (Brose et al., 2014a: 333) – made it implausible to identify risk with volatility.[46] On a conceptual level, it is clearly to object that we ought to distinguish between what risk is and how to operationalize the concept (see Chapter 4.1.), given that variance and standard deviation are a *measure* of risk (like Value at Risk, see 2.2.2.) and not risk itself.

An overview of many different and material notions of risk including some of their major characteristics, strengths and weaknesses is given below (in Table 4) and a proper definition is invoked (4.1.), roughly saying that risk is the real or realistic possibility of a negative rare or very rare event with serious or even extreme consequences the occurrence of which is not certain, or expectable but only more or less likely.

---

46 Moreover, volatilities, whatever the measure, are elusive and they are unobservable (Bessis, 2010: 189f.). Volatility is volatile itself: "I try to measure the volatility. It changes all the time. Everything changes. Nothing is constant. It's a mess of the worst kind" (Mandelbrot & Hudson, 2008: 149). In addition to that, it is not clear that volatility is well-defined in a statistical sense, even for a time series (Granger, 2010: 40). Rothschild & Stiglitz (1970) show that the concept of increasing risk is not equivalent to that implied by equating the risk of *X* with the variance of *X*. Cf. also Goldstein & Taleb (2007) for another critique of volatility.

Turning to *systemic risks*, in particular, much ado has been made about defining the term. The current debate is not very satisfactory and, thus, illuminating (see Chapter 4.2.) because there is widespread dissent on the definition of "systemic risk" (Getmansky et al., 2015: 74; Bisias et al., 2012). For example, the iconic term "*black swan*", above all coined by Taleb (2007a) and going back to Popper and others, is often said to neatly capture the notion of systemic risk, but, in fact, it is understood in many different ways (Aven, 2013b; Johnson et al., 2012; Blyth, 2010). For now, before an appropriate definition is motivated in-depth, there is no need to differentiate between risk associated with (very) rare events with extreme consequences, and systemic risk.

At this point, an already important finding, a first out of four major research gaps,[47] can be gained from this laconic review on complexity, risk and systemic risk, which might remind the reader of Gilbert Ryle's provocative dictum: "many people can talk sense with concepts but cannot talk sense about them" (Ryle, 1949: 7f.).

> **Research Gap I:**
> Poor conceptualization of the terms "risk", "systemic risk", and "complexity", as well as knowledge deficits concerning the conceptual relationships between them, in a banking context.

This dissertation, therefore, follows the call of Heinemann (2014: 172), Grösser (2013: 211), Schwarcz (2008: 197), Helbing (2010: 2) and others for concept clarification and refinement. While not enough effort has been placed on circumscribing and explicating the concepts of risk and systemic risk, the field of modern finance has introduced seemingly sophisticated tools for measuring and managing risks. Financial risk management is the industry's analytical response to the challenges presented by an imperfect and uncertain world (Brose et al., 2014a: 369): "The analysis requires information as its key input, which in turn seem to require enormous amounts of data. The output is an array of concrete decisions, such as whether to make or deny a loan, whether to add capital to the firm, or how to hedge a position" (ibid.).

The definition of risk management that forms the basis for the development of risk measurement and management tools is wide and general. Based on a con-

47 The other three research gaps are presented on page 56, 63 and 71, respectively.

solidated review of different articles and papers in the literature of economics & finance, we propose to summarize the definition with the following sentence by Hubbard (2009): Risk management encompasses "the identification, assessment, and prioritization of risks […] followed by coordinated and economical application of resources to minimize, monitor, and control the probability and/or impact of unfortunate events" (Hubbard, 2009: 46; cf. also Saunders & Cornett, 2010). Accordingly, risk management may be broken down into a number of subprocesses:

1) *Risk identification*: Internal and external events that would or might affect the financial performance of a bank or the achievement of a bank's objectives must be identified (Brose et al., 2014a: 367; COSO, 2004).
2) *(Quantitative) risk assessment*:[48] Risks are analyzed, considering likelihood and impact, as a basis for determining how they should be addressed (ibid.).
3) *Communication* of risks from the risk management unit / department to senior management (and possibly the board of directors): Material information is beheld, captured (e.g., in a risk report) and conveyed in a form and time frame that enable people to carry out their responsibilities – 'risk owners' must be specified, see Part IV. The final decision to take (analyzed) risks "rests not with the risk manager, but with top management [in some firms, there is a chief risk officer; C.H.]" (Stulz, 2008: 59). This decision depends on the bank's strategy, which in turn depends heavily on its *risk appetite* or the tolerance of the institution, and both strategy and risk appetite are the prerogatives of senior or top management (Greenbaum, 2015: 170f.; Wiggins & Metrick, 2014): "It is at the heart of the firm's strategy and how it creates value for its shareholders" (Stulz, 2008: 59).[49]
4) *Risk response planning*: Management selects risk responses, including: averting, accepting, reducing or sharing risk, developing a set of actions to align risks with the bank's risk tolerances and risk appetite (Brose et al., 2014a: 367; COSO, 2004).

48 Part II of this dissertation deals with qualitative risk assessment.
49 Unfortunately, senior executives often do not have the time or are often not equipped to evaluate the results that mathematical models generate (Boatright, 2011: 8).

5) *Risk monitoring and control*: Monitoring or control is accomplished through ongoing activities like modifications to the risk management process, or separate evaluations, or both (COSO, 2004).

There is a lucid emphasis on strategic issues (risk appetite, objectives/goals), awareness (event identification, risk assessment, monitoring) and reaction (control activities, risk response planning, communication). In the context of this dissertation, the focus lies on step 2, on risk evaluation, because "the main responsibility of risk management is to assess the firm's risks" (Stulz, 2008: 59). Risk analytics is a critical first step towards managing it and McKinsey research suggests that by 2025 the risk function's staff are principally dedicated to risk measurement (Härle et al., 2016: 3). Within this piece of work, "risk assessment / evaluation" is used synonymously with "risk measurement", and measurement, tout court, is "the process by which numerals, numbers, and other symbols are assigned to defined attributes of the [not necessarily real, C.H.][50] world in such a way as to describe[51] them according to further clearly defined rules" (Flood & Carson, 1993: 39). If we wish to represent risks using, for example, probability theory (see below), then we must abide by these rules. Later on, it will be useful to distinguish between different *scales of measurement* (Chapter 18).

At the heart of the body of knowledge on financial risk management and practices is a collective of financial economic theories, employing a variety of stochastic models to assess and calculate the risks associated with a plethora of events, financial assets and contracts. Judging from briefly synthesizing several leading textbook in financial economics (McDonald, 2006; Hull, 2010; Stulz, 2002), there appears to be much evidence of the predictive powers of modern financial economics: "the accuracy and validity of risk models and the applications that use them are said to be tested and revalidated literally millions of times

50 Because there is a major controversy among risk experts about the nature of (objective vs. subjective) risks. See Chapter 4.1.

51 From a more critical and philosophical point of view, it might be noteworthy that, contrary to risk assessment, risk management is not a scientific undertaking. Hansson (2007: 22) argues that its starting point is the outcome of risk assessment, which it combines with economic and technological information pertaining to various ways of reducing or eliminating the risk in question, and also with political and social information. Based on this, a decision is made on what measures (if any) should be taken to reduce the risk (ibid.). An essential difference between risk assessment and management, according to his view, is that values only appear in risk management. Ideally, risk assessment is a value-free process (ibid.). But is it value-free in practice? See Chapter 10 and Part IV of this thesis.

a day in the markets" (Millo & MacKenzie, 2009: 638). This study adds, however, critically that probability-based risk models suffer from principal flaws when applied to extreme and systemic events (Chapter 7).

2.2.1. Risk modeling

As *unit of analysis* for this Part I, we consider probabilistic modeling of extreme or systemic risk. In very broad terms, modeling can be said to be a device that helps its users to spot the systems they are dealing with. Insofar, a *model* can be defined as a representation of a system – a group of functionally interrelated elements forming a complex whole (Mitchell, 2009: 209; Sterman, 2000: 89); but for a model to be useful, it must address a specific problem and must simplify rather than attempt to mirror a system replete with elements in detail. The use of models can fulfill different functions, such as description, explanation, design, decision and change (Schwaninger, 2010).[52]

In the context of this Part I of the dissertation, we deal with *formal* or *mathematical* models. A formal model is a set of assumptions plus the resulting body of pure theory which apply to an idealized system which seems closely enough like the real system so that the theory of the idealized system will "explain" or organize and simplify or describe the real phenomena or predict or prescribe their future behavior (Weaver, 1963: 39).[53] Probabilistic models are formal models that utilize probability theory. Like all models, they are supposed to correspond in a useful way to some real phenomena.

In order to contribute to the understanding of risk, and extreme or systemic risk in particular, and not just the understanding of "models", we have to extend the formalist definition with a reference to the concept that is being modeled, i.e., to (extreme or systemic) risk. It can therefore be said:

52 According to Schwaninger (2010), descriptive models represent what is the case; they make the issue under study comprehensible. Explanatory models elucidate why the real system at hand behaves as it does and not differently (ibid.: 1421). "They try to capture interrelationships, e.g. causalities, interactions and dependencies. Models of analysis and diagnosis, which are among the explanatory models, inquire into the implications of system behavior and of the structure underlying it." (ibid.). See also Chapter 8. Finally, design models are "instruments that support the conceptual development of systems" (ibid.).

53 If one is a very pure theoretician, one may be interested only in inventing and developing pure theories, "leaving it to others to look around in the real world to see if there is any 'application' for the theory" (Weaver, 1963: 39); i.e., whether there is a body of real phenomena behaving in accordance with the theory.

Definition 2.1:
(Extreme or systemic) risk models are sufficiently[54] *accurate descriptions of (extreme or systemic) risk given in a formal language.*[55]

In terms of Schwaninger (2010), risk models as defined here fulfill the following functions:[56]

- *Descriptive* (per definition: "descriptions of risk")
- More or less *explanatory*: The ability of risk models to explain and analyze the risk that a peculiar institution, individual, etc. is exposed to depends on the choice of the formal language and comes from the interpretation of the *right*, i.e., well-chosen, formal language, which allows one to arrive at causal claims about how certain aspects of a real system function or to make inferences; e.g., about future developments of the system behavior (hence, *predictions*).
- *Predictive*: Non-causal (i.e., their mathematical relations are not based on a theorized causal mechanism), but statistical and correlational models can also be used for prediction by simply expressing observed associations (in the form of statistical correlations) among various elements of a real system.

The *quality* or *usefulness* or *validity* of a risk model is then determined by, above all, two aspects: first, by the accuracy of predictions, i.e., how adequately the inferences from the model match reality, and second, by the plausibility of the model assumptions. More precisely, it has been stressed and argued that a (risk) model must generate the "right output for the right reasons" (Barlas, 1996: 186;

54 A broad concept of "model" would subsume theories, frameworks and the like. The concept of "model" used here, however, is a more operational one. In accordance with Schwaninger & Grösser (2008: 450), we conceive of modeling as a process by which models are built, whereby we will focus on computational models.

55 A formal language (e.g., mathematical formula, proposition in logic, computer program, etc.) is essentially a modeling language. Formal languages have precise syntax and semantics (interpretation in another formal language). For example, a set of random variables describing gains and losses (à la Artzner et al., 1999) is a risk model. Even the "model-free" measures of risk in Artzner et al. are subsumed under our definition since a portfolio or list of securities is also given in (semi-)formal language.

56 Rapoport (1953: Part III), for example, presents two further functions. The first he calls *heuristic* function (which leads the modeler to new (research) questions). The second he calls *measuring* function, which allows to quantify hitherto qualitative concepts.

Forrester, 1968; see also section 19 in Part III of this thesis for a more thorough discussion of model validation). It remains a legitimate question though why often rather unrealistic models in the social sciences remain matters of academic discussion (von Bertalanffy, 1968/2013: 112)?[57]

> **Definition 2.2.:**
> Furthermore, we define a *risk measure* as *a mapping from a risk model to a real number*. More formally: Let $\mathbb{M}$ be the set of all risk models. A risk measure is a function $f: \mathbb{M} \rightarrow \mathbb{R}$.[58] Consequently, a risk measure is also a risk model (but not vice versa) since it is definitely a description of risk, namely as a mathematical function.

A large number of different risk models exist in order to primarily make forecasts of the likely losses that would be incurred for a variety of risks (Rebonato, 2007: 43, 107f.): "it is vital to remain mindful that it is the *forecast* that matters" (Brose et al., 2014a: 340). Such risks are typically grouped into *market risk* (= the risk of losses in positions arising from movements in market prices), *credit risk* (= referring to the risk that a borrower will default on any type of debt by failing to make required payments), *liquidity risk* (= a given security or asset cannot be traded quickly enough in the market to prevent a loss), and *operational risk* (= the risk of direct or indirect losses, incurred for inadequate or failed inter-

57 Some economists defend remote assumptions of "if, then" models on "as if" grounds, whereby "the philosophy of as if" traces back to Hans Vaihinger's monumental work from 1913: "As long as the model yields accurate predictions, it's fine to represent the world as if it had […] outlandish features" (Bhidé, 2010: 97). According to Milton Friedman, for example, the assumptions of a hypothesis need not be verified; a hypothesis is confirmed only by its predictive success. Given that such success is achieved, the validity of assumptions is irrelevant. Unrealistic assumptions may well have value, as he and other so-called neoclassical economists argue, in making *positive* theories concise (ibid.: 99). "But when carried over into *normative* domains, they can produce dubious prescriptions" (ibid.). And, at least, theories of the social sciences are laden with values (Ulrich, 2014: 5f. Ulrich, 1993): There is no neutral theory concerning human affairs (Shrader-Frechette, 1985: 69). And Cyert & Grunberg (1963) propose that we give much more emphasis to the *explanatory* ability of models (see Part III of this thesis).

58 This definition is similar to the one given by Artzner et al. (1999: 207). According to them, a measure of risk is a mapping from $\mathcal{G}$ into $\mathbb{R}$ where $\mathcal{G}$ is the set of all risks, i.e. the set of all real-valued functions on Ω. Note that it is for good reason that $\mathbb{M}$ is less specified and refined than $\mathcal{G}$: While Artzner et al. stand in the tradition of probabilism (what we call *Risk II* in 4.1.), we endorse a broader framework (*Risk I*). See also 15.1. for modeling implications.

nal processes, people and systems, or from external events (including legal risk))[59] categories.

In this regard, it is common to speak of risk silos (apart from risk categories) and risk silo management (e.g., Mikes, 2009a). Given the importance and the reliance that nearly all financial institutions place on specific analytical models of various types and uses (as outlined in the successive sections) for assessing risks into the future (e.g., Mehta et al., 2012), it is particularly important that models be understood, vetted and calibrated (Braswell & Mark, 2014: 203; Cassidy, 2010: 1). The category of *model risk* grasps this idea and it is paraphrased as the risk associated with using a misspecified and, ergo, inappropriate model for measuring risk (McNeil et al., 2005: 3; The Economist, 1999).[60]

While the financial risks like market or credit risk can be thought of as the *raison d'être* for a bank – "it is only by accepting, managing and optimizing one or more of these financial risks that a firm can make a profit" (Mark & Krishna, 2014: 58) –, firms assume non-financial risks like operational or model risk, in contrast, simply by being in business but there is usually no upside for assuming such risks.[61]

The following Table 2 provides an overview of the major risk categories banks are confronted with and indicates how they usually measure and manage them. Apart from the three basic silos of risk, counterparty (credit) risk is emphasized because it has proven to be one of the most important sources of "systemic risk" (Nathanaël, 2010; French et al., 2010: 45) and it will be elaborated on in Part III for an exemplary application of a logic-based risk modeling approach, developed, endorsed and promoted, after all, in this thesis. Another important role is taken on by the category of model risk which is located at a higher level and reflects, in a way, the combative spirit of this whole thesis, aiming at pointing to

59 Although efforts to define and determine this category's scope more positively are recognizable – whereas within early regulatory discourses on the subject, operational risk was seen as simply a residual category for "other risks" –, this definition does still leave open a range of interpretations of the scope of operational risk which different groups could exploit (Power, 2007: 111). Cf. also BCBS (2015) for admitted difficulties in measuring the notion.

60 In an insurance context, the term "*risk of error*" is often used to designate model risk. Risk of error can be separated into forecasting risks and diagnostic risks.

61 Note that there are, however, a number of firms that have made non-financial risk mitigation their business by successfully building a business model where certain essential functions may be out-sourced by financial firms at a lower cost than keeping the function in-house and assuming the resulting risk (Mark & Krishna, 2014: 58). In terms of operational risks, examples include "IT out-sourcing contracts, securities custody services", etc. (ibid.).

limitations of standard risk management approaches. Albeit specific risk assessment and measurement procedures exist, the table also highlights the fact that the technique Value at Risk (VaR) is applied across all major risk silos. As an interesting side note, it is finally hinted at an empirical study by Kuritzkes & Schürmann (2010) where the authors show that the risks less (credit risk) and least (operational risk) easy to quantify, i.e., those risk silos which present risk silo managers with the greatest quantitative challenge (see footnote 62), have the greatest impact on bank earnings volatility.

Given the large number of risk models (Lee, et al., 2010; Saunders & Cornett, 2010; McDonald, 2006; McNeil et al., 2005; Hull, 2005; Stulz, 2002), it is neither possible nor necessary to canvass each and every one here. Most of them are closely related to each other (Daníelsson, 2002), and we feel justified in shedding light on a carefully selected subsample only (depending on how prominent, established and frequently studied or used the risk models are) since the conceptual and principal critique, which is developed in Chapter 7, targets basic properties, namely the probabilistic nature of most, if not all, models employed to deal with (very) high impact risks linked to (very) rare events. The models that will be sketched, thus for illustration's sake only, are: Value at Risk (*VaR*) and Expected Shortfall (*ES*), as well as some remarks on Conditional Value at Risk (*CoVaR*), Systemic Expected Shortfall (*SES*) (Bernard et al., 2013: 167-173), and the Extreme Value Theory (*EVT*) (e.g., Diebold et al., 1998).

The review of risk measures and models serves three purposes: To make the reader aware of the intricacies of the conventional approaches to risk measurement, above all focusing on extreme and systemic risks; to exemplify blind efficiency seeking in risk management, which was condemned in the Introduction of this thesis; and (most importantly) to allow for a comparison with our own proposal for an innovative and combative logic-based risk modeling approach which will be presented below (Part III).

2.2.2. Value at Risk (VaR)

VaR is the most frequently cited technique of risk silo management (Riedel, 2013: 21; Litzenberger & Modest, 2010: 75; Jorion, 1997). Interestingly, it was originally suggested by a group of bankers (Flood, 2014: 25; Granger, 2010: 36). *VaR* is the primary statistical tool for measuring market risk (Daníelsson, 2003: 178). Simply put, it is a statistical composite measure of unanticipated loss, derived

Table 2: Risks banks face and how they measure and manage them (based on: Capponi, 2013; Kuritzkes & Schürmann, 2010; Bessis, 2010; Mikes, 2009a: 11; Cecchetti, 2008: 295; Bervas, 2006; McNeil et al., 2005: 3; Drzik et al., 2004; Rebonato, 2002).

	Risk categories / silos	Source of Risk	Risk assessment and measurement: General	Risk assessment and measurement: Specific
Three basic categories of risk	Market risk (Financial risk)	Movements in market prices		Value at Risk (VaR)
	Credit risk (Financial risk)	Change in borrower's credit-worthiness	VaR (Mikes, 2009a: 11)	Credit rating models for measuring expected loss , based on estimates of the probability of default, loss given default, exposure at default (Kuritzkes & Schürmann, 2010: 115)
	Operational risk (Non-financial risk)	Many sources: e.g., fraud, a failed internal IT system, a terrorist attack		- Extreme Value Theory techniques (De Fontnouvelle et al., 2006) - Basic Indicator Approach (Mark & Krishna, 2014: 60) - AMA/LDA approaches (BCBS, 2015)
	Counterparty risk (Financial risk) (see Part III)	Counterparty fails to meet their obligations in a financial contract[63]		- Potential Future Exposure, and the Expected Exposure Profile (Capponi, 2013: 489); actions: e.g., deciding on trade execution or setting credit risk limits - Exemplary application of a logic-based risk modeling approach proposed in Part III of this thesis
	Model risk ("Meta risk") (see Part I–IV)	Using a misspecified model for measuring risk	- Inhabits, by definition, the opaque area where ascertained (Rebonato, 2002) - Validation is a continuous process of testing - Design more appropriate, "more valid" risk	

62 Data is taken from Kuritzkes & Schürmann (2010: 138). The authors conduct empirical research on bank earnings volatility – they define risk in banking in terms of earnings volatility. Their analysis precedes the credit crisis and financial market turmoil that began in mid-2007. Nevertheless, it establishes, for the 300+ U.S. bank holding companies that had total assets of at least USD 1bn (2005Q1 dollars) from 1986Q2 to 2005Q1, what the total level of earnings volatility (as reflected by quarterly deviation in returns on Basel I risk-weighted assets) is at varying quantiles. The analysis includes tail observations out to the 99.9% level corresponding to a 0.1% one-year default probability. Kuritzkes & Schürmann estimate the relative contribution to bank earnings volatility from each of five sources of risk identified in their taxonomy. Apart from the three basic categories, they consider structural asset/liability risk (a financial risk, 18%) and business risk (a non-financial risk, 18%). They found, for example, that although the most is "known" about market risk – "knowledge of bank risk increases as our ability to quantify risk increases" –, it contributes the least to bank earnings volatility at the 99.9% level.

Our ability to quantify	Risk allocation (in %)[62]	Risk management actions
High	6	Mitigate market risk: e.g., liquidate tradable instruments or hedge their future changes
Medium	46	Mitigate credit risk: e.g., diversify to spread risk or screen for creditworthy borrowers
Low	12	Mitigate operational risk: e.g., set up a common classification of events that should serve as a receptacle for data-gathering processes on event frequencies and costs (Bessis, 2010: 36)
	Comment	
Low	Embedded in all financial contracts which are traded over the counter (OTC), where the credit quality of counterparties plays a key role. Counterparty credit risk as one of the major drivers of the credit crisis of 2007-09, evidencing that counterparty risk is one of the most important sources of system-wide failure (Nathanaël, 2010).	
Comment		
the value of instruments cannot be fully & directly & building confidence in models (see Part III&IV) models (Part III)		

63 The difference between counterparty risk and credit risk is that the latter can be effectively mitigated by requiring a security (collateral) from the borrower, whereas the former includes the potential loss incurred when the value of the security does not cover the value of the principal. "Unlike a firm's exposure to credit risk through a loan, where the exposure to credit risk is unilateral and only the lending bank faces the risk of loss, the counterparty credit risk creates a bilateral risk of loss, when both parties are default-sensitive" (Capponi, 2013: 485).

from the loss distributions of different risk types that institutions track (e.g., market losses, credit losses, operational losses, insurance losses). Phrased differently, *VaR* is the upper bound potential loss not exceeded with some predetermined high probability, called a confidence level α (Bessis, 2010: 201). It was designed to provide an answer to the following question (where the wording clarifies the reference of *VaR* to the tail of the distribution):

> *What is the **minimum** loss incurred in the 1–α least likely cases of our portfolio?*[64]

In formal terms: If $F_L(l)$ is the loss distribution, that is the probability that the loss L is smaller than or equal to l, a maximum loss value amount (e.g., lost in liquidating a position), or $F_L(l) = P(L \leq l)$, is

$$VaR_\alpha \;=\; \inf\,\{l \in \mathbb{R} \mid F_L(l) \leq (1-\alpha)\}.$$

□ □ □

VaR is a quantile of the loss distribution – of course a real VaR calculation on a so-called clean P&L (see Appendix A) is a highly complicated matter; it is not "just reading off a quantile", it is all about L. Usually it holds that $\alpha = 0.95$ or higher. To give an illustrative example, in the case of a bank whose senior management specifies a 99 per cent (%) confidence level, a one-day *VaR* of $150 million would mean that the firm has a 1% chance of making a loss in excess of $150 million – provided, of course, the *VaR* has been correctly estimated.[65] In other words, we have $VaR_{0.99} = \inf\{l \in \mathbb{R} \mid F_L(l) \leq 0.01\} = \inf(150{,}000{,}000, \infty) = 150{,}000{,}000$. The argument to inf □ contains all the losses that occur with a probability smaller than or equal to 0.01, and the *VaR* is the smallest of those.

Risk measurement takes place in the context of risk metrics like *VaR*. The choice of risk metrics has been named the *cornerstone* of risk management (Stulz, 2008: 60). *VaR* received critical examination from several papers (e.g., Rowe, 2009; Bookstaber, 2009; Johnson & Kwak, 2009; Daníelsson, 2002; Engel & Gizycki, 1999). The reasons for its popularity are many, but the following might be the most important: First, it was specified by regulators (BCBS, 1996).

64 The question does not have to be related to a portfolio. See below.

65 Although financial institutions generally report daily VaR measures, VaRs can also be estimated for longer periods of time (Stulz, 2008: 59).

Second, it is said to have the largest set of desirable properties compared to other possible risk measures (Daníelsson, 2003: 178) – surely, a statement we cannot agree with (see Part III). Third, unlike simple volatility measures, *VaR* is clearly focused on the tails of (the downside of) the returns distribution,[66] given that $\alpha = 0.95$ or higher (Brose et al., 2014a: 337), which makes it especially attractive in the context here. Fourth, it is also widely applicable, not just to equities, but also to bonds, commodities, derivatives (see Part III), and other financial instruments, to single assets, asset classes or portfolios, and to both individual and firm-wide risks (Nocera, 2009). Finally, fifth, it "utilizes sophisticated mathematical formulas to circumvent the need to perform an immense number of calculations about each asset in a portfolio" (Boatright, 2011: 12f.), for example, and hence, its wide-spread adoption is due to the convenience of a single dollar or franc figure that epitomizes a complex concept (which points to its weaknesses at the same time; cf. Rootzén & Klüppelberg, 1999, for example; and see Chapter 4).

However, *VaR* has drawbacks as well. In particular, one can behold three specific flaws of *VaR* as a mode of risk assessment, which rather concern its irresponsible and unwarranted application (points 1 and 2), less the risk measure *per se* (point 3).

1) Foremost, *VaR* does not give any information about the severity of losses that occur with a probability lower than $1-\alpha$. This is particularly interesting for this study since rare events whose probability is almost certainly less than, e.g., 5%, are targeted. If, on the other hand, a much higher confidence level was picked (e.g., $\alpha = 0.999$ etc.), the model results would be implausible: Rebonato (2007: 136) regards such quantiles as *science-fiction* (cf. also Das et al., 2013: 715). *VaR* remains unchanged by large risk exposures that occur sufficiently infrequently to fall beyond the *VaR* threshold, and the ubiquity of *VaR* as a tool for setting risk limits thus encourages traders, *users*, to take on large tail risks (Brose et al., 2014a: 337; Rowe, 2009).
2) Some common, not all, implementations of *VaR* (e.g., by means of the so-termed variance-covariance technique; see 7.2.) implicitly and unre-

66 While a simple variance framework is often criticized for failing to distinguish between the downside of the return distribution (usually considered to be risk, see 4.1.) and the upside (usually considered to be potential), VaR is one (of several) ways of focusing on the downside.

alistically assume 'normally' distributed returns (so-called because it has been long viewed as the norm in nature; for a critical reply, see 2.5.), arriving independently from day to day with no jumps in the process. "In a normal distribution the likelihood that an observation many standard deviations beyond a 95% or even a 99% confidence interval will occur is infinitesimal" (Crotty, 2009: 571). In fact, "security prices follow a distribution in which the preponderance of observations are 'normal', but every five to ten years observations occur that are so far from the mean that they are virtually incompatible with the assumption of a normal distribution" (ibid.; cf. also Fama, 1965, 1970; Heri & Zimmermann, 2001: 1005; Buchanan, 2013: 436f.; Redak, 2011: 449ff.; Mandelbrot & Hudson, 2008: 134ff., 186ff.; Helbing, 2010: 4; Erben & Romeike, 2006). Taleb (2013: 37) baptizes this phenomenon the "masquerade problem" – "a fat tailed distribution can masquerade as a low-risk one, but not the reverse". Examples of this well-acquainted trouble with '*fat tails*'[67], i.e., high kurtosis[68] or significant outliers[69], of extreme events that are much more likely than for normally distributed data with the same mean and variance (see 2.5. and Figure 17 and 18) include the distortions brought on by the collapse of the giant hedge fund Long Term Capital Management (see 5.2.), the Asian crisis, or the demise of Lehman Brothers etc. Such common *VaR* implementations are recipes for underestimating tail risks (Brose et al., 2014a: 337; BCBS, 2011). See IIIc) in Chapter 2.4. and Chapter 7 for a fundamental issue behind this admonition. In face of this conceptual critique (Chapter 7), a regime-switching volatility model that assumes different market regimes with various volatilities (Papaioannou et al., 2015: 25) and that has been suggested in response to this issue of procyclicality is not convincing.

3) Artzner et al. (1999) present and vindicate a set of four desirable properties for measures of risk, and mark the measures satisfying these properties "*coherent*". They demonstrate that *VaR* measures, or more

67 The literature also speaks of heavy or long tails and there is no need to differentiate between those terms.

68 A normal distribution will have a kurtosis of 3.

69 An outlier is an observation that lies an abnormal distance from other values in a random sample from a population (Sornette, 2009: 5).

generally, quantiles-based risk measures, are not coherent since they do not satisfy postulate Nr. 2, sub-additivity. Sub-additivity reflects the idea that risk can be curtailed by diversification – in the words of Miguel de Cervantes Saavedra's Don Quixote (1605): "it is the part of a wise man to keep himself today for tomorrow, and *not to venture all his eggs in one basket* [emphasis added]" –, a time-honored principle in economics and finance (for technical details, cf. their paper).[70] Many researchers (e.g., McNeil et al., 2005; Bertsimas et al., 2000; Embrechts, 2000; Pflug, 2000) and practitioners / regulators (Yamai & Yoshiba, 2002) take these axioms seriously in terms of regarding these axioms as defining the concept of risk or risk measure itself. As a consequence, VaR is sometimes considered as not being a risk model at all.

2.2.3. Expected Shortfall (ES)

VaR is only the smallest potential loss that occurs with a given probability of less than or equal to $1 - \alpha$, and does not contain any information about the distribution of loss beyond α. This can be seen in the definition of VaR (see above), which takes the infimum (inf□) of all losses with sufficiently low probabilities. Assume, for example, a α=99%-VaR of $150M. This could mean that, for example, the chance of losing $150M is 0.9% and the chance of any losses greater than $150M is 0.1%. However, the following scenario is also possible and results in exactly the same VaR: Assume the probability of losing exactly $150M is 0.001 (a tenth of one percent), but the probability of losing, say, $300M is 0.009 (nine tenths of one percent). In this latter case, the VaR value of $150M would be delusive since there is a higher loss ($300M) with a much higher probability than that of $150M. For this reason, the Expected Shortfall (ES) or the tail conditional expectation (sometimes also named conditional VaR; Söderlind, 2014)[71] considers *all* losses that occur with low probabilities, by integrating over the entire tail of the distribution. It is geared to provide an answer to the following question:

---

70 More precisely, the non-subadditivity of VaR holds for so-called non-elliptical portfolios (Embrechts et al., 1998). More about coherent risk measures follows in a later section of Part III. See Chapter 15.1.

71 Here, we use the two different terms for two different concepts. See 2.3.1.

What is the ***expected*** *loss incurred in the 1–α least likely cases of our portfolio?*

$$ES_\alpha = \frac{1}{1-\alpha}\int_\alpha^1 q_u(F_l)du$$

$$\square = \frac{1}{1-\alpha}\int_\alpha^1 VaR_u(L)du$$

where α is the confidence interval and F_l stands for the loss distribution.

The primary improvement of ES over VaR is that ES (through integrating over the tail of the distribution) considers the expected value of *all* losses with a sufficiently low probability, rather than the *minimum* loss that might occur. ES_α depends only on F_L and $ES_\alpha \geq VaR_\alpha$.

ES addresses some of the theoretical drawbacks of VaR by tackling the problem of ignoring loss exposures in the tail of a loss distribution. It is able to overcome some of the conceptual deficiencies of VaR related to sub-additivity. Indeed, the coherence of ES can be proved (McNeil et al., 2005: 243f.; Acerbi & Tasche, 2001).

ES (i.e., the expected loss, conditional on being in the tail) also forms a useful complement to VaR (Brose et al., 2014a: 338). It is preferred to VaR by more and more risk professionals for several reasons (McNeil et al., 2005: 44): Like VaR, ES is universal: it can be applied to any instrument and to any underlying source of risk. ES is complete: it produces a global assessment for portfolios exposed to different sources of risk. Being a sub-additive measure of risk, ES values, e.g., of different trading desks, can be aggregated to firm-levels in a way that respects portfolio diversification. ES is (even more than VaR) a simple concept since "it is the answer to a natural and legitimate question on the risks run by a portfolio" (Acerbi & Tasche, 2001: 8). Furthermore, "any bank that has a VaR-based Risk Management system could switch to ES with virtually no additional computational effort" (ibid.). Finally and most importantly, in the sense of proper risk management which takes place, not in the world of 'If'-thinking, but in a world of "What if" thinking (see also Chapter 5.1.: event-oriented world-view vs. feedback view of the world), ES can be regarded as a step in the right direction due to its severity, not frequency orientation (attributed to discussions with Prof. Paul Embrechts). In this (after efficiency aspiring) sense, ES vis-à-vis VaR constitutes a certain progress in financial risk management.

Yet, the fundamentals are not undermined, the potential of "What if" or systemic thinking is not fully tapped as Part III of this thesis reveals. ES is still susceptible to improper distributional assumptions, misleading estimation windows and, foremost, this is due to it being grounded in statistics and classical probability theory which will lead us to our central objection to conventional quantitative management tools of extreme risks in general (Chapter 7).

2.3. Systemic Risk Assessment

Many so-called systemic risk models with different functions, designs and groundings exist. Two major approaches can be distinguished. The first major approach, the so-termed Extreme Value Theory (*EVT*), is a branch of statistics dealing with extreme quantiles and probabilities "by fitting a 'model' to the empirical survival function of a set of data using only the extreme event data rather than all the data, thereby fitting the tail, and only the tail" (Diebold et al., 1998: 2).[72]

The second has more heterogeneous manifestations. There are mainly two subgroups. One consists of chiefly network analysis and agent based models (e.g., Bookstaber et al., 2015; Cristelli, 2014; Thurner & Poledna, 2013) and works directly on the structure, the nature of relationships between banks in the market (Bernard et al., 2013: 166). King et al. (2014: 108f.) provide a good exposition of such explanatory systemic risk models, designed for, above all, regulators which they group into three broad families: 1) High level analyses which focus on a few causes and effects, 2) Network and institutional analyses (cf. Bernard et al., 2013), and 3) Granular analyses encompassing simulation as a tool and System Dynamics (SD) Modeling. In the broader context of the discussion of mathematical models in general, Barlas & Carpenter (1990: 148) add with regard to this first subgroup that these models base their mathematical expressions on postulated causal relations within the modeled system and are committed to substantiate causal claims about how certain aspects of a real system function. They can be used for both prediction and explanation (ibid.). Explanatory

72 The survival function is simply one minus the cumulative density function, 1 – P(x). Note, in particular, that because P(x) approaches 1 as *x* grows, the survival function approaches 0 (Diebold et al., 1998: 1f.).

systemic risk models for regulators, basically frameworks for systemic risk (in the narrow sense, see 4.2.) monitoring (e.g., King et al., 2014), are however not discussed in this context for mainly three reasons.[73]

Another systemic risk approach, principally different, is to investigate the impact of one institution on the market and its contribution to the global systemic risk (Bernard et al., 2013: 166). Similarly, Barlas & Carpenter (1990: 148) refer to these models' counterparts (i.e., on more general grounds) as non-causal, which simply express observed associations (in the guise of statistical correlations) among various elements of a real system. They call them purely empirical or correlational, their mathematical relations are not based on a theorized causal mechanism.

In any case, we refrain from an exact definition or a comprehensive characterization of the models in these rubrics due to many reasons. For example, Extreme Value Theory (EVT) is an entire branch of statistics and its full presentation would go far beyond the boundaries of current work. Conditional Value at Risk (CoVaR), and Systemic Expected Shortfall (SES) are just derivatives of VaR and ES, respectively. On top of that, the Central Argument of this Part I and the critique it puts forward is fundamental, rather than specific to peculiar risk models or measures. Therefore, only some brief conceptual remarks on CoVaR, SES, and EVT follow in the frame of this work.[74]

---

73 Firstly, following Bernard et al. (2013) and Weistroffer (2012: 12), CoVaR and SES are definitely the more prominent, established and more frequently studied or used systemic risk models (in the classical or narrow sense of "systemic risk") and this might not be unjustified. Because interestingly, it is secondly far from clear whether or not explanatory systemic risk models *for regulators* are more useful in a systemic risk management and monitoring context than their counterparts which are purely empirical or correlational (as Barlas & Carpenter (1990: 148) would put it). For example, Adrian & Brunnermeier (2011: 9) view it as a virtue rather than as a disadvantage that the CoVaR measure does not distinguish whether the contribution to systemic risk is causal or simply driven by a common factor. Be that as it may (i.e., even if Adrian & Brunnermeier (2011) are right in preferring their non-causal measure CoVaR to alternatives of *certain* explanatory systemic risk models, this does not entail that *all* explanatory systemic risk models would be inferior), the primary subject of this thesis are thirdly models for assessing extreme financial risks or systemic risks *in the sense of 4.2.* from market participants' or banks' (not regulators') point of view (see also 8.2.). The question of which *other* systemic risk models to consider is subordinate.

74 Formal details and numerical examples are provided by Bernard et al. (2013: 172f.).

2.3.1. Tools primarily for regulators: Conditional Value at Risk (CoVaR) and Systemic Expected Shortfall (SES)

Conditional Value at Risk (CoVaR)

Contributing to that second subgroup of (non-causal) approaches, Adrian & Brunnermeier (2011) invoke, on the one hand, the *CoVaR* measure. They pursue two objectives: first, to construct a measure that identifies "the risk to the system by 'individually systemic' institutions, which are so densely interconnected and large that they can cause negative risk spillover effects on others, as well as by institutions that are 'systemic as part of a herd'" (ibid.: 1; cf. also Brunnermeier et al., 2009b). Second, to provide regulators with measures that "recognize that risk typically builds up in the background in the form of imbalances and bubbles and materializes only during a crisis" (Adrian & Brunnermeier, 2011: 1). The idea of CoVaR now is to compare the VaR of the system under "normal conditions" and the VaR of the system "conditional on institutions being under distress". Adrian & Brunnermeier (2011) define an institution's contribution to systemic risk as the difference between CoVaR conditional on the institution being under distress and the CoVaR in the median state of the institution. Their proposal of CoVaR allows, for instance, to ventilate the question of "which institutions are most at risk [of default, for example; C.H.] should a financial crisis occur" (ibid.: 8).

CoVaR conditions on the event that an individual institution is at its VaR level, occurring with probability $1-\alpha$. The systemic risk is then measured by the difference with the unconditional VaR or by the difference with the "median" situation. The difference between the VaR of the financial system conditional on the distress of a particular financial institution and the VaR of the financial system conditional on the 'normal' or median state of the institution captures the marginal contribution of a particular institution (in a non-causal sense) to the overall systemic risk (ibid.: 2), whereas previous risk measures like VaR or ES only focus on the individual risks of individual institutions.

Systemic Expected Shortfall (SES)

Similarly, one main stimulus for Acharya et al. (2010: 2) to develop *SES* is the tension between the fact that financial *regulations*, such as Basel I and Basel II, and risk measures in this connection, on the one hand, are designed to assess and limit each institution's risk seen in isolation; and, on the other hand, a focus on systemic risk which "is often the rationale provided for such regulation". Systemic risk is linked in their view to financial contagion (see also 4.2. for a discussion of different understandings). In contrast to Adrian & Brunnermeier's (2011) proposal, they define a systemic risk measure, SES, in terms of the marginal expected shortfall (MES), i.e., a financial firm's "losses in the tail of the aggregate sector's loss distribution" (Acharya et al., 2010: 3). For example, MES can be specified to be "the average return of each firm during the 5% worst days for the market" (ibid.: 4).[75] "A financial system is constituted by a number of banks, just like a bank is constituted by a number of groups. We can therefore consider the expected shortfall of the overall banking system by [replacing a certain bank's return by; C.H.] the return of the aggregate banking sector or the overall economy.[76] Then each bank's contribution to this risk can be measured by its MES." (Ibid.: 6f.).

SES is measurable because it "increases in the bank's expected losses during a crisis" (ibid.: 3). This creates a systemic risk index among banks based on their individual contribution to the capital shortfall of the financial system (Acharya & Steffen, 2013: 247). The SES measures, and is conceived of as, the propensity of a bank to be undercapitalized when the system as a whole is undercapitalized (Bernard et al., 2013: 170; Acharya & Steffen, 2013: 248). The measure increases with the bank's leverage and with its expected loss in the tail (ES) of the system's loss distribution (SES).

Acharya et al. (2010: 1) show empirically "the ability of SES to predict emerging risks during the financial crisis of 2007-2009". A lesson for regulators might be that financial institutions internalize the cost that affects the financial system or its players, respectively (who did not choose to incur that cost which results e.g. from a bank's demise)[77], i.e., internalize their externality, if they are "taxed" based on their SES (cf. also Poledna & Thurner, 2016).

In this stream of literature, systemic risk seems to be (narrowly, see 4.2.) ascertained by the dependency between the individual institution and the finan-

75 An empirical extension is given by Brownless & Engle (2011).

76 The return of the aggregate banking sector can be seen as a weighted sum of the returns of each bank (out of a total number of banks) and the weight of each bank is relative to the total aggregated value of the market (it could be interpreted as each bank's assets divided by the aggregate value of the market).

77 Of course, distress costs can occur even if a firm does not actually default.

cial system or the economy in a state of stress (Bernard et al., 2013: 166). Other tail dependence measures alternative to *CoVaR* and *SES* exist (cf. Joe, 1997; Juri & Wühtrich, 2003; Embrechts et al., 2003; McNeil et al., 2005; Nelsen, 2006): e.g., co-exceedances and exceedance correlations between the financial system and an individual financial institution.

2.3.2. Extreme Value Theory (EVT)

Longin (1996, 2000) is one of the main promoters of EVT and he has advocated its use for risk management purposes. As stated earlier, we will not attempt to depict EVT in a 'short summary' form; cf. Embrechts et al., 1997; Embrechts et al., 1999 and the references therein. The key point is that EVT deals with the description (rather than the explanation)[78] of extremes (maxima, minima, longest runs, longest time, …) of random phenomena (Embrechts, 2000: 7). It focuses on extreme deviations from the median of probability distributions. It is a territory of statistics that is devoted to modeling the maxima of a random variable (e.g., the potential extreme profits and losses made by a bank's portfolio) or to "estimating what happens to a distribution in the far-out tails (i.e., to assessing the probability of exceedingly rare events)" (Rebonato, 2007: 167). In its easiest form, EVT "yields the canonical theory for the (limit) distribution of normalised maxima of independent, identically distributed random variables" (Embrechts, 2000: 7). "In its more advanced form, EVT describes the behavior of extremal events for stochastic processes, evolving dynamically in time and space" (ibid.).

In particular, it provides a general foundation for the estimation of the VaR for very low-probability 'extreme' events (Johansen & Sornette, 2001: 1). Indeed, EVT can be used to model tail-focused risk measures such as VaR, but also ES (Gilli & Kellezi, 2006). EVT is in antagonism to traditional parametric statistical and econometric methods that are typically based on the estimation of entire densities, and which have been considered ill-suited to the assessment of extreme quantiles (especially, $\alpha > 0.999$) and event probabilities (see above; Christoffersen et al., 2003: 166). On the one hand, these parametric methods implicitly strive to attain a good fit in regions where most of the data fall, potentially "at the expense of good fit in the tails, where, by definition, few observations fall" (Diebold et al., 1998: 1).[79] On the other hand, "seemingly sophisticat-

78 Strictly speaking, we should not call it a *theory* then, see footnote 15.

79 This includes, for example, the fitting of stable distributions, as in McCulloch, 1996.

ed non-parametric methods of density estimation, such as kernel smoothing, are also well-known to perform poorly in the tails" (ibid.: 1f.).[80] By contrast, Diebold et al. (1998: 2) underline that EVT has a number of attractive features, including:

- The estimation method is tailored to the object of interest, the tail of the distribution, rather than the center of the distribution.
- An arguably-reasonable functional form for the tail can be formulated from a priori considerations (however, see Chapter 7 for the manifesto of an outspoken partisan).
- Moreover, Embrechts (2000) stresses that the main virtue of EVT is that it gives the user a critical view on, and a methodological toolkit for, issues like skewness, fat tails, rare events, stress scenarios, etc.

The concerns of EVT are in fact wide-ranging and comprise fat-tailed distributions, time series processes with heavy-tailed innovations, general asymptotic theory, point process theory, long memory and self-similarity (see 2.5.), and much else (Diebold et al., 1998).

However, although it has been claimed that EVT holds promise for accurate estimation of extreme quantiles and tail probabilities of financial asset returns, there are also a number of severe pitfalls associated with the use of EVT techniques (Diebold et al., 1998):

- For example, whereas the EVT literature usually assumes *independent* returns, which implies that the degree of fatness in the tails decreases as the holding horizon lengthens, Johansen & Sornette (2001) demonstrate that this is not the case: "returns exhibit strong correlations at special times precisely characterized by the occurrence of extreme events, the regime that EVT aims to describe" (ibid.: 1). See also IIIb) and IIIc) in 2.4.
- In the light of widespread complexity, it is also fatal that "nonlinearities can ruin the heavy-tailed modeler's day" (Resnick, 1998). See also Chapter 6 and 7.
- In addition, the reliance on *elusive* estimations of tail probabilities poses serious difficulties for the use of extreme value distributions for risk

80 Cf. Silverman, 1986.

management (Johansen & Sornette, 2001). One has to make mathematical assumptions on the tail model which are very difficult (if at all) to verify in practice (Embrechts, 2000). Hence, there is intrinsic *model risk*. See Part I-IV.

The problem as relevant for the present context – applications of statistical methods like EVT in financial risk management – is that "for estimating objects such as a 'once every hundred years' quantile, the relevant measure of sample size is likely much better approximated by the number of non-overlapping hundred-year intervals than by the number of data points. From that perspective, our data samples are terribly small relative to the demands we place on them" (Diebold et al., 1998: 8). As a consequence, current risk evaluation is more based on confidence intervals and tolerance ranges and less on exact tail probabilities.

2.4. General Appraisal

Extant systemic risk models and measures are used to predict *what* happens *when* the system is under stress. Some (CoVaR, SES) are based on standard risk measures (VaR and ES), and others (EVT) are designed specifically for tail risks. In contrast to VaR, ES, and EVT, SES and CoVaR, as the perhaps most prominent representatives of *systemic* risk measures or models, were primarily initiated for improving the work of regulators (King et al., 2014: 118, 136; Adrian & Brunnermeier, 2011: 4). This is not surprising since systemic risk is usually defined narrowly and systemic risk in *this* sense is usually seen as the concern of regulators (see Chapter 5.1. for a critical reply).[81]

However, none of the systemic risk models presented hitherto in this thesis, be it SES and CoVaR (according to the classical and narrow comprehension of systemic risk) or VaR, ES, and EVT (according to the broad use of the term proposed in Chapter 4.2.), explain *why* the system is under stress or what the *causes* of stress are (Bernard et al., 2013: 177). For example, VaR and ES pose and answer a *What* question and not a *Why* question. Or in terms of SES and CoVaR, a company may indeed be culpable for creating systemic risk or producing a certain state (stress) or behavior of the financial system without being under

81 For example, such traditional systemic risk models serve as a rationale for which institutions should be considered systemically relevant or the main policy implication might be that minimum capital standards for banks should be higher than they have been to date.

stress when the system is under stress (e.g., consider the role of Goldman Sachs or of Fabrice Tourre, VP at Goldman Sachs, during the financial crisis of 2007-09; ibid.: 178; Le Monde, 2013). Those models hinge on big amounts of data (Brose et al., 2014: 369; see also 7.2.) and do not distinguish whether the contribution to potential losses is causal or simply driven by a common factor. They are explanatorily impotent (Schwaninger, 2010: 1421).

Albeit managing risks is inevitably directed by evidence claims (Renn, 2008: 4): e.g., what are the *causes* and what are the *effects*?, and even though the plea for taking dynamics, interrelations and interdependencies in risk modeling into account is not new (e.g., Acharya et al., 2013: 204; Thurner & Poledna, 2013; Helbing, 2010; Stulz, 2008: 62), the literature has not yet amply identified and discussed the need for explanatory models (see Appendix A for a definition/characterization) to describe, quantify and explain systemic risks in and to the financial system – especially from market participants' and not regulators' stance. Accordingly, the second out of four research gaps says the following.

> **Research Gap II:**
> Lack of understanding of *what* sort of explanatory models are required for banks' in-house systemic risk management purposes, *why* they are needed, and *in what sense* existing systemic or extreme risk measures and models turn out to be insufficiently explanatory.

Table 3 summarizes and organizes the different kinds of systemic risk models, what purposes they are able to serve and how they should reasonably be categorized.

2.4.1. Advantages of conventional risk models and measures

According to McNeil et al. (2005), reasons for using statistical risk models that are derived from probability or (profit and) loss distributions (see Chapter 7.2.), in general, include:

1) Losses are the central object of interest in risk management and so it is *natural* to base a measure of risk on their distribution.
2) The concept of a loss distribution makes sense on all levels of *aggregation* from a portfolio consisting of a single instrument to the overall position of a financial institution.

Table 3: Overview of systemic risk models and how they might be classified.

Systemic risk models	Underlying systemic risk concept	Users	**Category of mathematical models (Barlas & Carpenter, 1990)** **Causal or theory-like models** • Mathematical expressions based on postulated causal relations • Seek to make causal claims about how certain aspects of a real system function **Category of systemic risk models (Bernard et al., 2013)** Focus on structure, nature of relationships between banks in the market (network analysis is seen as predominant)	**Non-causal, statistical / correlational models** • Simply express observed associations (statistical correlations) among elements of a real system • Mathematical relations are not based on a theorized causal mechanism Investigate the impact of one institution on the market and its contribution to the global systemic risk	Purpose / Function
Value at Risk (**VaR**)	Broad (see Chapter 4.2., definition on p. 74)	Both banks & possibly regulators	--	Non-causal but not a systemic risk model in the sense of Bernard et al. (2013)	- Description - Prediction
Expected Shortfall (**ES**)	Broad (see Chapter 4.2., definition on p. 74)	Both banks & possibly regulators	--	Non-causal but not a systemic risk model in the sense of Bernard et al. (2013)	- Description - Prediction
Extreme Value Theory (**EVT**)	Broad (see Chapter 4.2., definition on p. 74)	Both banks & possibly regulators	--	Non-causal but not a systemic risk model in the sense of Bernard et al. (2013)	- Description - Prediction
Conditional Value at Risk (**CoVaR**)	Narrow (see Chapter 4.2., the 3 types of concepts 1) to 3))	Regulators	Direct **LBR** rivals → Data-driven --	X	- Description - Prediction
Systemic Expected Shortfall (**SES**)	Narrow (see Chapter 4.2., the 3 types of concepts 1) to 3))	Regulators	--	X	- Description - Prediction
Not further considered here: Explanatory systemic risk models for **regulators** (King et al., 2014)	Narrow (see Chapter 4.2., the 3 types of concepts 1) to 3))	Regulators	Divided into three broad families: 1) High level analyses which focus on a few causes and effects, 2) Network and institutional analyses (cf. Bernard et al., 2013), 3) Granular analyses encompassing simulation & System Dynamics (SD) Modeling	--	- Description - Prediction - *Explanation*
Novel approach proposed here: Logic-Based Risk modeling (**LBR** in Part III)	Broad (see Chapter 4.2., definition on p. 74)	Here: Banks (future research required for other results)	- Rather *logical* than causal modeling, and not network analysis modeling - *Structure-oriented* instead of data-driven	--	- Description - Prediction - *Explanation*

derived

3) If estimated properly, the loss distribution reflects *netting and diversification effects*.
4) Loss distributions can be *compared* across portfolios.

Yet, none of these reasons *require* the use of statistical models. Indeed, symbolic and logic-based risk modeling, as we are going to invoke and summarize it (Part III), provides very similar benefits; however, purged of appealing on loss/probability distributions. Furthermore, the latter add additional benefits – for example, knowledge reusability, which diminishes the cost of developing risk models. See Chapter 19.

2.4.2. Weaknesses of conventional risk models and measures

In general terms and as the discussion in Stulz (2008) suggests, there are five types of risk management failures:

1) Failure to use suitable risk metrics
2) Mismeasurement of known risks
3) Mismeasurement stemming from overlooked risks
   3.1) Ignored known risks (wrongly viewed as immaterial)
   3.2) Unknown or undetected risks
4) Failure in communicating risks to top management
5) Failure in monitoring and managing risks.

In this dissertation, we will focus on the first three mentioned of these failures in turn since 4) and 5) would form the object of another analysis while the problem areas 1) to 3) specify what is meant by "*the ineffectiveness and inappropriateness of risk models*" in this study. They all point to limitations of statistical risk measurement techniques.

According to the failure to use suitable risk metrics, a risk metric or model does not provide the right information to senior or top management, information tailored to their needs, not because it is calculated incorrectly, but because, for example, it answers the wrong question (which is true for, e.g., VaR; Acerbi & Tasche, 2001: 4). Accordingly, this weakness of a risk model would amount to its diminished applicability if, on the one hand, it does not pick up the (strategic) questions which guide risk management in banking. On the other hand, there might be difficulties to *interpret* model results, because it might be difficult to discern the reasoning behind the sophisticated calculations (Boatright, 2011: 8).

In this case, the model is perhaps more complicated and (skill-)demanding than necessary[82] or does not achieve highest levels of transparency in the formalizations.[83] For instance, "due to their [structural; C.H.] complexity,[84] analytical models are often viewed as 'black boxes' that emit 'correct' results. Models are often accepted or relied upon without sufficient understanding or checks and balances." (Braswell & Mark, 2014: 203).

The second issue, beheld by Stulz (2008) but which we want to understand in slight difference to him, says that risk managers could make a mistake in assessing the *likelihood* of a large loss, or they could be wrong about the *size* of the loss (the *impact*), *given* that the respective risk can be identified and quantified *ex ante*. Or they could use the wrong distribution altogether or may mismeasure the *correlation* across different risks or among the different positions of a bank (ibid.). The vulnerability of the bank or of a portfolio to low-probability events with extreme consequences, resulting not only from an increase of correlations (Stulz, 2008), but also from the mismeasurement, may be critical. Hence, a risk model might be poor at assessing and analyzing certain already identified possible risk events correctly in terms of likelihood and impact although they can basically be identified and quantified in advance.

Finally, third, a bank's risk managers may either ignore a known risk, whose extent and full implications might remain unclear, "perhaps because of a mistaken assumption that it is immaterial, or because of the difficulty of incorporating it in the existing risk models" (Stulz, 2008: 62f.). Or a significant risk is "truly unknown, or at least completely unanticipated" (ibid.: 63). The corresponding weakness of a risk model would be to neglect the installation of *new* risks and

---

82 As Einstein is supposed to have said when asked how complex a theory or a model should be: "Everything should be made as simple as possible, but not simpler."

83 However, one should not disregard that results of mathematical finance are based on centuries of development in mathematical logic and that the conditions under which certain (very) precise conclusions hold are an integral and crucial part of any theorem. Therefore, from a more technical, methodological point of view, another reading of the fact that non-suitable risk metrics have been used might be provided: "The Crisis saw numerous examples where 'practice' fully misunderstood the conditions under which some mathematical concepts or results could be applied" (Das et al., 2013: 702; cf. also Angius et al., 2011: 2). As a result, another important lesson to be learned is to always understand in detail the premises and conclusions of a mathematical theorem (ibid.; see Chapter 7).

84 For example, according to Snowling (2000: 2), "*model complexity*" "describes the level of detail in the relationships describing the processes in a system. Model complexity is higher in models with greater numbers of state variables, parameters and processes, and fewer simplifying assumptions."

some major sources of uncertainty or to be unable to assess risks meaningfully at present.[85]

Specific weaknesses of extreme and systemic risk modeling

More precisely, by looking more closely at extant extreme or systemic risk models and measures, we find that we overall lack good methods of describing and measuring systemic and extreme risks (cf. also Helbing, 2013: 57). State-of-the-art risk analysis still appears to have a number of shortcomings out of which the following are addressed.

The first and second flaw below correspond to Stulz's (2008) mismeasurement problems 2) and 3) above. And the third risk assessment issue which is approached and tackled in this study pertains to his first overall problem area, namely what he baptizes "the failure to use appropriate risk metrics".

IIIa) *Problem statement*: Estimates for probability distributions and parameters describing rare events, including the variability of such parameters over time, are often poor as there is not enough and/or no reliable or pertinent *historical data*. Put differently, by relying on historical data, orthodox stochastic procedures tend to be *pro-cyclical*, in the sense that they extrapolate future movements based on past experience; future events, however, that are "diverse" from the available data (Collier, 2008: 233).[86]
Systemic explanation: The underlying structure of the financial system can change dramatically, especially during times of stress (Liechty, 2013: 163; see Chapter 6). For such cases, a statistical model would get it horribly wrong. On the one hand, the rareness of the events under study (extreme or systemic events; see Chapter 4) makes it virtually impossible to estimate these probabilities exclusively based on past data (Litzenberger & Modest, 2010: 97). On the other hand, the changing nature of financial systems and crises (e.g., due to the rapid pace of innovation) poses huge challenges for risk modeling, especially if solely

85 Some experts (e.g., Kuritzkes & Schürmann, 2010: 104) would probably like to add a further category of *un-knowable* risks. However, by definition, little can be done to learn about or manage the unknowable.

86 It is a commonplace that the information we can gain from the past indicates only what observers expect in the future, not what the future will be. It is a problem, however, that "[t]hese predictions, based on this information, affect real movements, although nobody knows how" (Esposito, 2011: 138; cf. also Lucas, 1976).

with recourse to data and without regard to the *structure* of the system and current trades (ibid.).

IIIb) *Problem statement*: The likelihood of *coincidences* of multiple unfortunate, rare events is often underestimated (e.g., Thurner, 2012; French et al., 2010: 45; Perrow, 1984), even though their *interaction dynamics* may lead to *amplification effects* and *feedback loops* (such as procyclicality or positive feedback loops; cf. also Daníelsson et al., 2001: 3).

Systemic explanation: Systemic or financial risk moves in a not fully random way (contrary to the works following the pioneers of classical finance: Bachelier, 1900; Black & Scholes, 1973) because of forms of dependence (Battiston et al., 2016), where the past influences the future non-linearly, i.e., not in the sense of continuity: *natura non facit saltus* (Esposito, 2011: 150; von Linné, 1751/2012). Interconnections (e.g., of the players in the market) and correlations (e.g., of risks or bank positions, also correlations along many dimensions) are somewhat opaque or may be poorly understood as their precise nature may be entirely different in a stressed scenario than under 'normal' conditions (Acharya et al., 2013: 204). Within finance, correlations are not only difficult to assess, as they can change over time, at times abruptly (Stulz, 2008: 62), but overall correlations are very badly understood due to the falsity of some commonly held views on correlation (Embrechts et al., 1998). In complex systems, we are dealing not only with interactions among the components at the same level. The character of complex systems is a consequence of interactions of system parts with each other; interactions of parts of the system with the system as a whole; and interactions of the (*open*) system with other systems with which it intersects, within which it is nested, and with which it may share interpenetrating components (Byrne & Callaghan, 2014: 173). Eventually, we have to look at the forest (system) rather than the trees (system elements), and too few really do that (Sornette, 2009: 15).

IIIc) *Problem statement*: Common assumptions underlying established ways of thinking are not questioned enough. In particular, conventional statistical risk assessment approaches not only assume that probabilities can be expressed by numerical values and that those values can be accurately ascertained, which is already challenged by the two preceding points, but also the following is often taken for granted (cf. Mandelbrot & Hudson, 2008: 85ff.):[87] First, statistical *independence*:[88] Two events are said to be independent if the occurrence of one does not affect the probability of the other.[89] This implies, for instance, that any information that could be used to predict tomorrow's market price is contained in today's price, so there would be "no need to study the historical charts" (ibid.: 87). This supposition lies behind most statistical narratives (Blyth, 2010: 458). A second delicate supposition is statistical *stationarity*: According to this principle, the statistics (statistical properties such as mean, variance, autocorrelation, etc.) are independent of the time origin.[90] And third, many risk models assume a *normal* distribution of data, returns, prices, etc. This means that changes follow the proportions of the so-called bell curve (because the normal distribution is the distribution whose density function (which defines the distribution) is epitomized by the famous bell or Gaussian[91] curve), a

87 For example, Modern Portfolio Theory assumes that price changes follow a so-called Brownian motion (Mandelbrot & Hudson, 2008: 87). From this assumption, independence, statistical stationarity and a normal distribution can be derived (ibid.). Many other problematic assumptions that accompany probability theory exist and are well-documented. For example, the so-called Principle of Indifference, given a canonical formulation by Laplace in 1814 and which is prominent in decision theory, suffers from a number of grave defects (Salmon et al., 1992: 74-77) and may lead to inconsistent probability assignments (Frigg et al., 2015: 3999f.; Halpern, 2005: 18).

88 This shall not exclude that probability theory has also been most fruitfully applied to series of dependent trials, i.e., to cases where past events do influence present probabilities and which constitute Bayesianism.

89 More precisely, if, for two events *A* and *B*, $0 < P(A)$ and $0 < P(B)$, then, A and B are *statistically independent* if, and only if: $P(A \mid B) = P(A)$. Hájek & Hall (2002) point to two cautions: firstly, the locution "*A* is independent of *B*" is somewhat careless, encouraging one to forget that independence is a relation that events, variables or sentences bear *to a probability function*. Secondly, this technical sense of "independence" should not be identified unreflectively with causal independence, or any other pre-theoretical sense of the word.

90 "If you assume coin tosses decide prices [a hypothetical mechanism generating price changes, C.H.], the coin does not get switched or weighted in the middle of the game. All that changes are the number of heads or tails as the coin is tossed; not the coin itself" (Mandelbrot & Hudson, 2008: 87). Please note that the fact that this assumption does make sense in a coin tossing game does not entail that the same holds for financial systems where we do not find such a mechanism for price changes. See Chapter 6.3. Cf. also Gottman, 1981: Chapter 8.

91 The normal distribution was discovered in 1733 by the mathematician Abraham de Moivre as an approximation to Jacob Bernoulli's binomial distribution when the number of trials is large. The distribution is more usually associated with the name of Gauss who derived it in 1809, in his *Theoria motus corporum coelestium*, as the law of errors of observations, with particular reference to astronomical observations (Bulmer, 1979: 108).

symmetrical graph that represents a probability distribution, – most changes are small and extremely few are large, in predictable and rapidly declining frequency.

This is what theory, among other things, presupposes in order to allow for the emergence of 'elegant and sophisticated' risk models. However, in reality, life is more *complex*.

Surely, risk models and some of their shortcomings – especially, the inadequacy of objective interpretations of probability for many situations in risk management; black swans that cannot be measured / predicted, etc.; Taleb, 2007a; Rebonato, 2007; Pergler & Freeman, 2008; Pergler & Lamarre, 2009; Helbing, 2010 – have been widely discussed in the literature and even though more and more attention has been devoted to systemic and extreme risks in the aftermath of the financial crisis that erupted in 2008, these three deficits have not yet been amply debated; nevertheless, they refer to not less pressing problems. On the contrary, it is one of the main contributions of this study to show that they can be exacerbated to provide evidence for the *conceptual* inadequacy of probability-based models of systemic and extreme risks (Chapter 7). Albeit our argument directs the spotlight not on probability theory or statistics itself, but on its scope, it will nonetheless impair the trustworthiness of many risk model results dramatically and, therefore, this is nothing short of a methodological disaster, given that probabilistic forecasts of extreme events are used in many places and all the time. Hence, the third gap can be formulated as follows.

Research Gap III:
Minimal insights on linking IIIa)-c) with the fundamental inadequacy of probability theory as a foundation for modeling systemic and extreme risk in a banking context.

2.5. Excursus: Benoît Mandelbrot's Plea for Fractal Methods

The mathematician Benoît Mandelbrot, a protagonist of chaos theory, elaborated a flourishing mathematical systems theory and asserted to have already given a satisfactory reply to the three challenges IIIa)-c). Therefore, we will examine in the following briefly to what extent our third research gap can be closed by drawing on Mandelbrot's fractal methods.[92] *Fractal* (from the Latin "fractus") is the term coined by Mandelbrot (1983, 1968) and used to describe curves, sets or objects with the following properties: "1) fine structure (detail at all scales, however small); 2) self-similarity (made up of small scale copies of itself in some way); 3) classical methods of geometry and mathematics are not applicable; 4) 'size' depends on the scale at which it is measured; 5) a simple recursive construction; 6) a natural appearance" (Falconer, 2013: 7).[93] The concept of fractals is related to, but distinct from, the notion of *hierarchy* in systems theory (e.g., Simon, 1962).[94]

Mandelbrot's work is driven by the insight that irregular objects should be regarded as the norm rather than the exception, which includes that our comprehension of how markets work, how prices move and how risks evolve has been very limited. With regard to our challenge IIIc), he found that critical assumptions underlying standard financial (Mandelbrot & Hudson, 2008: Part I; Engle, 1982; Mandelbrot, 1963b) and risk models (Mandelbrot & Hudson, 2008: 272-275) are wrong, by pointing at conspicuous and strong symptoms of non-independence (*The Joseph Effect*, a long-term memory of time series)[95], non-stationarity ("Market time is relative"; ibid.: 22)[96] and non-normality (*The Noah*

92 Schwaninger (2011: 755) elucidates that several mathematical systems theories have been elaborated, e.g., ma-thematical general systems theory (Klir, Pestel, Mesarovic and Takahara), as well as a whole stream of theoretical developments which can be subsumed under the terms "dynamical systems theory" or "theories of non-linear dynamics"; for example, catastrophe theory (Zeeman, 1977; Thom, 1975), chaos theory (Lorenz, 1963) and complexity theory (Kauffman, 1993). Under the latter, branches such as the theory of fractals are subsumed.

93 "Is there a more precise definition of a fractal? There has been considerable debate about this ever since the term was introduced. Mandelbrot originally proposed a technical definition in terms of dimensions, but this was abandoned because there were plenty of objects that did not fit in with the definition but which clearly ought to be considered fractals. The current consensus is to regard something as a fractal if all or most of the properties listed above [...] hold in some form." (Ibid.: 8).

94 Introductions to fractals with some mathematical details are found in Sayama (2015) and Peitgen et al. (2004).

95 "Price changes are not independent of each other. Research over the past few decades, by me and then by others, shows that many financial price series have a 'memory', of sorts" (ibid.: 11f.). For example, "[s]ometimes a trend will continue just because traders expect (or fear) that it will" (Lowenstein, 2002: 72). Furthermore, Mandelbrot showed that dependence can be infinitely long.

96 "[...] I came to think of markets as operating on their own 'trading time' – quite distinct from the linear 'clock time' in which we normally think. This trading time speeds up the clock in periods of high volatility, and slows it down in periods of stability." (Mandelbrot & Hudson, 2008: 22).

Effect, the fatter tail syndrome)[97]. Mandelbrot tackled those symptoms one by one: first, by incorporating heavily non-Gaussian marginal distributions (1963a, b), then by focusing on strong long-term dependence (1965), and finally by bringing those two features together by introducing the new notion of *multifractality* (Mandelbrot & van Ness, 1968; and since).

Fractal and multifractal geometry[98] is the study of roughness, of the irregular and jagged (see Figure 3). Its objects are not reduced to a few perfectly symmetrical and smooth shapes as in Euclidean geometry. Instead, it explores the *asymmetry*, *roughness*, and *fractal* structures of nature, which Mandelbrot regards as no mere imperfection from some ideal, but indeed as the very essence of many natural objects. Based on Falconer's (2013: 7) definition or characterization of fractals, they can be said to be objects that have structure on many different scales; the same shapes repeat at larger and smaller sizes. More precisely, fractal processes are self-similar and invariant in distribution with respect to changes of time and space scale.[99] The occurrence of self-similarity, roughness and fractality can be highlighted in a wide range of settings: "clouds are not spheres, mountains are not cones, coastlines are not circles", (Mandelbrot & Hudson, 2008: 124), and financial markets do not harbor smooth bell, but much wilder curves. Small portions of a coastline or a cloud or a brick's fractured surface resemble larger parts, and these larger parts in turn resemble the whole; irregular structures in nature are often "self-similar" in this way.

Impact on finance and risk management

The power of Mandelbrot's approach comes from its unique ability to "express a great deal of complicated, irregular data in a few simple formulae" (Mandelbrot &

97 "Price movements do not follow the well-mannered bell curve [...]; they follow a more violent curve [e.g. obeying a so-called 'power law' where the tails do not become imperceptible, see below; C.H.]"; ibid.: 20.

98 Mandelbrot (1997a) studies, for example, financial charts as geometric objects.

99 The self-similarity index or scaling coefficient is a non-negative number denoted by H, the Hurst index. For more details, cf. the references to Mandelbrot's work. The most important interpretation of H is that "it reflects the statistical predictability, or *long-term dependence* of phenomena that arise as a combination of many competing effects" (Falconer, 2013: 100). For instance, if H (which is defined between 0 and 1) lies between 0.5 and 1, then there is a positive correlation between the past and future (ibid.). Yet, this interpretation is tremendously problematic not so much due to a superficial difficulty of estimating Hurst exponents from empirical data, but because this inductive procedure presupposes a uniformity of nature which is very critical (see Chapter 7).

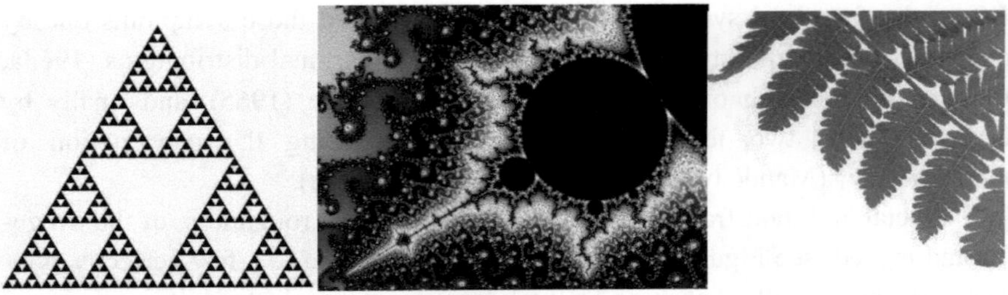

Figure 3: Images of three different fractals: two pure mathematical objects – the Sierpinski triangle (left) and the Mandelbrot set (center) – and a natural fern, which is only approximately fractal.
If you zoom in on one of these fractal objects, it will look similar or exactly like the original shape.

Hudson, 2008: 117). It describes the observed behavior of financial markets (e.g., capital or equity market returns) in a more accurate way that encloses, for example, jumps, heavy-tails, and skewness (measure of asymmetry of the probability distribution) observed in the real financial world, which, euphemistically, are much too often considered as 'anomalies' by standard theory; what made Mandelbrot (1983) speak of "suicidal" statistical methodologies.

Mandelbrot adopts a complexity perspective as it is suggested in this study as well (although chaos theory is not countenanced, see 6.2.2. and thereafter). With regard to our challenge IIIb), it should, therefore, be noted that his work in finance has been largely devoted to the roles of *discontinuity* and closely related forms of *concentration* (Mandelbrot, 1997b): Even in the absence of actual jumps, market price changes, which cause market risk, do not occur evenly over time, but tend to be concentrated in short 'turbulent' periods. One of the lessons of this finding for risk management is that the procedure of eliminating an option's risk through continuous dynamic hedging is incompatible with fractal discontinuities (Mandelbrot & Taleb, 2010: 54; Taleb, 2007a).

All things considered, it has been argued that Mandelbrot's innovative ideas enrich risk management research as well as present an opportunity to professionals in the territory of banks' risk management to improve their quantitative and qualitative tools (e.g., Mandelbrot & Taleb, 2010). Some of the implications of his work for both risk management in banking and this study include:

- Given empirical evidence, fractional or self-similar processes like fractional Brownian motion, a generalization of Brownian motion allowing for dependent increments (Mandelbrot & van Ness, 1968), have advantages over simplistic or ordinary Brownian motion models for 'measuring' or (better) estimating the magnitude of risks in actual financial systems more reliably (e.g., Sun et al., 2009).[100] This is the case because the former exhibit both the *Joseph Effect* and *Noah Effect* which characterize modern financial systems and, therefore, because they give up the common, but at least contestable, if not untenable, suppositions behind the latter (Mandelbrot & Hudson, 2008: 87ff.; Mandelbrot, 1997a). Yet, accounting for some non-normal distribution forms or the *Noah Effect* and the *Joseph Effect* is undeniably a valuable contribution to enhance risk modeling capabilities for real-world applications, but Mandelbrot's approach might turn out to be too short-sighted: dynamics and feedback in complex systems deserve further investigation and *wilder* distribution forms than those that follow from fractal models are conceivable. See Chapter 6 and 7.
- A concrete application of fractal methods to risk management has been proposed by Mandelbrot & Taleb (2010) to evaluate the robustness of a portfolio over an entire spectrum of extreme risks (Diebold et al., 2010: 26). They expect of a stress test analysis complemented with fractal methods that it will give us a much clearer idea of a bank's risks by expressing them as a series of possibilities. For more details, cf. their article; for an overview of scenario analysis in general, see Chapter 11 and 12.

---

100 The so-called Brownian movement of very small particles suspended in a liquid, caused by accidental bumps from the liquid's moving molecules, can be seen in the light of a very general 'random walk' problem (cf. e.g. Gottman, 1981: 75 and Hughes, 1995; Weiss, 1994.). In other words, Brownian motion can be thought of as a random walk with infinitely many infinitesimally small steps and a random walk, in turn, is basically a mathematical formalization of a path that consists of a succession of such random steps, which has had serious applications in many fields. There are different types of random walks: e.g., so-called lattice random walks, continuous-space short jumps / discrete time, discrete-space short jumps / continuous time, continuous space & time (diffusion), or non-stationary random walks (i.e., with shrinking/growing steps), etc.; the first four types lie in the domain of the celebrated *Central Limit Theorem* (see footnote 222). It is essential to bear in mind that Pearson (1905) who originally proposed the term "random walk" seems to have been referring to pure and genuine randomness (by the phrase "through any angle whatever"; cf. also Suppes, 1984: 34). As stressed in Chapter 6, another kind of randomness exists, demanding a different (compared to the work by Bachelier, 1900, for example) and special treatment. (This distinction goes, of course, far beyond the truism that there is no true attainable randomness in *practice*, but only in *theory*.)

- The essential property of fractals, their self-similarity can be translated into the jargon of probability distributions, which are central to conventional risk assessment (see Chapter 7): There is one single class of probability distributions which are scale-free (i.e., they look like the same at all scales) or self-similar, namely so-called *power law distributions*. And the study of power laws has had a strong impact on risk management in the sense that the power law has been found to be a good description of the *heavy* tails of many distributions (of losses) that are encountered in practice (Hull, 2010: 198; Helbing, 2010; Mandelbrot & Taleb, 2010; Sornette, 2009; see above 2.2.2. and Chapter 7.2. below).
- For many power laws means or variances do not exist (see the next sections). The moral of this story for risk management is not only that we should not take averages for granted; but that, in situations described by such power laws, reporting a mean from a finite set of data, although it is mathematically well-defined for *this* sample, can be bewildering, in the sense that it is not an expression of a valid generalization (which is a problem because most of the time when we describe a situation, we use an average to make a general statement, not about the sample, but about the population). While the more data we get, the better our estimate is for an average if this mean of a random variable x exists; *big data* is delusive when a mean does not exist, which invades the citadel of conventional and, thus, data-driven risk assessment. See Chapter 6, 7 and 8 for a follow-up.

Some first remarks on power laws

Tout court, a power law is a function or a mathematical relationship of this form:[101]

$$p\,(x) = A \times (\frac{1}{x})^D = A\,x^{-D}$$

101 At this point, it is important to differentiate between "*p*" and "*P*". *p* in the formula here is a probability distribution function while the capital letter would denote a (complementary) *cumulative* distribution function (= fraction that are equal to or greater than *x*), for which a power law must be defined in a slightly different way:
P (x) = [A/(D-1)] x - (D-1).

This mathematical relationship is called a power law because the variable x is *raised to the (fixed) power* $-D$. Through data analysis the exponent D and the constant A can be determined.[102] x can be, for example, the frequency of occurrence of unique words in a text like the novel "Moby Dick" by Herman Melville.[103] We then ask ourselves how the distribution of the word frequencies (a histogram) looks like or how likely it is that a certain word has frequency x. Around 210000 words in total and 18855 different words appear in *Moby Dick*. Some of them appear very frequently like "the", which can be found 14086 times, or "of" (6414 times), while other words are much rarer, all in all indicating a wide range of frequencies or data. A histogram of word frequencies for *Moby Dick* would tell us that 9161 different words appear only once, there are around 3200 words that appear twice and there are fewer words still that appear three times, four times and five times. The most common frequency is thus 1 and then it drops off very quickly. Accordingly, the probability of a randomly chosen (in the genuine sense) word from a list of unique words in *Moby Dick* to appear only once is almost 0.5. Circa 17% of the words appear only twice and so on. Or by using the formula from above, if we suppose (or ascertain through meticulous data analysis), for instance, that D is approximately 1.95 and A is approximately 0.59 and if we are interested in $x = 10$ (i.e., what is the probability that a word has the frequency 10), then we obtain: $p(10) \approx 0.59\ (10^{-1.95}) \approx 0.0066$. This means that there are around 18800 different words that appear in *Moby Dick* and if we select one of these 18855 words at random, then the probability that this word appears 10 times in the novel is very small, namely 0.0066.

Power law distributions look similar to exponential or geometric functions and different from normal distributions (see 7.2.). It is the special property of power laws though that they are scale-free or self-similar. Furthermore, they possess heavy or long tails, i.e., it takes a relatively long time for power law distributions before their tails get so close to zero that they become practically indistinguishable; power law distributions decay and get smaller, but linger for a long time (compared to bell curves or the curves of exponential functions that decay much more quickly in the tails, see Figure 17). The superscript D (also

---

102 The superscript D is given by the slope of the line on a log-log plot. A can be calculated from the intercept. Powers of numbers are closely related to logarithms (Falconer, 2013: 44).

103 The *Moby Dick* data can be obtained at http://tuvalu.santafe.edu/~aaronc/powerlaws/data.htm (20/11/15). This data is analyzed and discussed in Clauset et al., 2009.

referred to as the 'scaling parameter') characterizes the nature of the tail; the scaling parameter typically lies in the range $2 < D < 3$ (Clauset et al., 2009). For $D \leq 2$, the mean of x does not exist and if $D \leq 3$, the standard deviation (= a measure of average departure from the mean) of x is theoretically not defined (Sornette, 2009: 2). Mandelbrot argued, based on his observations of stock and real asset price movements, that a power law distribution would characterize them better (see also 7.2.). Power laws are often viewed as 'signatures' of specific mechanisms, namely, critical phase transitions (Bak, 1996) and preferential growth (Barabási, 2002), but also many others would be to name (some multiplicative processes that can yield power laws; or optimal distribution networks; etc.). Yet, real objects only behave as fractals over a restricted range of scales – "we call this the *range of fractality*" (Falconer, 2013: 49) or, put differently, few empirical phenomena in practice obey power laws for all values of x (Clauset et al., 2009: 662).

Résumé

In partial response to the need for explanatory risk models in the sense of Schwaninger (2010), expressed in research gap II, it is noteworthy that Mandelbrot's fractal methods are less a tool for *prediction* of, e.g., price changes (and, hence, the development of (market) risks), but rather an enabler of a better *understanding* of the variables that drive risk factors (Mandelbrot & Hudson, 2008: 121ff.; Mandelbrot, 1963a).

This being so, we would basically embrace the insights that have been gained by Mandelbrot and his fellows. However, we do not share a common ground, there is a principal disagreement (see also Conjecture 4): While Mandelbrot calls himself a true believer in the power of probability – "probability is the only tool at our disposal" (Mandelbrot & Hudson, 2008: 30) –, this study will be more radical and do nothing less than to refute the usefulness of probabilistic reasoning in the field of risk management (see Chapter 7). Thus, even though Mandelbrot focuses much of his work on dealing with the objections IIIa)-c), he misses to link them with the fundamental ineptness of probability theory as a theoretical framework for modeling systemic and extreme risk.

Moreover, if this fundamental inadequacy can be shown, there arises the need for developing models of risk that are not probabilistic in nature. Therefore, in terms of Part II and III of this thesis, one further research gap stands out.

Research Gap IV:
Knowledge deficits concerning risk models that do not rely on a specific notion of uncertainty (such as in probabilistic terms), but that are based upon alternative measures of uncertainty.

The research gaps I to III, which have been identified and motivated in the previous sections, and IV remain to be closed and, therefore, they are addressed by the successive research questions.

3. Research Questions

Based on this literature synthesis, this dissertation sets out to contribute to the existing literature by answering two overarching research questions **RQ1** and **RQ2** throughout this dissertation.

> **RQ1**:
> Are the taken-for-granted quantitative risk assessment and management approaches, including VaR, CoVaR, ES, etc., effective; if not, under what conditions are they useless and do become themselves a risk object for banks?
>
> **RQ2**:
> How can the measurement and management of systemic or extreme risk be improved to compensate for the shortcomings of conventional quantitative approaches and to account for the financial system's dynamic complexity?

Questions of how to increase the effectiveness with which systems serve their purposes are singled out as central in the so-called Systems Age (Ackoff, 1974: 18). RQ1 is central in Part I, RQ2 in Part III, and Part II represents an indispensable *stepping stone* between the response to RQ1 on the one hand and RQ2 on the other. The final Part IV serves as a concluding paragraph and embeds the preceding study in a larger context or system.

Pursuing RQ1 properly requires to raise certain more specific or sub-questions that guide our research activities in the remaining chapters of this Part I, in order to operationalize the objectives set out in the Introduction and to close the research gaps *I* (in terms of concept clarification and refinement), *II* (in terms of the need of explanatory models), and *III* (in terms of the objections IIIa)-c)), respectively.

Sub- or Specific Guiding Questions:

RQ1.1: What is an adequate concept of risk in the realm of banking?
➔ Answered in Chapter 4.1.

RQ1.2: What is an adequate concept of systemic risk in the realm of banking?
➔ Answered in Chapter 4.2.

RQ1.3: Why should banks (and not only regulators) take account of, and try to deal with, systemic risks?
➔ Answered in Chapter 5.1.

RQ1.4: What are concrete systemic risk scenarios for banks?
➔ Answered in Chapter 5.2.

RQ1.5: What is an adequate concept of complexity for examining the suitability of quantitative risk assessment and management approaches and how can it be applied?
➔ Answered in Chapter 6.1. and 6.2.

RQ1.6: Wherein lies the complexity of modern financial systems and of problems of risk assessment therein?
➔ Answered in Chapter 6.3.

RQ1.7: To what degree is error of risk measurement averted when the data from complex systems is treated statistically?
➔ Answered in Chapter 7.

RQ1.8: In what sense point the objections IIIa)-c) in the literature to the fundamental inadequacy of probability theory as a foundation for modeling systemic and extreme risk in a banking context?
➔ Answered in Chapter 7.

RQ1.9: In what sense and why are existing systemic or extreme risk measures and models insufficiently explanatory? What sort of explanatory models are required for banks' in-house systemic risk management purposes?
➔ Answered in Chapter 8 and Part III.

By ventilating these questions we construct this first of four pillars of the dissertation.

4. On an Adequate Concept of Risk and Systemic Risk in the Realm of Banking

The purpose of this chapter is to outline and discuss different concepts of risk (4.1.), systemic risk (4.2.), and to define a proper meaning of the two terms in the realm of banking. This is essential as the central research question RQ1 revolves around quantitative *risk* assessment and management approaches and it should be clear what the object of interest, of assessment and management endeavors is.

4.1. The Notion of Risk

In non-technical contexts and contexts of common parlance, the word "risk" refers, often rather vaguely, to situations in which it is possible but not certain that some undesirable event will occur (Hansson, 2011; Heinemann, 2014).[104] More precisely, the philosopher Sven O. Hansson distinguishes five particularly important and more specialized uses and meanings of the term, which are widely used across academic disciplines and/or in everyday language (Hansson, 2011).

1) risk = an *unwanted event* which may or may not occur.
   An example of this usage is: "The risk of a financial collapse is vast."
2) risk = the *cause* of an unwanted event which may or may not occur.
   An example of this usage is: "Subprime lending is a major risk for the emergence of a housing bubble." Both (1) and (2) are qualitative senses of risk. The word also has quantitative meanings, of which the following is the oldest one:
3) risk = the *probability* of an unwanted event which may or may not occur.

---

104 The origin of the concept of risk is not clear. Etymologically, the term is, among other things, derived from the Greek word "rhiza" which can be translated with "cliff", supporting the above negative mode of explanation, and from the Latin vulgar expression "risicare" / "resecare", meaning "to run into danger" or "to wage / to hazard". Cf. Heinemann, 2014: 59.

This usage is exemplified by the following statement: "The risk that a financial collapse will occur within the next five years is about 70%."

4) risk = the statistical *expectation value* of an unwanted event which may or may not occur.

   The expectation value of a possible negative event is the product of its probability and some measure of its severity. It is common to use the total amount of monetary costs as a measure of the severity of a financial crash. With this measure of severity, the "risk" (in sense 4) laden with a potential financial collapse is equal to the statistically expected number of monetary costs. Other measures of severity give rise to other measures of risk.[105]

5) risk = the fact that a decision is made under conditions of *known probabilities* ("decision under risk" as opposed to "decision under uncertainty").[106]

All concepts of risk have in common what philosophers call contingency, the distinction between possible and actual events or possible and chosen action (Renn, 2008: 1). In addition to these five common meanings of "risk", according to Hansson (2011), there are several other more technical meanings, which are well-established in specialized fields of inquiry. With regard to economic and particularly relevant analyses for the purposes of this study, *nota bene* that the current debate on risk resembles a Babylonian confusion of tongues. The present situation is characterized by many weakly justified and inconsistent concepts about risk (Aven, 2012: 33). Some of the many different definitions that are circu-

105 "Although expectation values have been calculated since the 17th century, the use of the term 'risk' in this sense is relatively new. It was introduced into risk analysis in the influential Reactor Safety Study, WASH-1400, (Rasmussen, 1975)." (Hansson, 2011). Today, Hansson (2011) regards it as the standard technical meaning of the term "risk" in many disciplines. Some risk analysts even think that it is the only correct usage of the term (ibid.).

106 "Most presentations of decision theory work from Luce & Raiffa's (1957) [building on Knight, 1921; C.H.] classic distinction between situations of *certainty* (when the consequences of actions are known), *risk* (when the probability of each possible consequence of an action is known, but not which will be the actual one) and *uncertainty* (when these probabilities are unknown)" (Bradley & Drechsler, 2014: 1229).
This taxonomy has also had a major impact on other literature streams. For example, the literature of management science on risk and uncertainty typically distinguishes between risks of two types: risks with known probabilities ("risk proper") and risks with unknown probabilities of the outcomes ("uncertainty"). Cf., e.g., Abdellaoui et al., 2011; Van de Kuilen & Wakker, 2011; Zimmermann, 2014.

lating are triaged and a subsumption system for them is given in Table 4. The purpose of this overview is to lay out the variety of material risk notions, rather than to claim that the categories proposed are exhaustive or mutually exclusive.

In light of this ambiguity, some notes on the epistemology of risk are in order to escape possible snares before we will deduce our own definition of risk.

The epistemology of risk

When there is a risk, there must be something that is unknown or has an unknown outcome. Therefore, knowledge about risk is knowledge about lack of knowledge (Hansson, 2011). This combination of knowledge and lack thereof contributes to making issues of risk difficult to grasp from an epistemo-logical point of view.

Second, it is sensible to acknowledge that risk not simply refers to something unknown, but to draw a conceptual framework distinguishing between the *k*nown, the *u*nknown, and the *u*nknowable ("*KuU*" as it is labeled by Diebold et al., 2010). Accordingly, Kuritzkes & Schürmann (2010: 104) call a risk *known* (*K*) if it can be identified and quantified *ex ante*; *unknown* (*u*) if it belongs to a collective of risks that can be identified but not meaningfully quantified at present;[107] and *unknowable* (*U*) if the existence of the risk or set of risks is not anticipatable, let alone quantifiable, *ex ante*. *Nota bene* that there is no sharp definitional line to be drawn between these classes, maybe leaving the *KuU* classes lying along a continuum of knowledge.

Third, things are even more confusing because even "known" risks (in the sense of Kuritzkes & Schürmann, 2010) contain uncertainty: "[…] as recent evidence coming from the financial markets painfully shows, the view according to which a 'known probability distribution' contains no uncertainty is not quite right" (Fedel et al., 2011: 1147).[108] The authors strengthen their assertion as follows (ibid.): Suppose a die is being rolled. One thing is to be uncertain about the face that will eventually show up (a "known" risk). One quite different thing is to be uncertain about whether the die is fair or unbiased (is the ostensibly known risk

107 The unknown might, therefore, also be knowable insofar as there (will) exist mechanisms that allow transforming the unknown into the known. These mechanisms can be either known or unknown. It is often unknown whether a risk or circumstance is a "knowable unknown" or an "unknowable unknown", which might remind the reader of Donald Rumsfeld's dictum of known and unknown unknowns – another demarcation line.

108 Ellsberg (1961) speaks of the *ambiguity* of a piece of information.

Table 4: Classification system for risk definitions and characterization of different risk definition categories.[109]

Issue	R = EV	R = P ∨ OU	R = V
Definition	Risk is the *expected* value	Risk is (known) *probability* or *objective / measurable uncertainty*	Risk is *volatility* around the mean
Examples where this concept is found	- De Moivre, 1711 - Rasmussen, 1975 - Adams, 1995 - Mark & Krishna, 2014	- Haynes, 1895 - Knight, 1921 (»risk« proper) - Luce & Raiffa, 1957	- Markowitz, 1952 - Sharpe, 1966 - Rajan, 2006 - Cecchetti, 2008 - Saunders & Cornett, 2010 - Esposito, 2014
Literature Stream	- Classical Economics - Decision / Safety Analysis	- Modern Economics - Rational Choice Theory - Statistics	- Economics and Finance - Insurance Mathematics
Criterion	**R = EV**	**R = P ∨ OU**	**R = V**
Risk is defined quantitatively	X	X	X
Risk is a qualitative concept	O	O	O
Risk exists objectively (is subjective)	X (X?)	X (X?)	X (O)
Risk balances different attributes (e.g., consequences *and* likelihood)	X	O	O
Reference to probability calculus	X	X	O
Risk relates to undesirable consequences /	X?	O	O
Allows for distinction between the concept and how to measure / operationalize it	O/X?	O	X?

109 *x*: yes, *o*: no, *x?*: answer depending on the meaning of the terms or it is not specified. A similar, but not fully satisfactory summary is found in Aven (2012: 37).

R = (Sᵢ, Pᵢ, Cᵢ)	R = C	R = U	R = U&C
Risk is equal to a triplet of possible *scenarios*, their *probability* and the severity of their *consequences*	Risks are the possible negative *consequences* of agents' own decisions or actions	- Risk is uncertainty - Risk is the *effect of uncertainty on objectives*	Risk is the real or realistic possibility of a negative, (very) rare and *uncertain* event with serious or even extreme *consequences*
- Kaplan & Garrick, 1981 - Sheffi, 2005	- Nida-Rümelin, 2002 - Luhmann, 1991	- Keynes, 1937 - McNish et al., 2013 - Gronemeyer, 2014 - Heinemann, 2014 - ISO, 2009 - Helbing, 2013	- Steigleder, 2012 - Aven & Renn, 2009 - Taleb, 2007a - Stulz, 2008 - Power, 2009 - Mikes, 2011 - **Definition used here**
Engineering	Ethics - Luhmann's System Theory - Common parlance	- (Strategic) Management - Ethics in Finance	Critical Finance and Management - Ethics in Finance

R = (Sᵢ, Pᵢ, Cᵢ)	R = C	R = U	R = U&C
X	O	O	O
O	X	X	X
X (X?)	X? (X)	X? (X)	X? (X)
X	X	O/X?	X
X	O	O	O
X	X	O	X
O	X	X	X

really known?) (ibid). In other words, we can rather naturally differentiate between *first order* and *second order* uncertainty, respectively. In the former case, we are uncertain about some (presently unknown) state of affairs. In the latter, we are uncertain about our uncertainty, i.e., second order uncertainty refers to the assessment that an agent makes about her own uncertainty (Fedel et al., 2011: 1147f.).[110] It follows that (almost) all decisions are made "under uncertainty" if one abstracts from clear-cut and idealized textbook cases.[111]

Finally, fourth, Hansson (2011) observes that a major problem in the epistemology of risk, a problem which is paid special attention to in this study, is how to deal with the severe limitations that characterize our knowledge of the behavior of unique *complex* systems that are essential for estimates of risk (e.g., modern financial systems). Such systems contain components and so many, potentially shifting, interactions between them that it is in practice *unpredictable* (ibid.). However, in spite of this fundamental uncertainty, meaningful statements about some aspects of these systems and their behavior can and will be made (see Part III).

These four points already presage that the relationship between the concepts "risk", "knowledge" and "uncertainty" seems to be wide-ranging, multi-layered and elusive. Hereafter, we try to cope with these issues and, further, to establish four explicit conditions for defining a proper, i.e., a more useful and a consistent,[112] notion of risk.

Condition 1:
Risk should be defined in such a way that it can be distinguished between *risk per se* (what risk is) and *how risk is measured, described* or *managed* (Aven, 2012: 33; Bradley & Drechsler, 2014: 1226).

This condition is important because there exist perspectives on risk in which this distinction is not made (see Table 4 and cf., e.g., Beck, 1992: 21; Hansson, 2007:

110 In principle, even higher orders of uncertainty are conceivable.

111 If a decision problem is treated as a decision "under risk", this does not mean, as Hansson (2011) clarifies, that "the decision in question is made under conditions of completely known probabilities. Rather, it means that a choice has been made to simplify the description of this decision problem by treating it as a case of known probabilities. This is often a highly useful idealization in decision theory" but it is, at the same time, important to distinguish between those probabilities that can be treated as known and those that are genuinely uncertain (ibid.).

112 Following Rothschild & Stiglitz (1970: 226f.), it is, of course, impossible to prove that one definition is better than another. Instead, they point out that definitions are chosen for their usefulness as well as their consistency.

27). Like MacKenzie (2006: 143-179), George Soros (2008: 3) notes how "our understanding of the world in which we live is inherently imperfect because we are part of the world we seek to understand" and he focuses on "how our knowledge of the world is interdependent with our measurements of it" (Blyth, 2010: 460).[113] In principle, every (measurement or description or management) tool in use (which could be based on stochastic models) should be treated as such. Every such tool has its limitations and these must be given due attention. By a distinction between risk as a concept, and its descriptions or assessments "we will more easily look for what is missing between the overall concept and the tool" (Aven, 2012: 42). By the same token, if a proper framework clarifying the disparity between the overall risk concept, and how it is being measured or operationalized etc. is not established, it is difficult to know what to look for and how to make improvements in these tools (ibid.). In addition to that, it is a central principle of systems science to examine issues from multiple perspectives – "to expand the boundaries of our mental models" (Sterman, 2000: 32) – and, as a consequence, the risk concept should not be illuminated by one theoretical perspective only (e.g., mere probabilistic underpinnings); it should not be founded on one single measurement tool. Because in the various scientific environments, application areas or specific contexts, there might not be one best way to measure / describe risk. This appears to be, therefore, a reasonable and uncontroversial premise.

The second condition purports the following:

Condition 2:
Risk should be defined in such a way that it can be distinguished between *what risk is* and *how risk is perceived* (Aven, 2012: 34)[114] as well as that the definition does not presuppose an interpretation of either *objective* or *subjective* risk (Hansson, 2011).

113 An impressive example of how knowledge is interwoven with our measurement tools can be taken from fractal geometry: Intuitively, we would assume that a question like "How long is the coast of Britain?" is well-defined and can be answered clearly and precisely by pointing to a certain fact. However, by adding to the observations by Lewis Richardson (1881-1953), Mandelbrot (1967) shows that the length of a coastline, a self-similar curve or fractal object, depends on the scale at which it is measured (which has become known as the 'coastline paradox').

114 According to Aven (2012), this premise is not in line with *cultural theory* and *constructivism* (cf. also Jasanoff, 1999; Wynne, 1992; and critical comments in Rosa, 1998). Beck (1992: 55), for example, writes that "because risks are risks in knowledge, perceptions of risks and risk are not different things, but one and the same".

There is a major debate among risk professionals about the nature of risks: are risks social or subjective constructions (human ideas about reality, a feature of the agent's informational state) or real-world, objective phenomena (representations of reality, a feature of the world itself;). Willett (1901/1951) and Hansson (2011), for example, speak up for a strong objective component of risk: "If a person does not know whether or not the grass snake is poisonous, then she is in a state of uncertainty with respect to its ability to poison her. However, since this species has no poison there is no risk to be poisoned by it" (Hansson, 2011). On the other hand, it is obvious to others that risks constitute mental models (Renn, 2008: 2). They are not veritable phenomena, but originate in the human mind (ibid.). As Ewald (1991: 199) notes: "Nothing is a risk in itself; there is no risk in reality. […] [A]nything *can* be a risk; it all depends on how one analyses the danger, considers the event." The definitional framework should, hence, try to "avoid the naïve realism of risk as a purely objective category, as well as the relativistic perspective of making all risk judgments subjective reflections of power[115] and interests" (Renn, 2008: 3).

There are at least two more requirements for a good risk definition.

> **Condition 3:**
> Risk should be defined in such a way that it is helpful to the decision-maker in lieu of misguiding her in many cases (Aven, 2012: 42), and, thereby, the risk definition should capture the main *pre-theoretic* intuitions about risk (Rothschild & Stiglitz, 1970: 227).

At first glance, this condition might sound vacuous. But if proposals such as R = P v OU (see Table 4) are taken into account, then Aven (2012: 41) objects that, "referring to risk only when we have objective distributions would mean we exclude the risk concept from most situations of interest". Moreover, it must not be forgotten that risk cannot be confined to the ivory tower of scholarly deliberations. Even though it might be a theoretical and abstract concept, risk has forged a direct link with real-life management challenges and actual decision-making. It has a direct impact upon our life: Speaking for the banking context, banks, tax-payers, governments lost a lot of money (and much more; e.g., credibility) because risk managers (in a broad sense) ignored or misjudged risks, miscalculated the uncertainties or had too much confidence in their ability to master dangerous

115 Power, for example, to the extent that what counts as a risk to someone may be an act of God to someone else, resigned to her/his fate (Bernstein, 1996b).

situations (FCIC, 2011). Ultimately, only time and feedback from the economic practice can tell whether or not this premise is fulfilled.

In conjunction to this third premise, opening the debate to a wider (namely, to a non-academic) audience, one can also see the following ethical demand.

> **Condition 4:**
> Risk should be defined in such a way that it does not divert attention away from, but emphasizes (very) low-frequency events in a high-dimensional space or systemic effects that have an impact on not only the actor, but also on other actors (Rehmann-Sutter, 1998: 120).

Rehmann-Sutter (1998: 122) bemoans that in some economic concepts of risk, "there is only one personal position: the decision-maker", whereas most risks are not individual but rather social (Sen, 1986: 158f.), i.e., there might be negative consequences for others from "taking risks". He adds, however, that we have difficulty in adequately including those other persons (e.g., taxpayers in our context) affected by the consequences of the (risk management) decision (of a bank) in the decision-making process, where the concept of risk is worked out in reality (Rehmann-Sutter, 1998: 122). "These other participants are abstract; attention is diverted away from them. These participants are conceptually hidden." (Ibid.). While we cannot regard this critique as fundamental in terms of the economic risk concepts taken into consideration in Table 4 – e.g., the definition R = EV does not entail a narrow reading of the consequences. Nevertheless, an important lesson can be learned from this admonition, among the most prominent of which was drawn by Kristin Shrader-Frechette.

Shrader-Frechette (1991) points to the unease we feel when we are using a concept which was elaborated for optimization of entrepreneurial behavior in an unpredictable market to describe interventions into the (financial) system with potential or actual adverse effects to other persons and institutions. What is *prima facie* rational might *secunda facie* not be rational if a *feedback view* of the world is adopted (Sterman, 2000; see Chapter 5 and 6). Since only those risks enter standard probabilistic risk measurement procedures that (directly!) affect the respective bank, risk managers or traders etc. often do not see a direct connection between their actions and other actors (Garsten & Hasselström, 2003: 259) or with significant changes in the financial system or even the global economy, which, in the end, bounce back on the individual institutions themselves (see below in 5.1.).

This problem will be explicitly taken up by extending the discussion of an appropriate risk notion (with a strong focus on low-frequency/high-severity losses) to the debate on a sound concept of systemic risk which includes our argument that (private) banks (as opposed to e.g., regulators) should also account for systemic risk and should actively address it for in-house risk management purposes (Proposition 1).

Prior to that, a bottom line is that, unfortunately, many extant definitions of risk do not even meet the first two basic requirements (see Table 4, Criteria 3 and 7). In terms of Table 4, only risk in the sense of *uncertainty* (R = U) and risk as the real or realistic possibility of a negative, (very) rare and *uncertain* event with serious or even extreme *consequences* (R = U&C) remain in the game. Since seeing risk as uncertainty can be considered a special case of U&C, the latter seems to be the most promising candidate whereas the other risk concepts presented do not only turn out to not have some desirable properties, but also suffer from other shortcomings. For example, the especially in a banking context relevant identification of risk with volatility or the variance of returns (R = V) is clearly unsatisfactory (see also Chapter 2.2.): "We can construct distributions that have identical variance but with which we would associate very different degrees of 'riskiness' – and risk, as the saying goes, is one word but is not one number" (Rebonato, 2007: 237; cf. also Rootzén & Klüppelberg, 1999); "[i]n any case, anyone looking for a single number to represent risk is inviting disaster" (Taleb et al., 2009: 80; cf. also Power, 2007: 121; and see the section on reductionism vs. reduction in Chapter 21, Part IV).

Before we shed some more light on U&C, it makes sense to first look closer at another example, namely the field of the risk definition R = P v OU where Knight (1921) made one of the first large-scale distinctions between risk and uncertainty, for what became known as 'Knightian risk' (= *measurable* uncertainty) and 'Knightian uncertainty'. Albeit there might be good reasons for regarding Knight's original argument for distinguishing between risk and uncertainty as going astray (see condition 3),[116] it is nevertheless important to bear it in mind due to several reasons. First, it is very puzzling to see how different economists, risk experts and others have reacted to Knight's oeuvre, how they

116 Taleb & Pilpel (2004) and Aven (2012), for example, argue that we should leave the Knightian nomenclature once and for all: "[...] the distinction is irrelevant, actually misleading, since, outside of laboratory experiments, the operator does not know beforehand if he is in a situation of 'Kightian risk'" (Taleb & Pilpel, 2004: 4).

interpreted it and what conclusions have been drawn. A good example is that while both groups like Heinemann (2014), Stout (2012), Bhidé (2010), Aven & Renn (2009), Bäcker (2008), or Taleb & Pilpel (2004), on the one hand (critical and modest), and Friedman (1976), Ellsberg (1961), Savage (1954) on the other (economic mainstream and imperialistic), consider Knight's distinction between risk and uncertainty as invalid because his risk perspective is too narrow, the interests of these two groups are diametrically opposed to each other: Whereas the former repels probability based definitions of risk ("risk as a concept should not be founded on one specific measurement tool [such as probability, C.H.]", Aven, 2012: 42) in favor of uncertainty, the latter maintains that Knightian risk, i.e. risk measured by probability, would prevail instead of "uncertainty" ("for a 'rational' man *all* uncertainties can be reduced to *risks* [because it is believed that we may treat people *as if* they assigned numerical probabilities to every conceivable event, C.H.]", Ellsberg, 1961: 645).[117]

Second, Knight's seminal work might, therefore, be seen as very influential or even path-breaking for the more recent history of economic thought (Heinemann, 2014: 61f.; Aven, 2012: 41; Esposito, 2011: 32) and as laying the grounds for a common meaning of "risk" (Hansson, 2011), especially relevant in economics and decision theory (Luce & Raiffa, 1957). Indeed, the tie between risk and probability is seen as so strong that only few seem to question it: "Risk can only be found in situations that have to be described by probabilities" (Granger, 2010: 32). Moreover, Knight (1921) introduced a simple but fundamental classification of the information challenges faced in banks' risk management, between Knightian risks which can be successfully addressed with statistical tools (VaR, ES, etc.), and Knightian uncertainties which cannot (Brose et al., 2014a: 369). Good risk management, thus, calls for toolkits that handle both Knightian risk and uncertainty (ibid.; see Chapter 13).

Hence, it is third in turn important to have a risk concept based on probability models to be able to participate in, and contribute to, the discourse of risk if a great number of participants and economists or people interested in risk management in banking, in particular, should be reached. Since such a definition of risk would not do justice to the requirements set above (e.g., the first condition), however, it will not be the one which is pursued and embraced in this study after all.

117 However, the agent's acting *as if* the representation is true of her does not make it true of her. Cf. Hájek, 2009: 238.

Hence, it would be premature to simply and uncritically take on Taleb & Pilpel's (2004) or Aven's (2012) position of pleading in favor of leaving the Knightian nomenclature once and for all. Instead, our strategy is twofold. We first conclude that the kind of definitions by Heinemann (2014), Steigleder (2012), Aven & Renn (2009), etc. are the most appropriate before we approve a narrow notion of risk that is compatible with how risk discussions are commonly held.

Understanding risk

As an answer to RQ1.1, risk, in this dissertation, is paraphrased broadly as…[118]

> … the real or realistic possibility of a positive or negative event the occurrence of which is not certain, or expectable[119] but only more or less likely. However, the probability that the positive or negative event will occur does not have to be known or be subject to exact numerical specification.

Thus, the term "risk" is not used as an antonym to "uncertainty", as is customary in decision theory, but rather as a generic concept that covers both "risk in a narrower sense" (what Knight, 1921, calls measurable uncertainty) and "uncertainty". This is because we frequently lack a sufficient basis to determine the probabilities with any precision (Greenbaum, 2015: 165) as it will be clarified below. From a systems theoretical perspective, it is furthermore interesting to see that an event-oriented worldview (see 5.1.) might be underlying this definition.

This broad notion of risk is designated by *Risk I.* Structurally, risk in this sense captures:

- What can happen?
  - Answering this question requires the identification or description of consequences or outcomes of an activity.
- Is it more or less likely to happen (in contrast to *how* likely is that to happen)?
  - Attention is restricted to rather rare or very rare events.[120]

---

118 These first two passages are taken from Steigleder (2012: 4).

119 We follow Steigleder (2012: 4) in calling an event expectable here "if it is known to be a normal and common consequence of certain circumstances or actions. Whenever an event that is expectable in this sense does not occur, that is something abnormal and needs explanation."

120 Weaver (1963: 222) says that probability and *degree of rarity* are essentially identical concepts.

- If it does happen, what is the impact?
    - Answering this question requires the evaluation of consequences which are rather serious or even extreme.

We thereby follow the call of Das et al. (2013: 715) that quantitative risk management research will have to dig deeper "in going from more frequency oriented 'if' questions to a more severity oriented 'what if' approach, and this at several levels". The focus lies on (very) low-frequency events in a high-dimensional space or, in particular, on low-frequency, high-severity (monetary) losses for several reasons. For example, pushing natural phenomena to an extreme unveils truths that are ensconced under normal circumstances.

As stressed in Johansen & Sornette (2001) and following the 16th century philosopher Francis Bacon, the scientific appeal of extreme events is that it is in such moments that a complex system offers glimpses into the true nature of the underlying fundamental forces that drive it (Johnson et al., 2012: 3).

Accordingly, the need to address unexpected, abnormal or extreme outcomes, rather than the expected, normal or average outcomes is a very important challenge in risk management in banking (McNeil et al., 2005: 20; Malevergne & Sornette, 2006: 79; Greenbaum, 2015: 164); because improving the comprehension (of the distribution) of extreme values, which cannot be dismissed as outliers because, cumulatively, their impact in the long term is dramatic, is of paramount importance (Mandelbrot & Taleb, 2010; Joint Central Bank Research Conference, 1995).[121]

Benoît Mandelbrot uses a nice metaphor for illustration's sake (cf. also Churchman, 1968: 17): "For centuries, shipbuilders have put care into the design of their hulls and sails. They know that, in most cases, the sea is moderate. But they also know that typhoons arise and hurricanes happen. They design not just for the 95 percent of sailing days when the weather is clement, but also for the other 5 percent, when storms blow and their skill is tested." (Mandelbrot & Hudson, 2008: 24). And he adds: The risk managers and investors of the world are, at

121 The need for a response to this challenge also became very clear in the wake of the LTCM case in 1998 (McNeil et al., 2005: 20). John Meriwether, the founder of the hedge fund, clearly learned from this experience of extreme financial turbulence; he is quoted as saying: "With globalization increasing, you'll see more crises. Our whole focus is on extremes now – what's the worst that can happen to you in any situation – because we never want to go through that again." (*The Wall Street Journal*, 2000). See also 5.2.

the moment, like a mariner who "builds his vessel for speed, capacity, and comfort – giving little thought to stability and strength. To launch such a ship across the ocean in typhoon season is to do serious harm". (Ibid.: 276).

Clearly, this does not mean that (very) low-probability risk events matter simply because they have a very low probability. For example, there is some probability that a pink elephant will fall from the sky. But such a risk does not affect managerial decisions in banks. The known or unknown risks that matter for our purposes are, of course, those that, had senior or top management been aware of them, would have resulted in different actions (Stulz, 2008: 64) – e.g., the bursting of a pricing bubble or an escalating political conflict etc. (see Chapter 5.2.).

Second, a narrow concept of risk is invoked (*Risk II*); it is basically circumscribed by two key variables, the severity of the consequence and its probability of occurrence,[122] and it presupposes that possible / significant consequences and the corresponding values of severity and probabilities are known.[123] Risk II encompasses Hansson's (2011) risk definitions 3 to 5[124] and it can be regarded as a special case of the broad risk definition (Risk I):

A Taxonomy of Uncertainty

In our broad risk definition, risk is grounded in uncertainty. Apart from the different orders of uncertainty (Fedel et al., 2011: 1147; Ellsberg, 1961), different types of uncertainty need to be taken into account. In Figure 4, we distinguish three qualitatively different types of uncertainty: (*a*) what decision theorists or phil-

122 The probability of occurrence or at least the subjective probability must be less than 1 and more than 0, otherwise there would be *certainty* about the event or the possible outcomes of an action. (Going back to Lewis 1980, the principle that, roughly, one's prior subjective probabilities conditional on the objective chances should equal the objective chances is called the *principal principle.*) Moreover, the probability should be seen in relation to a fixed and well-defined period of time. For the concept of probability including objective and subjective probabilities, in general, cf. Hájek (2011).

123 For readers well versed in economic theories of decision sciences, it should be added that, depending on the particular theory, probabilities are not always assigned to the consequences of action alternatives (e.g., Jeffrey, 1983), but also, for example and actually more often, to so-called states of the world (e.g., Savage, 1954).

124 The risk formula "Risk = probability * measure of severity (e.g., utility, monetary unit, etc.)" directly follows from the Risk II concept (Hansson's fourth definition). Since Risk II presupposes known probabilities (with $0 < p < 1$), decisions under "risk" are made, and not decisions under conditions of "uncertainty" (Hansson's fifth definition). And, finally, seeing risk as probability (third definition) can be considered a special case of Risk II.

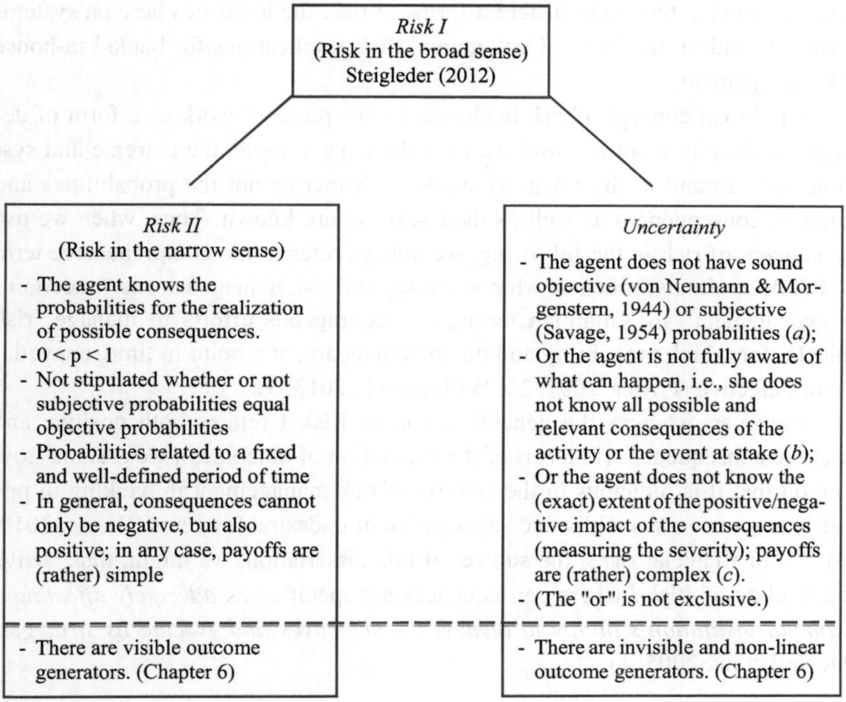

Figure 4: Two relevant risk concepts: Risk I encompasses Risk II and uncertainty.[125]

osophers might call *state uncertainty*, (*b*) what they might call *option uncertainty* and/or *state space uncertainty*, and (*c*) what corresponds to *ethical uncertainty*, a form of normative uncertainty (cf. Bradley & Drechsler, 2014). On top of that, many different kinds of risk (business risk, social risk, economic risk, etc., Kaplan & Garrick, 1981: 11) or categories of risk (market, credit, operational risk, etc.), as briefly mentioned above, are discussed in the literature and many more classification systems are introduced. It will be argued, however, that, even though some of the taxonomies offered for bank risks or for knowledge (or the lack thereof) are persuasive, e.g., the conceptual framework "*KuU*" by Diebold et al. (2010), at least the silo-treatment of risks should be overcome. Instead of

125 A similar illustration (but insufficient explanation of the concepts) is found in Heinemann (2014: 61).

devoting much attention to different forms of risk, the focus lies here on systemic risks in and to the financial system and their implications for banks' in-house risk management.

The broad concept of risk is chosen in this piece of work as a form of description since it is not *a priori* clear for the risks at issue, the extreme and systemic risks in and to the financial system, whether or not the probabilities and potential consequences as well as their severity are known. Thus, when we use the concept of risk in the following, we always refer to the comprehensive term *Risk I*. Accordingly, much of what we today call risk management is "uncertainty management" in Knightian terms, i.e., courageous efforts to manage 'risk objects' for which probability and outcome data are, at a point in time, unavailable or defective (Power, 2007: 26; Willke et al., 2013: 9).

However, whereas the general notion of Risk I retains both positive and negative consequences (in terms of the evaluation of outcomes), we assume from now on that it is judicious in the context of risk management in banking to primarily associate risks with adverse, negative or undesirable events (Bessis, 2010: 26).[126] For financial risks, the subject of this dissertation, we might, thus, arrive at a reading of *Risk I* where consequences are specified as *adversely affecting a financial institution's ability to achieve its objectives and execute its strategies* (McNeil et al., 2005: 1).[127]

126 Even though it makes much sense in this special context of risk management in banking, the general definition of risk should actually not distinguish between positive and negative consequences (desirable and undesirable consequences), the point being that the activity results in some *significant* consequences (whatever they are). In practice, there are always some outcomes that are judged as undesirable (Aven, 2012: 42). "The activity runs, and there is a possibility of undesirable consequences, but the consequences could also be positive. When taking risk, we balance these concerns." (ibid.). Of course, it would have been possible to generally and strictly restrict the consequences to undesirable consequences. However, by doing this we would need to determine what is undesirable, and for whom (ibid.). An outcome could be positive for some stakeholders and negative for others. "It may not be worth the effort and energy discussing whether an outcome is classified in the right category, and therefore most general risk definitions allow for both positive and negative consequences" (ibid.).

127 Note that this narrower reading of Risk I, that a restriction to negative consequences does not contradict the statement made above, namely that in the financial universe, risk and return are two sides of the same coin or that it is special for financial institutions that risk management not only focuses on the negative, but also on opportunities and successes. Because, of course, banks can make a good deal by absorbing, repackaging and passing on risks (with its negative connotation) to others.

Furthermore, Knight's important distinction between risk and uncertainty is esteemed by separating Risk II from uncertainty. This dichotomy is made explicit in sections of this study where a differentiated and nuanced view is desirable or reasonable.

It will become obvious that this differentiation is, in some cases, indispensable for the discourse of risk (management) in banking because different implications arise. The risk perspective chosen strongly influences the way risk is analyzed and, hence, it may have serious effects on risk management and decision-making (Aven, 2012: 42).

4.2. The Concept of Systemic Risk

Not very surprisingly, the current situation in the literature, regarding the definition of *systemic* risk, is not satisfactory either (Getmansky et al., 2015: 74). The precise meaning of systemic risk is ambiguous; there is a perplexing cacophony of conflicting opinions. The very definition of systemic risk "is still somewhat unsettled" (Schwarcz, 2008: 196).

Albeit the increase in theoretical, empirical and policy analyses of financial instability has been substantial and while systemic risk is now widely accepted as the fundamental underlying concept for the study of financial instability, there has been little attention paid to what is endogenous to the financial system[128] and events that are external (Fouque & Langsam, 2013: xx). The recent crisis has painfully demonstrated that it is not so robust that one can ignore systemic risks (ibid.). One of the lessons taken from it is that "the conceptual way we think about risk in the financial sphere needs to be changed by taking an economic system wide perspective" (Detken & Nymand-Andersen, 2013: 753).

Given this starting point, we develop an elaborated concept of systemic risk or, at least, a plausible working definition of systemic risk in order to establish a *modus vivendi* "in handling and managing a pressing perennial problem" (Willke et al., 2013: 10) by, first, explicating and analyzing existing concepts and, se-

128 Systemic risk in a very general sense is by no way a phenomenon limited to economics or the financial system. De Bandt & Hartmann (2000: 6, 13f., 26) identify three interrelated characteristics that may justify why financial systems can be more prone to systemic risk than other sectors of the economy: First, the structure of bank balance sheets, second, the complex network of exposures among financial institutions and, third, the inter-temporal character of financial contracts and related credibility problems.

cond, synthesizing relevant factors. The term's general meaning is "[o]f, or pertaining to, a system" (Oxford English Dictionary 499 (1989)).

Up to date, a search of the literature revealed three frequently used types of concepts (e.g., Heinemann, 2014; Anand, 2010; Schwarcz, 2008; Kaufman & Scott, 2003).

1) According to the first, systemic risk is described as the *result of causal relationships between market participants*. Systemic risk is the probability that cumulative losses will accrue from a single internal event, usually the default by one market participant, that sets in motion a series of successive losses along a chain of institutions or markets comprising a system (Kaufman, 1995: 47). That is, systemic risk is the risk of a "*chain reaction* of falling interconnected dominos" (ibid., cf. also Helbing, 2010).[129] Sometimes it is distinguished between *a)* the failure of a chain of markets or institutions or *b)* a chain of significant losses to financial institutions, "resulting in increases in the cost of capital or decreases in its availability, often evidenced by substantial financial-market price volatility" (Schwarcz, 2008: 204). This type of definition is sometimes also known as the so-called *domino model of financial contagion* (De Bandt & Hartmann, 2000: 10ff.). These definitions emphasize correlation with causation (the triggering event and the reactions to it), and they demand close or direct connections among institutions or markets (Kaufman & Scott, 2003: 372f.). Banks are, for example, closely linked to each other through the interbank market. Linkages are rather direct, e.g., if several institutions are connected to

129 This definition is consistent with the one given by McNeil et al. (2005: 15): "Systemic risk is the danger that problems in a single financial institution may spill over and, in extreme situations, disrupt the normal functioning of the entire financial system"; and with that of the Federal Reserve (the *Fed*): In the payments system, "systemic risk may occur if an institution participating on a private large-dollar payments network were unable or unwilling to settle its net debt position. If such a settlement failure occurred, the institution's creditors on the network might also be unable to settle their commitments. Serious repercussions could, as a result, spread to other participants in the private network, to other depository institutions not participating in the network, and to the nonfinancial economy generally." (Board of Governors of the Federal Reserve System, 2001: 2).
Likewise, the Bank for International Settlements (BIS) defines systemic risk as "the risk that the failure of a participant to meet its contractual obligations may in turn cause other participants to default with a chain reaction leading to broader financial difficulties" (BIS, 1994: 177). Etc.

each other by mutual obligations and liabilities, but they could also be indirect in nature when institutions have similar risk structures and are thus affected by market fluctuations in the same way (see definition type 3): "By synchronizing the actions of market participants, the feedback effects are amplified" (Brunnermeier et al., 2009a: 17). In thinking about systemic risk, one must therefore go beyond considerations of individual players and incentives and pay attention to issues of systemic interdependence (Fouque & Langsam, 2013: xxi; Hellwig, 2008).

2) The second discerns systemic risk as a possible trigger of an unexpected "big" shock or macro-shock "that produces nearly simultaneous, large, adverse effects on most or all of the domestic economy or system" (Kaufman & Scott, 2003: 372). Concomitantly, Adrian & Brunnermeier (2011) treat systemic risk as the risk that the intermediation capacity of the entire financial system is damaged, "with potentially adverse consequences for the supply of credit to the real economy" (ibid.: 1). Here, "systemic" refers to "an event having effects on the entire banking, financial, or economic system, rather than just one or a few institutions" (Bartholomew & Whalen, 1995: 4).[130] Put differently, the shock is rather systematic than idiosyncratic (De Bandt & Hartmann, 2000: 11). This kind of definition does not further specify the nature of the sudden event and how effects are transferred from a macro-shock to individual units (banks). Instead, emphasis is placed on the event occurring unexpectedly, causing a misallocation of capital or financial instability that can[131] become so widespread that it compromises the functioning of the financial system to the point where economic growth and welfare are materially impaired (ECB, 2010; Oet et al., 2013: 792; Group of Ten, 2001).

According to this definition type, any risk that threatens the financial system, can be referred to as "systemic". This encloses risks, such as „economic downturn, borrower defaults, pressures in funding markets, sovereign risk, failure of financial institutions, regulatory and account-

130 Likewise, Mishkin (1995: 32) defines systemic risk as "the likelihood of a sudden, usually unexpected, event that disrupts information in financial markets, making them unable to effectively channel funds to those parties with the most productive investment opportunities".

131 A shock does not have to result in a crisis (Varnholt, 1995: 11).

ing changes, financial market dislocation, loss of confidence in authorities, tight credit conditions, disruptions to derivatives and insurance markets, loss of confidence in pitching, disclosure and ratings, operational risk, property price falls and infrastructure disruption" (Bank of England, 2008/2009: 231).

3) The third definition type focuses on systemic risk as an *(after-)effect or spillover from an initial exogenous external shock*, but it does not (in contrast to definition 1) involve direct causation and depends on weaker and more indirect connections (Kaufman & Scott, 2003: 373). In the same vein, Illing & Liu (2006: 244) postulate that systemic risk or financial stress "is the product of a vulnerable [market] structure and some exogenous shock". Exogenous sources originate from outside the financial system and be intensified and impacted by other financial systems within other economic areas and/or other political and business events failing to contain the systemic risk within the local financial system (Detken & Nymand-Andersen, 2013: 754). This definition 3) stresses similarities in third-party risk exposures among the units involved (Kaufman & Scott, 2003: 373), which increases losses or the number of defaults in bad scenarios (i.e., if the external shock occurs), depending on how similar the risk profiles and (investing, risk exposure) strategies are (see also 5.1.). Moreover, when one bank experiences adverse effects from the shock, this shock prompts not only direct severe losses at this bank and other banks with similar risk profiles, but also uncertainty is created about the values of other units *potentially* also subject to adverse effects from the same shock. These other units will be canvassed by market participants to see whether and to what extent they are at risk. "The more similar the risk-exposure profile to that of the initial unit economically, politically, or otherwise, the greater is the probability of loss, and the more likely it is that participants will withdraw funds as soon as possible" (Kaufman & Scott, 2003: 373).[132] This response by the players in the market may induce

132 Even worse, at this stage, common-shock contagion may appear indiscriminate, potentially affecting more or less the entire universe and reflecting a general loss of confidence in *all* units (Kaufman & Scott, 2003: 374). Solvent parties, i.e., those which are perceived to be economically sound and not overly leveraged, might not be differentiated from insolvent (ibid.).

liquidity problems or even more fundamental solvency problems and it might also result in a 'bank run' (Schwarcz, 2008: 199). Kaufman & Scott (2003: 373) refer to this pattern as a "*common shock*" or "reassessment shock" effect and it "represents correlation without direct causation (indirect causation)".

Even though the pertinent literature potentially contains other types of concepts, we embark on discussing these three main proposals for defining "systemic risk" at this point.

Common ground: The definitions have in common, for example, that they all describe a triggering event, followed by a series of negative economic consequences (Heinemann, 2014: 171). More importantly, however, there are a range of inconsistencies and weaknesses of the proposals made in the literature. Some are pointed out in what follows.

Inconsistencies:

- In the first definition risks are *endogenous*, i.e., they are provoked *within* the financial system or by the interdependencies and correlations between its components (e.g., financial intermediaries, markets and instruments and/or financial infrastructures). The second allows for the possibility of risks originating from within the financial system while the third excludes this possibility.
- In contrast to Def. 2), Def. 1) and Def. 3) focus more on the micro level and on the transmission of the shock and potential spillover from one unit to others.
- In contrast to Def. 1), the network of system elements does not play a major role in Def. 3).
- Unlike in the second (macro shock) definition, only one bank needs to be exposed in direct causation to the initial shock in the first definition. "All other banks along the transmission chain may be unexposed to this shock. The initial bank failure sets off the chain or knock-on reaction" (Kaufman & Scott, 2003: 373).

- The trigger event in the first is a "default by one market participant"; in the second, merely a "big" and unexpected "event", not further specified, and in the third definition an "exogenous external shock".[133]

Specific weaknesses:

- With regard to Def. 1), Brunnermeier et al. (2009a: 17) contend that the so-called "domino model of contagion is flawed, and is not useful for understanding financial contagion in a modern, market-based financial system". First, it is only with implausibly large shocks that the simulations engender any meaningful contagion (ibid.: 16). Second, the reason is that the domino model paints a *non-dynamic* picture of passive banks that stand by and do nothing as the sequence of defaults unfolds (ibid.). In practice, however, they "will take actions in reaction to unfolding events, and in anticipation of impending defaults" (ibid.). Third, defaults need not even be necessary to generate contagion (French et al., 2010: 67). While price changes themselves may actually be enough, the model ignores reinforcing feedback loops – e.g., "[…] changes in prices lead to losses […], [l]osses worsen funding liquidity for many financial institutions, forcing them to shed even more assets which further depresses prices and increases losses, and so on" (Brunnermeier et al., 2009a: 17).
- Following Brunnermeier et al.'s (2009a) third caveat to the domino model of contagion, it can be noted that also the second definition is guilty of over-emphasizing the role of a big shock for the emergence of systemic risks. However, a relatively unremarkable risk exposure can have a big impact on a bank's business if its ability of absorbing losses is not given (Varnholt, 1995: 11). If a dynamic perspective is adopted, this implies that different states of the financial system are considered and, obviously, this comprises phases of relative stability of the bank or of the bank's environment (e.g., 2004-07), where minor or major shocks might be absorbed, as well as situations where the system is unstable and fast-changing (e.g., since 2007) and the bank is vulnerable.
  Moreover, definition type 2) leaves (too) many things open: Not only is the nature of the sudden event and how effects are transferred from a

133 Moreover, it is not the case that the initial shock to the system must be a single shock. There can also be independent shocks simultaneously affecting all banks (e.g., Battiston et al., 2012), or correlated shocks (e.g., Amini et al., 2012; Ladley, 2011).

macro-shock to individual units not specified, but it also remains unclear whether the "big" shock epitomizes the risk event itself or merely its cause (Heinemann, 2014: 172).

- In terms of the third proposal, it needs to be objected that a system may get into a critical state not only via external influences affecting its stability (Haldane & May, 2011: 351; Sornette, 2003: xv).[134] 'Extreme events' can be "a result of the inherent system dynamics rather than of unexpected external events" (Helbing, 2013: 52; cf. also Albeverio et al., 2010). Senge (2006: 46) bemoans that assumptions of an "external cause" pervade non-systemic thinking. Again, relatively *small* initial shocks have the potential to make strong contributions to systemic risk (Haldane & May, 2011: 353; Lorenz, 1963). The misconception that crises and disasters in social or anthropogenic systems are 'natural', or accidents emanating from external disruptions is *dangerous*.[135]

General weaknesses:

- The three proposals suggest that systemic risks are linked to single and big or major shock events whereas catastrophic or systemic risk events often result *not from a single cause* but from inter-connected risk factors and multiple causes and conditions (Bonabeau, 2007: 64). Each (perhaps, minor) risk factor taken in isolation might not cause a disaster, but risk factors working in synergy can (Sargut & McGrath, 2011: 72). Consequently, complex, dynamic and interconnected systems like modern financial systems (Neave, 2010; see Chapter 6) conjure up many, sometimes unexpected or counter-intuitive vulnerabilities.

134 "Events external to the banking system, such as recessions, major wars, civil unrest or environmental catastrophes, clearly have the potential to depress the value of a bank's assets so severely that the system fails. Although probably exacerbated by such events […], the present crisis seems more akin to self-harm caused by overexuberance within the financial sector itself." (Haldane & May, 2011: 351). Bonabeau (2007: 64) would agree by adding that "[a]n external trigger must not be confused with the cause of – or be blamed for – a catastrophic event. […] [E]xternal triggers merely served to highlight the existence of internal flaws, which deserve the true blame for those catastrophes."

135 Helbing (2013: 57) provides the explanation that "[f]or a long time, humans have considered systemic failures to originate from 'outside the system', because it has been difficult to understand how they could come about otherwise. However, many disasters in anthropogenic systems result from a wrong way of thinking and, consequently, from inappropriate organization and systems design". For the role of *systems thinking* in this study, see also Chapter 5.1. and 6.

- In none of the systemic risk definitions triaged, "risk" is understood in a way that would be compatible with how the term is used here (*Risk I*). It appears that not much thought and care have been put into the underlying concept – "risk" is simply read as "event" or "probability", for example – while relatively detailed views on the meaning of "systemic" have been presented. The risk notion in Def. 1) – 3) is too narrow because risk is identified with probability or it is simplistic when equated with "event".

All in all, a more appropriate definition of systemic risk is needed. In particular, the critique suggests that more attention ought to be devoted to focal (dynamic and complex) systems and their attributes. For example, Brunnermeier et al. (2009a) indirectly affirm that financial systems are dynamic and complex by emphasizing, for example, that they are governed by feedback and that a dynamic viewpoint would be desirable. It is also to acknowledge that sources of systemic risks can be endogenous or exogenous. In addition to that, it can be noticed that the importance of systemic risk has at least two dimensions, the severity of systemic events as well as the (not necessarily quantifiable) likelihood of their occurrence, referring back to our definition of risk and cf. also, De Bandt & Hartmann (2000: 13): "Strong systemic events, in particular systemic crises, are [very; C.H.] low probability events, which might lead some to consider them as less of a concern. However, once a crisis strikes the consequences could be very severe." (Ibid.). In consonance with *Risk I*, systemic risks may be regarded as *systemic uncertainties* (Heinemann, 2014: 195; Willke et al., 2013: 9; Bailey, 2005: 84).

What is Systemic Risk instead?

The different types of risk, such as market risk and credit risk, describe risk arising from different sources. What the risk types have in common is that they are caused by change: Market risk is created by changes in market prices and credit risk arises from changes in the creditworthiness of borrowers. Needless to say, markets change all the time and default events are also not unheard of in day-to-day lending, but the kind of change that creates significant risk – and is of interest to risk management – is an unexpected, unanticipated change of conditions for the worse. In this spirit and as an answer to RQ1.2, a (at least temporary working) definition for systemic risk may be (cf. also Johansen & Sornette, 2010: 206f.):

Definition 4.

"Systemic risk is either endogenous risk caused by a significant change of the system in which a business operates; for banks, this system is the financial system.[136] Or it is induced by a significant change of *another* system (an exogenous shock)."

While some authors, as seen above, miss the point of reaching the systems part of systemic risk – e.g., by foregrounding individual institutions (often called 'systemically important') rather than the financial system as a whole, or events / system behavior in lieu of system structures, etc. (cf. also the critique by Thurner & Poledna, 2013: 1; Rossi, 2011: 62, 75; French et al., 2010: 26, 135) –, this broad definition of systemic risk underscores its roots in systems. "System" is its essential element in at least four ways, which at the same time aid to clarify the definition further.[137] *First*, from a systems perspective there is no absolute difference between internal (endogenous) and external (exogenous): what is internal for the system is generally external for its subsystems. It all depends on where one draws the boundary between the system and its environment (Heylighen in Gershenson, 2008: 70f.; see also 2.1.).

Second, this definition does not lead to a too big class of elements, e.g., excluding risk entities simply associated with (very) rare and (very) impactful events – i.e., events caused by a significant change of the system – but that are well understood. Since, above all, systemic risks within modern financial systems (Neave, 2010) are the subject of this study and as these systems are usually characterized as complex (Chapter 2.1. and 6.3.), which includes that their behavior is not well understood, it follows that the resulting systemic risk events under study are not well understood. Dynamic complexity imposes certain restrictions on how to interpret systemic risks.

136 Strictly speaking, different financial systems exist, e.g., in geographical terms. As a consequence, the geographical reach of systemic risk can be regional, national or international (De Bandt & Hartmann, 2000: 11). To the extent we are concerned with the risk implications of the global financial crisis of 2007-09 and its consequences, our focus is on the international or global financial system – "international" and "global" can be seen as interchangeable here.

137 Another clarification would be that systemic risk is an economic, not a political, definition (Schwarcz, 2008: 204): "It should not be used uncritically as an ex post political label for any large financial failure or downturn."

Third, we refer to systemic risks as systemic risks because they are *cause*d by a change or changes[138] of the financial system and not because their realization would have the *effect* that the whole system would be affected. The latter would be rather unwarranted as many authors, if not all, repudiate that a systemic risk *must* concern the whole system (e.g., McNeil et al., 2005: 15; Sornette, 2003: 75; De Bandt & Hartmann, 2000: 11; Varnholt, 1995: 11; Heinemann, 2014; Group of Ten, 2001)[139]. Apart from that, a systemic risk might have an impact on *several* systems, i.e., going beyond the financial system (Oet et al., 2013: 792; Detken & Nymand-Andersen, 2013: 754; Haldane & May, 2011: 351). By contrast, it is a common, but not necessarily necessary, effect of systemic risks that the ability of the system to function as intended is seriously degraded. Furthermore, by taking changes in the system to be the *cause* of systemic risk – e.g., "risk arises not through the failure of individual components in the system […], but rather due to the 'herd behavior' and network effects contained in the actions of large fractions of market participants" (Thurner, 2012: 7) –, our definition is consistent with those of other risks, e.g., market risk (caused by, not resulting in, changes in the market; Artzner et al., 1999: 205). And highlighting that risks "are produced because of changes" reveals their *dynamic* nature (Trieschmann et al., 2005: 5).

Finally *fourth* and most importantly, systemic risk should be distinguished from downturns that are caused by 'normal' changes of the system (e.g., regular market swings). "Although these downturns are sometimes conflated with systemic risk, they are more appropriately labeled *systematic risk*, meaning risk that cannot be diversified away and therefore affects most, if not all, market participants" (Schwarcz, 2008: 204; cf. also Harry Markowitz's Modern Portfolio The-

138 For the latter, think of, for example, the numerous relatively small, distinct but interconnected changes of the financial system that, taken together, describe a change of the sort of (very) low-frequency, (very) high severity because they resulted in the financial meltdown of 2007-09; e.g., the relaxation of banking regulations, monetary policies that kept interest rates low, ignorance on the part of borrowers, etc.

139 A counter-example is Willke et al. (2013: 10) who demand even more – more than an effect on the whole financial system – from systemic risk and its definition: "Bankruptcy of a financial firm, a local financial crisis or the breakdown of a large investment fund are *normal accidents* and normal events in a competitive financial market characterized by ups and downs and by successes and failures. As long as these volatilities do not impinge on the economy at large […], and as long as they do not impinge on the political system, these financial crises can strictly be seen as results of market dynamics. *Only when a financial crisis is threatening the political system and thus forces politics to save private firms with public money, the term systemic risk comes into play*."

ory).[140] Indeed, as stated earlier, the significance of systemic risk, and, therefore, of the corresponding change of the system, has two dimensions, the severity of events possibly resulting from the change of the system as well as the likelihood of their occurrence (Brose et al., 2014a: 367; Willke et al., 2013: 9; De Bandt & Hartmann, 2000: 13). Systemic risks are found in the (very) low-frequency, high-dimensional space (Thiagarajan et al., 2015: 115). Therefore, systemic risks can be said to be tantamount to certain extreme risks.

What makes risk in complex systems different from other types of risk is that it cannot be captured in isolation (unlike market risk or credit risk in a simple or complicated, but not interdependent world), which might almost be counted as an axiom according to systems science. Instead, it has to be scrutinized at the higher level of interactions between parts of the system and between parts and the whole. This being so, systemic risk is systemic and not merely extreme.

Moreover, a *systemic risk event* is defined as the realization of systemic risk in form of a (very) rare event with extreme consequences; or put differently, events induced by a significant change of the system, endangering the functioning of the whole (financial) system, possibly resulting in a crash or '*black swan*' or '*dragon-king*'.[141] Given that the ties between events and times are loose,[142] it is

---

140 "System" has two adjectives, *systemic* and *systematic*. In a general sense, "systemic" refers to holistic thinking whereas "systematic" refers to step-by-step procedures.

141 Systemic risks are well captured by the image of *black swan* (Taleb, 2007a; Aven, 2013b) or by Sornette's important *dragon king* terminology (Sornette, 2009). Taleb (2007a) refers to a black swan as an event with the following three attributes.

1) Firstly, it is an *outlier*, as it lies outside the realm of regular expectations, because nothing in the past can convincingly point to its possibility.
2) Secondly, it carries *an extreme impact*.
3) Thirdly, in spite of its outlier status, human nature makes us *concoct explanations for its occurrence* after the fact, making it explainable and predictable.

However, we do not agree with Taleb's extreme view (as exposed in Taleb, 2007a) according to which he doubts whether any value can be given to a scientific/rational approach to finance (cf. also Das et al., 2013: 715).

The term "*king*" has been introduced by Sornette to *emphasize the importance* of those events, which are beyond the extrapolation of the fat tail distribution of the rest of the population. Sornette (2009: 5) also likes to refer to these exceptional events as "*dragons*" to stress that we deal with a *completely different* kind of animal, beyond the normal, with extraordinary characteristics, and whose presence, if confirmed, has profound significance.

142 Events can be construed as times *cum description*, i.e., as temporal instants or intervals during which certain statements hold (van Benthem, 1983). On this view, for example, the occurrence of the 2007-09 financial crisis is identified by an ordered pair $<i,\varphi>$ where i is the relevant time period (corresponding to the descriptor "2007-09") and φ is the sentence "The financial crisis occurs". Cf. also Casati & Varzi, 2014.

unproblematic to speak of, for example, the financial crisis of 2007-09 as a systemic risk event on a relatively abstract level, on the one hand, and, at the same time, of the fact that the financial meltdown can be traced to numerous distinct but interconnected events, which, taken by themselves, might not be considered as the realization of systemic risks because and provided that they are not of the sort of (very) low-frequency, (very) high severity: the relaxation of banking regulations, the invention of instruments that entitled lenders to shift risk off their balance sheets, monetary policies that kept interest rates low, the evaporation of reasonable credit standards and conventional down-payment requirements, and so on.

These definitions may need further refinement by future work, but they already capture the hallmarks of systemic risk at this stage. The definition provided for systemic risk will underlie this study in the remainder. The absence of an accepted definition of systemic risk in the literature is not simply an abstract academic ivory tower issue. Systemic risks in and to the financial system are regarded as triggers of global financial crises (Schwarcz, 2008: 193-249; Kelly, 1995: 221ff.). Having lucid definitions is a fundamental requirement for management and modeling (Fouque & Langsam, 2013: xxviii). Without a well-thought notion of systemic risk and approaches for measuring and managing the amount and nature of the risks, it would be difficult to effectively target indispensable (e.g., mitigating) action without running the real risk of doing more harm than good (ibid.).

5. On the Relevance of Systemic Risks for Banks

The purpose of this chapter is to argue for the relevance of systemic risks for (private) banks (as opposed to regulators) (5.1.) and to provide empirical evidence for systemic risk events (5.2.) by drawing on an illustrative case which will reappear in the course of this work. This chapter is essential, not only for contextualizing RQ1 as this study is interested in banks', and primarily in-house, risk management approaches, but also for clarifying the centrality of RQ1 for all participants in financial markets.

5.1. Why should Banks take account of, and try to deal with, Systemic Risks?

Systemic risks affect financial market participants in many ways. However, the literature insists firmly that they are and, in fact, should be of little concern to (private) banks (as opposed to regulators). For example, the *Bank of England* clarifies in its *Financial Stability Review* (2005: 3) that "private firms cannot be expected voluntarily to take full account of the possible consequences of spillovers from their actions for the overall stability of the financial system as a whole […]". In other words, "because systemic risk, by definition, breaches the boundaries of individual firms, the task of monitoring these risks falls to the regulatory community" (Brose & Flood, 2014: 6.). To the extent that systemic risk is "the concern of regulators [e.g., European Systemic Risk Board (ESRB), Financial Stability Board (FSB), C.H.], they should have no obvious role to play in actively managing the day-to-day affairs of the bank […]" (Rebonato, 2007: 224). In the same vein, it might be impossible to determine a price for the general risk, which could be incorporated in banks' respective calculations (LiPuma & Li, 2005: 416; Pryke & Allen, 2000: 271). Alan Greenspan, thus, concludes that "the management of systemic risk is properly the job of the central banks" (ibid.: 249;

cf. also Willke et al., 2013).[143] According to this view, systemic risk is not just beyond the interest and power of any one firm to manage, but is also a risk that affects all groups in an economy (see the systemic risk definition type 2, and cf. Bartholomew & Whalen, 1995: 4) and that should, therefore, be monitored and managed by regulatory bodies (only). These and many more accounts have been given to enunciate this assertion.

On the other hand, there are plenty of *actual* cases where systemic risks are disregarded by banks. Varnholt (1995: 6) observes that the risk of a system collapse is usually irrelevant for decision-making processes of market participants because there is a very low subjective probability of occurrence: Most of the risk experts from the economic practice who were interviewed by Nocera (2009) confirm that there is "a great deal to be said for being able to manage risk 99 percent of the time, however imperfectly, even though it [means] you [cannot] account for the last 1 percent [if standard tools like VaR are employed, C.H.]" (ibid.: 15). "[T]he individuals who flourish are those who have demonstrated expertise solving current problems, not those addressing systemic concerns that may never materialize" (French et al., 2010: 38). In the recent financial crisis, the risks of loans, including subprime mortgages and collateralized debt obligations or CDOs (see also the glossary at the end, Appendix A) that were securitized from them, "were of little concern to banks once these risks were transferred to other parties" (Boatright, 2011: 6). The main risks that were managed were (directly) "confined to the banks own portfolios; the losses that might result from these toxic assets were someone else's problem" (ibid.).[144] In the current *regulation* context, "financial institutions do maximize their risk-adjusted returns" without taking systemic risks into account (Acharya et al., 2010 in Bernard et al., 2013: 170; cf. also Schwarcz, 2008: 198). This entails that banks which are in default impose losses on creditors and externalities on the society at large,[145] in case of a systemic crisis (Acharya et al., 2010).

143 Cf. also Financial Times, 2009a: 4.

144 Similarly, the moral hazard that the implicit government guarantee provided to so-called too-big-to-fail institutions or institutions of systemic relevance (i.e., too-interconnected-to-fail) were "opportunities" to be exploited, without regard for the consequences to others (ibid.).

145 Private costs of an initial failure can be lower than the social costs. Then, "individually rational bank management may lead to a higher level of systemic risk than would be socially optimal" (De Bandt & Hartmann, 2000: 16).

As documented above, the response to this socially unwelcome situation (e.g., negative external effects) which is usually put forward in the literature is that regulators or policy makers should intervene to deal with systemic risks because banks will not or cannot be expected to do so, unless at least their incentives are altered (which calls for again regulators to improve the regulatory framework). In this chapter, by contrast, we show that this response is in need of completion, that the arguments in the literature are flawed and that not only regulators or policy makers, but also banks should indeed account for, and deal with, systemic risks (irrespectively of the regulation context). This thesis may be espoused on moral grounds (Heinemann, 2014; Boatright, 2011), e.g., if banks have a corporate social responsibility,[146] but here we argue that morality follows from reasons of rationality; in particular, if a so-termed feedback view of the world (Sterman, 2000) is adopted. In reference to RQ1.3, asking for the need to look at systemic risks from banks' point of view, two answers are provided.

First, the view usually adopted in the literature is based on an arbitrarily narrow interpretation of, perspective on, the term "systemic risk" and a systemic risk event does not only comprise the default, failure or bankruptcy of (a) certain bank(s). Since one of the foremost purposes of risk management in banking is to evaluate risks of the category „high severity, low likelihood" (Banks, 2009: 17f.; Arnoldi, 2009: 15; McNeil et al., 2005: 20; Posner, 2004: 6; Moss, 2002: 31; Stulz, 1996: 7), a minimal goal for private-bank risk managers (Rebonato, 2007: 249), it is clear that (private) banks should take account of systemic risk and should try to deal with it, given how the term is defined here. In opposition to Taleb's (2007a, 2007b, 2012) extreme view according to which he doubts whether systemic risks or black swans can be reckoned or calculated at all, a scientific and rational approach is possible (Part III).

Second, even if we stuck with a narrow reading of systemic risk, the management of systemic risks in banks does make sense because the frequently made distinction between individual risks (banks' business) vs. systemic risks (none of banks' business) usually goes astray. This dichotomy is often found in the literature (see above and also the next paragraph) and the reasoning behind it can be captured by a systems theoretical model (see Figure 5). However, this reasoning

146 Note that corporate social responsibility can be an expression of systems thinking, namely *environmentalization*: "the process of putting into a system's mind its relationship to the whole of which it is part" (Ackoff, 1974: 55).

and the corresponding model do not do justice to how the real system behaves, which is better modeled in Figure 6. By following the 'logic' of this latter model, it becomes obvious that systemic risks and their management are highly relevant to banks, regardless of how exactly the term "systemic risk" is specified.

In terms of the flawed argument in favor of the dichotomy between individual vs. systemic risks, it is often asserted (even by the Queen of England; Helbing, 2013: 53) that individual risks may *rightly* have been viewed as small regarding the occurrence of a financial meltdown – because single banks perceived their individual risk (e.g., of default or insolvency) *diminish* as a result of cooperation (i.e., *risk sharing*[147] by diversification) – while the risk to the system as a whole was *vast* or *increasing* (Garnier et al., 2013: 432; Helbing, 2013: 53; Haldane & May, 2011: 353).

This reasoning in the literature appears to suggest that individual banks did not need to be on red alert, that their risk management was effective, and that no further (mitigating) action or special attention to systemic risk was required by them. The following causal loop diagram (CLD) interconnects the variables that were found important according to this flawed reasoning with arrows that are supposed to indicate causal relationships.[148]

147 Interbank lending constitutes risk-sharing as Staum (2013: 532) explains: "it enables banks to survive liquidity shocks by borrowing, but it drains liquidity from lenders, leaving them more exposed to future liquidity shocks".

148 How to read a CLD: The arrows indicate the causal relationships. The + (–) signs at the arrowheads indicate that the effect is positively (negatively) related to the cause: e.g. an increase in systemic risks causes risk management efforts to rise above what it would have been (and vice versa). The *B* in the center of a loop denotes a balancing feedback, a *negative feedback loop* which is self-correcting. The overall polarity of a loop is the product of the signs on the arrows constituting that loop. All systems, no matter how complex, consist of networks of positive and negative feedbacks, and it is often stated that all dynamics arise from the interaction of these loops with one another (Sterman, 2000).
Even though this piece of work makes use of CLDs, the debate over the use and usefulness of CLDs still goes on (e.g., Warren, 2004; Homer & Oliva, 2001) and their fundamentally limited character should not be disguised. For example, despite their comparative advantage of explicitly representing feedback loops, they cannot represent the fact that the effects of a cause may show up in a smoothed way (Schaffernicht, 2007; Richardson, 1997). Moreover, causal loop models are supposed to contain and represent only causal relationships as opposed to correlations (Sterman, 2000: 141); yet, the notion of causality, including the concept, its role, and function in CLDs (and other System Dynamics modeling contexts), have not received much attention in the literature (Pedercini, 2006). On the other hand, CLDs concisely visualize the (both obvious and hidden) interconnections (and, thus, in some sense complexity), they can be used to elicit and capture the *mental models* of individuals or groups, and CLDs also capture hypotheses about dynamic behavior (Morecroft, 2007: 51). Due to these reasons they can be useful in spite of their weaknesses, which are rather insignificant here because our CLDs are used for illustration purposes only.

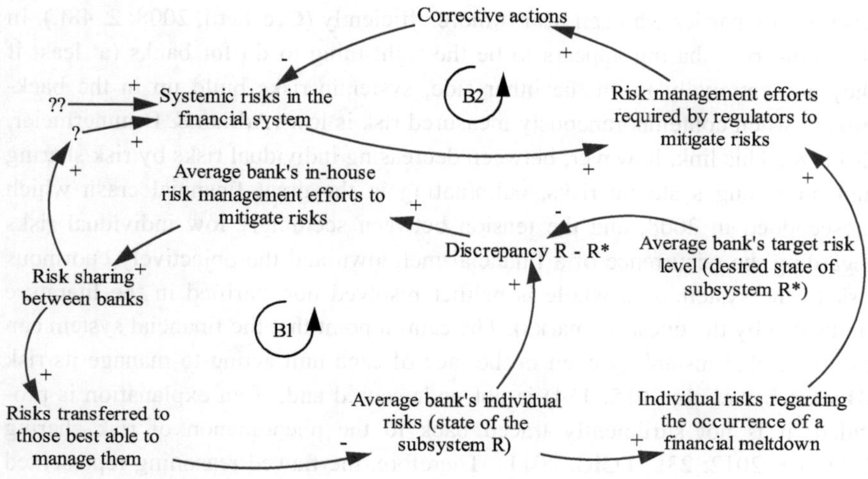

Figure 5: Risk sharing and systemic risks I: As the textbook reasoning goes, banks perceive their risks decrease as a result of cooperation.[149]

This figure reflects how textbooks and the literature (e.g., Saunders & Cornett, 2010; Bessis, 2010; Cecchetti, 2008) describe (and overestimate) the function of 'risk sharing between banks' which is outlined as being beneficial for the parties involved and which is the variable in focus in this model (see footnote 149). In *financial theory*, hedging and transferring of risk are possible because the risk is

149 This model consists of two causal feedback loops which are balancing. "Risk sharing between banks" is the key variable that expresses the degree to which financial risks are diversified among market participants. It is embedded in the causal circuit B1. Its logic is as follows: A comparison between banks' target risk level, a desired minimum value R*, and the actual level R results in a gap. The gap determines the magnitude of banks' in-house risk management efforts to mitigate risks which in turn positively affects the intensity of risk sharing between banks (i.e., more/less of the cause leads to more/less of the effect), etc., all along the loop. The logic of the other feedback loop B2 in the diagram is that more (less) risk management efforts and actions are required by regulators to mitigate risks if systemic risks in the financial system increase (decrease), which in turn depends on actions taken by the regulators. However, the crucial weakness of the model, of the underlying reasoning found in the literature, is that it neither establishes nor explains the link between rising (declining) individual risks or risk sharing initiatives and rising (declining) systemic risks, which is indicated by the question marks in the CLD. To be precise, this weakness is not a weakness of the model, but arises from the shortcomings of the reasoning which it is meant to depict. By contrast, it is indeed a flaw of this diagram that not all variables seem to be operationali-zable (e.g., "average bank's in-house risk management *efforts* to mitigate risks"); a flaw, however, which we consider as negligible since the CLDs in this study are used for illustration purposes and clarification of arguments only.

assumed by parties who can bear it more efficiently (Cecchetti, 2008: 2, 48f.). In this light, risk sharing appears to be the right thing to do for banks (at least if they act 'rationally'). On the other side, systemic risks build up in the background when contemporaneously measured risk is low (Adrian & Brunnermeier, 2011: 8). This link, however, between decreasing individual risks by risk sharing and increasing systemic risks, culminating in the great financial crash which crescendoed in 2008, and the tension between seemingly low individual risks regarding the occurrence of a financial meltdown and the objectively enormous risk to the system as a whole is neither resolved nor clarified in the literature (indicated by the question marks). The central point that the financial system can exhibit global instability even in the face of each unit acting to manage its risk (Bookstaber et al., 2015: 154) is not underscored and, if an explanation is provided, it is not sufficiently traced back to the phenomenon of risk sharing (Thurner, 2012: 23f.; FCIC, 2011). Therefore, the flawed reasoning represented by Figure 5 ought to be discurtained as such and, hence, a more appropriate and realistic picture or diagram needs to be drawn, respectively.

Indeed, risk sharing has not worked out in *practice*: The proposition that sophisticated modern risk management was able to transfer risk to those best able to manage it has failed (Crotty, 2009: 572). The paradigm is, instead, that "risk has been transferred to those least able to understand it" (ibid.; Financial Times, 2009b). Systemic risks occur then "because financial agents do not understand (or care) how their behaviour will affect everyone else and how synchronization of behaviour builds up" (Thurner, 2012: 24). Interconnectedness through risk sharing (or spreading) poses substantial threats to the stability of the financial system (Bookstaber et al., 2015: 147). To the extent systemic risk affects markets or the whole financial system (the Wall Street) or the real economy (the Main Street) etc., it is positively correlated with the markets etc. and cannot be diversified away (Schwarcz, 2008: 200). Risk sharing entails a kind of nonlinearity that causes *robust-yet-fragile behavior* in financial systems (Bookstaber et al., 2015: 147; Staum, 2013: 532).[150] In other words, risk sharing decreases the expected number of bank defaults, it is beneficial unless a *tipping point* is passed. Then it turns into a disadvantage because the interconnectedness of banks no longer dampens a shock, buth rather amplifies and distributes the damage

150 A property of a system is *robust* if it is invariant with respect to a set of perturbations (Alderson & Doyle, 2010: 840). Fragility is the opposite of robustness, i.e., the lack of invariance.

throughout the system (Willke et al., 2013: 30). The disadvantage is that risk sharing "increases the variance of the number of defaults and it increases the number of defaults in bad scenarios" (Staum, 2013: 532). In the extreme case of complete risk-sharing, there are no defaults (i.e., robustness) unless the aggregate shock, a systemic risk event, "exceeds the capacity of the system as a whole to absorb it, in which case every firm fails [i.e., fragility]" (ibid.). Higher connectivity leads to more extreme robust-yet-fragile behavior (ibid.: 534).[151] For example, when the strategies of (bank) companies all over the world become more and more similar due to inviting the same consultancy companies, the result is a lack of variety or heterogeneity in the system, which implies that "the number of defaulting companies is either negligible, or many companies fail at the same time" (Helbing, 2010: 12).

The successive CLD substitutes the previous diagram and illustrates that important feedback has been neglected which operates in *real life*,[152] as opposed to text book cases, highlighting that "[f]inancial instability typically results from positive feedback loops intrinsic to the operation of the financial system" (Bookstaber et al., 2015: 147).

Although banks thought that they had transferred the risks in their own portfolios successfully (e.g., by means of credit default swaps) – such banks have perceived themselves as smart (see loop B and the differences in comparison to the similar loop B1 in Figure 5) –, the risk *returned* to them after a while (see R1 to R5 in Figure 6) – and to taxpayers – when the counterparties were unable to pay claims (Boatright, 2011: 6). Hence, risk sharing might be regarded as a blessing and a curse in the course of time, which corresponds to Staum's (2013) robustness-vs.-fragility distinction as to financial systems.

Basically, this CLD in Figure 6 might be traced back to a simple generic structure, namely a systems archetype which Senge (2006: 103) calls "*Shifting the Burden*". Because for both cases it is characteristic that symptomatic solutions (like risk sharing) tend to have short-term benefits (for the "smart" banks) at best while in the long term, the problem (of coping with risks effectively) resurfaces and there is then increased pressure for symptomatic response. And Senge (2006: 22) has a good point when he warns: "Today, the primary threats to our

151 Empirical evidence for this phenomenon can be provided, cf. Vitali et al. (2011: 7).
152 The model could be further extended to incorporate more feedback, variables and interconnections between them.

survival, both of our organizations and of our societies, come not from sudden events but from slow, gradual processes."

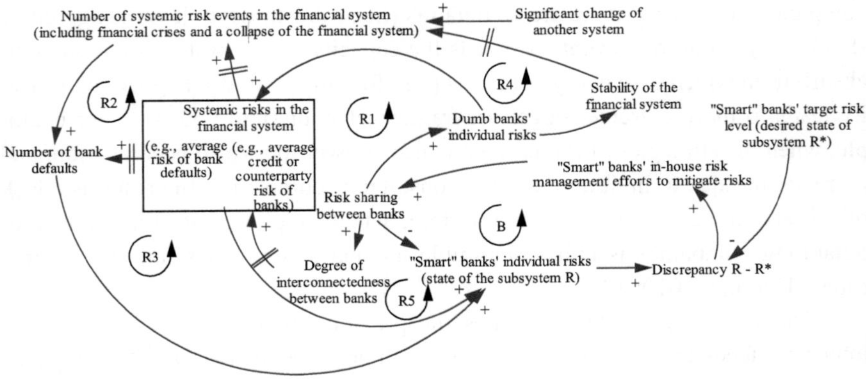

Figure 6: Risk sharing and systemic risks II: In reality, the distinction between individual vs. systemic risks usually goes astray.[153]

Why systemic risks have been viewed as immaterial for/by banks

One cause of not comprehending the full range of feedbacks operating in a system, of not seeing the inter-connections, relationships or the structures that underlie situations, is our tendency to interpret experience as a series of events, our so-called event-oriented worldview, which leads to an event-oriented approach to problem solving (Sterman, 2000: 10). Figure 7 shows how we often try to solve problems.

153 This model consists of six causal feedback loops. The loops which are added here are self-reinforcing, hence the loop polarity identifier *R*. They are called *positive feedback loops*. *Delays* between "systemic risks in the financial system" (cause) and "number of systemic risk events in the financial system" (effect), etc. are pervasive and denoted by the orthogonal dashes on several arrows. "Risk sharing between banks" is still the key variable. This time, however, it is embedded in several causal circuits. On the one hand, the functioning of the loop B is very similar to the logic of B1 in Figure 5, with two peculiarities though: first, this CLD is more abstract in the sense that some steps or variables are skipped; second, it is more specific in the sense that a differentiation is made between "smart" and "dumb" banks. On the other hand, the five reinforcing feedback loops work in a similar way. They all show that some banks ("dumb" banks) do not profit from risk sharing, their individual risks increase with risk sharing. This results in growing systemic risks in the financial system, which on one way or the other bounces back to banks that thought they would be smart because they transferred risk to those "least able to understand it" in the first place.

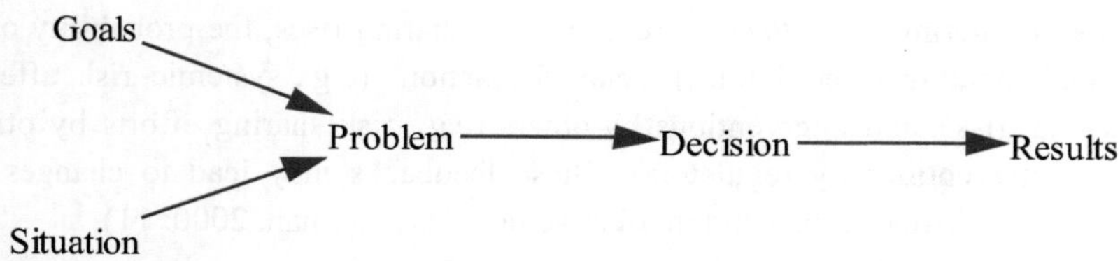

Figure 7: Event-oriented view of the world (Source: Sterman, 2000).

According to this view, as Sterman (2000: 10) describes, we assess the state of affairs and compare it to our goals. The gap between the situation we desire and the situation we perceive defines our problem (ibid.). For example, suppose that a bank wishes to minimize its individual risks (R* in Figure 5 and 6). The problem is that individual risks are higher than desired. The bank then considers various options to correct the problem. It might share or diversify its risks by selling CDOs or doing *xyz* (Cecchetti, 2008: 47), it might stop taking high risks in the first place, or take other actions. The bank selects and implements the option it deems best. It might observe its risks decline: problem solved. Or so it seems.

However, "[p]roblems and solutions are in constant flux; hence *problems do not stay solved*" (Ackoff, 1974: 31). Yesterday's 'solution' can become today's problem. Namely, it is important to see that actors in the financial system are not puppet masters influencing a system *out there*. There is feedback (see Chapter 6): The results of banks' risk management activities define the situation they face in the future. The new situation changes their assessment of the problem and the decisions which will be taken tomorrow. Their decisions alter the state of the system, leading not only to new decisions,

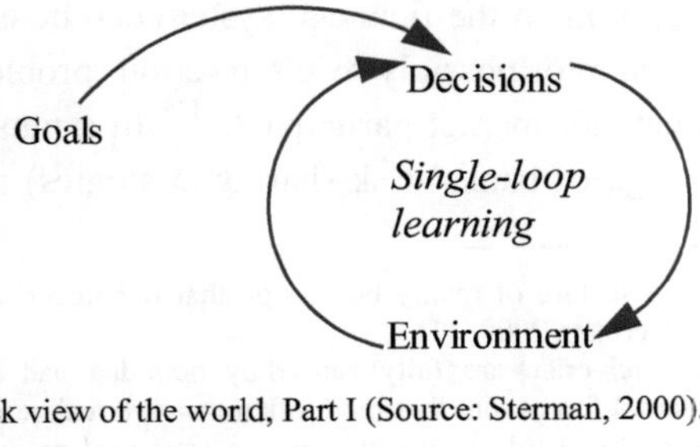

Figure 8: The feedback view of the world, Part I (Source: Sterman, 2000).

but also triggering *side effects*[154] (e.g., as risk sharing rises, the probability of a financial meltdown deteriorates), delayed reactions (e.g., systemic risk affects individual risk), and interventions by others (e.g., risk sharing efforts by other banks, interventions by regulators). These feedbacks may lead to changes in goals, unanticipated results and ineffective policies (Sterman, 2000: 11).

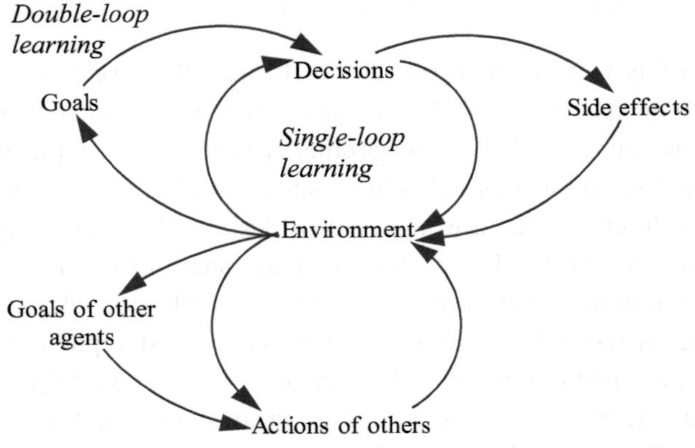

Figure 9: The feedback view of the world, Part II (Source: Sterman, 2000, 1994): Information feedback about the environment not only alters our decisions within the context of existing frames and decision rules, but feeds back to alter our mental models and decision goals. "The development of systems thinking is a double-loop learning process" (Sterman, 1994: 297; cf. also Stacey, 2010: 119f.).

If risk managers are not able to grasp and spot the factors determining the behavior of the system, if they do not adopt a feedback view of the world (Figures 8-9), then they do not only disregard systemic risks for in-house risk management purposes, but their interventions in the financial system can be even responsible for the instability of the system or possibly result in serious problems like a financial crisis that (badly) affects all market participants.[155] In a nutshell, to understand individual decisions (e.g., of banks' risk-sharing strategies) and their impact on

154 "Side effects are not a feature of reality but a sign that our understanding of the system is narrow and flawed" (Sterman, 2000: 11).

155 This is not to say that such crises are (fully) caused by individual bad decisions, by mistakes of individuals or by external forces, but that more often than we realize systems cause their own crises. However, Forrester (1961) maintains that the causes of many pressing public issues (like a financial crash) lay in the very well-intentioned policies designed to alleviate them (i.e., what he refers to as contra-intuitive behavior of social systems).

the system in which the actors are embedded, to cope with dynamic complexity, which is pervasive and a central organizational issue (Anderson, 1999; see Chapter 6), and to perceive system changes, which cause systemic risks, a feedback view of the world is prerequisite. It entitles risk managers, especially in the practice, to become aware of the relevance of systemic risks for in-house risk management purposes, which is of utmost interest to themselves and society at large (see 5.2.; cf. also Soros, 2013; NZZ, 2016 for a current case at hand: Falcon Private Bank).

Summa summarum, this argumentation allows to derive the *first proposition* to pioneer on uncharted terrain.

Proposition 1:
(Private) banks should adopt a feedback view of the world, they should account for systemic risk and actively address it for in-house risk management purposes.

Bottom line

By putting this postulation forward, it is not meant to replace the activities and the engagement of regulators, but to complement them. Admittedly, bright-line bank regulations have their advantages: Metaphorically speaking, "it is usually better to specify a speed limit than to enjoin drivers from speeding" (Bhidé, 2010: 289). Yet, in many situations of bank regulations considerable reliance on broad, as opposed to tight, rules is unavoidable. For example, one set of capital requirements does not fit all: "If bankers are given a precise definition of activities that fall under the rubric of casino banking, they will surely find other ways to gamble" (ibid.). Regulation and the law are rather crude instruments, and the law "is not suited for regulating all aspects of financial activities, especially those that cannot be reduced to precise rules" (Boatright, 2008: 9). In addition to that, regulation often develops as a reaction to activities that are considered to be socially undesirable or unacceptable. It would be perverse to encourage people in banks to "do anything that they want until the law tells them otherwise" (ibid.). Therefore, a certain amount of self-regulation is requisite, not as a surrogate for legal regulation, but as a supplement for territories which the law cannot easily touch upon and as an ideal for rising above the law (ibid.).[156] In other words, rather than solely placing our bets on new 'super' or 'systemic' regulatory bodies, the effective and fair implementation of broad rules calls for decentralized, case-by-case judgments (Bhidé, 2010: 289) and must be fostered by in-house approaches towards managing systemic risks in the financial system.

Furthermore, the implications of this first central research finding (Proposition 1) should not be underestimated. In particular, as stated earlier, the starting point for all common risk-management frameworks in banks is the classification of risks into risk categories (Mikes, 2009a). There is market risk, there is operational risk, there is reputational risk, there is credit risk – all separately discussed and managed in banks (ibid.; Detken & Nymand-Andersen, 2013: 759–761). On the one hand, such subsumption and categorizations may appear to be compulsory in order to present manageable information to executive management (Braswell & Mark, 2014: 245). Likewise, it is often thought to be the case that the creation and introduction of risk silos is an important part of the effort to make an otherwise ill-defined risk measurable, manageable and transferable since "[e]ach category of risk calls for distinct sets of risk management skills which are often used to define, delegate and organize the risk management activities of an FI [financial institution]" (Mark & Krishna, 2014: 35).

But, on the other hand, the reality in light of the systemic viewpoint here is different from the picture drawn by these practices: All the risk categories interact (Mikes, 2011: 239). The danger is that risk has been compartmentalized too much – for example, Kuritzkes & Schürmann (2010) dedicate all their efforts to identifying room for risk management improvements by ventilating all the risk silos separately.

Yet, the only viable way forward for a successful handling of financial risk consists of a *holistic* approach, i.e., an integrated approach taking all types of risk and their interactions into account (McNeil et al., 2005: 3). Whereas this is a clear goal, current models do not yet allow for a fully satisfactory platform (ibid.). Along these lines, investigating systemic risks of the financial system transcends the usual risk silo management approach and focuses on changes of

156 More critically, regulation might even be *harmful* and contra-productive: Implementing different regulation scenarios, such as the Basel accords, may deepen crisis when leverage levels are high, which is due to enhanced synchronization effects induced by the regulations (Thurner, 2012).

dynamically complex financial systems, including interdependencies and spillovers between risk clusters. As a result, Proposition 1 provides a strong reason for overcoming the silo-treatment of risks, at least to some extent. Moreover and still on the theoretical side which is foregrounded in this thesis, the perspective of complexity and well-grounded systems theories, that is required due to the dynamic complexity (Byrne & Callaghan, 2014: 39; Schwaninger, 2005: 32), is hardly compatible with the standard categorization of risks, which is aggravated anyway by new emerging risk categories (Härle et al., 2016: 6).[157]

To use an analogy, risk management is chemistry (complexity science, global), not particle physics (mechanical science, local). You cannot separate the risks!

5.2. What are concrete Systemic Risk Scenarios for Banks?

Many different concrete systemic risk scenarios can be composed to illustrate the relevance of systemic risks for banks (ad RQ1.4). Taken from the more recent past and apart from the recent financial crisis of 2007-09, these might involve events like the collapse of Barings Bank in 1995 or of the giant[158] hedge fund Long Term [!][159] Capital Management in 1998, and the Asian crisis in 1997/98. Countless more (very) rare events with extreme consequences exist or can be envisioned, ranging from natural disasters (e.g., an earthquake in Tokyo from the point of view of a bank with its headquarters in Tokyo's financial district) over severe political conflicts (e.g., Western sanctions against Russia over the Ukraine

157 An empirical reason is that the standard categorization has proved to be unhelpful and, indeed, dangerous. For example, credit and market risks are often monitored independently from each other along functional responsibility lines for credit risk and asset-liability management (ALM). Although it is stressed in this case that it is absolutely critical that both groups periodically share reporting strategy, methodology and data in order to ensure alignment to the greatest extent possible (Rossi, 2014: 79), reality all too often departs from this ideal. One observer noted that in the recent financial crisis, the risk of CDOs (i.e., collateralized debt obligations which are securities that bundle together large numbers of loans and divide them into tranches with different risks and rates of return) "was not widely recognized because they fell between market and credit risks, and the parties responsible for each of these risks thought the problem belonged to the other" (Boatright, 2011: 9).

158 In terms of personnel, LTCM was of limited size: initially, eleven partners and thirty employees; by September 1997, fifteen partners and around 150 employees (MacKenzie, 2003: 354). These people, however, managed a considerable body of assets: in August 1997, LTCM's assets totaled \$126 billion, of which \$6.7 billion was the fund's own capital (ibid.).

159 The fund existed for no more than four years. Apart from that, Taleb (2005: 54) objects that under (utter) leverage there is no such thing as long term.

crisis from the stance of a Russian bank) to homemade failures (for the latter, think, e.g., of the rogue trader in the case of Barings Bank (Nick Leeson),[160] Société Générale (Jérôme Kerviel) or UBS (Kweku Adoboli); Jacque, 2015: 143-196). Yet, the diversity of extreme and systemic events underscores that they necessitate very different management and hedging approaches, at least on a detailed level (Bhansali, 2014: 152).

The well-studied case of the fall of the hedge fund[161] *Long Term Capital Management* (cf., Lowenstein, 2002) and its impact on banks and the international banking system is presented in this context and discussed as a systemic risk event in-depth. This means that an explanation is provided of in what sense the event of LTCM's fall is or can be considered as (very) rare, as producing disastrous consequences and of what is really systemic and not only extreme about it. But first, the impressive story of LTCM, containing defining moments of the economic history of the 1990s, runs in a short form as follows.[162]

LTCM was a hedge fund management firm, founded in 1994 by John W. Meriwether, the former vice-chairman and head of bond trading at Salomon Brothers and by common consent the most talented bond trader of his generation (MacKenzie, 2003: 352). Members of LTCM's board of directors included Myron S. Scholes and Robert C. Merton, who shared the 1997 Nobel Memorial Prize in Economic Sciences for a "new method to determine the value of derivatives" (The Royal Swedish Academy of Sciences, 1997). This might explain why LTCM has been labeled the "probably [...] best academic finance department in the world" (Mandelbrot & Hudson, 2008: 106). Therefore, it is not perplexing that sophisticated investors, including many large investment and commercial banks, flocked to the fund, investing $1.3 billion at inception (Drobny, 2006: 24). LTCM was hugely successful: "at its peak, it deployed what is almost certainly the largest single concentration of arbitrage positions ever" (MacKenzie, 2003: 352).[163] This one obscure arbitrage fund amassed an amazing $100 billion in assets, virtually all of it borrowed from not more than one hundred investors

160 Note that both Leeson's fraudulent, unauthorized and speculative practices (as a whole) and the collapse of Barings Bank itself (which in turn was caused by his trading activities) can be regarded as systemic risk events.

161 For a selective review of the recent academic literature on hedge funds as well as updated empirical results for this industry, cf. Getmansky et al. (2015).

162 For a longer version, cf. Lowenstein, 2002.

163 Arbitrage refers to trading that seeks to profit from price discrepancies.

(Lowenstein, 2002: xix). Against this background of a huge amount of capital, it entered into thousands of derivative contracts, essentially side bets on market prices, which covered an astronomical sum of more than $1 trillion (ibid.). And yet in the late 1990s the firm's master hedge fund collapsed, ultimately due to the Russian financial crisis in 1998 (Jorion, 2000), in which the Russian government imposed a moratorium on foreign debts, defaulted on some domestic debts, and ended the Rubel's peg on the dollar which led to a large fall in the Russian currency's value (Stiglitz, 2002: 145f.). (But unsurprisingly, as we do not inhabit a mono-causal world, LTCM also faced other problems like on the Danish mortgage market.) These events happened during a more general financial crisis in Asia that had begun a year before, and together they led to a flight of capital towards US Treasury bonds, causing the spread between them and underlying interest rates to widen, contrary to the expectations of LTCM. At the same time, other market participants were aware of LTCM's strategy and intentionally tried to increase the spread even further, which caused LTCM to have to post more and more collateral until it had used up all its capital and required a bailout by other banks (Roubini & Mihm, 2011: 29; Greenspan, 2007; Mac Kenzie, 2003: 367). In Chapter 16, we are going to analyze exactly the kind of trade that resulted in the fund's demise, and show that our model would have been able to capture some of the consequences of the 1998 events, without having to make difficult assumptions such as pinpointing a probability for a default of the Russian government, which in the end denounced LTCM as "a catastrophe that was caused by the pseudo-science of economics" (Taleb, 2005: 54).

It is *prima facie* beyond dispute that LTCM's crisis – the firm was driven to the brink of bankruptcy – can be classified as a systemic risk event. First, the event is or can be considered as (very) rare in reference to similar situations or situations perceived as similar. While it might be impossible to specify an objective probability for LTCM's collapse considering high scientific standards of rigor – the "true" probability of a loss of 77% in a certain interval may have been 0.1% or 25% or it may have been more or less probable but since LTCM lost 77% on only one occasion, nothing can be concluded from this fact; neither 'the true value' nor anything about the effectiveness of LTCM's risk management (cf. Stulz, 2008: 62; and see also Chapter 7) –; the subjective degrees of belief concerning the fund's failure were very small. Especially, the fund's managers, who considered themselves to be smarter than others (Lowenstein, 2002: 89), believed that such a scenario would be negligible. LTCM did not merely concede the possibility of loss, it reckoned the supposed odds of its occurring, and to precise mathematical degrees (Lowenstein, 2002: 61): "Just as [in] a handbook of poker […], the professors calculated that Long-Term would lose at least 5% of its money 12% of the time (that is, in twelve of every hundred years). The letter went on to state that "[o]nly *one year in fifty* should it lose at least 20 percent of its portfolio – and the Merton-Scholes encyclical did not entertain the possibility of losing more" (ibid.: 63). On this basis, it is clear that a collapse was not on their radar. In fact, the partners explained the blowup of LTCM as the result of a 'ten sigma event', which should take place once per lifetime of the universe. It would be more convincing, however, to consider that, *rather, they used the wrong distribution* (Taleb & Pilpel, 2004: 3).[164] In addition to that, LTCM's letter represented a dramatic leap: While it heartily acknowledged risk in the sense of *Risk II* (see also Appendix A), it banished uncertainty or risk in the broad sense by putting numerical odds on its likelihood of loss.

Second, the event's consequences were extreme. LTCM's losses were stunning in their size and rapidity: for example and yet this was only a foretaste of what was to come, in August 1998, it lost 44% of its capital (MacKenzie, 2003: 365). LTCM's final, cumulative loss was staggering (see Figure 10). Through April 1998, the value of a dollar invested in the firm quadrupled to $4.11 (having grown to $2.85 after deducting the partners' fees). By the time of the bailout, only five months later, precisely 33 cents (23 cents) of that total remained (Lowenstein, 2002: 224; Jacque, 2015: Chapter 15).

In net terms, the greatest fund ever had lost 77 percent of its capital while the ordinary stock market investor had been more than doubling his money (ibid.: 225). LTCM experienced a flight-to-quality and a cascade of self-reinforcing adverse price movements (MacKenzie, 2003: 353). The result was "a downward spiral which fed upon itself driving market positions to unanticipated extremes well beyond the levels incorporated in risk management and stress loss discipline" (Lowenstein, 2002: 219). In the end, in terms of the firm itself and its internal stakeholders it is noteworthy that the partners' investment in LTCM – once

164 "As the crisis [of 2007-09] began, reports of '10-sigma' or '20-sigma' events were commonplace until a sort of ennui set in, and it became understood that models designed to characterize the behavior of asset prices during normal market conditions had little relevance in a crisis so extreme that the need to survive trumped many financial institutions' normal profit-seeking behaviors." (Getmansky et al., 2015: 62).

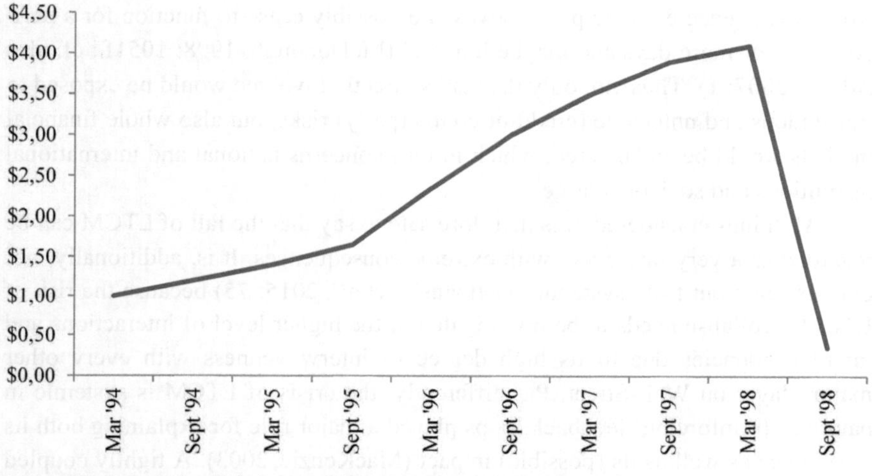

Figure 10: Gross value of $1 invested in LTCM, March 1994 – September 1998 (Source: Lowenstein, 2002; cf. also Fung & Hsieh, 1999: 329).

worth $1.9 billion – was totally gone, most of it lost in a mere five weeks (ibid.: 208). The fund's employees received most of their pay in the form of year-end bonus money. Most of those bonuses had been invested in the fund and went down the drain as well (ibid.: 225). A month after the rescue, LTCM laid off 33 employees, almost a fifth of the staff (ibid.). After that, there was a steady stream of defections (ibid.).

On the other hand, the crisis was extreme for external stakeholders, respectively. Greenspan (1998: 1046), for example, speculates that if "the failure of LTCM triggered the seizing up of markets […] it could have potentially impaired the economies of many nations, including our own". LTCM's monstrous indebtedness (almost $100 billion) and its notional derivative exposure ($1 trillion) had endlessly intertwined it with every major bank on Wall Street. If LTCM defaulted, all of these banks would be left holding one side of a contract for which the other side no longer existed (Lowenstein, 2002: xix). In the words of William J. McDonough, the former President of the Federal Reserve Bank of New York: "Had Long-Term Capital been suddenly put into default, its counterparties would have immediately 'closed out' their positions […]. [I]f many firms had rushed to close out hundreds of billions of dollars in transactions simultaneously […] there was a likelihood that a number of credit and interest rate markets would experience extreme price moves and possibly cease to function for a period of one or more days and maybe longer." (McDonough, 1998: 1051f.; cf. also Adrian, 2007: 1). Thus, not only the banks directly involved would be exposed to tremendous and untenable (credit or counterparty) risks, but also whole financial markets would be endangered, which in turn concerns national and international institutions and society at large.

All things considered, it is therefore safe to say that the fall of LTCM can be regarded as a very rare event with extreme consequences. It is, additionally, not only extreme but truly systemic (Getmansky et al., 2015: 75) because the risk of LTCM's collapse needs to be investigated at the higher level of interactions and interdependencies due to its high degree of interwovenness with every other major player on Wall Street. Put differently, the crisis of LTCM is systemic in nature as (reinforcing) feedback loops played a major role for explaining both its emergence as well as its (possible) impact (MacKenzie, 2003). A tightly coupled system as a set of elements, here: LTCM and its contractual or trade partners, standing in heavy interrelation was established (von Bertalanffy, 1968/2013: 38).

LTCM's crisis has aroused widespread comment (cf., Lowenstein, 2002) and this case study is particularly interesting in the context of this thesis for a couple of reasons.

1) "Risk is a critical component of hedge fund strategies [even more than elsewhere; C.H.], so the way in which it is measured is extremely important" (Adrian, 2007: 2). Moreover, "[e]ver since the demise of LTCM in 1998, hedge funds have become inextricably linked to systemic risk, though the links are still not yet well defined" (Getmansky et al., 2015: 62). On top of that, it has been purported that tail or extreme risk is a distinctive facet of hedge-fund risk management (ibid.: 55).
2) Merton saw LTCM not merely as a "hedge fund", "a term that he and the other partners sneered at, but as a state-of-the-art *financial intermediary*", a financial-technology company, that provided capital to markets just as banks did (Lowenstein, 2002: 30). More specifically, its partners and managers fell prey to "managing risk by the numbers" (ibid.: 65; see Chapter 10). Therefore, very interesting lessons can be learnt from studying this case. For example, the partners assumed that, *all else being equal*, the future would look like the past (ibid.: 59) which serves as a nice illustration for the target of the objection IIIb)

and for invoking Chapter 7. Another lesson is that there were misbeliefs about risk. For instance, LTCM's press spokesman, glibly explained: "Risk is a function of volatility. These things are quantifiable" (ibid.: 64). Third, in opposition to some accounts which claim that LTCM's partners had blind faith in the accuracy of risk management or finance theory's mathematical models (cf. MacKenzie, 2003: 352), it appears to be the case that the traders at LTCM knew the models were imperfect – "'we know this doesn't work by rote', said Robert Stavis, the former member of the Arbitrage Group at Salomon; 'but this is the best model we have'" (Lowenstein, 2002: 75). The response given here is that there might be a more appropriate modeling approach compared to orthodox methods (Part III) and that even if no persuasive alternatives could be found, this would not make up for the applied methods' shortcomings (Part IV). Etc.

3) The rise and especially the fall of LTCM were presented in such detail because in later sections the case of LTCM is taken up in the following ways.
   a) This thesis looks at LTCM's collapse not only as a general systemic risk event, but as a counter-party credit risk crisis (the reason why intervention by the Fed was a *sine qua non* for preventing it) from banks' point of view in particular.
   b) This thesis is not interested in LTCM's (investment) strategy *per se* but rather an example trade is provided (Chapter 16.1.) to form the starting point for an illustration for the applicability of a novel and enhanced conceptual program towards responding to systemic risks in the financial system (introduced in Part III).
   c) The case of LTCM is employed as empirical evidence for our Central Argument in Chapter 7.

Ultimately, the overriding importance of systemic risks for banks also results from the importance of managing complexity in banks.

6. Dealing with Quantitative Risk Management in Banking as a Complex Systems Problem

Ideas thus made up of several simple ones put together, I call Complex; such as are Beauty, Gratitude, a Man, an Army, the Universe.
(John Locke, 1689)

The whole is more than the sum of its parts.
(Aristotle, 384 – 322 BC)

True wisdom comes to each of us when we realize how little we understand about life, ourselves, and the world around us.
(Socrates, 470/469 – 399 BC)

"Risk is like a polished gem with different facets: each facet reflects the light in different colors; but the whole gem can be appreciated only if the images of all the facets are being absorbed" (Renn, 2008: xv). Indeed, risk is a truly interdisciplinary, if not transdisciplinary, phenomenon and difficult questions about risks often depend upon a transdisciplinary vision of the risk concept. None of the single discipline-based approaches to grasp the entire substance of the risk issues can thrive (ibid.). Only if they combine forces, one can expect an adequate approach towards understanding and managing risks (ibid.). Thus, investigating risks necessitates a multi- or (better) transdisciplinary, i.e., disciplines brought together in an integrated fashion, approach which renders a systems / complexity perspective an appropriate choice for comprehending and managing systemic risks in and to the financial system. Because it is important to recognize that the discipline of 'systems science'[165] in fact claims to be a *meta-discipline* (Flood & Carson, 1993: 21). In other words, systems science is not, strictly speaking, multi-disciplinary, it is not concerned with lots of disciplines *separately*, but rather it is an interdisciplinary meta-subject (ibid.). Systems science grew out of the need

165 It is controversial if such a thing as systems or complexity *science* exists. Bruce Edmonds or W. Brian Arthur, to name just two skeptics, would rather call it a movement or an approach to do science (cf. Gershenson, 2008). Therefore, we use the term "systems / complexity science" only in a loose way.

to communicate across disciplinary boundaries as a counter-current to the increasing fractionation of science into highly specialized branches: "We must stop acting as though nature were organized into disciplines in the same way that universities are" (Ackoff, 1960: 6).

When, however, asked to expound what systems science or theory (better: theories) is all about, many systems scientists are confronted with a rather daunting task.[166] The discipline tends to be presented and understood in a fragmented way (Flood & Carson, 1993: 1). Figure 11 tries to give a consolidated overview of the many and broad-ranging subject areas and the systems movement's evolution in general (which is not meant to be exhaustive).

"Systems movement" – often referred to briefly as "systemics" – is a broad term, which takes into account the fact that there is no single or royal road to systems theory, but a range of different approaches (Schwaninger, 2011: 753). Returning to the quest for an overview understanding of systems science, a standard answer might be twofold. First, it is noteworthy that a very close relationship exists between the different systems theories, on the one hand, and an underlying methodological holistic way of thinking on the other. The common denominator of the different systems approaches in our day is that they are aligned around a worldview which is an integrating, an analytical as well as a synthesizing (Ulrich & Probst, 1990: 34), form of thinking, expanding one's horizon, starting from larger contexts and taking many factors into account, compared to a more isolating and decomposing analytical procedure. Rather, to be an effective systems scientist, we must at the same time be both a *holist*, looking at the system as a whole (e.g., the financial system and its dynamic complexity), and a *reductionist*, discerning the system in more detailed forms (e.g., analysis of financial systemic and extreme risks) (Flood & Carson, 1993: 17). The various systems approaches originate from a form of thinking which involves "seeing" interconnections and relationships, i.e., the whole picture as well as the component parts (Ulrich & Probst, 1990: 11f.). Systems theories are then formalizations of holistic, systemic or *systems thinking* (Flood & Carson, 1993: 4),

166 There exist several definitions of systems science, which are often unsatisfactory. For example, Klir (2001: 5) defines it as "a science whose domain of inquiry consists of those properties of systems and associated problems that emanate from the general notion of systemhood", where he traces "systems science" to the not less nebulous term of systemhood, which is not even a correct English word according to The Oxford English Dictionary (OED Online, accessed April 14, 2015).

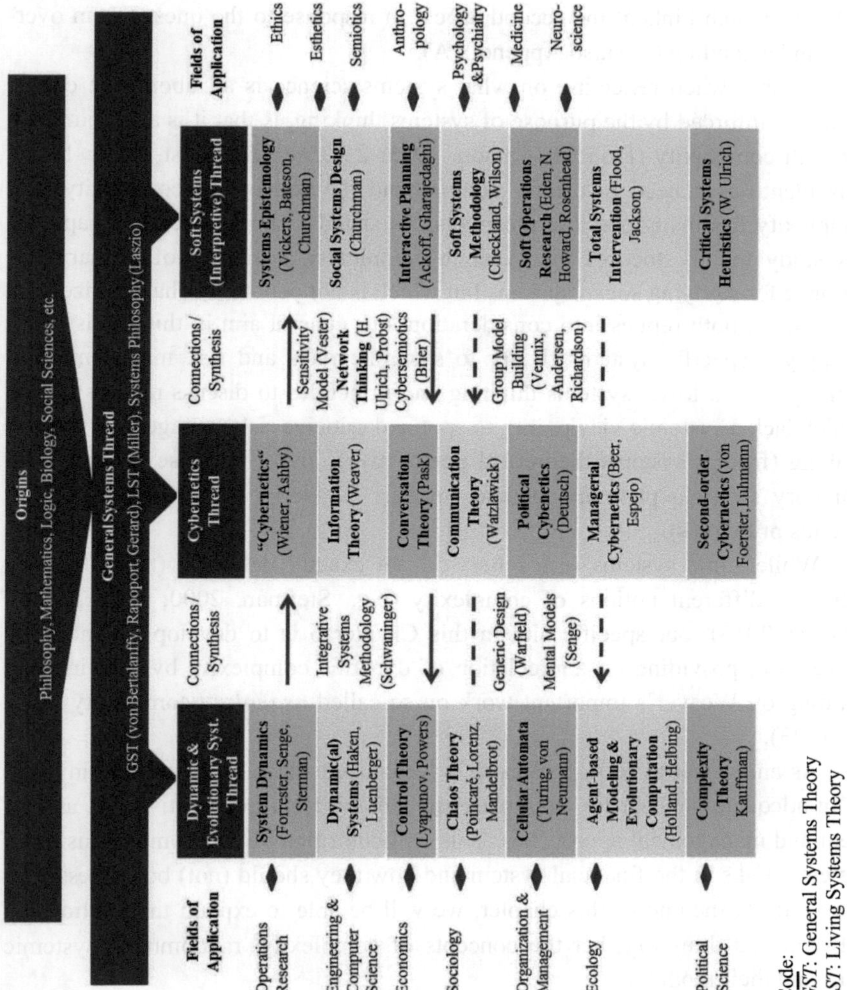

Figure 11: The evolution of the Systems Approach (based on Schwaninger, 2011).

not systematic thinking (Ulrich & Probst, 1990: 20). It has been said that systems thinking is a framework of thought that helps us deal with complex things in a holistic way (e.g., Schwaninger, 2011: 753; Senge, 2006: 69; Flood & Carson,

1993: 4), which hints at the second aspect in response to the quest for an overview understanding (see also Appendix A).

Second, when reflecting on what systems science is all about, the classic answer, reinforced by the purpose of systems thinking, is that it is all about dealing with complexity (Flood & Carson, 1993: 2; Ulrich & Probst, 1990: 19).[167] This identifies a need to clearly comprehend the concept of complexity. But complexity has many possible meanings. As stated and explained in Chapter 2, this study mainly focuses on dynamic complexity, which is of primary importance for studying social systems but which is not yet amply characterized.

Taking both replies into consideration, our general aim in this thesis is *not* to apply a specific systems theory to systemic risks and risk management in banking, but to foster systems thinking and principles to discuss notions of risk (which lack a systemic viewpoint), to spot and criticize risk management tools in banking (from a systems theoretical perspective), and to propose an exact, explanatory scenario planning method (in Part III, derived from complexity or systems principles).

While some systems researchers do not exactly delineate (the difference between) different notions of complexity (e.g., Sterman, 2000; Senge, 2006; Grösser, 2013), our specific aim in this Chapter 6 is to develop a conceptual framework, providing an appreciation of dynamic complexity by drawing and building on Weaver's important work on so-called *organized* complexity (Klir, 1991: 23).

As an answer to RQ1.5, Weaver's "organized complexity" will be invoked as an adequate concept for examining the suitability of quantitative risk assessment and management approaches. This will contribute to our comprehension of systemic risks in the financial system and how they should (not) be addressed or managed. At the end of this chapter, we will be able to explain the relationship between and draw together the concepts of complexity, randomness, systemic risks and their modeling.

The following figure summarizes the line of argumentation as well as the storyline in this Chapter 6 and its purpose, the latter by integrating and pointing to Chapter 7 where the Central Argument is presented.

167 Note that the inversion does not hold: Not every mode of dealing with complex issues is systemic.

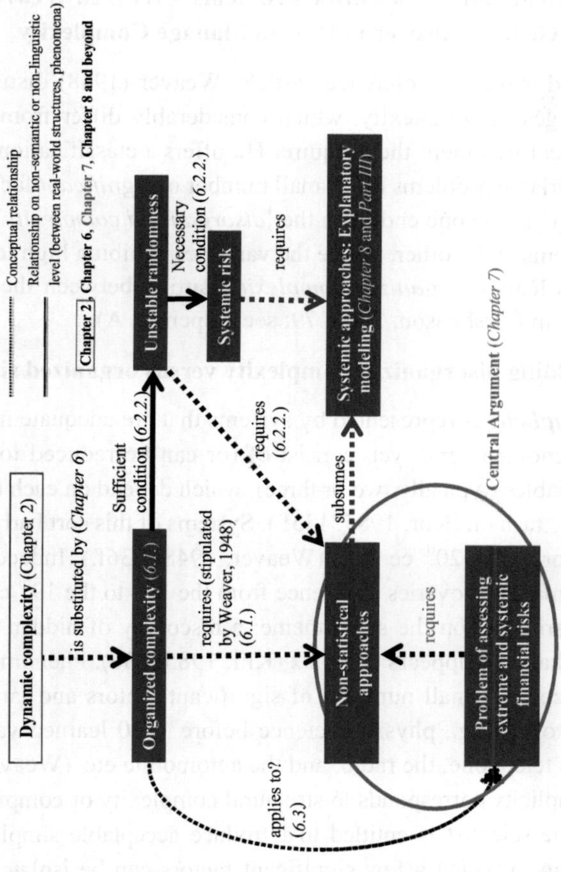

Figure 12: The line of argumentation in Chapter 6 and its embeddedness: In a nutshell, the storyline runs as follows: Taking the presentation of dynamic complexity in Chapter 2 and its insufficient characterization as a starting point, we refine and replace the term by Weaver's "organized complexity" in the following. According to him, problems of organized complexity require non-statistical approaches, including, for example, explanatory models (which is picked up in Chapter 8). Against the background of demonstrating the ineptness of statistical instruments in risk management, which is a main aim of this study, it would be expedient to deploy the Weaverian concept of organized complexity. Unfortunately, Weaver leaves (too) many questions open. And even though introducing unstable randomness into the picture is illuminating, as it proves to be both necessary for the emergence of systemic risk and the existence of organized complexity as well as necessary and sufficient for the inadequacy of statistical methods, obscurities remain. Therefore, we seem to be obliged in the end to propound a separate argument (Chapter 7).

6.1. A Trichotomy of Scientific Problems – Warren Weaver's Scheme as a General Answer to How to Manage Complexity

In a classic and massively referenced article, Weaver (1948) distinguishes three significant ranges of complexity, which considerably differ from each other in the mathematical treatment they require. He offers a classification that separates simple, few-variable problems (or a small number of *significant* factors) of '*organized simplicity*' at the one end from the '*disorganized complexity*' of numerous-variable problems at the other, where the variables exhibit a high level of random behavior. This leaves '*organized complexity*' sitting between the two extremes (cf. Huberman in Gershenson, 2008: 79; see Appendix A).

6.1.1. Tackling disorganized complexity versus organized simplicity

Organized simplicity is represented by systems that are adequate models of some real-world phenomena and, yet, consist of (or can be reduced to) a very small number of variables (typically two or three), which depend on each other in a highly deterministic fashion (Klir, 1985: 135f.). Systems of this sort had been pervasive in science prior to the 20th century (Weaver, 1948: 536f.). Indeed, the recorded history of the main discoveries in science from the 17th to the 19th century consists basically of variations on the same theme: a discovery of hidden simplicity in a phenomenon that only appears complex (Klir, 1985: 136). Phenomena of this sort are characterized by small numbers of significant factors and large numbers of negligible factors – e.g., physical science before 1900 learned variables, which brought us the telephone, the radio, and the automobile etc. (Weaver: 1948: 536). Organized simplicity corresponds to structural complexity or complicatedness (see 2.1.), where the scientist is entitled to introduce acceptable simplifying assumptions, according to which a few significant factors can be isolated from a large number of presumably negligible factors, which in turn describes an analytical or reductionist procedure. Application of the analytical procedure depends on two conditions. The first is that interactions between parts are non-existent or weak enough to be omitted for certain research purposes. "Only under this condition, can the parts be 'worked out', actually, logically, and mathematically, and then be 'put together'. The second condition is that the relations describing the behavior of parts be linear [for basic aspects of linearity, cf. Zadeh & Desoer, 1979: 132f.; C.H.]; only then is the condition of *summativity* given [i.e., an equation describing the behavior of the total is of the same form as the equations describing the behavior of the parts; C.H.]" (von Bertalanffy, 1968/2013: 19). "Due to their nature, systems with the characteristics of organized simplicity are perfectly suitable for *analytic* mathematical treatment, usually in terms of the calculus and differential equations. They are best exemplified by systems based upon *Newtonian mechanics*." (Klir, 1985: 136; cf. also Gomez, 1981: 15f.).

Disorganized complexity[168] possesses attributes that are exactly opposite to these: it is represented by systems with very large numbers of variables and high degrees of *randomness* (Weaver, 1948: 537f.).

Preliminaries on randomness

We follow Eagle (2005: 775) in defining randomness as a strong or utter form of unpredictability: an event is *random* if, and only if, the probability of an event, conditional on evidence, equals the prior probability of the event (cf. also Kyburg, 1974: Chapter 9; Suppes, 1984: 31f.; Klir, 1991: 20; and for some conceptual problems with "randomness", cf. Churchman, 1961: 156ff. and Eagle, 2012 for an overview).[169] Likewise, "a random process is one for which we are not able to predict what happens next" (Frigg, 2004: 430).[170] On the other hand, while McNeil et al. (2005: 4) appear to neglect conceptual differences between randomness and chance[171] when they foreground that the former "has eluded a clear, workable definition for many centuries; it was not until 1933 that the Russian mathematician A.N. Kolmogorov gave an axiomatic definition of randomness and probability";[172] this study questions that there is a tight and unbreakable connection between

168 In essence, what Weaver called *disorganized complexity* was ultimately a way to extend the "simple" to large ensembles and, in his thinking, was not really about complexity at all (Alderson & Doyle, 2010: 847).

169 That something is 'predictable' implies that there exists a constraint (Ashby, 1956: 132). Neither chaos nor disorder nor indeterminism is a synonym for randomness (Earman, 1986: 145; Eagle, 2012).

170 Following Eagle (2012), it is important to clarify that "for this kind of view to yield the right results, we cannot count as 'being able to predict a process' if we merely guess rightly about its outcomes. For that reason, prediction must involve some notion of *reasonableness*; it must be rational for the agent to make the predictions they do. […] [S]imply guessing will not be reasonable, even if it's correct."

171 This position appears to be endorsed in the scientific literature too (Eagle, 2012 – cf. Futuyma (2005: 225) as an example). Some authors might be subject to an unthinking elision, but others deliberately use "random" to mean "chancy" (prominent examples include: Earman, 1986: 137; Suppes, 1984: 27; von Mises, 1957).

172 Note that Kolmogorov did indeed develop an important definition of randomness (see *Appendix C*), however not in 1933 (when his oeuvre on probability was published), but in the 1960s (in the field of *algorithmic information theory*, cf. Kolmogorov, 1963, 1965).

randomness and probability – they indeed overlap in many cases, but are separate concepts (Eagle, 2012). It poses the counterquestion (see 6.2.2.) whether such formal definitions used in the fields of probability theory and statistics do not turn out to be too narrow or whether they should not be complemented by other definitions. Indeed, if McNeil et al. (2005) suggest that randomness in general (and not only probability) should conform to Kolmogorov's (1933) axiomatization of the probability calculus, this would be inconsistent with the research results in Chapter 7, *Proposition 5* in particular (as Kolmogorov's (1933) work is there not questioned as standard mathematical theory of probability as such). *Appendix C* deepens our understanding of randomness (cf. also Eagle, 2012 and see Appendix A for a synopsis).

Interest in systems of this sort of disorganized complexity began in the late 19th century with the investigation of systems representing the motions of gas molecules in a closed space (Weaver, 1948: 538). “Such a system would typically consist of, say, 10^{23} molecules. The molecules have tremendous velocities and their paths, affected by incessant impacts, assume the most capricious shapes. It was obvious that systems with these characteristics could not be explored in terms of the ideas and methods developed for dealing with systems in the category of organized simplicity”. (Klir, 1985: 136).

While organized simplicity is quantifiable by analytical mathematics concentrating on specific elements, the latter class of problems is apt for analysis by probabilistic or statistical means, calculating average properties of many variables. The demarcation line between simplicity and disorganized complexity is that the problem becomes unmanageable as soon as one tries to analyze many instead of few variables (e.g., the motion of ten or fifteen vs. two or three balls on a billiard table), not because there is any theoretical difficulty, but just because the actual labor of dealing in specific detail with so many variables turns out to be impracticable (Weaver: 1948: 537). The flipside is that the problem now becomes easier, as long as we are interested only in aggregate quantities (Somfai, 2013: 210). This is the realm where the methods of *statistical mechanics* are applicable, emanating from the work of Ludwig Boltzmann and Josiah W. Gibbs.[173] The radically new paradigm of statistical methods eventually emerged at the begin-

173 The early work in probability theory, on which much of current economic theory is based, predates the development of the notion of *ergodicity*, and it assumes that expectation values reflect what happens over time (Peters & Gell-Mann, 2016).

ning of the 20th century. Their purpose is not to deal outspokenly with the individual variables – for example, the detailed history of one special billiard ball or the motions of the individual molecules – but to use a small number of calculated *average* properties – focusing on questions such as, on the *average* how many balls per second hit a given stretch of rail? Etc. (Weaver: 1948: 537). This is the section of probability theory, namely the Laws of Large Numbers, that is vaguely but not always properly understood by those who talk of the "law of averages", and who state that the probabilities "work out" in the long run (Weaver, 1967: 145; Huberman & Hogg, 1986: 376). Calculations are based on the suppositions of large numbers of randomness. "Disorganized complexity is thus best exemplified by systems based upon principles of statistical mechanics" (Klir, 1985: 136).

6.1.2. Disorganized complexity and statistical techniques

Statistical techniques are not restricted to situations where the scientific theory of the individual events is very well known, as in the billiard example where the impact of one ball on another can be precisely explained. In principle, there are two different – or at least apparently different – fields or types of problems to which probability theory and statistical techniques reasonably apply (Weaver, 1967:147f.).

For the first type of problem probability theory is used not so much because we are convinced that we are to use it but because it is so very convenient (ibid.). Probability-based methods can then be applied to, on the one hand, situations which may be considered deterministic[174] but where the individual event is shrouded in mystery; like the life insurance example, where the insurance company can have no knowledge whatsoever concerning the approaching death of any one individual, but has dependable knowledge of the average frequency with which deaths will occur (Weaver, 1948: 538). Probability statements are possible, useful, and sufficiently robust. Since new people are steadily being added to the system, actuaries rely on samplings. They are not perfect, but they work, because the sample of people is very large and mortality rates change only slowly. It is one of the most striking and fundamental things about probability theory and statistics that it leads to a comprehension of the otherwise peculiar fact that

174 This means that observed randomness may be no (true) randomness after all.

even events which are individually capricious and unpredictable can, when treated *en masse*, lead to stable *average* performances (Weaver, 1963: 273); whereby the relevance and precision of statistical methods increase with a rise in the number of variables and their degree of randomness (Klir, 1985: 136).

On the other hand, there are many situations of this sort in serious everyday life where we use probabilities not because it is clear that 'chance' plays some cryptic and mysterious role – e.g., there seems to be no essential mystery about why a coin lands heads or tails – but primarily because the situation is so *complex*, so intricately affected by so many small causes, that it is prohibitively inconvenient to attempt a rigorous analysis (Weaver, 1967: 148). "[W]e merely mean that, conveniently for us, the very complexity that makes a detailed analysis practically impossible assures an overall behavior which is describable through the laws of probability" (ibid.). The causes are too numerous, too complicated, and/or too poorly understood to permit a complete deterministic theory (ibid.: 149). We therefore deal with these subjects through probability. But in all these cases we would say, with Henri Poincaré, that chance "is only the measure of our ignorance".

The second type of probability problems, appears very different at first glance because probabilistic reasoning seems to be even theoretically unavoidable (ibid.: 147). It is a more foundational use which (physical) science makes of statistical techniques.

> The motions of the atoms which form all matter, as well as the motions of the stars which form the universe, come under the range of these new techniques. The fundamental laws of heredity are analyzed by them. The laws of thermodynamics, which describe basic and inevitable tendencies of all physical systems, are derived from statistical considerations. The entire structure of modern physics, our present concept of the nature of the physical universe, and of the accessible experimental facts concerning it rest on these statistical concepts.
>
> (Weaver, 1948: 538).

Moreover, most scientists, in contrast to Einstein who has remarked in a characteristically appealing way that "I shall never believe that God plays dice with the world", believe that some of the most elementary occurrences in nature are essentially and inescapably probabilistic (Ismael, 2015). They adhere to quantum mechanics.[175] Thus, with regard to modern physics and the problems the discipline addresses, "probability notions are essential to any theory of knowledge itself" (Weaver, 1948: 538).

All things considered, the crucial point is that both problem areas pertain to the class of *disorganized complexity* because the common denominator of the two types of problems is a high number of variables that (at least) appear to display a high level of random behavior.

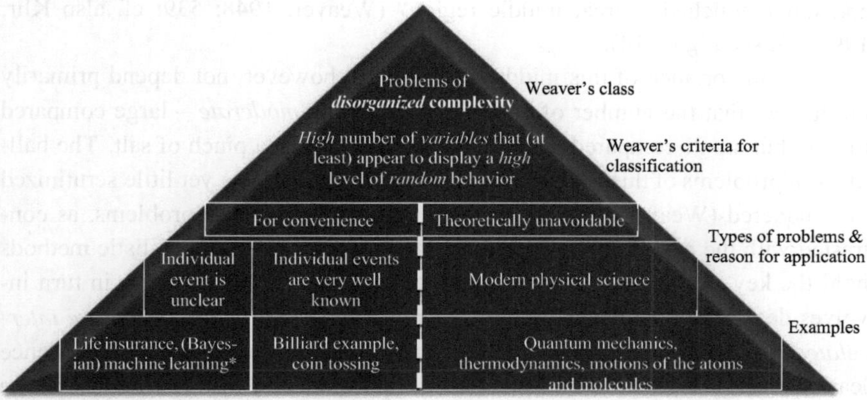

Figure 13: Weaver (1948, 1963, 1967) on probability theory, statistics and fields of application: The demarcation line between "for convenience" and "theoretically unavoidable" is only dotted because the division is not strict and rigid (cf. Beer, 1959: 28).
* in stable environments with plenty of data only: e.g., chess (cf. Lai, 2015)

Organized complexity, by contrast, is principally different: here, complexity is not determined componentwise or by variety, but by other factors, above all by, of course, the degree of organization.

175 However, the distinction between the two problem areas, while of practical value, might turn out to be illusionary (Weaver, 1967: 147). On the one hand, one could doubtless deal quite successfully from a large-scale and practical point of view with large-scale phenomena which depend ultimately on small-scale probabilistic phenomena; for example, with coin tossing on the basis of very careful actual measurements, plus all the analytical resources of dynamical theory; it remains true yet that "the coin is made of elementary particles whose positions and motions can be known, as science now views the matter, only in a probability sense" (ibid.: 150). On the other hand, quantum mechanics can be interpreted as a deterministic theory (Holland, 1993).

6.1.3. Tackling organized complexity: open questions remain

In addition to, and in-between 'problems of simplicity' that are solvable with hard sciences and 'problems of disorganized complexity' to be dealt with by probability theory and statistics, Weaver beheld a third kind and, therefore, a trichotomy of scientific problems – maybe for the first time at all (Seising, 2012: 61): "One is tempted to oversimplify, and say that scientific methodology went from one extreme to the other – from two variables to an astronomical number – and left untouched a great middle region" (Weaver, 1948: 539; cf. also Klir, 1991: 23; see Figure 14).

The importance of this middle region does, however, not depend primarily on the fact that the number of variables involved is *moderate* – large compared to two, but small compared to the number of atoms in a pinch of salt. The hallmark of problems of this middle region, which science has as yet little scrutinized or conquered (Weaver, 1948: 539), lies in the fact that these problems, as contrasted with the disorganized situations where statistical or probabilistic methods hold the key, show the essential feature of *organization* (ibid.). This in turn involves dealing simultaneously with a *sizable number of factors which are interrelated to form an organic whole*. Interactions and the resulting interdependence lead to *emergence*, i.e., to the spontaneous appearance of features that cannot be traced to the character of the individual system parts (Anderson, 1972), and, therefore, cannot be fully captured in probability statistics nor sufficiently reduced to a simple formula. Something more is needed than mathematical analysis or the mathematics of averages (Weaver, 1948: 540; Huberman & Hogg, 1986: 376).

Weaver (1948: 539) lists examples of problems of organized complexity where in each case a substantial number of relevant variables is involved that are varying simultaneously, and in subtly interconnected ways; that "are all interrelated in a complicated, but nevertheless not in helter-skelter, fashion" (ibid.). In particular, the economic is viewed as being within the realm of organized complexity (Klir, 1991: 119).

- On what does the price of wheat depend?
- How can currency be wisely and effectively stabilized?
- To what extent is it safe to depend on the free interplay of such economic forces as supply and demand? …

That statistics turns out to be 'impotent' to deal with such cases of organized complexity has been underlined by not only Weaver, but other authors as well. Three prominent examples with different backgrounds (Friedrich August von Hayek (economist and philosopher), Fredmund Malik (management cybernetics), and Lotfi A. Zadeh (mathematician and systems theorist)) suffice to clarify this point.

> Because statistics is designed to deal with large numbers it is often thought that the difficulty arising from the large number of elements of which complex structures consist can be overcome by recourse to statistical techniques. Statistics, however, deals with the problem of large numbers essentially by eliminating complexity and deliberately treating the individual elements which it counts as if they were not systematically connected. It avoids the problem of complexity by substituting for the information on the individual elements information on the frequency with which their different properties occur in classes of such elements, and it deliberately disregards the fact that the relative position of the different elements in a structure may matter. In other words, it proceeds on the assumption that information on the numerical frequencies of the different elements of a collective is enough to explain the phenomena and that no information is required on the manner in which the elements are related. The statistical method is therefore of use only where we either deliberately ignore, or are ignorant of, the relations between the individual elements with different attributes, i.e., where we ignore or are ignorant of any structure into which they are organized. Statistics in such situations enables us to regain simplicity and to make the task manageable by substituting a single attribute for the unascertainable individual attributes in the collective. It is, however, for this reason irrelevant to the solution of problems in which it is the relations between individual elements with different attributes which matters.
>
> (Von Hayek, 1967: 29f.) (Cf. also Malik, 1996: 201)

As Weaver did already more than a decade before, Zadeh denied in 1962 that probability theory is an adequate mathematical tool to manage the analysis of highly complex systems (Seising, 2012: 55).

> [T]he fundamental inadequacy of the conventional mathematics – the mathematics of precisely-defined points, functions, sets, probability measures, etc. – [is reflected in its inability of] coping with the analysis of biological systems [more generally, systems which pervade life sciences, social sciences, philosophy, economics, psychology and many other 'soft' fields; Zadeh, 1969a: 1], […] which are generally orders of magnitude more complex than manmade [complicated, C.H.] systems. [W]e need a radically different kind of mathematics, the mathematics of fuzzy or cloudy quantities which are not describable in terms of probability distributions.
>
> (Zadeh, 1962: 857; cf. also Zadeh, 1969b: 199)

Nonetheless, the diagnosis that probability theory is not of use and success in this realm of organized complexity, which was already reached by Weaver, von Hayek, Malik, Zadeh and others, still remains vague and is, therefore, revised in Chapter 7.3. and clarified in the following sense: the thesis will be (a) exactly deduced by providing an explicit argument and (b) broken down to risk management of extreme and systemic events in banking.

On the constructive side, Weaver (1948), in contrast to Zadeh who has put forward his theory of fuzzy sets and systems and fuzzy logic, respectively (see Part III, Chapter 15.2.), also remains vague in his responses to the challenge of organized complexity. Basically, his answer revolves around harnessing the power of computers and cross-discipline collaboration. While the former, among others, points to simulation runs (as, e.g., performed by System Dynamics researchers (e.g., Sterman, 2000; Grösser, 2013; Forrester, 1961)) and the latter to systems science at large as a linking element between several theoretical perspectives, much more work is needed to widen Weaver's scheme.

6.1.4. Synopsis

The inclusion of Weaver's trichotomy in this chapter allows to examine more closely what complexity is, how to tackle different forms of complexity (cf. also von Bertalanffy, 1968/2013: 34, 93) and, thereby, to bring together in one single framework concepts of complexity, on the one hand, and statistical or probability-based methods, which are essential to conventional quantitative risk management in banking (e.g., McNeil et al., 2005), on the other. Weaver's answers forges what has been stated earlier in Chapter 2.1.: Complicated or structurally complex worlds are *reducible*: The general Weaverian proposition is that by reducing complicated systems to their constituent parts (ad organized simplicity) or their orderly and analyzable average properties (ad disorganized complexity), and fully comprehending each part or statistical key figure, we will then be able to understand the world. As the parts begin to connect with one another and interact more, however, the scientific underpinnings of this approach begin to fail.

Dynamically complex systems and systems of organized complexity, respectively, resist simple reductionist analyses, because interconnections and feedback loops preclude holding some subsystems constant in order to study others in isolation (Anderson, 1999: 217). We then move from the realm of complication and structural complexity to dynamic and organized complexity, and reduction no longer gives us insight into construction (Miller & Page, 2007: 27); systems thinking is required.

Figure 14 extends the picture of the decomposition of the complexity concept drawn in Chapter 2 by consolidating the findings and impulses from Weaver's work (1948, 1963, 1967) which was summarized in the previous sections of Chapter 6.

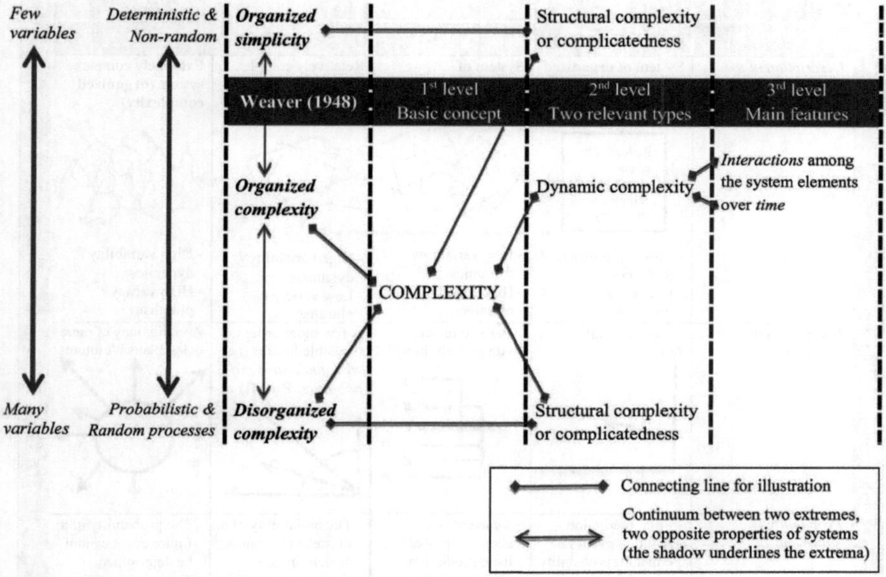

Figure 14: The disassembly of complexity II: The extended framework.[176]

Furthermore, Table 5 resumes the relationship between Weaver's notions of complexity and the suitability of stochastic methods in terms of the respective status of probabilistic statements. This already points to different corresponding states of uncertainty, which paves the way for bringing risk and extreme/systemic risk into the scheme (elaborated on in 6.2. and 6.3. and cf. also Rzevski & Skobelev, 2014: 7).

176 The diametrical opposition between randomness and determinism, which Weaver (1948) declares, is not really in existence, considering *chaotic systems* where randomness and lack of chance or probability go hand in hand: In the classic example of the *baker's transformation* (Earman 1986: 167f.) or Lorenz' (1963) model of the weather, we have random sequences; yet none of these outcomes happens by chance; chaotic systems like the baker's transformation are entirely *deterministic* (Eagle, 2012). Furthermore, the possibility of *deterministic chance* (Loewer, 2001) would also render a stringent Weaverian contradistinction untenable. See also 6.2.2. below for an argument against assuming a fundamental split between the two endpoints on the scale.

Table 5: A suggested taxonomy of uncertainties and complexities based on Weaver (1948). (* see Appendix A)

Simplicity of the system → Complexity of the system

	Layer 1	*Layer 2*	*Layer 3*	*Layer 4*
	Certainty	*Risk II*	*Risk I:*	*Deep uncertainty**
Description of the system	System of **organized simplicity**	System of **disorganized complexity**	Relatively complex system (**organized complexity**)	Extremely complex system (**organized complexity**)
	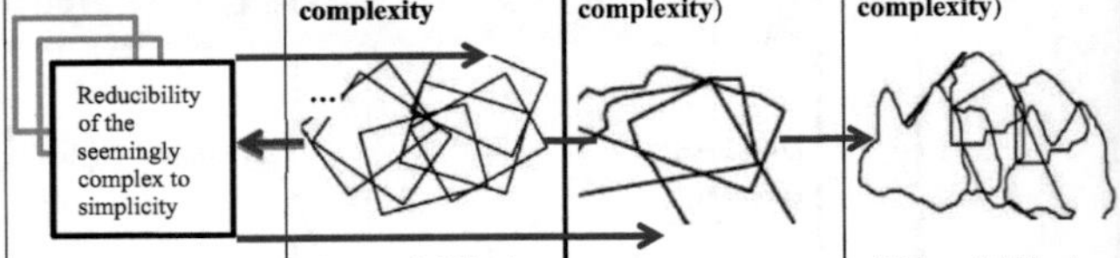			
	- Low variability / dynamics - Low variety / pluralism	- Low variability / dynamics - High variety / pluralism	- High variability / dynamics - Low variety / pluralism	- High variability / dynamics - High variety / pluralism
Future system behavior	A clear enough future 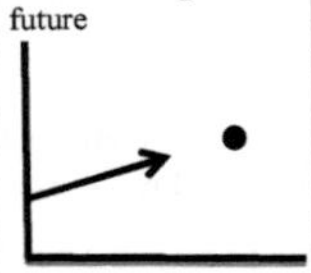	Alternate futures (with probabilities) 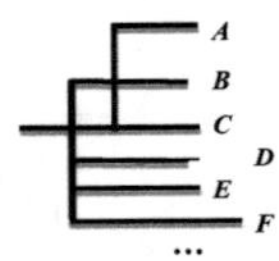	A few more or less plausible futures (i.e. with *qualitative probabilities*, Part III) 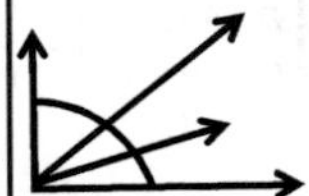	A multiplicity of more or less plausible futures 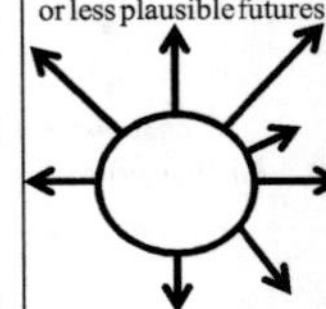
Probability statements	- Point prediction - A future event has either the probability of 1 or 0; i.e., *determinism* - One can become certain of the truth-value of the proposition if one has the right data	- *Informative* or *accurate* probabilistic prediction - The probability of a future event can be clearly determined - Not truth-value of proposition, but probability of it being true	- The probability of a future event cannot be determined - Truth-value of the proposition cannot be find out - Meaningful probability can only be given it in a *qualitative sense* (see Part III)	- The probability of a future event cannot be determined - Truth-value of the proposition cannot be find out - Meaningful probability can only be given it in a *comparative sense* (see Fig. 36)
Decision-making	Under "certainty" (Luce & Raiffa, 1957)	Under risk (ibid.)	Under uncertainty (ibid.)	Under uncertainty / "ignorance" (ibid.)
Example	- Automobile - Diesel engine	- Life insurance (informative) - Deck of cards[177] (accurate)	- Subsystem of a financial system - Local financial syst. - See Chapter 6.3.	Modern international financial system See Chapter 6.3.

177 Suppose one wants to know whether or not *P* is the case for some proposition *P* – "The next card I will draw from a standard deck of cards will be black". The beauty of cards is that the universe is known; there are 52 cards in the deck, and only 52 and the rules of the game are set. One cannot find out the truth-value of *P*, but one can find out the probability of it being true. Under certain conditions (e.g., a complete deck) one can conclude that p('black') = p('red') = 0.5. One is then in a state of *decision-making under risk* in the classical decision-theoretical sense of the phrase (Luce & Raiffa, 1957), or as it would be put here: *decision-making under risk II*.

6.2. Weaver's Taxonomy Revisited: Attempts of Clarification, Extension and Refinement

As seen, Weaver introduced a classification of scientific problems which entitles us to distinguish the simple, the complicated, and the genuinely complex. This study now seeks to unveil that the concept of organized complexity applies to the problem of assessing extreme or systemic risks, which would debunk orthodox methods of quantitative risk management in banking as inadequate. Before this objective could be met, the issue of how to employ Weaver's concept needs to be tackled. Two strategies can be separated. The approaches in the literature towards operationalizing "organized complexity" prove to be insufficient (6.2.1.). Therefore, a novel proposal for identifying so-called unstable randomness as a sufficient condition for organized complexity is put forward, which, however, in the end turns out to be not satisfactory either because, rather, the latter is sufficient for the former and not vice versa (6.2.2.). Nonetheless, introducing unstable randomness into the picture is enlightening since it can reasonably be viewed as both necessary and sufficient for the inadequacy of statistical methods.

6.2.1. Approaches towards the operationalization of Weaver's concept of organized complexity

How to understand organized complexity and organization is not much discussed, and it is far from trivial: Not only lies complexity on a spectrum from less organized to increasingly organized, somewhere in between the extremes of organized simplicity and disorganized complexity, but moreover, organization in its most general form – when activities and entities each do something and do something together to provoke a certain phenomenon – itself comes in a *multi-dimensional spectrum* of increasingly complex organization (Illari & Williamson, 2012: 128). "Our world seems to involve different forms of organization, more or less *complex*, in different cases. In the simplest cases organization might be simple or trivial, but it is still present." (ibid.). This interwovenness of more or less organized complexity and more or less complex organization poses the warning that the attempt of operationalizing "organized complexity" is at least a problematic matter. In addition, it is reasonable to assume that a system's complexity is purely *relative to a given observer*, which renders untenable the undertaking to measure an absolute or intrinsic complexity; in favor of regarding complexity as something in the eye of the beholder (Ashby, 1973).

One of the first who accepted the challenge was Herbert Simon. In an influential article titled "The Architecture of Complexity", he follows the distinction made by Weaver between unorganized and organized complexity in avoiding a formal definition of complexity, suggesting only that complex systems are ones "made up of a large number of parts that interact in a nonsimple way" (Simon, 1962: 468). Simon (1962) views organized complexity as complexity with an architecture. More specifically, the architecture that seems to characterize complex systems in the behavioral and life sciences is one of hierarchical composition (or modularity), whereby a system "is composed of interrelated subsystems, each of the latter being in turn hierarchic in structure until we reach some lowest level of elementary subsystem" (ibid.). Above all, he argues that such an architecture allows us to make sense of the rapidity with which complexity has evolved. In partial accordance with Simon (1962), Huberman & Hogg (1986) invoke a physical measure of the complexity of a system based on its diversity, while ignoring its detailed specification. It applies to discrete hierarchical structures made up of elementary parts and provides an accurate, readily computable quantitative measure. This measure of complexity is maximal for systems which are intermediate between perfect order and complete disorder, and which might thus be labeled as organizationally complex.

Norbert Wiener (1961) worked on the formalization of organized complexity in his development of cybernetics as a common theoretical core to the integrated study of technological and biological systems (Seising, 2010). By the 1960s, it became clear to many engineers, mathematicians, biologists, and social scientists (at least) that organization was more than the statistics of random ensembles (Alderson & Doyle, 2010: 848). For example, Jacobs (1961: Chapter 22) argues that cities should be identified, understood, and treated as problems of organized complexity but that the theorists of conventional modern city planning have consistently misjudged cities as problems of simplicity and of disorganized complexity, and have tried to analyze and treat them thus.

More recently, Keller (2009), Crutchfield & Wiesner (2010), or Alderson & Doyle (2010) stress the need to extend Weaver's scheme if, e.g., one wishes to detect a demarcation line between organic wholes and physical systems (Keller, 2009: 27).

Finally and most interestingly, La Porte (1975a) builds on Weaver (1948) directly and comprehensively. He attempts to provide initial operational grounds for treating organized complexity as an independent variable; i.e., as a condition which if altered would in turn alter other important relationships. La Porte (1975a: 6) offers a working definition of *organized social complexity*, i.e., his concern is limited to *social* systems possessing the characteristics of organized complexity.

> The degree of complexity of organized social systems (Q) is a function of the *number* of system components (C_i), the relative *differentiation* or variety of these components (D_j), and the degree of *interdependence* among these components (I_k). Then, by definition, the greater C_i, D_j, and I_k, the greater the complexity of the organized system (Q).

La Porte (1975a: 6f.) illuminates the different parts of this definition one by one. First, a *component* of an organized social system is paraphrased as "a *person* or *group* occupying a position within the system and evincing these characteristics: (1) sufficient mutual agreement or consensus about this position so that he or she or it is the object of expectations and actions from other members and (2) recognition on the part of the person or group of the legitimacy of the others' expectations and positive response to those expectations, at least to the degree required for maintaining membership in and avoiding expulsion from the system" (ibid.).

Second, *differentiation* of components is circumscribed as "the number of different social roles or positions within the system, based on the degree of mutual exclusiveness of the activities distributed among the roles in an organization" (ibid.: 7).

The most difficult element of his definition is, third, the *interdependence* of components, which is by far the most important and the least developed. "Interdependence among persons or groups assumes varying degrees of *reciprocal* relationships between them. Interdependence means an exchange relationship of at least one resource between at least two persons. Interdependent relationships can vary between any two members (a, b) exchanging resource r_1 as follows:

1) member A dominant over member B, i.e., B depends on A for some desired resource $(a >> b)_{r1}$
2) A and B mutually dependent upon one another for a resource both parties desire $(a << >> b)_{r1}$
3) B dominant over A $(a << b)_{r1}$." (Ibid.).

This basic illustration contains only one resource; however, in many situations several resources may be exchanged with all three dependence relationships obtaining between two or more persons. Moreover, on the operational level, determining the degree of interdependence would require that the persons in question recognize their relatedness (ibid.: 8). For more details, several anticipated analytical difficulties with his proposal, and some examples, cf. La Porte's (1975a) contribution. The crucial point is that, even though his approach is very interesting, the purpose of the function La Porte is proposing seems to be rather illustrative. In other words, to realistic or real-world cases, i.e., what transcends his artificial or designed examples, his explication of Weaver's concept of organized complexity appears to not hold the key – imagine the overwhelming task of identifying *all* components and subsystems of modern financial systems (not more than a glimpse is given in Figure 1), of comparing the complexity of different systems over *time*, or of accounting for the *multi-layered and multifarious complexity* of real social and financial systems (see 6.3.). Thus, the application of La Porte's (1975a) function to show that a system is of organized complexity might turn out to be practically extraneous. At least up to now, the same seems to hold for other approaches found in the literature. Another strategy might thus be required to make use of Weaver's notion of organized complexity.

Hereafter, we argue that it is important to clarify the disparity in approaches to managing organized vs. disorganized complexity by paying some more attention to randomness and the fact that, while similar degrees of effective randomness are given, different generators can be very differently organized (Crutchfield & Wiesner, 2010: 37). In other words, we must become aware that there are "different algorithmic structures that use different amounts of memory organized in different ways" (ibid.).

6.2.2. The bigger picture of complexity and randomness

According to Alderson & Doyle (2010: 851), the views of organized and disorganized complexity continue to be so incompatible that there is no veritable dialogue between them. This section is committed to contribute to creating a basis for dialogue and a common denominator by pointing to random processes which are characteristic for *both* disorganized and organized complexity. Two different kinds of random processes or mechanisms need to be separated though: *stable* vs. *unstable randomness*.

Yet, this distinction is anything but familiar. While the idea behind the term "stable randomness" can be regarded as well-established because it is basically old wine in a new bottle (and a new bottle is needed as another type of wine has been discovered), "unstable randomness" is hardly appreciated and singled out.

This marks a poor basis for defining the dichotomy exactly, but fortunately characterizing and paraphrasing the two cases in a first conceptual approach is sufficient to design a proposal for how this distinction might help enhance the applicability of the notion of organized vs. disorganized complexity: If unstable (stable) randomness proved to be a sufficient condition for organized (disorganized) complexity, then demonstrating the existence of unstable random processes in modern financial systems would automatically show that these systems are of organized complexity and save the trouble of dealing directly with the concept of organized complexity (see 6.2.1.).

Stable random mechanisms correspond to disorganized complexity

Albeit the name "stable randomness" is not very common, the phenomena denoted by it seem to be well-known. While Eagle (2005: 775), as seen in 6.1.1., defines randomness, in general, as a strong form of unpredictability (see also Appendix C), explicitly allowing for greater or lesser degrees of unpredictability/randomness (ibid.: 772), Brose et al. (2014a: 330) specify that there are "*stable* random processes", on the one hand, which simply means that there exists a mechanism generating the observations or observable events and it exhibits a *stable* mean, dispersion, symmetry[178], etc. Put differently, it has been argued in the literature on randomness (see Appendix C) that a genuinely random process should satisfy all of the various "properties of *stochasticity*" (Martin-Löf, 1966: 604) and Brose et al. (2014a) clarify that, ideally, randomness is time-invariant or indifferent to history because, as we might add, the property of large numbers is named among those properties (Eagle, 2012), i.e., "the claim that the limit frequency of a digit in a random sequence should not be biased to any particular digit" (ibid.; see also Appendix C). Brose et al.'s (2014) specifications render explicit what is commonly, but sometimes diffusely associated with genuine randomness (Pearson, 1905) and, therefore, help refine our understanding. It is namely "our curious tendency to take independent identically distributed trials, like the Bernoulli process of fair coin tossing [where all those beautiful *properties of stochasticity* can be observed over time; C.H.], to be [...] the paradigm of random sequences" (Eagle, 2012; cf. also Dasgupta (2011: 656) who immerses himself in stochastic laws of randomness in view of an underlying fair coin mod-

178 It is open to debate if classical randomness allows for skewness (as lack of symmetry) and for *biased* chance processes, respectively (cf. Eagle, 2012).

el). A formal definition of stable (vs. unstable) randomness goes hand in hand with a mathematical discussion of issues of stationarity and ergodicity that is beyond our scope here.[179]

According to stable randomness, there are visible outcome generators, where sampling the past causes convergence to the 'real mean' and 'real variance' of the type of event in question (Blyth, 2010: 452).[180] The repeated realizations of random events are produced by a stable stochastic mechanism, or, at least, one with a high degree of stochastic *inertia*; i.e., where the structure of the randomness changes only slowly over time (Brose et al., 2014a: 331). The practical consequences are that any two large samples of random events from the same mechanism will resemble one another;[181] the larger the sample size, the smaller the discrepancy between samples (ibid.: 330; Hoffmann, 2009; Bernoulli, 1713). The mechanism is not perfectly known, but one might say that it is measurable in this sense (Brose et al., 2014a: 330).[182]

Examples of these stable random processes abound. Above all, they enclose Bernoulli's (unbiased) urn experiments (*with* replacement) (Hoffmann, 2009: Chapter 2.2) and the many games of chance (coins, dice, etc.), known since the early days of probability theory, where, for example, one can describe – and assign probabilities to – all possible future paths that might ensue in an unfinished game of chance. Or in another field, the actuaries have seen how individual uncertainties can *add up*, when large numbers of cases are involved, to dependable behavior (Weaver, 1967: 152; see also footnote 222 on the *Central Limit Theorem*) – e.g., in terms of (only slowly changing) mortality rates.

In this regard, we add that it is this category of randomness, characterized as 'distributional' in nature, which is typical for Weaver's disorganized complexity – i.e., it is what Weaver actually had in mind when he undifferentiatedly spoke of randomness. The name "Risk II" is assigned here in this study to the unknown events which are brought about by this first and classical type of random mechanisms.

179 For details, cf. Tsay, 2010 and the references therein. Cf. also Gottman, 1981: Chapter 8.

180 Only the metaphysicians will wish to pursue further the question as to whether a 'true value' *really* exists or not (Weaver, 1967: 151). Cf. also Bhidé, 2010: 96f.

181 It is notable that von Mises' (1919) initial description of randomness was expressly constructed with this in mind – "for him, a random sequence is one for which there is no admissible subsequence having a frequency differing from the frequency in the original sequence" (Eagle, 2012).

182 For a discussion of a direct vs. an inverse application of Bernoulli's theorem, the Weak Law of Large Numbers, cf. Hoffmann, 2009: Chapter 4.2.

Unstable random mechanisms correspond to organized complexity

In reviewing pertinent economic and mathematics journals, business and management journals from the ISI[183]-database, it has been found that the notion of *unstable randomness*, on the other hand, is vastly understudied. To the best of our knowledge, it has been introduceded, but barely coined by Brose et al. (2014a) who bring in a *dynamic* perspective. Corresponding to Weaver's organized complexity, this category of unstable randomness refers to situations where the mechanism is *not measurable*, "either because observations are *too rare* (or even unique), or because *the mechanism itself is unstable*, perhaps because human agents are in the mix disrupting the process" (Brose et al., 2014a: 330f.). Following Danielsson (2002), this in turn is related to *Goodhart's Law* (cf. also the *Lucas critique*; Lucas, 1976).[184]

Put differently, dealing with an organized complex system means that we have invisible (Taleb, 2007b: 40; see also Figure 15 "below the waterline") and non-linear (Blyth, 2010: 452) outcome generators because, for example, organized complexity normally comprises feedback loops, which themselves entail non-linearity (Richardson, 1999: 308). Sampling the past does not converge to a real mean or real variance, since no such mean and variance exist (Blyth, 2010: 452; Taleb, 2013: 6). This is true for power laws (with $D \leq 2$ and $D \leq 3$, respectively). But power laws are just one example and there is a whole range of other probability distribution forms which are 'wild' in the sense that they exhibit fat, long or heavy tails (e.g., log-normal distributions), which means that the variance is indeed immense or infinite. In addition to that, there can also exist distributions which are 'wilder' and, thus, have a more irregular form – for example, *multi-modal* distributions (i.e., they have multiple peaks) due to regime shifts of the system.[185]

Generated events, which are typically rare or non-recurring, are sometimes designated by "black swans" – especially if economically significant – and are then considered in this study as *Risk I* events and systemic risk events, in particular. One

183 Institute for Scientific Information.

184 Goodhart's Law mandates that any statistical relationship will break down when used for policy purposes.

185 Yet, many theorists appear to be unimaginative in this regard; for example, when the generation of a multi- or bimodal distribution is the result of mixing two or more normal distributions, each from a different regime (cf. Bhansali, 2014: 130).

could also deem risk in the broad sense to remain unpredictable to a high extent, pointing in turn to high randomness, "precisely because it [risk] does *not* follow a random walk" (Esposito, 2011: 135). Rather, "it presents a series of correlations and stickiness that makes it partly predictable (albeit only locally and in reference to contingent situations), and a reflexivity that produces sharp discontinuities and abrupt changes" (ibid.: 150; cf. also Mandelbrot & Hudson, 2008).

But although such systems do change radically from time to time, they will often, in the absence of significant perturbations, follow a 'normal' linear trajectory or exhibit regular patterns (e.g., cycle-like phenomena such as Kondratieff Waves or Pork Cycles; cf. also Buchanan, 2013: 435f.; Rapoport, 1986: Chapter 3.2, 3.7-3.8; Ashby, 1956: 78; Sterman, 1994: 298).

In this light, the lack of attention towards unstable randomness in the literature is not very surprising for at least two reasons. First, "unstable randomness" might be regarded as even a *contradictio in adjecto* or an *oxymoron* because randomness is usually assumed to be indifferent to history (see the section on stable randomness), while unstable randomness is not, as its name already tells: The simplest way in which unstable randomness is history-dependent is when the conditions that may be responsible for a certain event change over time (i.e., become unstable). Second, to many, "it is very natural to reject the idea that the observed outcomes are random" (Eagle, 2012) at all if the "'stochastic law of unbiasedness' as a 'stochastic law of randomness'" (Dasgupta, 2011: 656) does not hold.

While it might be true that biased sequences, which characterize unstable randomness (given, for example, non-linear outcome generators), really are less disorderly (Eagle, 2012), a then lesser, but possibly still high degree of randomness, i.e. unstable randomness, is *prima facie* compatible with both our/Eagle's (2005) definition of randomness and Kolmogorov complexity as a standard measure of randomness (see Appendix C); and examples in favor of generalizing the notion of randomness can be provided.

Apart from manipulated cases of games of chance (for example, such that the outcome x_1 is the result of a generator G_1 (a fair coin) at time t_1, outcome x_2 that of generator G_2 (a biased coin) at later time t_2, and so on), the case of modern Western banking systems can be provided as an original example of 'unstable random processes' in 6.3., which is based on Blyth (2010: 452) and Daníelsson (2002).

Necessary and sufficient conditions

Unfortunately, the proposal does not work. Rather than identifying unstable (stable) randomness as sufficient for organized (disorganized) complexity, the situation appears to be just the other way around: First, if unstable randomness was sufficient for organized complexity, then organized complexity would be necessary for unstable randomness, but, as the examples of manipulated cases of games of chance show, the latter is not the case.

Second, organized complexity is instead a sufficient condition for unstable randomness because Brose et al. (2014a) introduced the term "unstable randomness" in a way that it is both necessary and sufficient for the inadequacy of probability-based methods and Weaver (1948) shaped "organized complexity" such that it is sufficient for probability-based methods not holding the key. Hence, focusing on unstable randomness does not allow to surrogate the examination of organized complexity, but it does answer why probabilities and statistics do not work when organized complexity is present.

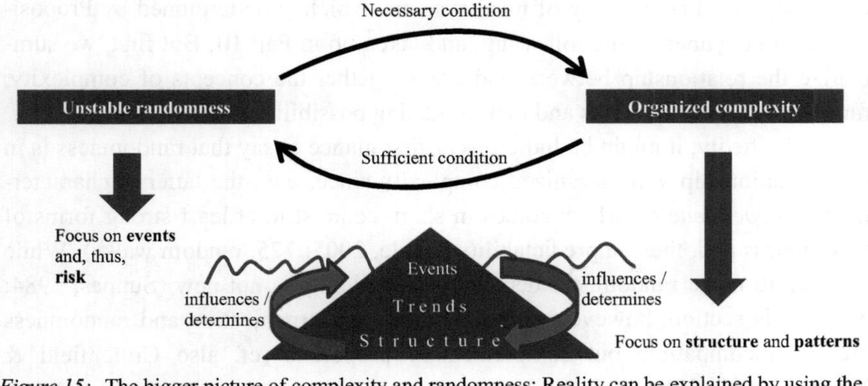

Figure 15: The bigger picture of complexity and randomness: Reality can be explained by using the iceberg metaphor (Van der Heijden, 2009: 104) which basically means that events are above the waterline (and thus visible) whereas trends and structures are beneath the surface (invisible). Systems science then mandates that events are just the tip of the iceberg while the underlying structures and patterns are the core elements of the system that lead to the creation of events (Probst & Bassi, 2014: 25; Warren, 2004: 333; Richardson, 1999: 299). Relations in their entirety, between system elements and between them and the whole constitute the system's structure and patterns are a set of relationships that allow the description of a system to be shorter than the set of descriptions of its parts. Vice versa, the system behavior also influences the structure (Ulrich & Probst, 1990: 70). Risk ("the real or realistic possibility of a positive or negative event…") and randomness (Eagle, 2005; Appendix C) are defined in relation to events while a system's property of organized complexity refers to its structure and patterns.

Figure 15 summarizes the mutual relationship between unstable randomness and organized complexity and clarifies the different levels (events vs. structure) they refer to.

Lessons learned

In this Chapter 6.2., the attempt was undertaken to develop further the still undertheorized Weaverian characterization of organized vs. disorganized complexity in order to render the notions applicable to real-world systems, modern financial systems in particular. While the arguments in the literature to operationalize "organized complexity" do not stand up to diligent scrutiny (6.2.1.), the widening of Weaver's scheme to include first conceptual remarks (which need to be enlarged upon in future work) on the separation of "stable" vs. "unstable randomness" (6.2.2.) is insightful despite the initial suspicion (unstable randomness being a sufficient condition for organized complexity) turning out to be not confirmed. Our proposal (in 6.2.2.) helps treat quantitative risk management in banking as a complex systems problem by tracing financial systemic risks back to the organized complexity of focal systems, which is underpinned by Proposition 2, to be gained in the following, and taken up in Part III. But first, we summarize the relationship between and draw together the concepts of complexity, randomness, systemic risks and their modeling possibilities (see e.g., Figure 16).

Admittedly, it might be ludicrous at first glance to say that randomness is in close relationship with organized complexity since, e.g., the latter is characterized by *dependencies*, which comes in sharp contrast to at least strong forms of randomness and, thus, unpredictability (Eagle, 2005: 775; random walks). While the idea to make randomness depend on complexity is not new (Suppes, 1984: 30)[186], this section, however, aimed to argue that organization and randomness are not incompatible but complementary properties (cf. also Crutchfield & Wiesner, 2010: 37):

> "Randomness" is a gradual concept and unstable randomness is random or unpredictable to a high, but lesser degree than stable or genuine randomness. The structures of organized complex systems are the mechanism of unstable random processes.

---

186 The intuitive idea is that only sequences that are highly complex in the sense of so-called *algorithmic complexity* or *Kolmogorov complexity* (see 2.1. and Appendix C) are random. Early important papers have been those of Kolmogorov (1963, 1965), Martin-Löf (1966), Solomonov (1964) and Chaitin (1969). See Appendix C.

Considering the attributes of the two different forms of randomness and how the uncertainty of events produced by the corresponding mechanisms can/should be managed, unstable randomness, Risk I (Appendix A) movements or situations of organized complexity remain risky. It is therefore particularly risky to think that they can be controlled. And furthermore, through the transition from Risk I to systemic risk, uncertainty is raised in a twofold sense. First, systemic risks, qua definitione, are more uncertain: compared to non-extreme risks, they are realized less frequently and, thus, less is known about them. Second, if the importance of systemic risk is increasing (if they become less remote or more frequent), then the system will assume more different states, i.e., be more complex, for a given period of time, and therefore, there will be more uncertainty. In other words, "if [a random variable, C.H.] *X* and [a random variable, C.H.] *Y* have density functions *f* and *g*, and if *g* was obtained from *f* by taking some of the probability weight from the center of *f* and adding it to each tail of *f* in such a way as to leave the mean unchanged, then it seems reasonable to say that *Y* is more uncertain than *X*" (Rothschild & Stiglitz, 1970: 226).

Simply put, Risk II embedded in situations of disorganized complexity and engendered by stable random processes can be *analyzed* in a distributional or statistical framework and Risk I within the organized complexity framework cannot. It would be problematic – even counter-productive – to force a distributional apparatus into the study of such non-recurring events (Brose et al., 2014a: 331; and see especially Chapter 7). Therefore, organized complexity, Risk I and systemic risk, respectively, require a principally different evaluation approach which is described in Chapter 8 and spelled out in Part III.

Note that Mandelbrot (1997a) also distinguishes between different "states" of randomness: "Any attempts to refine the tools of [conventional risk management, C.H.] by relaxing [some standard] assumptions, or by fudging and adding the occasional jumps will not be sufficient. We live in a world primarily driven by random jumps, and tools designed for [mild] random walks address the wrong problem." (Mandelbrot & Taleb, 2010: 47). According to them, randomness can be either in a *mild* or *wild* state, two mutually exclusive types of randomness (ibid.). On the one hand, mild randomness is exemplified by the Gaussian or 'normal' distribution. The corresponding bell curve has 'thin tails' in the sense that large events are considered possible but far too rare to be consequential. On the other hand, wild or fractal randomness is epitomized by *power law distribu-*

tions (Mandelbrot & Taleb, 2010). The power law exemplifies a "second stage of indeterminism" (see 2.5. above and 7.2. below). Simply put, wild randomness is an environment in which a single observation or a peculiar number can impact the total in a disproportionate way due to the 'fat tails' of power law distributions. Recall, in particular, that in case of most power laws (i.e., for $D \leq 3$), the standard deviation of the random variable x does not exist, which means that the fluctuation around the mean (if a mean exists at all) is immense; in fact, it is infinite (see 2.5.). There is no convergence and, therefore, gathering more or big data is worthless in cases of wild randomness (specific power laws) or unstable randomness (wild distributions in general) because no general statements about x or the situation / phenomena / processes described by it and its distribution can be earned.

Nonetheless, Mandelbrot does not repel probabilistic or statistical analysis, the distributional apparatus, for situations engendered by wild or fractal randomness, but sheds light on the peculiarities of this type, which calls for a special treatment (cf. Mandelbrot's work). By contrast, Chapter 7 contains a plea against the use of probability distributions in financial risk management contexts and against the representation of financial quantities (such as profits and losses) with *random* variables.

The whole picture, where complexity, randomness and risk are brought together, is drawn in Figure 16.

Even though to some scholars it is beyond dispute that complexity is a source of risk and uncertainty or systemic risks (e.g., Bonabeau, 2007: 64), this stance deserves some scrutiny and reflection, which was delivered in this Chapter 6.2.2. Moreover, that systemic risks, the concept of which derives from *Risk I*, result from organized or dynamic complexity is already suggested by our definition of systemic risk (see 4.2.): "Systemic risk is […] caused by a significant change of the system" (cf. also Diebold et al., 2010: 12); *change* entails dynamism and *significance* refers to other components or implications of organized complexity, nonlinearity (Richardson, 1999: 308) and potential for abrupt change (due to unstable randomness) in particular.

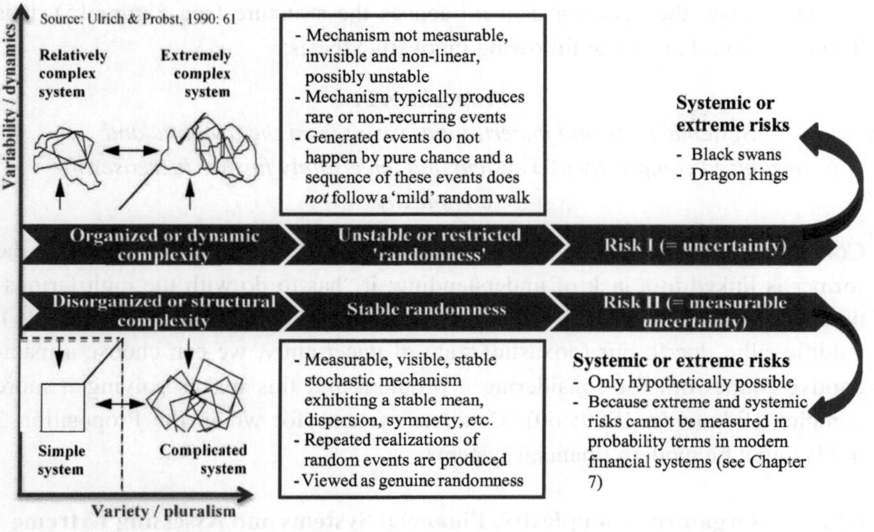

Figure 16: Bringing complexity, randomness and risk together: On a profound level 'beneath the waterline', different system structures can be identified. Truly complex systems with a high variability or dynamics and a more or less high variety are separated from complicated and disorganized complex systems which exhibit a high variety, but remain rather invariable (of course, what appears to be unchanging is, over a longer time horizon, seen to vary too). The former generates unstable randomness above the waterline while the latter can be viewed as a mechanism for stable randomness (whereas simple systems are dispensable in this regard and only included for the sake of completeness). Randomness, in turn, is the direct source of risk. As extreme and systemic risks cannot be measured in probability terms (we see that in Chpt. 7), they spring from uncertainty.

To suppose then that systemic risk and uncertainty originate in complexity is in line with many other accounts.[187] Furthermore, following Rzevski & Skobelev (2014: 11) and, first and foremost, the acknowledged principle that the system structure (complexity) influences or even determines the system behavior (risk),

187 For example, Helbing (2013: 51) reasons that systemic failures and extreme events are consequences of the highly interconnected systems humans have created. Similarly, Ulrich & Probst (1990: 60) highlight and elaborate that high dynamic complexity has the unfortunate consequence that a system behaves so different over time that we are unable to predict what state it will assume next. This causes the observer to be in a (doxastic) state of high uncertainty (ibid.). According to Bernstein (1996b: 232), game theory says that the true source of uncertainty lies in the intentions and the behavior of others which, too, points to dynamic and organized complexity since it results from the interactions among the agents of a system over time (cf. also Sterman, 2000; Edmonds, 1999: 60).

and vice versa, the behavior also influences the structure (see Figure 15), it is hence safe to establish the following innovative thesis:

Proposition 2:

Systemic risks and uncertainties result from the dynamic and organized complexity of a system and uncertainty further increases the complexity.

Complexity and uncertainty seem to be closely and strongly interrelated as the former is linked to a lack of understanding: it "has to do with the multifariousness and uncertainty of an object we have to deal with" (Schwaninger, 2009: 11). Additionally, due to our (doxastic) state of uncertainty, we can choose a maladaptive framework for considering a problem and this makes solving it more complex (Edmonds, 1999: 60). Concrete systems for which the Proposition 2 holds might be modern financial systems.

6.3. Organized Complexity, Financial Systems and Assessing Extreme and Systemic Risks

Over the last few decades, systems in a socio-economic context that used to be separate are now interdependent and interconnected (Schwaninger, 2009; Levy, 1994), which means that they are, by many definitions (including the one by Weaver), more complex. This affects organizations, banks in particular, in two different ways (ad *RQ1.6*).

On the one hand, they themselves are systems because they consist of interconnected components (e.g., departments, teams, etc.) that work together and form a dynamic (e.g., changes in enterprise size, portfolio structure, strategies, etc.) and open (e.g., importing information on borrowers from the external environment and exporting some financial products into the environment) whole (Anderson, 1999: 216; Ulrich & Probst, 1990: 52; Ackoff, 1971: 670). And most of these systems have gone from relatively complicated to complex: Thompson (1967: 6) describes a complex organization as a collective of interdependent parts, which together make up a whole that is interdependent with some larger environment (e.g., through the interbank trading system). Daft (1992: 15) equates complexity, as it relates to organizations, with the number of activities or subsystems within the organization, noting that it can be measured along three dimensions:[188] (1) *Vertical complexity* deals with the number of levels in an organizational hierarchy, (2) *horizontal complexity* deals with the number of functions, units, or jobs across the organization, and (3) *spatial complexity* is the number of geographical locations. On this basis, it must be concluded that: "[l]arge banks and financial institutions are by far the largest corporations in the world by asset size, and they are also arguably among the most complex" (Admati & Hellwig, 2013: 89, 76) and that "it cannot be emphasized enough that banks [...] have become horrendously complex" (Boot, 2011: 28; cf. also Paulson, 2011: 99; Williams, 2010).[189]

On the other hand, the environment banks are facing consists of complex instead of merely simple or complicated systems. With respect to environments, Scott (1992: 230) equates complexity with the number of different items or elements that must be dealt with simultaneously by the organization. Needless to say, the fact that (literature leaves no doubt that) many large banks and financial institutions as parts of the larger financial system are complex already suggests that the financial system itself is complex (Simon, 1962).[190] Indeed, to some authors it is obvious that "any sensible observer is ready to agree that modern financial systems are complex objects" (Gaffeo & Tamborini, 2011: 80; cf. also Helbing, 2010: 12; Taleb et al., 2009: 79; Malik, 2008: 210). As an answer to RQ1.6. and in terms of organized complexity in particular, the claim of organized complex financial systems and problems of risk assessment, respectively, can be supported by shedding light on the structural features of such systems and problems (6.3.1.) as well as on unstable randomness and the corresponding events in modern financial systems to which risks and systemic risks of banking are linked (6.3.2.).

---

188 Other conceptualizations of organizations as complex systems can be found, e.g., Siggelkow, 2001.

189 Admati & Hellwig (2013) add that, of the largest companies in the world, in 2011 the top seventy-nine corporations in the world by asset size were all banks. Saunders & Cornett (2010: 2) bring in the example of J.P. Morgan Chase and according to UBS (2013), the UBS Group comprises the Corporate Center and five business divisions (Wealth Management, Wealth Management Americas, Retail & Corporate, Global Asset Management and the Investment Bank), each consisting of many more layers (ad vertical complexity) and offering a whole range of financial services or products (ad horizontal complexity). Overall, the bank had 60205 employees (as of 31 December 2013, ad vertical and horizontal complexity), active in more than 50 countries (in terms of own offices) (ad spatial complexity).

190 "[A]s one moves to considerations of larger and larger systems, the problems of complexity become enormous" (Churchman, 1968: 77).

Unfortunately, in spite of the much evidence in the literature for regarding those systems as organized complex, it cannot be shown, demonstrated or proved that a concrete system is organized complex. This is not surprising though because the fact that a system cannot be described accurately and in detail just expresses its extreme complexity (Beer, 1959: 27, 32; Ulrich & Probst, 1990: 108f.). On the other hand, it might indeed be even more problematic to explicate and apply Weaver's concept of organized complexity than, e.g., La Porte (1975a) thought. Namely, especially with regard to social (including financial) systems, it seems rather *simplistic* or *reductionistic* if organized complexity is determined on just two scales (Weaver: number of variables and their degree of organization) or by three arguments (La Porte: the number of system components, their degree of differentiation and of interdependence).[191]

6.3.1. On the level of structures

La Porte (1975a: 17), for example, would consider a modern financial system as organized complex if its elements have a very high degree of interdependency. And indeed, modern financial systems are made up of components that are so tightly coupled that, should one component fail, e.g., Lehman Brothers (Williams, 2010) or another so-called systemically important financial institution,[192] the whole system either collapses or becomes inoperative. Bookstaber et al. (2015: 152) stress that the system for a bank is more interconnected than that of a business in another sector because some system elements that receive the output

191 Such a simplistic proposal would not do justice to the much more multi-layered and multifarious complexity of social or financial systems. They are characterized by many more aspects where it is at least *prima facie* not clear how they can be captured on Weaver's two scales or by La Porte's three arguments; e.g., highly developed forms of adaptation, communication, people and their risk attitude, observations, regulation, motives, intentions, antici-pation, fears, hopes, etc. This author is grateful to Andreas Hieronymi for the thought-provoking idea that our inability to understand modern financial systems, which he sees as a major source of systemic risk, originates from an insufficient engagement in studying Weaver's middle region. "The difficult part of understanding social systems is that they develop properties beyond the mere interaction of people" (Willke et al., 2013: 19).

192 For the example of Bear Stearns, Henry Paulson describes tight coupling in these terms: "A Bear Stearns failure wouldn't just hurt the owners of its shares and its bonds. Bear had hundreds, maybe thousands, of counterparties – firms that lent it money or with which it traded stocks, bonds, mortgages, and other securities. These firms – other banks and brokerage houses, insurance companies, mutual funds, hedge funds, the pension funds of states, cities, and big companies – all in turn had myriad counterparties of their own. If Bear fell, all these counterparties would be scrambling to collect their loans and collateral." (Paulson, 2011: 99; cf. also Thurner & Poledna, 2013: 1).

from a bank are at the same time sources of inputs: "A hedge fund that is borrowing in order to buy securities might also be lending other securities. A pension fund that is providing funding might also be using the bank/dealer for market making. Hedge funds and related institutional investors are on both sides of the production in that they are both buyers and sellers of securities, and in that sense provide inputs as well as output in market making." (Ibid.).

As seen, Simon (1962) is also concerned with Weaver's organized complexity and proposes to conceive of complexity as degree of hierarchy. Accordingly, modern financial systems are organized complex because they are made up of interrelated subsystems (e.g., the interbank lending market) that, in turn, have their own interrelated subsystems (e.g., banks), and so on.[193]

How then does the term "organized complexity" apply to problems of assessing extreme and systemic risks in banking or within modern financial systems? More precisely, the question is to what extent risk assessment and management activities involve studying systems which are organic wholes, with their parts in close interrelation: Organic or viable systems (Ulrich & Probst, 1990: 62, 101; Gomez, 1981: 87f.; Beer, 1959) comprise ecosystems and socio-economic systems (including financial systems) which consist of living entities as essential components (such as human beings or banks in a certain sense (Ulrich & Probst, 1990: 242f.)). They meet the demands of surviving in changing environments; in other words, they are adaptive. And modern financial systems as organic wholes with their parts in close interrelation are central to measuring systemic risks, given that systemic risk is defined in this study in reference to primarily such systems (see 4.2.). The same also holds for extreme risks and financial risks tout court because the respective events (risk (e.g., loss) events) occur in the financial system.

6.3.2. On the level of events

Churchman (1961: 163f.) highlights that the supposition that the process of generating outcomes is like a stable random-number process appears to be extremely dubious in case of business executives' ventures: "[I]t is absurd to picture the drama of the business executive as made up of 'random' scenes, so that today's

193 Does this not contradict the earlier statement that the complexity of the whole cannot be accurately traced to individual parts of the system? Cf., for example, the quote by Aristotle ("the whole is more than the sum of its parts") and see also the second last footnote.

ventures are merely random draws from a large urn consisting of equivalent ventures of yesterday and tomorrow. No doubt many decision-makers do rationalize their choices on this basis." (ibid.: 163). Churchman affirms that "no manager can feel sure that the events that he faces come from a system that generates [stable] randomness" (ibid.: 164). Indeed, a risk manager's situation should rather be conceived of as being triggered by unstable randomness.

"The major flaw of our type of [financial] economy is that it is unstable" (Minsky, 1986/2008: 11), which is due to the internal processes that in turn are the manifestation of complex, sophisticated, and evolving financial structures (ibid.; Minsky, 1992; Bhattacharya et al., 2015; Shefrin, 2013; Fisher, 1933). Blyth (2010: 452) considers the Western banking system in this light:

> If you took a monthly time series average of financial-industry profits in the West from, say, June 1948 until June 2008, you could talk with some degree of accuracy about the mean rate of return, the "standard" deviation, and all the rest up until about July 2008. But if you included returns from July-December 2008 in the sample you would have included an outlier so large that it would blow your earlier historical measures out of the water.

In financial systems, we are never sure that the sample is complete or reliable because an unstable and drastically changing stochastic mechanism or a high degree of unstable randomness is responsible for sample sizes which are too small and samples, respectively, which cannot represent the population. For example, as Lowenstein (2002: 71) straightens out, the universe of all trades looked one way throughout the 1920s and another way after the Great Depression. The pattern changed again during the inflationary 1970s, yet again in the effervescent 1990s. After which of these periods was the picture 'representative', 'normal' or 'complete', and how do we know that the next new period will not change the story again (ibid.)? Moreover, when extreme financial events in particular are considered, "[…] the relevant measure of sample size is likely much better approximated by the number of non-overlapping hundred-year intervals than by the number of data points" (Diebold et al., 1998: 8). Thus, from that perspective, our data samples or the number of data points would be terribly small in contrast to those of disorganized situations, with which statistics can cope, and therefore relative to the demands we would place on them if statistical methods were applied. The example of the complex Western banking system embodies an unstable random process and a system of organized complexity.

Esposito (2011: 148) adds and expounds that, until the mid-1980s, it was realistic to expect the financial system and risk to behave in a predictable way as "there was a high correlation between theoretical predictions and the behaviour of the markets. Since 1987, however, things have begun to change." (See also footnote 36.) Today, the finding of some nonlinearity in financial data, which expresses among others organized complexity, appears to be a robust result (Lux, 1998: 144; MacKenzie, 2006: 183ff.).

That financial markets react to themselves through the operation of feedback *loops* (such as seen in Chapter 5.1.) distorts the calculation of risk (if it was set without considering this reflexivity). In the same vein, Daníelsson (2002) differentiates the statistical process of risk from that of the weather in at least one sense: forecasting the weather does not (yet) change the statistical properties of the weather, but forecasting risk does change the nature of risk, which is related to *Goodhart's Law* (and cognate ideas known as *Campbell's law* or the *Lucas critique*). To Goodhart is attributed the insight that "any statistical relationship will break down when used for policy purposes because the behavior of people following the policy will systematically alter the statistical relationship" (Boatright, 2011: 10). The corollary drawn by Daníelsson (2002) is that risk management systems (which rely on statistical relationships) will break down when used for its intended purpose (ibid.). Events in financial history demonstrated the limitations of risk models which adhere to stable randomness and disorganized complexity[194] in lieu of embracing the challenge of unstable randomness and organized complexity.

6.4. A Tentative Bottom Line

The story of this chapter can now be briefly retold. We began with the hope that, by falling back on Weaver's "Science and Complexity", the inadequacy of orthodox (hence, probability-based) quantitative risk management instruments (VaR, ES, etc.) can be disclosed by recourse to the notion of organized complexity which has been coined by Weaver (*6.1.*) and others (*6.2.*). We realize that no

194 "There is commonly an underlying assumption that the future will resemble the present in some statistical sense. All our tomorrows are assumed to be sampled from the same distribution as today" (Lee, 1976: 152). However, we do not live in a simple statistical world; "it is more the world of T.S. Eliot's *Four Quartets*. There is plenty to think about." (Ibid.: 153). First ground is broken in the subsequent Chapter 7.

matter how we grasp and try to make use of the concept of organized complexity, we seem to be always driven to the necessity of introducing *judgement*: the operation of verifying that modern financial systems or problems of assessing extreme and systemic financial risks, in particular, are members of the class of systems of organized complexity is ultimately based on judgement (*6.3.*). This finding alludes to the subjectivity of complexity and its multifariousness or multilayeredness which appears to escape conceptual *analyses* (as suggested by e.g. La Porte). In a certain sense, we have taken a long route to arrive at an apparent truism: complexity is complex (Cilliers, 1998: 9; cf. also Cilliers in Gershenson, 2008: 28f. and Lloyd in Gershenson, 2008: 87). Wide off the mark, this self-reference is highly explosive as well as insightful, and constitutes therefore a central, but negative research result of this study.

Proposition 3:

*The concept of organized complexity **seems**[195] to be complex itself. If it is complex, only characteristics of complexity can reasonably be discussed and a definition or an explication of complexity, which is analytic and reductionist in nature, cannot be achieved. This interferes with the application of the concept because it remains somehow nebulous.*

Thus, the recourse to Weaver's notion of organized complexity entitles us to cast (vehement) doubt, but is unfortunately not viable enough to allow the stronger and crude conclusion that probability-based models are truly inadequate for measuring extreme and systemic risks. A separate argument is required and, indeed, propounded in the next Chapter 7.

195 Just as it cannot be *shown* that any other system is complex, it cannot be shown that the concept itself is complex.

7. The Fundamental Inadequacy of Probability Theory as a Foundation for Modeling Systemic and Extreme Risk in a Banking Context

Cum ex aliquo observationum numero indagamus lineam cometae, supponimus eam esse ex conicarum aut alio faciliorum genere. Datis quotcunque punctis inveniri possunt lineae infinitae per ipsa transientes.
(Gottfried Wilhelm Leibniz, 1703)[196]

The comet may have taken an infinite number of other trajectories from point to point, the finitely many points observed on its previous path do not say how the actual trajectory continues in the future or at the other points, respectively. In a similar way, a finite number of statistical data may not be safely extrapolated into the future. Nonetheless, we may rely on the "habits of nature", which, as experience according to Leibniz shows, let her causes recur in a similar manner throughout time[197] – put in the image of the comet: it may be safely assumed a path with no wild or radical changes. The empirical estimation will be useful and sufficient in practice (Leibniz, 1703/1962: 84). Only an exact mathematical model of contingent events cannot exist from his point of view.

Without wishing to undermine Leibniz' caveat – the opposite is true –, it must be noted that, from today's perspective, his example is an unfortunate choice. Because to bring the tenet of physics, that a comet's trajectory corresponds to a simple and regular geometric shape, into question would mean nothing less than to raise doubt on the gravitational force (in a thought experi-

196 Leibniz, 1703/1962: 84.

197 According to Leibniz, *natura non facit saltus* ("nature does not make a jump"). Nature obeys laws, hence the laws of nature. But there always exists the possibility that God suspends these laws of nature (since He is not amenable to the laws). In other words: Laws of nature are not necessarily valid, but only stand for "habits of nature".
However, cf. also the work of 2016's laureates of physics who opened the door on an unknown world where matter can assume strange, unaccustomed states (which is more in accordance with a complexity worldview).

ment).[198] Instead, this chapter of the thesis presents a more suitable case or example where the so-called *problem of induction* applies; namely the problem that "the habits of nature" do indeed allow to estimate probabilities, but never with quantifiable or even asymptotically increasing precision and reliability. But in addition, we go beyond many philosophical accounts – what began with Hume was induction as a problem of philosophical skepticism (Hacking, 2006: Chapter 19) – and uncover that here we do not tackle a mere 'skeptical problem', where the 'pragmatist' or 'realist' can accept the skeptic scenario[199] and continue to work with what he perceives as reality. By contrast, we deal with an issue of high practical relevance, from which it follows that probability theory loses its claim to be a breeding ground for the management of systemic and extreme risk in banking.

This research endeavor of Chapter 7 is an important contribution to enlarge upon the argumentation in the previous sections. For example, the finding that probabilistic reasoning is not of use and success in the realm of organized complexity, which goes back to Weaver, von Hayek, Malik, Zadeh and others (see Chapter 6.1.), but turned out to be afflicted with vagueness (see e.g., Proposition 3), is refined in 7.3. in this sense: it will be (a) exactly deduced by providing an explicit argument and (b) verified for the measurement of extreme and systemic risks in financial systems.[200]

Our Central Argument thereby exceeds the truism by far that there is simply not enough historical data (not to speak of enough *reliable* and *pertinent* historical data) to obtain an estimate of the 'true' probability distribution of, say, financial crises, with reasonable accuracy. Because merely pointing to the fact that systemic, i.e., extreme events, only take place *extremely* rarely would obviously

198 Gravitation is one of the four fundamental forces of nature and to imagine a world without gravitation would require, according to the prevailing scientific model of the Universe known as the Big Bang, to draw a picture of the 'world' in the Planck epoch, a brief period extending from time zero to approximately 10–43 seconds after the Big Bang (which took place ca. 13.7 billion years ago).

199 For example, we cannot be absolutely sure that the sun will rise tomorrow, that our favorite dish will not be poisonous tomorrow, that pink elephants will not fall from the sky, etc. However, we can accept the possibility that things might be suddenly otherwise without changing our everyday lives. The practical or acting man has no reason to attach any importance to such logical and epistemological precariousness (von Mises, 1957/2005: 201).

200 Another implication of the reasoning in this Chapter 7 for the topic of the previous Chapter 6 would be, for example, that certain notions of complexity, foremost, *statistical complexity* (which measures the minimum amount of information about the past behavior of a system that is needed to *optimally* predict the statistical behavior of the system in the future; see 2.1.), become rather untenable.

result in nothing more than telling an analytic truth. By contrast, the point we make is much more fundamental (see 7.4.) and says that it is, with necessity, *not* even *possible* to estimate a 'true' probability distribution of gains and losses in modern financial systems.

In the following, we will first delineate the philosophical problem of induction and briefly review its development in a systematic (not historical) manner (7.1.). Because "[n]owhere is the problem of induction more relevant than in the world of trading [in the branch of financial economics, more generally; C.H.] – and nowhere has it been as ignored" (Taleb, 2007b: 116; cf. also Spitznagel, 2013: 98, 178, 243; von Mises, 1949/1998: 31)[201]. Before pointing out its concrete and practical implications for the risk management in banking context by developing the Central Argument of this chapter (7.3.), we explain in a few words the meaning of probability theory as being germane in this context and as being subverted by the Central Argument (7.2.). The chapter is closed by linking this conceptual critique with IIIa)-c), which can be viewed as 'signs' or 'signatures' of the principal inadequacy of probability theory as a foundation for modeling systemic risk in banking (7.4.).

7.1. Philosophical Roots of the Problem of Induction: some Preliminaries

Arguably, David Hume's greatest single contribution to contemporary philosophy of science has been the so-termed problem of induction (1739-40/1888).[202] At a first pass, induction concerns inferences whose conclusions are not validly entailed by the premises (Hájek & Hall, 2002: 149). This contemporary notion of induction should not be confused with the too narrow understanding of what we now know as *enumerative induction* or *universal inference*; inference from particular inferences:

201 Indeed, "[a]t the heart of the Austrian methodology is healthy skepticism of data and, in particular, how economics (and, equivalently, investing) uses data to back-fit a story around spurious relationships found in the data [i.e., data mining; C.H.]. Admittedly, we do take a peek at the data […], but we do not rely upon statistical and historical information to form our understanding. […] I might go so far as to call myself an antiempiricist, because empiricism often creates illusions and obfuscates the true underlying mechanism at work." (Spitznagel, 2013: 177). The most experience can teach us is that there might be an ascertainable regularity in all the cases witnessed in the past (von Mises, 1957/2005: 4), but beyond, regularity is a desideratum which is far from being actualized when it comes to human action (ibid.: 6, 57, 203, etc.).

202 The problem of induction is to be distinguished from 'mathematical induction', a deductive argument form.

$a_1, a_2, \ldots, a_n$ are all *F*s that are also *G*,

to a general law or principle

*All F*s are *G*.

Because there are, of course, many counterexamples that may suggest the increased breadth of the contemporary notion: e.g., (good) inductions with general premises and particular conclusions (see footnote 199). On the other hand, it would be a bit too inclusive to take inductive inference to enclose all non-deductive inference (as Rudolf Carnap suggested; Vickers, 2014). But albeit inductive inferences are not easily characterized, we do have a lucid mark of induction: "Inductive inferences are *contingent*, deductive inferences are *necessary*" (Vickers, 2014);[203] inductions are *ampliative*, i.e., they "can amplify and generalize our experience, broaden and deepen our empirical knowledge"; whereas deduction is *explicative*, i.e., it "orders and rearranges our knowledge without adding to its content" (ibid.).

The original problem of induction now can be simply put; it concerns "the support or justification of inductive methods" (Vickers, 2014); methods that predict or infer, in Hume's words, that "instances of which we have had no experience resemble those of which we have had experience" (Hume, 1739-40/1888: 89), i.e., nature continues always uniformly the same. The problem is how to enunciate or vindicate the principle and it leads to a dilemma: it "cannot be proved deductively, for it is contingent, and only necessary truths can be proved deductively" (Vickers, 2014). Nor can the principle "be supported inductively – by arguing that it has always or usually been reliable in the past – for that would beg the question" (ibid.), i.e., it would result in a *petitio principii*,[204] by assuming just what is to be proved.

This Humean problem of induction must be separated from at least another one, which has been labeled *new riddle of induction* (Goodman, 1955; Mill, 1843) and which is that of amplifying what distinguishes *good* from *bad* inductions. The old, or traditional problem of induction was to warrant induction; "to show that induction, typically universal and singular predictive [...] inference, leads always, or in an important proportion of cases, from true premises to true conclusions"

203 Of course, the contingent power of induction brings with it the risk of error; good inductions may lead from true premises to false conclusions (ibid.).

204 A petitio principii or "begging the question" is a logical fallacy and means assuming just what is to be proved, i.e., a type of circular reasoning.

(Vickers, 2014). This problem, says Goodman, is, as Hume demonstrated, not soluble, and "efforts to solve it are at best a waste of time" (ibid.): We have been looking at the wrong problem: "It is not the least of Goodman's accomplishments to have shown that three questions all issue from the same new riddle" (ibid.):[205]

- What is the difference between those generalizations that are supported by their instances and those that are not?
- Which generalizations support counterfactual conditionals?
- How are lawlike generalizations to be distinguished from accidental generalizations?[206]

Many different replies to the problems of induction can be found in the literature and it would be beyond the scope of the present study to present and agitate them. Two concise comments shall suffice at this point. First, there is an extended debate revolving around probability and induction.[207] Second, one of the most influential and controversial views on the problem of induction has been that of Karl Popper who held that induction has no place in the logic of science (Popper, 1959a).[208]

The gist of the matter put forward in 7.3. is a problem of induction as inspired by the reading of 'Kripkenstein' on rules and the rule-following paradox (Kripke, 1982; see 7.3.).

---

205 The wording of these questions is also taken from Vickers (2014). Cf. also Freitag (2015).

206 Goodman's own response to the new riddle was that those generalizations that are supported by their instances involve predicates that have a history of use in prediction. Such predicates Goodman called *projectible*.

207 For example, on Reichenbach's view (1949), the problem of induction is just the problem of ascertaining probability on the basis of evidence. Cf. Kyburg & Teng (2001) for an overview.

208 While agreeing with Hume that no rational justification of induction can be found, Popper insists that this result is innocuous, simply because induction forms no part of the practice of science (Barlas & Carpenter, 1990: 154). According to Popper, scientists propose 'conjectures', "and then subject these conjectures to severe observational tests in an effort to falsify them" (Hájek & Hall, 2002: 154). He claims that "we are never rationally warranted in considering such an hypothesis to be probable, given that it has passed such tests" (ibid.). And since, according to the simplest version of falsificationism, deductive relations are all we need attend to in order to check that a hypothesis has been refuted by some piece(s) of evidence, "the problem of induction poses no threat to the rationality of scientific practice" (ibid.). As a descriptive claim about what scientists, *qua* scientists, actually *do* – let alone about what they *believe* about what they do – Popper's view strikes Hájek & Hall (2002) as absurd. But even as a normative claim it fares little better: "The simplest and most devastating point was nicely emphasized by Putnam (1974): Popper seems willfully blind to the fact that we use evidence from the past and present as a basis for making practical decisions, decisions whose rationality is hostage to the rationality of the inferences drawn about their likely consequences on the basis of the given evidence" (ibid.: 154).

7.2. Probability Theory in a Nutshell, its Embeddedness and its Applications

The Latin root of probability is a combination of *probare*, which means to test, to prove, or to approve; and *ilis*, which means able to be, something like "worthy of approbation" (Bernstein, 1996b: 48). Probability has always carried this *double meaning*, one looking into the future, the other interpreting the past, one concerned with our opinions and beliefs (interpretation as *subjective* probabilities), the other concerned with what we actually know or with frequencies in the real world (*objective* concept) (Hájek, 2011; Hacking, 2006: Chpt. 2; Jaynes, 2003: 39). But even though the interpretation of probability is an important foundational problem (ibid.) and even though the inadequacy of frequency interpretations of probability for many situations in risk management deserves appreciation (Rebonato, 2007),[209] it plays no major role in motivating and developing the Central Argument in 7.3. Nor does probability theory in some strict sense represent the object of criticism. Because what *ought to* be referred to as "probability theory" is the branch of mathematics and the standard formalism concerned with probability as axiomatized by Kolmogorov (1933) (cf. Schneider, 1988: Chapter 8). To be sure, Kolmogorov's axiomatization, which we shortly present in what follows, has achieved the status of orthodoxy, it provides the lingua franca for discourses on risk (II) (McNeil et al., 2005: 1f.) and it is typically what economists, risk experts and others have in mind when they think of "probability theory" (but also Jaynes, 2003: xi, 44).[210]

Following Kolmogorov (1933) and the outline by Hájek (2011), let Ω be a non-empty set ('the universal set'). A *field* (or *algebra*) on Ω is a set **F** of subsets of Ω that has Ω as a member, and that is closed under complementation (with respect to Ω) and union. Let P be a function from **F** to the real numbers obeying:

1) (*Non-negativity*) $P(A) \geq 0$, for all $A \in \mathbf{F}$.
2) (Normalization) $P(\Omega) = 1$.

209 The point is still worth making since, astonishingly enough, some writers "have come to realize that many everyday events, including those in economics, finance, and even weather forecasting, are best thought of as analogous to the flip of a coin or the throw of a die" (Cecchetti, 2008: 92). The "generator will toss a coin; *heads* and the [investment] manager will make USD 10,000 over the year, *tails* and he will lose USD 10,000" (Taleb, 2007b: 152).

210 Alternatives to Kolmogorov's probability calculus exist (e.g., Skyrms, 1980; Jeffrey, 1983; Spohn, 1986 and see Chapter 15.2. and 18). For an overview and an introduction to probability theories, cf. Reichenbach, 1949; Fine, 1973; Schneider, 1988.

3) (*Finite additivity*) $P(A \cup B) = P(A) + P(B)$ for all $A, B \in \mathbf{F}$ such that $A \cap B = \emptyset$.

Call P a *probability function*, the bearers of probabilities "events", "sentences (of a formal language)", or "outcomes", and $(\Omega, \mathbf{F}, P)$ a *probability space*. The assumption that P is defined on a field guarantees that these axioms are non-vacuously instantiated, as are the various theorems following from them (ibid.).

In the words of Hájek (2011), let us now strengthen our closure assumptions regarding **F**, requiring it to be closed under complementation and *countable* union; it is then called a *sigma field* (or *σ-algebra*) on Ω:[211]

3') (*Countable additivity*) If A_1, A_2, A_3 … is a countably infinite sequence of (pairwise) disjoint sets, each of which is an element of **F**, then

$$P\left(\bigcup_{n=1}^{\infty} A_n\right) = \sum_{n=1}^{\infty} P(A_n)$$

The non-negativity and normalization axioms establish, by and large, a convention for measurement, although it is non-trivial that probability functions take at least the two values 0 and 1, and that they have a maximal value (unlike various other measures, such as length, volume, and so on, which are unbounded). It is now easy to see that the theory applies to various familiar cases. For example, we may represent the results of tossing a single fair die once by the set $\Omega = \{1, 2, 3, 4, 5, 6\}$, and **F** be the set of all subsets of Ω. Under the natural assignment of probabilities to members of **F**, we obtain such welcome results as $P(\{6\}) = 1/6$, $P(\text{even}) = P(\{2\} \cup \{4\} \cup \{6\}) = 3/6$, $P(\text{odd or less than 4}) = P(\text{odd}) + P(\text{less than 4}) - P(\text{odd} \cap \text{less than 4}) = 1/2 + 1/2 - 2/6 = 4/6$, and so on (ibid.).

To the extent that Kolmogorov's first two axioms are simply matters of convention (which is not undisputed)[212], they are not controversial. And albeit the third postulate ('finite/countable additivity') is therefore seen as the most puzzling one for debate, that is indeed taken up in Chapter 15.1., 15.2. and 18 –

211 "It is controversial whether we should strengthen finite additivity, as Kolmogorov does. [… He] comments that infinite probability spaces are idealized models of real random processes, and that he limits himself arbitrarily to only those models that satisfy countable additivity. This axiom is the cornerstone of the assimilation of probability theory to measure theory." (Hájek, 2011). For probability theory without measure theory cf. Shafer & Vovk, 2001.

212 For example, physicists such as Dirac, Wigner, and Feynman have countenanced negative probabilities.

and establishing it is rightly regarded as one of the main achievements in many contexts, e.g., of Bayesian scholarship (Bradley, 2010)[213] – it is not the target of the Central Argument either. Naturally, the same holds for the theorems derived from the axioms. Hence, we temporary adopt a standard view by not bringing the Kolmogorovian probability calculus into question; namely, both in terms of its soundness and basic applicability and as long as we speak of probability theory *simpliciter*. But if the Central Argument does not deal with either the classical formalism or its interpretation, what, it may fairly be asked, is the objection about at all?

The gist of the plea against probability-based risk models is not that they are invalid[214] (in terms of the deductive reasoning), but that modeling systemic or extreme risks lies outside the scope of classical probability theory (7.3.). In a nutshell, the problem is with *that* application, not with the theory itself.

Thus, what we ought to bear in mind when the difficult task is attempted to expose the principal ineptness of probability theory as a foundation for modeling systemic risk in banking and when it is referred to probability theory in this context is that it was stimulated by games of chance in the 17th and the early 18th century and inaugurated by the Fermat-Pascal, Bernoulli-Leibniz (see the introduction of this chapter), etc. correspondences (Hacking, 2006; Bernstein, 1996b). While this playground where dice, coins, urns, playing cards, etc. are found, has offered a stable, sterile, and ideal environment to study probabilities and 'laws of probability', parts of reality, modern financial systems in particular, are not only quite different (see Chapter 6), but are characterized by conditions which do not allow to reasonably and meaningfully employ probabilities or stochastic methods (7.3.). Stated more compactly, although it should be a truism, it is all too often ignored or underestimated that life is *not* like Jacob Bernoulli's jar experi-

213 According to Bayesians, basically probability theorists who support the subjective view of probability, rational degrees of belief are probabilities. Probability axioms can be said to characterize rational belief. Contemporary Bayesianism, after Thomas Bayes and going back to F.P. Ramsey in 1930, is not only a doctrine, or family of positions, about probability. It applies generally in epistemology and the philosophy of science as well (Vickers, 2014). In terms of Kolmogorov's third postulate, arguments for saying that degrees of belief, when represented by fractions, should be additive have not been undisputed (Hacking, 2006: 152f.; see also 15.2. and 15.3.).

214 In another sense, it is right to say that validation and verification of models *with empirical content* is impossible or to point out that all such models are wrong because these models, mental or formal, are limited, simplified representations of the real world or of a real system, respectively (Sterman, 2000: 846; Forrester, 1961: 123). See also the sections on model validation in Part III.

ments,[215] that in the real financial world very few problems (if any) are akin to coin-tossing problems because the right implications have not yet been drawn.

It is well-rehearsed at the very least that, for a long time after its inception, the theory of probability was largely concerned with gambling games of various sorts (Weaver, 1963). In addition, there are other fields or types of problems to which probability theory reasonably applies and which have been classified as *disorganized* and *complex* (see Chapter 6, Figure 13). Now, after having delineated what probability theory is, where probabilities and probability theory (according to the Kolmogorov system) *should* be applied (1. situations of disorganized complexity, including 2. games of chance, and 3. the microcosm where quantum mechanics can explain phenomena etc.; see above and cf. also Renn, 2008: 16) and before arguing where they *should not* be applied (see 7.3.), the question arises in what sense probability theory *is* applied to (extreme) risk management in banking.

Commonly selected approaches to describe (extreme and systemic) risks, including VaR, ES, EVT, CoVaR, SES, are grounded in probability theory (Malz, 2011; McNeil et al., 2005 and see Chapter 2). More precisely, risk models are probabilistic models in at least the following two senses:

1) A (systemic) risk model is defined here as a sufficiently meticulous description of (systemic) risk given in a formal language. Kolmogorov's (1933) definition of probability and its accompanying theory provide the lingua franca for describing (systemic) risks, especially in terms of *Risk II*, which often corresponds to the standard view of risk (see 4.1. and cf. McNeil et al., 2005: 1f.).
2) Risk models are probabilistic models in the sense that they represent financial quantities such as profits and losses with random variables whose values are described by probability distributions (Pergler & Freeman, 2008: 3; Rebonato, 2007: 148). That quantities are expressed by random variables entails that the quantities are governed by (stable) randomness, corresponding to functions on the probability space (see below).[216]

215 Elsewhere the term "Bernoullian probabilities" has been coined to specify a certain class of probabilities that satisfy certain conditions – e.g., the Weak Law of Large Numbers, equiprobability, etc. (cf. Vickers, 2014).

216 Random quantities provide a convenient way to talk about many probabilities. The value taken by a (discrete or continuous) random variable is subject to chance, and the associated likelihoods are described by a function called the probability (mass or density) function (Grimmett & Stirzaker, 2001: Chapter 2). Cf. also Kyburg & Teng, 2001: 54f.; Rapoport, 1986: Chapter 3.3.

Or even more precisely, VaR and ES (and therefore also CoVaR and SES) are risk measures or models which are derived from the *loss distributions* (in relation to different risk types that institutions track), which of course are probability functions.[217] EVT, on the other hand, provides a general foundation for the estimation of the VaR or ES for very low-probability "extreme" events by dealing with extreme deviations from the median of probability distributions. It is devoted to estimating what happens to a distribution in the far-out tails.

Probability distributions, which are thus fundamental to the risk models discussed, can generally be understood as follows: Whenever there is an event E (e.g., a loss) which may have outcomes E_1, E_2, …, E_n whose probabilities of occurrence are p_1, p_2, …, p_n, we can speak of the set of probability numbers as the "probability distribution" associated with the various ways in which the event may occur (Weaver, 1963: 179).[218] A probability distribution in a purely formal sense is further a function that satisfies Kolmogorov's axioms of probability (Frigg et al., 2014: 5).

Compliant with Mark & Krishna (2014: 40f.), Rebonato (2007: 148f., 180) and Embrechts (2000: 449f.), there are basically three ways of building a probability distribution for some financial random variable.

1) *Historical method*: The distribution of the losses is simply constructed by 'brute force', i.e., by using the empirical distribution (frequencies) of past returns or losses.[219]

---

217 As seen above, *VaR* is the smallest potential loss occurring with some predetermined probability while ES considers *all* losses that occur with low probabilities (and not just the minimum value, by integrating over the entire tail of the distribution).

218 This is a very natural and sensible terminology, for it refers to the way in which the available supply of probability (namely unity) is distributed over the various things that may happen (different losses, in particular).

219 Suppose, following Rebonato (2007: 148f.), that we obtained 1000 observations of changes in the S&P index and, therefore, 1000 ranked hypothetical profits and losses. Let us take the tenth worst hypothetical outcome, and let us assume that it was −$20 millions (ibid.). We have 990 better (more favorable) outcomes and 9 worse outcomes (ibid.). By definition, we have just built from our sample an estimate of the true 99th percentile of the population (ibid.). Since the historical method appears to make use of no free parameters, "it is often referred to as a non-parametric approach" (ibid.: 148). Yet, an extremely important parameter *is* used; namely, the length of the statistical record or the length of the so-called 'statistical window' to be considered in the analysis (ibid.). This implicitly determines what constitutes the relevant past and does so in a binary manner – fully relevant and included in the data set or totally irrelevant and outside the boundaries of our data set (ibid.).

2) *Parametric techniques*, including the 'Variance-Covariance Approach' (Mark & Krishna, 2014: 40) 'Empirical Fitting Approach' (Rebonato, 2007: 150f.) and the 'Fundamental Fitting Approach' (ibid.: 152f.): These techniques assume that the market or the distribution of profits and losses obeys a simple statistical formula or is a member of one of the many families of distribution functions one finds in statistics books. For example, in the case of the elegant Gaussian distribution, there are then only two parameters, its mean and its variance or standard deviation, to describe the returns.
3) *Monte Carlo simulation method*: It randomly generates market factors such as interest rates and calculates the expected return on, e.g., the portfolio. This procedure is repeated many times (potentially hundreds of thousands of times). Ultimately, the resultant set of portfolio values form a distribution from which risk measures such as VaR can be calculated in the way earlier described.[220]

All three approaches have their weaknesses. In their article "On the Unfortunate Problem of the Non-observability of the Probability Distribution", Taleb & Pilpel (2004) elaborate on essential and principal problems with arriving at a probability distribution for some financial entities; in contrast to many other

220 Even though banks widely consider the Monte Carlo method as one of the best theoretical approaches to simulation of risk (Mehta et al., 2012; Pergler & Freeman, 2008), it should also be remarked that *if* we have strong *ex ante* reasons to believe that the probability distribution we are interested in is of a particular type and that we exactly know what its parameters are, *then* Monte Carlo simulations can indeed be a very powerful tool to sample the tails of this distribution. Rebonato (2007: 157f.) points out that in more common situations, however, ex ante information is not available or is of dubious validity (especially in the tails). "What we do have is a finite number of actual data points, painstakingly collected in the real world. On the basis of these data points I can choose an acceptable distribution and its most likely parameters given the data […]. This approach may well do a good job at describing the body of the distribution (where the points I have collected are plentiful); but, when it comes to the rare events that the timorous risk manager is concerned about, the precision in determining the shape of the tails is ultimately dictated, again, by the *quantity and quality of my real data* [emphasis added]." (Rebonato, 2007: 157f.). But there is worse news. A fatal trade-off is prevalent between the increase in accuracy coming from learning more precisely what the *relevant* conditions are and the loss of estimation power arising from the progressive loss of pertinent data (ibid.: 144). Moreover, what constitutes the relevant past is not 'contained in the data' (ibid.: 146). Consequently, there is also an assumption, implicit or explicit, about what constitutes relevance. Rebonato (2007: 159) concludes then that "if the underlying parametric model is not sound and trustworthy, a Monte Carlo simulation will only allow the very precise calculation of an incorrect percentile. There is no modeling content in Monte Carlo or other simulation techniques".

scholars who think that the central problem would reside in tackling the problem of *fat tails*, and therefore propose to surrogate the 'normal' distribution (with 'thin tails' or a small range of outcomes) by 'power laws', 'Pareto distributions' or 'Zipf's law' etc., or more generally, so-called 'heavy-tail distributions', allegedly better suited for describing many fundamental quantities such as stock and real asset prices (Hagel, 2013; Newman, 2013; Helbing, 2010; Mandelbrot & Taleb, 2010; Sornette, 2009).[221]

Since such more 'sophisticated' distributions imply that extreme events occur much more frequently than expected while orthodox risk models based on normal distributions have dramatically underestimated extreme risks (such as realized in the financial crisis which crescendoed in 2008), the problem of providing a sound basis for risk modeling in banking is solved; or so it seems. Figure 17 juxtaposes the 'old and denounced' normal distribution with a 'new and powerful' power law distribution – devoid of disguising that the former with its elegant properties (e.g., one can reasonably or meaningfully speak of the average of the distribution) keeps on playing a prominent role in statistics and probability theories.[222]

Adding to this contrasting juxtaposition, the following Figure 18 evidences that actual empirical data or an empirical return distribution conforms poorly to a prespecified theoretical normal distribution (cf. also Lux, 1998). (Obviously, the exact form of an empirical return distribution depends on the asset type and on the data frequency; Söderlind, 2014.[223] In other words, different data sets are differently well approximated by a certain prespecified theoretical distribution.)

---

221 The finding of fatter tails or of excess kurtosis in almost all financial data has generated much research in the attempt to fit stochastic processes with this feature to the data (Lux, 1998: 146). Candidates which have been proposed over the years include the stable Paretian distributions (Mandelbrot, 1963b, Fama, 1963), compound normal distributions (Kon, 1984), and mixed diffusionjump processes (Friedman & Laibson, 1989) to name only some alternatives.

222 It not only approximates many real-life situations well (e.g., the normal distribution of human body heights), but, even if a random variable *xi* is not distributed according to a normal distribution, the *Central Limit Theorem* states that, *given certain conditions* (e.g., random variables need to be independent, each with a well-defined expected value and well-defined variance, which is all in all critical in our context; see Chapter 2 and 6), the distribution of a *sum* of the random variables *xi* approaches a normal distribution as the number of variables in the sum becomes large. As a consequence, a variable that is the result of a number of *additive* influences should be normal. The real reason for the importance of the normal distribution lies in this Central Limit Theorem (Bulmer, 1979: 109). Henri Poincaré was among the first who recognized that many distributions are not normal.

223 An extreme example are options returns that typically have very non-normal distributions (in particular, since the return is -100% on many expiration days). Ibid.

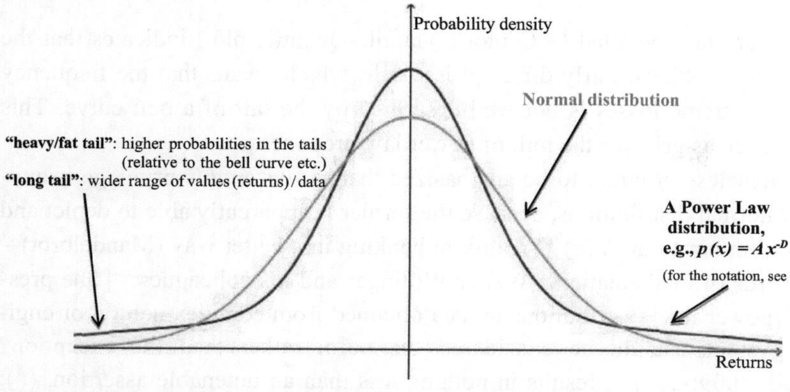

Figure 17: Heavy/fat and long versus thin and short tails: The value of the random variable according to the normal distribution or Gaussian distribution or the bell curve is practically zero when it lies more than a few standard deviations away from the mean. Insofar, the choice of a bell curve may not be appropriate when a significant fraction of outliers – values which lie many standard deviations away from the mean – is to be expected. A tricky problem is, as Taleb (2013: 9) states, that fat-tailed probability distributions can masquerade as thin tailed (see 2.2.2.).

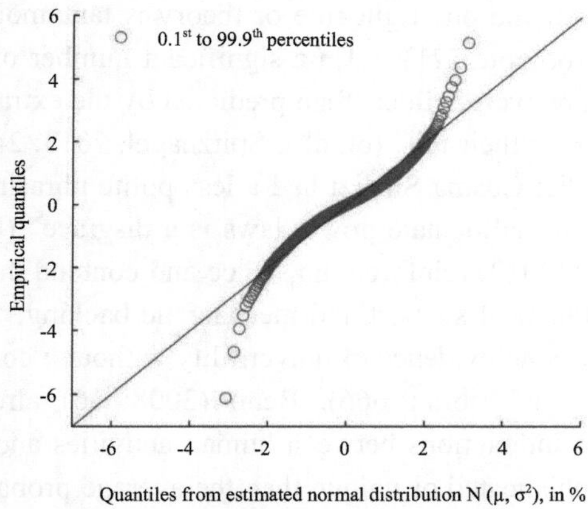

Figure 18: Normal distributions are not the (new) norm(al): A QQ plot of daily S&P 500 returns (the American stock market index Standard & Poor's 500), from 1957:Q1 – 2014:Q3; in general, a QQ plot is a way to assess if an empirical distribution matches reasonably well a prespecified theoretical distribution; for instance, a normal distribution (or a normally distributed continuous random variable N) where the mean (μ) and variance (σ^2) have been estimated from the data. Each point in the QQ plot shows a specific percentile (quantile) according to the empirical as well as according to the theoretical distribution. For instance, if the 0.02 percentile is at -10 in the empirical distribution, but at only -3 in the theoretical distribution, then this shows that the two distributions have fairly different left tails. The visual inspection of a histogram can also give useful clues for assessing the normality of returns. Source: Söderlind, 2014.

In particular, this so-called Q–Q plot (Quantile-Quantile plot) indicates that the two distributions have fairly different left tails, which means that the frequency of factual extreme losses is not well-described by the tail of a bell curve. This might be seen as grist for the mill of power law proponents.

Nonetheless, it ought to be emphasized that to *reasonably* privilege heavy-tail over normal distributions, because the former is apparently able to depict and describe (but not to *explain*)[224] reality in banking in a better way (Mandelbrot) – in the words of mathematician Walter Willinger and his colleagues: "[t]he presence of [power law] distributions in data obtained from complex natural or engineered systems should be considered the norm rather than the exception" (Mitchell, 2009: 269) –, results in nothing less than an untenable assertion, (*): namely, that *we now have a better (i.e., more reliable or trustworthy) or the right (?) extrapolation rule at hand; or, in the end, even an underlying theory of how bodies in the financial system behave and interact.*

Indeed, the following statement by Sornette (2009: 5) who embraces the abandonment of 'normal' distributions in favor of wilder distributions feeds the doubt that the search for the one right rule or theory is tantamount to a never-ending task (see also footnote 221): "[I]n a significant number of complex systems, extreme events are even 'wilder' than predicted by the extrapolation of the power law distributions in their tail" (cf. also Spitznagel, 2013: 244). The physicist and network scientist Cosma Shalizi had a less polite phrasing of his sentiments: "Our tendency to hallucinate power laws is a disgrace" (Mitchell, 2009: 254). Stumpf & Porter (2012) reinforce the stance and contend that most reported power laws lack statistical support and mechanistic backing: "[...] a statistically sound power law is no evidence of universality without a concrete underlying theory to support it" (ibid.: 666). Renn (2008: 16) already remarked fundamentally that the interactions between human activities and consequences are more complex, sophisticated or unique than the average probabilities used in technical risk analyses are able to capture. Alan Greenspan conceded "that nobody can predict the future when people are involved. Human behavior hasn't changed, people are unpredictable." (Cited in Sornette, 2003: 321). Churchman (1961: 164) differentiates that in the case of the gambler, such a theory [in the context of his discussion: a 'well-substantiated' theory of the manner in which

224 Capturing time series properties of data by some stochastic model does not explain the underlying regularities.

draws of various types occur for a given reference class] may be available; in the case of the executive [metaphorically speaking of real-world businesses and risk management], there is no such theory.[225] Von Hayek (1967: 30) makes a very similar point.[226]

To this author, the assertion (*) is therefore after all untenable since it has not yet been sufficiently accounted for the challenges posed by the complexity of modern financial systems:

While Mandelbrot and fellows have taken a step in the right direction by addressing some

- non-linearities (*The Noah Effect*) and
- some dependencies (*The Joseph Effect*),
- real *dynamics* or *unstable* time series (i.e., what is above the waterline, see Figure 15) – evolving or changing complex systems over time, which does not entitle us to pick a specific probability function because we do not have a good reason to prefer one to the other (see 7.3.) – and
- other *dependencies* such as *feedback* in *open* systems (i.e., what is beneath the waterline, see Figure 15) – self-similarity and invariance in distribution with respect to changes of time and space scale do *not* indicate systems whose parts interact and that exchange material, information, and/or energy with their environment across a boundary –[227]

225 Furthermore, it is "useless to say the economist should look at history and let the facts 'speak for themselves', because we need an antecedent theory to know which facts we should even consider, and to even know how to classify a 'fact' in the first place" (Spitznagel, 2013: 177).

226 Indeed, the unpredictability of human action (and the enormous influence individual choice wields in how economics works) is the core of the Austrian (or Viennese) School of economics (along with von Hayek, L. von Mises, Joseph Schumpeter, Murray Rothbard and many others). For example, von Mises (1949/1998: 31) writes: "No laboratory experiments can be performed with regard to human action. We are never in a position to observe the change in one element only, all other conditions of the event remaining unchanged. Historical experience as an experience of complex phenomena does not provide us with facts in the sense in which the natural sciences employ this term to signify isolated events tested in experiments. The information conveyed by historical experience cannot be used as building material for the construction of theories and the prediction of future events. Every historical experience is open to various interpretations, and is in fact interpreted in different ways."

227 Moreover, a system, at least a complex system, is more than the sum of its parts whereas, in the case of fractals, the parts are similar to the whole. "Viewed structurally, a system is a divisible whole; but viewed functionally it is an indivisible whole in the sense that some of its essential properties are lost when it is taken apart" (Ackoff, 1974: 14).

have not yet received enough attention (see Part III for an answer to some of those open challenges).

This finding can be packaged in a resounding, but in this form still underdetermined and more suggestive research statement (which is why we refer to it as a conjecture, not as a fully fledged proposition).

Conjecture 4:

There is no good theory of how bodies in the financial system behave and interact and, therefore, a scientific basis for proclaiming the accuracy, suitability, and commonality of power law distributions is missing.

From the perspective of organized complexity, it is not power laws *per se* that are important, but the presence of underlying high variability / dynamics (Alderson & Doyle, 2010: 849). Moreover, the foundational and epistemological problem of identifying and utilizing the 'right' probability distribution is not, and perhaps cannot be solved (7.3.). All in all, 'power law' proponents like other probabilists seem to be just poking around in the dark. Trying to predict future (extreme) losses with structurally wrong models is like trying to predict the trajectory of a comet with Newtonian models. These models will invariably make maladaptive projections beyond some lead time, and these errors cannot be erased by adding a discrepancy term derived from other Newtonian models (Frigg et al., 2015: 3997). Even though it might not hold for *every purpose* of scientific work, the exact functional form of the distribution matters for *our* purposes because we are keen to investigate whether or not probabilities of extreme losses can be meaningfully ascertained, whether or not extrapolation of data on rare or systemic events works well. We would receive very different probability estimations and extrapolation paths, depending on the functional form we assume for our observation range (i.e., if the data is best fitted by a power law or a log-normal distribution, etc.).

Taleb & Pilpel (2004: 3) prepared the way for relativizing and restricting the power of power laws and company by pointing to, what they call, the central problem, which serves as a direct input for the Central Argument that we are going to develop in the following; namely that one does not observe probability distributions, but merely the outcome of random generators.

7.3. The Central Argument against using Probability Theory for Financial Risk Management

In this section, we show that the determination of a probability (or loss) distribution for (extreme or systemic) risk management purposes in banking is not possible. This is due to a foundational *epistemo-logical* problem of induction concerning deep doxastic uncertainty (rather than an ontological problem as it took center stage in Chapter 6, see 6.1.3. and 6.3. above and the comment on Premise 5 below). The argument runs as follows (and, at a glance, it is displayed in a condensed form in Appendix D):

Premise 1:

In general, there are two ways that probabilities can be determined: *a priori* or *a posteriori*; e.g., either by inference from the physical shape of the respective object (e.g., coin, dice; i.e., *a priori*) and from the parameters of a controlled experiment (e.g., lotteries; i.e., *a priori*), respectively, or by empirical observations to obtain an *estimate* for the chance of certain events (*a posteriori*).[228]

Rationale:

This is a commonplace established since the early days of the emergence of mathematical probability theories (e.g., Bernoulli, 1713/1988: 65).

Premise 2:

In financial risk management, probabilities can only be gained and evaluated *a posteriori*. And in terms of empirical observations, only samples and no complete observation are possible.

Rationale:

- It is impossible to know all the parameters involved, especially considering that modern financial systems consist of a plethora of parts and elements (a very simplified extract is given in Figure 1) that are tightly coupled and in close interrelation (6.3.).

---

228 By the laws of large numbers, the accuracy of the estimate increases with the number of observations if certain conditions are met (Grimmett & Stirzaker, 2001: 193). And yet it is unclear why convergence among still inaccurate measurements should be taken as an indication of truth (Tal, 2015).

- Ultimately, every (risk) model invariably extrapolates from data of the past to the future (Heinemann, 2014: 194; Redak, 2011: 450ff.). In particular, there are basically three ways of building a probability distribution for some financial random variable (see 7.2.), which depend mainly on hindsight, the same holds for *evaluating* those probabilities (Stulz, 2008: 62), and which are thus based on 'empirics' or 'experience'.
- The importance of inductive reasoning depends on the basic fact that, apart from trivial exceptions, the events and phenomena in the financial world (and, in general, of nature) are too multiform, too numerous, too extensive, or too inaccessible to permit complete observation (Weaver, 1963: 234). So, we have to content ourselves with samples. An issue is that we seem to demand a sample that is 'representative' of the whole (Churchman, 1961: 154).

Premise 3:
For any finite set of (P&L) data, there is an infinite number of probability distributions that are in accordance with that data / those observations and describe possible portfolio values.
Rationale:

- There are infinitely many values of returns ((profits and) losses) to which probabilities can be ascribed. Suppose, for instance, that "so far the daily change in a stock's price have been limited to the range between 0 and 10 points. Is there any reason to suspect that it will not move 1000 points one way or the other in the future?" (Taleb & Pilpel, 2004: 30).[229]

229 In this respect, Taleb & Pilpel (2004: 35) point to an important distinction between physical and financial systems: While in the former, "it is often the case that we can tell in advance, due to external, purely deductive reasons, that the 'generator' must be bounded and therefore (relatively) benign; we can therefore use the past data for inductive inference about the future […]". In terms of the latter, however, this appears to be not the case: "There are potential events in many such [financial] systems that would cause losses (or gains) that are, in theory, unbounded. To convince oneself of this, one need only look at a simple 'option': the possibility exists of losing an infinite amount of money combined with the fact that such probability may remain unknown by us" (ibid.). Cf. also Lux (1998: 144) for a difference in time series between economics and natural sciences and von Mises (1957/2005: 61, 209) for differences between perennial laws of nature and praxeology or patterns of human action.

- The past usage of a certain function is susceptible to an infinite number of different interpretations or extrapolations (in analogy to Kripke, 1982)[230].

Premise 4:
If there is an infinite number of probability distributions to represent possible portfolio values, not all of them are equally suitable for probability-based risk modeling and a given risk management purpose. If a probabilistic risk modeling approach is selected, only a suitable function ought to be picked.
Rationale:

- Only suitable or correct probabilities (of occurrence) should be ascribed to the loss values of interest (allowing a certain margin of error) – otherwise it is useless to employ probabilities at all.
- Frigg et al. (2013: 483f.) present a case where one can explicitly see that a certain function $p_t\ (x)$ need not be the correct probability distribution. Taking a 'wrong' probability distribution as a guide to actions can be ruinous (ibid.): One example is the blowup of LTCM discussed in 5.2. The partners explained it as the result of a very rare event albeit it would be more convincing to consider that *they used the wrong distribution* (Taleb & Pilpel, 2004: 3; Jorion, 2000).

230 Kripke (1982) originally introduced the following scenario to illustrate Wittgenstein's paradox: Suppose that you have only added numbers smaller than 57 before (the point is that everybody gave themselves only a finite number of examples instantiating that function). Suppose further that you are asked to perform the computation "68 + 57". Our natural inclination is that you will apply the addition function as you have before, and calculate that the correct answer is "125". But now imagine that you encounter a bizarre skeptic who argues:
1) That there is no fact about your past usage of the addition function that determines "125" as the right answer.
2) That nothing justifies you in giving this answer rather than another.
After all, it is perfectly consistent with your previous use of "plus" that you actually meant it to mean the *wild* "quus" function, defined as (ibid.: 9):

$$x\ quus\ y\ = \begin{cases} x+y\ if\ x,y\ < 57 \\ 5 \qquad otherwise. \end{cases}$$

The skeptic questions whether there is any *fact* that you meant plus, not quus, that will answer his skeptical challenge; and second, he questions whether you have any reason to be so confident that now you ought to answer "125" rather than "5" (ibid.: 11). Your past usage of the addition function (a '*mild*' function like the Gaussian (so to speak)) is susceptible to an infinite number of different quus-like or outlandish (*wild*) interpretations (see 6.2.2.).

- An objection to the validity of Premise 4 might be that, from a Bayesian perspective, one could point out that by using one peculiar probability distribution to compute predictions a prior probability of one has been implicitly assigned to that function. Given that we have no reason to assume that this model is true, this confidence is misplaced and one really ought to take uncertainty about the model into account (Frigg et al., 2014: 28).
Frigg et al. (ibid.), however, refute the objection in several ways.[231]

Premise 5:
A probability distribution is suitable for probability-based risk modeling and a given risk management purpose if, and only if, it fits not only the past but also future observations (of, e.g., loss values) or least any one that matches future observations within an acceptable margin of error (*Definition*).[232]

- *Comment*: It is obscure what it means for a probability function to "fit the past": For example, following the historical method (see 7.2.), we take a certain period of time and record data (e.g., gains and losses in a certain context) and the frequencies, respectively. Relative frequencies and, in the end, probabilities can be derived. Yet, many problems arise: 1) The number of (completely countable) observations and sufficiently

231 The first problem is that "it is not clear how to circumscribe the relevant model class. This class would contain all possible models of a target system. But the phrase 'all models' masks the fact that mathematically this class is not defined, and indeed it's not clear whether it is definable at all" (ibid.). The second problem they point out is that "even if one could construct such a class in one way or another, there are both technical and conceptual problems with putting an uncertainty measure over this class. The technical problem is that the relevant class of models would be a class of functions and function spaces do not come equipped with measures. The conceptual issue is that even if the technical problem could be circumvented somehow, what measure would we chose? The model class will contain an infinity of models and it is at best unclear whether there is a non-arbitrary measure on such a set that reflects our uncertainty about model choice." (Ibid.).

232 Another version of this definition, which is closer to a subjective interpretation of probability, could be: A probability distribution is suitable or 'right' if, and only if, the agent is sufficiently convinced or justified in applying it to a certain set of data (specific loss values of interest). Because "sufficiently convinced or justified" could be translated with assigning prior probabilities to probability distributions and ultimately, after updating degrees of belief, one model stands out. However, see the previous footnote for some problems with this proposal.

similar circumstances[233] are critical for counting frequencies and deriving sound probabilities. 2) Objective probabilities are tacitly assumed and it is at best far from clear whether, e.g., the frequency notion is able to convey any fruitful meaning when reference classes are small, i.e., when it comes to rare events (Churchman, 1961: 148f.). 3) This approach may well do a good job at describing the body of the distribution (where the points we have collected are plentiful); but, when it comes to (very) rare events, it might or will fail. For example, as seen in 5.2., LTCM made a loss of more than 70% of capital. LTCM lost 70% on only one occasion and LTCM was capable of losing 70%, whether the 'true' probability of that loss was 1% or 25% (Stulz, 2008: 62). Etc.

In this light, it seems that speaking of a 'suitable' probability function does not make sense in the realm of dynamic, organized and complex systems where, e.g., sufficiently similar and stable circumstances cannot be assumed over time. If so and if modern financial systems are sufficiently dynamically and organizationally complex, the Central Argument would become redundant. Because then, not an epistemological (how to identify the 'right' probability function), but an ontological problem (there is no one 'right' distribution form) would take center stage – see 6.1.3. and 6.3.

- *Implication*: So, the problem is to choose by relying on experience from an infinite set of probability distributions the one that best matches future observations if such a function exists or is defined at all. The latter is a tacitly assumed premise here in 7.3., otherwise the conclusion follows more directly.

Premise 6:

The suitability of a probability distribution for describing some past and future P&L data as well as for a given risk management purpose cannot be determined from past data.

233 The importance of a stable 'chance set-up' (see 6.2.2.) becomes obvious if one adheres to Popper's (1959b) *propensity interpretation* of probability. For him, a probability p of an outcome of a certain type is a propensity of a repeatable experiment to produce outcomes of that type with limiting relative frequency p (Hájek, 2011). But to claim that "an experimental arrangement has a tendency to produce a given limiting relative frequency of a particular outcome, presupposes a kind of stability or uniformity in the workings of that arrangement" (ibid.) – for, considering unstable randomness from above, the limit would not exist in a suitably unstable arrangement.

Rationale:

- Skeptical reasoning: There is no fact about the past usage of a certain probability function P* that determines its 'suitability' for future applications (in analogy to Kripke's (1982: 8f.) argument).
- Practically relevant supplement: As argued in 6.3., modern financial systems possess structures, on the one hand, that single them out as complex in some sense. Accordingly, events in the financial system, on the other hand, seem to be generated by unstable random processes. In particular, modern financial systems not only have the potential to change (as a mere theoretical possibility as it is the case in Kripke's skeptic scenario, see footnote 230), but they *do* change *radically* and *non-linearly* (Bhansali, 2014: 20) where the past only has a limited influence on the future and where the past in fact influences the future not in the sense of continuity (Esposito, 2011: 150).[234] Similarity of the past to the future cannot be inferred (Taleb & Pilpel, 2004: 33f.). Many dependencies within the system may be opaque and poorly understood. Ergo: All things considered, this renders simple or naïve, including linear as well as nonlinear,[235] extrapolation fallacious and, ipso facto, relying on the past for determining the accuracy/suitability of a probability distribution turns out to be fallacious, too. In this sense, data can be said to be *toxic* (Taleb, 2012: 126).[236]
- Logical reasoning: "If one needs a probability distribution to gauge knowledge about the future behavior of the distribution from its past results, and if, at the same time, one needs the past to derive a probability distribution in the first place, then we are facing a severe *regress*

234 Moreover, history shows that financial markets can implode without perceived warning and precursory phenomena, not unlike 'phase transitions' (Bak, 1996) that occur in physical systems (Bhansali, 2014: 20).

235 The fact that organized complex systems change non-linearly does not say *how* they change non-linearly (cf. e.g. Gomez, 1981: 44f.).

236 Consider also that big data is misleading when we deal with wild or unstable randomness where e.g. the mean of the distribution does not exist (see 2.5.); and the fatal trade-off between more relevant vs. less limited amounts of data or issues like how to define the 'statistical window' which cannot be derived from the data (see footnote 220). Moreover, of what use would historical data be at all when it comes to a *new risk*, a risk that has not manifested itself in the past? For instance, "prior to the subprime crisis, there had been no experience of a downturn in the real estate market when large amounts of securitized subprime mortgages were outstanding" (Stulz, 2008: 62).

loop" (Taleb & Pilpel, 2004: 2); i.e., Hume's principle of uniformity of nature is designated as both conclusion and premise. See also the *petitio principii* presented in 7.1.

Conclusion 1:

Thus, any choice of a particular probability distribution for a given risk management purpose is necessarily arbitrary and cannot be justified.

Note that this finding is in line with the results reported by many mathematicians (mathematical finance) – in contrast to some applied scientists and practitioners (involved in the broader quantitative finance scene): "[…] The [Financial] Crisis [of 2007-09] saw numerous examples where 'practice' fully misunderstood the conditions under which some mathematical concepts or results could be applied. Or indeed where models were applied to totally insufficient or badly understood data; the typical 'garbage in, garbage out' syndrome." (Das et al., 2013: 702; cf. also Riedel, 2013: 23f., 33, 52, 180; Jaynes, 2003: 65f., 74; Daníelsson et al., 2001: 3). In the light of our Central Argument, however, they unfortunately phrased their concerns in a too reluctant manner.

Conclusion 1 is furthermore different from and stronger than the analogous result in Kripke's (1982) *skeptical* argument. While in the Kripkian case one can ignore the skeptical reasoning in a carefree manner because one has still *good reasons* to use the addition function in lieu of a *wild* quus or quus-like function (namely, for example, that the 'practical man' succeeds in life by employing the former, not the latter), our Central Argument, by contrast, is practically relevant in several regards.

It is important to see though that its correctness does *not* depend on the practically relevant supplement, i.e., on problems of systemic risk assessment being organized complex and escaping statistical analysis – otherwise, the reasoning would be circular. Rather, the practically relevant supplement is given because it emphasizes and locates the link between complexity and the inadequacy of probability-based modeling of extreme and systemic risks. The importance of the Central Argument has different facets.

First, it exposes the uselessness of probability-based models of predominantly extreme risks, as the differences between probability distributions are less significant in the body (see Figure 17). In other words, we clearly reveal a wrong track of risk modeling in today's world, namely one which cannot succeed by normal statistical means, when we push logic to the extreme. The output of risk measures like VaR or ES, for example, is a value for a loss of money the magnitude of which depends on *which* loss or probability distribution is assumed. Probability distributions are not directly observable and as long as we have no systematic way of drawing a line between the 'good' and the 'bad' distributions, we should not rely on our calculations of minimum or expected losses etc. when making provisions for the future (Frigg et al., 2013: 487). Conditional on the settings depicted by the Central Argument (excluding, for example, situations of disorganized complexity where the Premise 6 does not hold)[237], probabilistic forecasts are unreliable and do not provide a good guide for action as such (ibid.: 490).

Second, the probabilities of events such as potential loss values are unknown and since *Risk II* presupposes known probabilities (with $0 < p < 1$), the Central Argument makes a strong case in favor of *Risk I* as a more proper risk concept, in favor of non-orthodoxy (see 4.1.).

Third, this entire discussion on probability distributions would have remained completely theoretical if it was not occurring against the background of risk management practices in the financial industry. Any real-life risk calculations which hinge on knowledge about probability distributions are suspicious and as it can be very *expensive* to use the 'wrong' distribution (consider, for example, the collapse of LTCM; see 5.2.) which we cannot separate from a suitable one according to the Central Argument, it is finally to conclude:

Conclusion 2 / Proposition 5:
There is no point in drawing on probability theory for financial extreme and systemic risk management purposes.

This Central Argument is valid and the rationale beneath each of its premises should ensure that they are correct (or at least, very plausible) and that, therefore, the whole argument is sound. In that case, the house of modern risk management where probability theory and distributions are constituting elements is not in danger of collapsing, but has never been well-established since it lacks a theoretical foundation.

---

237 One explanation is this: In systems with very large numbers of variables and high degrees of (genuine) randomness, the laws of large numbers, the Central Limit Theorem and other so-called "properties of stochasticity" (Martin-Löf, 1966: 604) hold (see Appendix C).

7.4. Linking the Central Argument with the Current State of the Literature (IIIa)-c))

In Chapter 2, this thesis reviewed and discussed three objections to conventional, i.e., probabilistic, risk modeling (IIIa)-c)), which we are now able to expound as forming part of the problem of induction outlined by the Central Argument: On the one hand, it purports that the inference to obtain a certain probability distribution that (within a certain margin) describes some past and future P&L data and that can be used to calculate the minimum or expected loss is arbitrary and, therefore, an instance of an unsound or bad induction. On the other hand, it is problematic when bad inductions are embraced (be it consciously or not) so that it is no wonder that the (in theory as well as in practice) dominating probabilistic reasoning is closely associated with severe difficulties in the effectivity aspects of corporate, financial and other systems because its consequences are all too often disastrous (see 5.2., and cf., e.g., FCIC, 2011). Hence, we face a problem of induction.

If IIIa)-c) are symptoms or elements of this underlying and foundational problem of induction, they turn out to be *conceptual problems* (ad *RQ1.8*) – *conceptual* because then these issues are inherent in the concept of probabilistic financial risk modeling and result from risk models' grounding in probability theory, respectively.[238] Thereby, we unveil that the failure of standard risk models is not accidental (a *contingent* fact), but that it is caused by their reliance on probability theory (a *necessary* fact). With recourse to Chapter 2, IIIa)-c) can be briefly restated as follows:

IIIa) Estimates for probability distributions and parameters describing rare events, including the variability of such parameters over time, are often poor, because there is not enough and/or no trustworthy historical data.

IIIb) The likelihood of coincidences of multiple unfortunate, rare events is often underestimated, even though their interaction dynamics may lead to amplification effects and feedback loops (such as procyclicality or positive feedback loops).

IIIc) Common assumptions underlying established ways of thinking are not questioned enough: statistical *independence*; statistical *stationarity*; *normal* distributions of data, returns, prices, etc.

238 In general, to point at conceptual problems is the strongest form of critique.

Now, how can IIIa)-c) be grasped as symptoms or signs or elements that indicate the problem of induction pointed out by the Central Argument? Firstly, IIIa), namely that estimates for the 'true' probability distribution are often poor, follows from Conclusion 1. That there does not exist enough (reliable) historical data is naturally true for systemic or extreme risk events and relevant due to Premise 1 and 2. Secondly, IIIb) alludes to central characteristics of organized and dynamic complexity and is represented in (the motivation of) Premise 6. Finally, in terms of IIIc), assumptions should be questioned as a result of Conclusion 1 (the assumption of *normal* distributions) or should be given up because they are incompatible with dynamic or organized complexity (*stationarity* and *independence*), against the background of which the Central Argument is conducted.[239]

Commonly used risk models to describe risks are grounded in probability theory (Malz, 2011; McNeil et al., 2005). This makes available the elegant mathematical framework that probability theory is based on, but it comes at a cost: The strong supposition that probabilities can be expressed by (exact) numerical values and that those values can be accurately determined. While probability-based risk models usually share this principal assumption, many of them impose additional constraints. They may require, for example, that statistical variables be independent or assume that data from the past is an accurate or at least a reliable indicator of probability distributions. Standard risk models cannot accurately model the risk posed by especially rare, systemic events, as a number of financial crises in the past two decades have shown (Aven, 2012). Not only have such rare events occurred far more frequently than predicted, but they have brought with them strong interdependencies between institutions and rapidly increasing correlations between markets, for example, that would, under '*normal*'[240] circumstances, be deemed unrelated (Lowenstein, 2002; MacKenzie, 2003).[241]

Conventional risk models have, therefore, all in all failed and failed exactly when they were needed the most (namely, when to address extreme risks) since they have proved to be conceptually inappropriate.

---

239 Aven (2013b: 46) concludes that the probability-based approach to treating risks and uncertainties tends to hide critical assumptions and, thus, provides a delusive description of the possible occurrence of future events.

240 Is there a norm at all? See 6.3.2. and cf. Lowenstein, 2002: 71.

241 Their tendency to become highly correlated during times of market distress is sometimes regarded as a unique aspect of hedge-fund returns (Getmansky et al., 2015: 55).

This study thus proposes a new and subversive thesis:

Proposition 6:
Standard quantitative systemic and extreme risk assessment approaches are conceptually inappropriate.

8. Conclusion to Part I

In order to draw inferences from data as described by econometric texts, it is necessary to make whimsical assumptions [...]. The haphazard way we individually and collectively study the fragility of inferences leaves most of us unconvinced that any inference is believable.
(Edward E. Leamer, 1983: 43)

The Central Argument has shaken the house of modern risk management literature and practice with their standard extreme risk modeling approaches in banking to its very foundations; it further serves the purpose of shaking risk management professionals out of a 'dogmatic slumber' (with regard to Part III). In a broader sense, it also illustrates the confusion (folly and nonsense) that can occur when a concept that belongs properly to one realm, namely that of disorganized complexity and of gambling, wagering, betting and games of chance, in particular (Hacking, 2006), is uncritically and improperly applied to another (risk management in banking): the borrowing of any method on the sole ground that is has been successful somewhere else is inadmissible (Schumpeter, 1954/1994: 17; von Hayek, 1943).[242]

In fact, it has been rather popular for scientists to remark that people do not really understand anything until they know how to measure it (cf. Weaver, 1963: 275). It has to be declared clearly though that this statement is of limited usefulness.[243] Measurement in this imperfect world of ours is subject to error and one

242 There might be a temptation to respond that Chapter 7 does not show that probabilities are useless, not even in the realm of risk management in banking; common experience only shows that we should not use probabilities when they are misleading. The problem with this suggestion is that outside of thought experiments we have no means to tell when that happens. "The only thing we have is the model, which we know to be imperfect in various ways" (Frigg et al., 2014: 13). Examples show that model-probabilities and 'probabilities in the world' (if such things exist) can come unstuck dramatically, but we do not know where and when (ibid.). See also 7.3.

243 As Weaver (1963: 275) remarks, science has probably never measured anything as frequently or as accurately as intervals of time; but both, he and this author, are not aware that this persistence has at all increased an understanding of what "time" really is (ibid.). Furthermore, it is a myth, Aven & Krohn (2014: 4) say, a costly myth, that "if you can't measure it, you can't manage it".

cannot make progress towards precision unless we have some way of dealing with error (ibid.: 276). In the previous Chapter 7, the attempt was undertaken to enunciate the thesis, as a negative answer to RQ1.7 (about the degree of error prevention in risk measurement), that probabilities are not only not apt for dealing with errors of risk measurement, but that employing probabilities (at least) in the field of risk management in banking *implies* errors. This result opens the floor for the debate on a more promising and effective approach to dealing with financial systemic risks (see Part III).

Probabilistic reasoning is not worthless, not even in terms of its application to the real world (as opposed to gambling games of various sorts and text book cases); but, instead of using it not so much because we are convinced that we are to use it but because it is so very convenient, it is time, at the risk of boresome repetition, to use it with caution, deliberation, and restraint; the latter especially when facing organized and dynamic complexity (cf. also Peters & Gell-Mann, 2016).

8.1. Résumé

We are now able to answer the overarching question **RQ1** of this Part I:

> "Under what conditions are taken-for-granted quantitative risk assessment and management approaches, including VaR, CoVaR, ES, etc., ineffective and do become themselves a risk object for banks?",

In retrospect of the previous chapters, the following conditions can be identified:

- *Condition 1*: Improper risk concept is applied (*Risk II*) – Chapter 4.1.
  Explanation: Since we frequently lack a sufficient basis to determine the probabilities of certain risk or loss events with any precision (in favor of *Risk I* and reinforced by the result of Chapter 7), it would mean we exclude the risk concept from most situations of interest if the term was restricted to cases where probabilities are known. It would be dangerous to devote our risk management interests only to a clear minority of cases, which are not only of low frequency but also of relatively low severity (compared to systemic and extreme risk events that cannot be captured in probability terms, see Chapter 7). Good risk management, thus, calls for toolkits that handle both, Risk II (which can be success-

fully addressed with statistical tools, VaR, ES, etc.) and uncertainty, Risk I, (which takes center stage and cannot be ignored) – see Chapter 13.

- *Condition 2*: Narrow notion of systemic risk is employed – Chapter 4.2 and Chapter 5.1.
  Explanation: Systemic risk is usually defined narrowly (also in terms of the underlying risk concept) and systemic risk in *this* sense is usually seen as the concern of regulators. It is often said that systemic risks are or should be beyond the interest and power of any one bank to manage although systemic risks (even in the narrow sense) affect financial market participants in many ways and thus should in fact be actively addressed by banks for in-house risk management purposes (*Proposition 1*).
- *Condition 3*: Broad notion of systemic risk is employed – Chapter 4.2 and Chapter 5.1.
  Explanation: A broader notion is put forward in this study and it stands in stark contrast to the common compartmentalization of risk. Systemic risk has to be scrutinized at the higher level of interactions. Orthodox tools such as *VaR* are, by contrast, techniques of risk silo management.
- *Condition 4*: Event-oriented worldview is adopted – Chapter 5.1.
  Explanation: The full range of feedbacks which operate in a system has not been understood due to an improper event-oriented worldview. If risk managers are not able to grasp and understand the factors determining the behavior of the system they are operating in, if they do not adopt a feedback view of the world to perceive system changes causing systemic risks, then their interventions in the financial system, which they derive from VaR, ES etc. calculations among others, can even contribute to the instability of the system or possibly result in serious problems like a financial crisis.
- *Condition 5*: Lessons have not been learned from the past – Chapter 5.2.
  Explanation: The managers and partners of LTCM naively believed in the uniformity of nature, the conformity of future and past. There were misbeliefs about risk and pretense of knowledge (von Hayek), etc.
- *Condition 6*: Assessing and managing extreme and systemic risks in banking is *mistakenly* categorized as a problem of *disorganized complexity* – Chapter 6.

Explanation: Even though Weaver's concept of organized complexity must remain under-determined (*Proposition 3*), it seems fair to say that risk management activities involve studying modern financial systems which are organic wholes, with their parts in close interrelation. This organized complexity is different from disorganized complexity as it escapes statistical or probabilistic approaches, which is suggested by Weaver (1948) and others and which is underpinned by the introduction of unstable randomness into the picture. If assessing and managing extreme and systemic risks in banking represents an example of organized complexity and if stochastic methods do not hold the key in such cases, then conventional approaches to assess and manage extreme and systemic risks become untenable.

- *Condition 7*: Probabilistic reasoning is not an adequate foundation for modeling systemic or extreme risk in a banking context – Chapter 7.
  Explanation: Standard measures to describe (extreme and systemic) risks are grounded in probability theory and probability distributions because they are derived from loss distributions, which are ultimately associated with random variables. However, any choice of a peculiar probability distribution is invariably a display of despotism in the face of complexity and cannot be vindicated; a scientific basis is missing (*Conjecture 4*). Since the differences are more and primarily significant in the tails across different distributions, this leads to the conclusion that there is especially no point in falling back on probability theory for financial systemic and/or extreme risk management purposes (*Proposition 5*). Hence, we are left with the disastrous outcome that taken-for-granted quantitative systemic/extreme risk assessment approaches are conceptually inappropriate (*Proposition 6*).
- *Condition 8*: The systems part of systemic risks is grasped in not a merely metaphorical way and quantitative risk management in banking is treated as a complex systems problem.
  Explanation: The nature of systemic risk and complexity, the latter giving rise to the former and uncertainties (*Proposition 2*), requires explanatory modeling (*Proposition 7*) – Chapter 6, Chapter 2.4 and 8.2 – while actual modeling of extreme or systemic risk in banking (EVT, VaR, CoVaR, ES, SES) turns out to be insufficiently structure-oriented.

8.2. Outlook: Explanatory Models for In-House Risk Management in Banking

From the negative result that taken-for-granted quantitative risk assessment or management approaches proved to be non-effective, it arises the need for alternatives; alternatives which are inspired by the insight that describing and quantifying systemic risks in and to the financial system necessitates explanatory models: What makes systemic risk different from other types of risk is that it cannot be captured at the level of the individual components of a system (unlike market risk or credit risk, see 4.2.). Instead, it has to be studied at the higher level of interactions between parts of the system and between parts and the whole. These relations in their entirety constitute the system's structure (Kirchhof, 2003: 8; Probst, 1981: 112), which is addressed by explanatory models and disregarded by traditional risk models. The latter only tend to work at the component level (*under certain conditions*), and therefore do not adequately model systemic risk (see also Chapter 7).

On a more profound level, it is furthermore well-known in systems science that complexity (an organized complex system) requires a well-grounded systems theory (explanatory models; Schwaninger, 2005: 32; Byrne & Callaghan, 2014: 39; Schwaninger, 2010; Sterman, 2000). We learned that (financial) risks are the symptoms of problems of complexity (in financial systems) and that dynamic or organized complexity is their generator (see Figure 16 and *Proposition 2*). Hence, when it comes to assessing risk assessment approaches in this new light, problem articulation must be seen as the most important step in risk modeling: What is the real problem, not just the symptom of difficulty? (Sterman, 2000: 89). Our risk management attention should not be drawn to the symptoms of difficulty (certain possible and uncertain events), but rather to the underlying drivers (dynamic and organized complexity as well as their determinants, respectively).

On this basis and in partial anticipation of a comprehensive reply to RQ1.9, it should be clarified what explanatory models are and how those used by regulators might be different from those endorsed in Part III (LBR). In general, explanatory models elucidate why the real system at hand behaves as it does and not differently (Schwaninger, 2010: 1421). Instead of relying on big amounts of data, they try to capture interrelationships, for example but not limited to, causalities (Cartwright, 1983), interactions and dependencies, and "inquire into the implications of system behavior and of the structure underlying it" (Schwaninger, 2010: 1421).

Explanatory models express a systemic view, being aligned to complex, dynamic and organized systems, and an interest in describing, explaining and often designing or at least influencing them (Schwaninger, 2011: 753). In order to distinguish explanatory models from such that merely describe and allow to make predictions, the following Figure 19 illustrates the formal process which is said to model the natural process and it integrates the three different functions (descriptive, explanatory, predictive) a model can have.

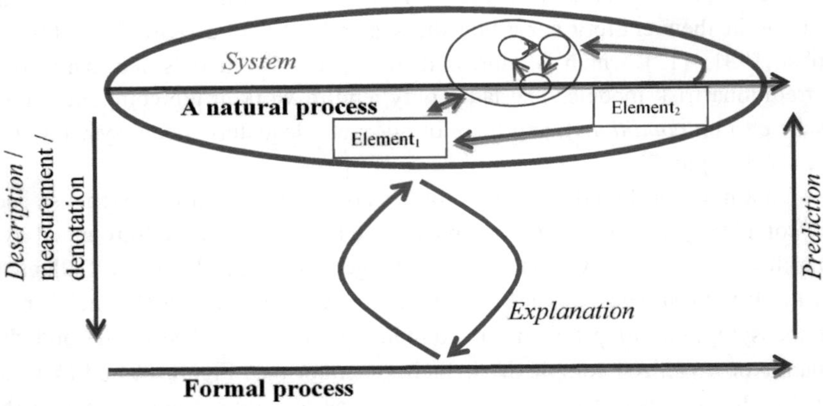

Figure 19: The modeling relations.

Explanatory models can obviously be of great value to regulators, striving to achieve financial stability (Schinasi, 2004), because they can be used to identify changes that influence the system in a certain way. Explanatory models of this kind focalize agents and networks in the system, often lending themselves to simulation. Their primary interest lies in the behavior of the system as a whole (for example, the likelihood that a default is contagious) and the behavior of its components is only relevant in relation to the system (King et al., 2014).

By contrast, individual market participants may also use explanatory models, but with a different outlook: Their main interest is the impact – direct or indirect – of changes in the system on their own exposure (for example, how a sharp decrease in market prices affects their liquidity). The system as a whole is therefore only relevant to the extent that it affects the individual.

As a consequence, requirements for explanatory models used by banks are different from those used by regulators. Market participants have to take into account their own position in detail, whereas regulators use aggregate values to represent individual participants. On the other hand, models for regulators try to represent the interactions between all parts of the system accurately, whereas market participants usually do not have the information, or are reticent to share information (Battiston et al., 2016), to model the interactions between third parties (Thurner & Poledna, 2013; Caballero & Simsek, 2009) albeit not only their own interactions with others might be relevant for them (e.g., envision direct and indirect contractual links between banks).

The risk models ventilated in this thesis are aimed at individuals and in-house risk management in particular, not at regulators. As such, their primary function is to explain the impact of systemic events rather than their cause within the system in which they occur. They are not primarily causal, but interested in logical connections. The desired focus on dynamic and organized complexity in our models is realized through analyzing complex financial instruments (derivatives), which (among others) drive the financial system's dynamic complexity. All in all, this study argues against unnecessary complexity in modeling endeavors (enunciated by, e.g., the inquiry of the nexus of complexity drivers in place of spotlighting complex derivatives only) as well as against the trends of endless specification (exact probability measurement) and big data movements (which does not make much sense in the realm of few and poor data) to create room for a novel approach.

Proposition 7:

An appropriate model of systemic risk should be explanatory and thus, structure-based in lieu of data-driven; i.e., for banks, it should explain the impact of systemic risk events on their own exposures.

Proposition 7 and its derivation provide a rationale for a shift from extant (mainly data-driven) to disruptive explanatory modeling in banks' risk management. This is not a side note in the theoretical frame-work of risk management, but rather a call for a Kuhnian paradigm shift. How a plea for explanatory modeling might then find its concrete way into risk modeling in banking, how such an approach is to be tested in a business setting, etc. is the topic of Part III. Part III elaborates on LBR (Logic-Based Risk modeling) against the background of financial trading and the LTCM counterparty credit risk crisis, exemplifying the kind of explanatory systemic risk model for market participants, and discloses that this proposal exhibits many strengths in contrast to conventional, merely descriptive and statistical models. We strive for explanatory models with sufficient richness and that, at the same time, are simple enough to remain manageable in particular. This opens the way for a convincing systematic in-house approach to examining, assessing and managing systemic risks in the financial system (Part III). The groundwork for that is laid in the following Part II.

Part II: The Transition to the Decision Level, Risk Assessment and Management

The Risk of Ineffective Risk Management II: Overcoming Limitations of the Qualitative Risk Analysis Approach in favor of Logic-Based Risk Modeling

9. Introduction to Part II

Problem solving has traditionally been taken to be
an essential function of management.
Through systems thinking, however, we have come to doubt
the existence of problems and solutions to them.
(Russell L. Ackoff, 1974)

[T]he development of systems thinking is crucial for the survival of humanity.
(John D. Sterman, 1994)

A steady stream of philosophers, scientists, and management gurus is observed by Sterman (1994: 291) to lament that "[c]omplexity had extended itself on immense horizons, [that] arithmetical ratios were useless for any attempt at accuracy [and] even mathematics [in general, C.H.] should soon succumb" (Adams, 1918: 490, 496). They call for leaps to fundamental new ways of thinking and acting since, when trying to solve problems successfully, "[w]e fail more often because we solve the wrong problem than because we get the wrong solution to the right problem" (Ackoff, 1974: 8). Many have advocated the development of systems thinking – "the ability to see the world as a complex system, in which we understand that 'you can't just do one thing' and that 'everything is connected to everything else'" (Sterman, 2000: 4). A holistic worldview, it is argued, could yield action that is in consonance with the long-term best interests of the system as a whole (ibid.), and be manifested through envisioning possible future behavioral paths of the systems; i.e., by articulating alternative futures and their implications for a certain business in order to foster discussion and debate among decision-makers in the context of risk management in banking, for example.

This Part II of the thesis looks at qualitative risk management and, under this heading, only at scenario planning, thinking or analysis as well as stress testing to some extent. This focus is chosen for several reasons:

1) In the end, it is all about decision-making competency in financial and systemic risk management (e.g., Brose et al., 2014a: 369; see also Chapter 21) and it has been argued by some authors that holistic quali-

tative tools in a larger learning process are better able to deal with decisions of great consequence than narrow and possibly reductionist quantitative approaches (e.g., Power, 2007: 120). This point is put forward in the literature of critical finance and reproduced in Chapter 10.

2) A lesson from the negative result that quantitative risk assessment and management techniques proved to be non-effective (Part I) could be that more room should be left for using 'softer' instrumentation with more qualitative calibration to frame (financial, especially extreme) risks. A critical finance society flourished, gaining new ground and new adherents. They have insisted on this shift of emphasis and highlighted that uncertainty should be tackled by scenario analysis (Mikes, 2011: 241). Their point (of view) is presented in Chapter 10.
3) The strong link between risk thinking and scenario planning deserves appreciation (e.g., Renn, 2008). This point is made in Chapters 10 and 11.
4) Scenario analysis has been declared as a key approach to master the challenges of today's global, complex and rapidly changing business environment (Varum & Melo, 2010; Roxburgh, 2009; Burt et al., 2006). It is, together with stress testing, the principal tool of risk analysis when quantitative instruments fall short (Diebold et al., 2010: 25). This point is sketched in Chapter 11.
5) Many strengths of scenario analysis exist: e.g., promotion of 'better quality thinking about the future', integration of hard and soft data with social judgments, emphasis on the decision level, on effective decision-making and learning. This point is worked out in Chapter 12.
6) Notwithstanding the many weaknesses of scenario planning, on the other hand, which do not allow to advocate it or qualitative risk management tools in general as panacea (Chapter 12), valuable implications can be derived for rethinking the approach to assessing extreme and systemic risks, which combines both quantitative and qualitative elements (in Part III). This point is stressed in Chapter 13.

Thereby, the stepping stone towards Part III is laid where the second guiding research question can then be tackled. The answer in Part III will stem from an insight gained in this Part II, namely that important issues in the world of the unknown or unknowables, of extreme and systemic risks, are more economic, philosophical and strategic than statistical and probabilistic (Diebold et al., 2010: 29).

10. The Critical Turn: The Renaissance of Practical Wisdom

Not everything that can be counted counts,
and not everything that counts can be counted.
(Attributed to Albert Einstein)

The moral of the story of the preceding discussion in Part I could well be that quantitative approaches to assessing and managing (extreme and systemic) risk ought to be abandoned, which goes beyond the conclusions reached in Part I. One might argue in favor of reinventing finance (Shiller, 2012: xii) and that uncertainties, as contrasted with clearly measurable risks which are not to be expected (see Chapter 7, where "our [supposedly] best tools [might have] prove[d] to be our worst instruments"; Blyth, 2010: 453), require a broader, more forward-looking and strategy-oriented approach to risk management.

Indeed, it is recognized by many that risk management in banks "is undergoing a quiet revolution, moving from an essentially compliance-driven, quantitative control function[244] toward a senior-management capability relevant at the highest levels of decision-making and strategy setting" (McNish et al., 2013: 1). In other words, senior management has shifted the notion of risk management from a disciplinary, backward-facing craft building on an exclusively defined technical expertise in risk management departments for the *counting of risks* to a forward-directed practice, offering knowledge and strategic advice tailored to management needs; proving that, even without elaborate calculations, *risks can count* (Mikes, 2011: 240; Power, 2007: 122). A critical finance, management and accounting society or community (or simply: critical finance society) emerged in the face of the recent crisis that erupted in 2008, which encouraged Power (2009) to conclude that the risk management of everything (Power, 2004b) turns out to be the risk management of nothing (cf. also Taleb, 2007a). We reproduce their views, critique, and learnings in a summarized form in this Chapter 10. To some

244 There often exists an illusion of control (Helbing, 2013: 51).

extent, we will build on their findings, which guide us, on the other hand, to an engagement with scenario analysis.

It has been witnessed by this community (e.g., by Brose et al., 2014a: 369; Mikes, 2009a; MacKenzie, 2006) that risk management has its own "calculative culture" determined by "cultural cartographers": Some draw the boundaries of quantitative risk management around the body of a loss distribution, others substantiate claims on the probabilistic modeling and control[245] of uncertainties, dragon kings, and systemic risks for which trustworthy measurements do not (yet) exist (Mikes, 2011: 230). The critics say that those *calculative idealists* display quantitative enthusiasm, glorifying "*optimization*" and "*efficiency*" ("doing things right") of a peculiar unchallenged strategy or course of action, without a preceding determination of a proper starting point (Drucker, 2006) for tackling extreme and systemic risks within dynamic and complex financial systems. Instead, they "aim to manage risk 'by the numbers', replacing judgmental risk assessments with risk quantification" (Mikes, 2009a: 8). The consensus, according to the observations of the critical finance community, seems to be that any risk model output is better than none – even if it is wrong (Mandelbrot & Taleb, 2010: 52). In this sense, "calculative idealists are reductivists" (Power, 2007: 120) and blinded. We strengthen and clarify this characterization of calculative idealism by the critical finance society through introducing the subsequent proposition.

Proposition 8:

Quantitative risk management, as practiced by banks that narrowly focus on probabilistic risk models and use them to colonize hitherto uncontrolled and wild (unstable) areas of uncertainty, extreme and systemic risks, has no functional, economic function, but seems to be ceremonial, a signaling exercise.

This thesis is in need of further evidence and arguments from the literature, as well as of examples abetting it. Scherer & Marti (2008: 279), for instance, appear to raise a similar objection when they reclaim that "[i]t has to be analyzed whose interests are served by the models developed with a technical cognitive interest". Rebonato (2007: 253) disillusions picturesquely that "banks were not battening

245 Focusing on risk control by measurement (Mikes, 2011: 241).

down the hatches against the perfect storm. Rather, much as a peacock parading its beautiful but ultimately useless tail, they were engaging in a *signaling exercise* [emphasis added]". "[T]hey wanted to send to bond-holders and shareholders signals that had become linked to the granting of credit ratings" (ibid.: 252).

McGoun (1995: 185) adds with regard to the ceremonial character of developing and applying (at least some) stochastic risk models that they set standards that facilitate exclusion: "Mathematics, like medieval Latin, is a medium of disputation in economics wherein those skillful in its use can subdue those who are not, independent of any substantive economic meaning". Attempts of quantifying and calculating risk "are very opaque, and appear to be 'a special kind of alchemy'" (Esposito, 2011: 131; Bougen, 2003). "The desire to have a 'magic formula', a single number capable of encapsulating and resolving the complexity of financial decision making, is understandable but does not improve the practice of risk management" (Rebonato, 2007: 256). Bernstein (1996a: 47) cautions, risk management could become "a new kind of religion, a creed that is just as implacable, confining, and arbitrary as the old". An *over*reliance on probabilities "may lead to errors as serious as those committed by ancient priests who relied on omens and offerings" (Boatright, 2011: 3; cf. also Ferguson, 2008; Bernstein, 1996b: 336).

In sharp contrast to this style of risk management of calculative idealism, the critical finance society places a much lesser degree of "trust in numbers" (Porter, 1995) accompanied by risk analytics because, for example, relying on a single number may itself be an operational risk (model risk; Wilson, 2001; Taleb et al., 2009: 80). The old narrative of the persuasive triumph of the undisputable efficiency "of risk scoring over the relative inefficiency of human 'judgmental' decision-making" (Marron, 2007: 113) needs to be replaced in their opinion. In light of probability-based risk models that have (all too) often failed in the past, it is tried to manage, to *verstehen*[246] uncertainty in academia (e.g., Mikes, 2011;

246 The juxtaposition of Erklären vs. Verstehen is well-known (e.g., Lane, 2000: 13; von Mises, 1949/1998: 49f.). Whereas natural scientific explanation is Erklären, Verstehen is the hermeneutical process of understanding and interpreting the subjective meaning that humans attach to objects and to their actions. Critical Theorists – and other humanities scholars – are profoundly suspicious of Erklären, of this form of determinism, believing that "social life [does] not lend itself to such causal explanation" (Morrow & Brown, 1994: 94).
"The balance of appropriate explanation in social sciences (Erklären versus Verstehen) is widely seen to vary with the detail of the phenomena studied" (Lane, 2000: 13).

Redak, 2011; Blyth, 2010; Power, 2009; Daníelsson, 2002) and in the economic practice (e.g., the Swiss Re Liability Risk Drivers™ model, cf. Swiss Re, 2016; Gotebank in Mikes, 2009a), which is a key aspect of organizational reality (Stacey, 2010: 53). According to the critical finance society, emphasis is on the decision level, on decision-making competence and *effective* decision-making and learning.

By using 'softer' instrumentation with more qualitative calibration (Power, 2004a) "to frame and visualize non-measurable uncertainties" (Mikes, 2011: 227), managers and leaders of financial firms should be sensitized for the myths of optimization, complexity and blind efficiency seeking. Advocates of such a critical turn can be regarded as quantitative skeptics (Power, 2003, 2007; Mikes, 2009b, 2011) that revolt against a "tyranny of numbers" (Boyle, 2001), a "new kind of religion" that has turned us into slaves (Bernstein, 1996a: 47) and the "quantificational spirit" of our age (Mikes, 2010: 2). They are "weary of promoting risk control as an 'answer machine'" (Mikes, 2009a: 8; Burchell et al., 1980). The critical finance community considers risk management to be more art than science, resisting "the urge to push metrics into carefully protected areas of judgment" (Mikes, 2011: 227). Risk figures are viewed as mere trend indicators (*calculative pragmatism*; Power, 2007), which they seek to complement, and often overwrite by practical wisdom (Schwartz & Sharpe, 2010), by senior managerial discretion, experience and judgment (Cassidy, 2010: 3; Bhidé, 2010).

Rather than falling prey to temptations of 'taming' Risk I (Appendix A) and reducing it to measurable silos of risk, this critical finance approach puts focus on risk anticipation and "envisioning risks" based on actors' mental models, prior experience and intuition (Mikes, 2011: 241). It manages uncertainty by first and foremost "articulating alternative futures and their implications for the business in order to encourage wider discussion and debate among decision makers" (ibid.: 237). This is the essence of scenario planning, as being introduced in the next chapter, that has been located in the realm of qualitative risk management activities.

But before we turn to this principal tool of qualitative risk management (e.g., Brose et al., 2014a: 369; Diebold et al., 2010: 25) which has been promoted by, among others, the critical finance society, Table 6 summarizes their insights and beliefs and provides from *this* angle a juxtaposition of quantitative risk modeling and qualitative risk analyses along different criteria.

Table 6: [247] A critic's comparison of quantitative risk modeling (theme of Part I) and qualitative risk analyses (theme of Part II).

	Quantitative risk modeling	*Qualitative risk analyses*
Underlying worldview	Mechanical worldview (see 6.1.1. & 6.1.2.) and 'analytical' approach	Complexity worldview*?* At least, more holistic view
The function of risk management	Computation tool	'Learning machine'
Span of quantitative risk management (attempts)	Risks I, including extreme and systemic risks	Only quantifiable risks (e.g., corresponding to the body of a return or loss distribution)
Tools of risk assessment / management	- Value at Risk (VaR) - Expected Shortfall (ES) - …	- Scenario planning - Stress testing - …
Time perspective	Modeling based and depending on historical data	More forward-looking, risk anticipation
Strategic significance of risk management	Derived from the integration of risk management with planning and performance management	Derived from influencing top-level decision-making (providing a 'strategic view' of risks)
Calculative culture	*Quantitative enthusiasm*: - Risk numbers are deemed representative of the underlying economic reality - Emphasis on the 'robust' and 'hard' nature of modeling - *Calculative idealism* and *economic imperialism*: Replacing judgmental risk assessments with risk quantification - Risk control by measurement	*Quantitative skepticism*: - Placing a much lesser degree of "trust in numbers" (Porter, 1995) - Risk numbers are taken as trend indicators - Focus on "softer" instrumentation and envisioning risks - Emphasis on learning about the underlying risk profile from the trend signals

In the following, the strong link between risk thinking and scenario-thinking, as perceived for example by Renn (2008), is esteemed and illuminated. As humans have the ability to design different futures, they "construct scenarios that serve as tools for the human mind in order to anticipate consequences in advance and to change, within the constraints of nature and culture, their course of actions accordingly. If the future were either predetermined or independent of today's human activities [i.e., if there was no reason to engage in scenario planning; C.H.], the term 'risk' would make no sense." (Ibid.: 1).

247 A simpler form of Table 1 can be found in Mikes (2009a: 35).

Considering risk management to be more art than science (Mikes, 2011: 237), that uncertainty should be diminished as far as it can be, but no further (Schoemaker, 2002: 66), and given the necessity of (expert) judgment (Power, 2007: 202; Bhidé, 2010), alternative futures in terms of their implications for the business or venture should be developed, articulated and made use of in order to foster wider discussion and debate among decision-makers.

11. Scenario Planning in a Nutshell and its Role in Risk Management in Banking

The distinctions between qualitative (see this Part II) and quantitative (see Part I above) approaches have been sharply etched and, as underscored by Forrester (1975: 48) or Rapoport (1953), somewhat exaggerated.[248] Yet, "the proper impression emerges – the 'art' of the former is still better able to deal with decisions of great consequence than the 'science' of the latter" (Forrester, 1975: 48). The anthropomorphic desiderata of good and effective (risk management) decisions, resilience, and flexibility (Brose et al., 2014a: 369; Helbing, 2013; Detken & Nymand-Andersen, 2013; Sheffi, 2005) become more important than preciseness, efficiency and optimization under conditions of *v*olatility, *u*ncertainty, *c*omplexity, and *a*mbiguity that characterize our world, a so-named "VUCA world" (Bennett & Lemoine, 2014; Kleindorfer, 2010: 185; see Chapter 6 for a deeper analysis of complex systems). In situations under these conditions, where single forecasts often pretend false certainty (Burt et al., 2006; Roxburgh, 2009), scenario planning has been honored as a key approach to cope with the challenges (Kleindorfer, 2010: 187; Varum & Melo, 2010; Roxburgh, 2009; Postma & Liebl, 2005) as it provides descriptions of multiple possible futures (Brummell & Macgillivray, 2008) and appears to recognize today's global business environment as complex and rapidly changing (Burt et al., 2006; Georgantzas & Acar, 1995). In particular, it is, together with stress testing, the principal tool of analysis in the domain of "Unknowns" and qualitative financial risk management (Diebold et al., 2010: 25); although scenario planning and stress testing are fa-

248 An example of overstating the juxtaposition would be to regard scenario analysis as a purely qualitative tool while scenarios are in fact often quantified (e.g., "in terms of volume, price, impact on individual oil producers [etc.]"; Wack, 1985a: 82). In addition to that, scenario analysis can be combined with other 'qualitative' uncertainty coping tools, e.g. Delphi analysis, a structured, interactive group communication and judgmental forecasting process (Donohoe & Needham, 2009; Linstone & Turoff, 1975) by means of which quantitative probabilities of each scenario can be gained (Walsh, 2005; Schoemaker, 2002: 106).

vored by regulators (ibid.) while banks' risk managers still privilege quantitative approaches (Pergler & Freeman, 2008: 13; Mehta et al., 2012).[249]

In the late 1960s and early 1970s, the oil company Shell pioneered a technique known as "scenario planning". "By listening to planners' analysis of the global business environment, Shell's management was prepared for the eventuality – if not the timing – of the 1973 oil crisis" (Wack, 1985a: 73). The main lines on which the Shell scenario approach operates would not be that it would yield meticulous forecasts, but rather that "it focuses attention on the specification of different sets of reasonable, or even unreasonable but not ignorable, assumptions" (Lee, 1976: 151) that result in *ex ante* forecast outcomes which should be read as counterfactuals or potential histories, serving in turn as basis for decision-making. The decision-maker needs "to confront multiple futures and consider them all equally plausible" (Van der Heijden, 2009: 99; Schoemaker, 2002: 15). In the interim, Shell's scenario planning approach has disseminated widely from Shell. It is now a standard tool for planning activities that span the medium and long term (Probst & Bassi, 2014: 156). Scenarios have become popular and reached banking among others.

The word "scenario", however, is not very well defined in the literature; it is used for many different contexts, approaches and tools (Van der Heijden, 2009: 113). A scenario can be circumscribed as a coherent but contrasting (with regard to at least one other) picture of a future which the company might have to face or to express "expectations of possible future events […], used to analyse potential responses to new and upcoming developments" (Probst & Bassi, 2014: 155). (Cf. also Brummell & Macgillivray, 2008; Comes et al., 2011.)

Scenarios serve multiple purposes

First of all, they draw comprehensive pictures of possible futures and enhance the comprehension of the environment; "better quality thinking about the future" (Van der Heijden, 2009: 6; Vecchiato, 2012; Johnston et al., 2008). Scenario planning as a speculative exercise does not claim that scenarios will materialize as such; "they are not meant to be tested against what actually will happen" (Van der Heijden, 2009: 110). The test is so to speak "whether they represent our current best knowledge of the situation and outlook, our current process theories,

249 This can serve as a rationale for Part II being much smaller than Part I. See also Conjecture 9.

and thereby lead to better strategies" (ibid.). As part of the future analysis, drivers of relevant future developments are identified (Gudonavičius et al., 2009; Brummell & Macgillivray, 2008; Burt et al., 2006). In addition to that, scenarios may uncover the effects that different drivers might have as well as the dynamic interrelations of these drivers and allow for the derivation of strategic implications (Johnston et al., 2008; Burt et al., 2006; Walsh, 2005). Scenario development widens executives' horizons by opening their eyes for strategically relevant possibilities that would otherwise be ignored (Walsh, 2005). In this regard, "[t]he scenarios are an important tool in a larger learning process" (Van der Heijden, 2009: 118). The aim is to prompt "decisions that are more robust under a variety of alternative futures [i.e., '*multifuture robust*' instead of 'single-future robust' decisions]" (ibid.: 5); to challenge prevailing mental models and change given mindsets, thereby triggering organizational learning (Johnston et al., 2008; Postma & Liebl, 2005). "[U]nless we influenced the mental image, the picture of reality held by critical decision makers, our scenarios would be like water on a stone" (Wack, 1985a: 85). Designing scenarios is thus closely bound to the decision level. Good scenarios push to action, respond to managers' deepest concerns and supply a vital "bridge"; "they must encompass both managers' concerns [the world of perceptions] and external reality [the world of facts]. Otherwise, no one will bother to cross the bridge." (Ibid.: 87).

Moreover, application of the scenario approach allows for identifying, testing, refining and evaluating strategic options and their payoffs across different situations (Ram et al., 2011; Johnston et al., 2008; Brummell & Macgillivray, 2008; Postma & Liebl, 2005) if "(1) [scenarios] are based on a sound analysis of reality, and (2) they change the decision makers' assumptions about how the world works and compel them to reorganize their mental model of reality" (Wack, 1985a: 74). This is said to lead to improved organizational preparedness (Roxburgh, 2009; Brummell & Macgillivray, 2008), the acknowledgement, structuring, understanding and possibly reduction of uncertainty, and the enhancement of strategic decisions (Varum & Melo, 2010; Brummell & Macgillivray, 2008).

Process of developing and using scenarios

Albeit there is no completely standardized process of developing or using scenarios and different approaches may show individual characteristics (Postma & Liebl, 2005), the following key steps are considered essential: (1) determination of a focal question, field of interest, (2) identification and analysis of key driving forces, (3) generation and description of scenarios, (4) derivation of strategic implications (Wright & Cairns, 2011; Brummell & Macgillivray, 2008; Kosow & Gaßner, 2008). These four steps can be extended and refined from a systemic viewpoint (see Figure 20 below).

For generating and describing scenarios (step 3), literature defines some quality criteria. Each scenario needs to be plausible, which means that it does not transcend what is realistically possible and coherent. It should contain descriptions of specific developments, i.e., sequences of events, actions, etc. (Kosow & Gaßner, 2008); and the constellation of a set of influencing factors that forge this scenario and affect the result of a chosen (business) strategy within this scenario (Klein & Scholl, 2004; Thomas, 2001; Gausemeier et al., 1998). Structure and patterns – usually captured "as the need for internal consistency in scenarios" (Van der Heijden, 2009: 102; Lee, 1976: 152) – as well as a challenging narrative description of possible futures in the external world play a decisive role in all scenario design. Causal links indicating why a scenario might arise are made obvious, clear, and consistent (Comes et al., 2011; Kosow & Gaßner, 2008). Furthermore, the entire set of scenarios, which should not be too big (otherwise, it becomes unmanageable for most decision makers; Wack, 1985b), is requested to be mutually exclusive and collectively exhaustive (Klein & Scholl, 2004). Finally, "scenarios should be as value free as possible" (Van der Heijden, 2009: 128).

Scenario planning and systems thinking

Lee (1976) was early in advocating a mixed approach to forecasting in which regularities from the historical record are assembled with various possible assumed *structural* changes. "Events are the raw material we work from to build up our understanding. While considering multiple events we have observed we start seeing trends and patterns. [...] [W]e wonder where this order comes from. This is the origin of causal thinking. It leads to implying an underlying structure behind the events we are observing." (Van der Heijden, 2009: 103). And this is basically where the art of *systems thinking* sets in, which is all about "the ability to see through the complexity to what is really essential" (Senge, 1992: 62). In effect, it "lies in seeing through the detail complexity [the sort of complexity in which there are many variables or events, see 2.1., Chapter 6, and Senge, 2006: 71f.; C.H.] to the underlying structures generating change. Systems thinking does not mean ignoring detail complexity. Rather, it means organizing detail complexity into a coherent story that illuminates the causes of problems and how they can be remedied in enduring ways." (Senge, 2006: 124, 69). "[I]n systems thinking an attempt is made to evaluate performance of a system as a part of the larger system that contains it" (Ackoff, 1974: 15).

Scenario planning *without* systems thinking would end up "painting lovely pictures of the future with no deep understanding of the forces that must be mastered to move from here to there" (Senge, 2006: 12).[250]

Scenario planning has become an important tool of systems theories (Ulrich & Probst, 1990: 158-173): Scenarios are part of a larger, holistic and systemic problem solving process, which is iterative (ibid.: 114; 224, Abb. 91); they explore the structure of the system to provide a comprehension of how it may react to imposed and/or emerging changes (Probst & Bassi, 2014: 161).

From a systems perspective, scenario analysis not only involves developing scenarios (steps 1-3 in the following), but also analyzing interventions and system responses (steps 4-6). "The art of scenarios is not mechanistic but organic; whatever we had learned after one step advanced us to the next" (Wack, 1985a: 74). Wack (1985a: 77) distinguishes, for example, between "exploratory first-generation scenarios", on the one hand, and "proper decision scenarios", on the other, throughout the iteration (see Figure 20). The former is especially systemic

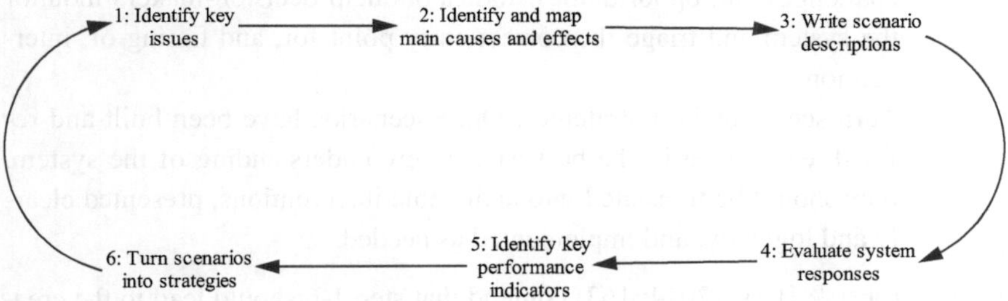

Figure 20: Scenario planning as a circular and iterative process from a feedback view of the world (Source: Probst & Bassi, 2014: 162).

250 However, one might also concede that systems thinking is a popular and shimmering, but also a poor and delusive concept. For example, in contrast to the sometimes endorsed reduction of systems thinking to CLD (e.g., at the International Systems Dynamics Conference 2014 in Delft; cf. also Warren, 2008: 191f.), it must be said that drawing a diagram of interdependencies in terms of feedback loops is not systems thinking. It is a diagram.

in nature as their goal is not action but understanding. "Their purpose is to give insight into the system, to identify the predetermined elements, and to perceive connections among various forces and events driving the system. As the system's interrelatedness became clear, we realized that what may appear in some cases to be uncertain might actually be […] *not* possible" (ibid.: 78).

Following the lead of Probst & Bassi (2014: 162f.), the individual steps along the circle can be described as follows.

1) Identify the issue to be analyzed: Scenarios are best suited to look at the future through the lens of a specific issue.
2) Identify key causes and main drivers of systems: These are the factors that are most relevant for the focal issue and are responsible for generating the system's observed and future patterns of behavior.
3) Write scenario descriptions, fully explaining the underlying drivers (e.g., feedbacks) of each scenario. These are the stories that try to explain how driving forces interact and what effects they have on the system and the analyzed problem.
4) Evaluate the system responses of each scenario. Each scenario, describing occurrences and processes in the system, is likely to trigger different feedbacks and response mechanisms.
5) Identify the main indicators to be monitored to anticipate upcoming challenges and opportunities. Indicators help decision-makers monitor the system and triage the correct entry point for, and timing of, intervention.
6) Turn scenarios into strategies. Once scenarios have been built and refined, expressing in the best case a new understanding of the system, they should be translated into actionable interventions, presented clearly and logically, and implemented as needed.

Finally, Probst & Bassi (2014: 163) contend that step 1-6 should lead to the creation of scenarios and derived actions that are plausible, consistent, relevant, creative and challenging.

Scenario planning in a risk management context

Above all, scenario planning finds its way into banks' risk management in the guise of *stress testing*. Stress testing concerns formulating and calibrating scenarios used to determine the stability of a given (financial) system or entity (e.g., a bank) within the system; scenarios that put the spotlight on extreme and systemic risks and expose potential vulnerabilities (Mark & Krishna, 2014: 53; Diebold et al., 2010: 25; Sheffi, 2005: 20). A real-world example of a (by their own account) "forward-looking" modeling approach that operates with loss scenarios is Swiss Re's proprietary Liability Risk Drivers™ scheme (Swiss Re, 2016). Another impactful, intuitively appealing proposal comes from Rebonato (2010) who positions stress testing as a bridge between the statistical areas of Risk II, where VaR, ES etc. can be effective, and the domain of Risk I and deep uncertainty by laying down the quantitative foundations, i.e., Hierarchical Bayesian Networks, for stress tests to obtain a coherent output that can satisfy the needs of industry users and regulators.

In terms of the identification of the main system drivers for forging scenarios (step 2 in Figure 20), careful attention should be directed to which relationships will continue to hold and which relationships will break down in times of stress (Diebold et al., 2010: 25). Therefore, it would be sensible to couple stress testing and scenario planning or qualitative risk analysis, in general, with a systems theoretical (modeling and simulation) approach, like not only Dynamic Bayesian Networks (which is however probabilistic), but also System Dynamics (Garbolino et al., 2016), favoring the development of a dynamic risk assessment framework. Stress testing helps bank firms "assess major changes in one or two specific variables whose effects would be major and immediate, although the exact timing is not forecastable" (Kaplan & Mikes, 2012: 57f.). They employ stress tests to assess, for example, how an event such as a large swing in interest or exchange rates, the tripling of prices for stocks, commodities etc., or the default of a major institution (e.g., LTCM, see 5.2.) or sovereign country (e.g., Greece) would affect trading positions and investments. Banks usually place limits on the outcome of stress tests, which "should anticipate and compensate for an attempt to model a participant's (e.g., management or trader) behavior and potential actions to stay below a stress test limit in a stress environment" (Mark & Krishna, 2014: 54).

"Scenarios can be created based on perceived risks to the portfolio (e.g., a scenario of sharply rising interest rates may be relevant to a yield-curve sensitive portfolio). Alternatively, historical or hypothetical events can be used to determine the effect on underlying risk factors (interest rates, equity indices, commodity prices, etc.), which can then be applied against the firm's portfolio. In practice, firms often use a hybrid approach by creating hypothetical scenarios informed by market behavior during real events." (Mark & Krishna, 2014: 54f.). Stress testing, the consideration and simulation of shocks and crises, is not dependent on their realization and may be of help even if such extreme events never occur. "The data necessary to simulate a crisis may prove useful in monitoring vulnerability [i.e., the inability of a system to withstand the effects of the environment; C.H.] and a careful consideration of the consequences of such a crisis may lead to changes in strategy and/or risk management. Crises seldom unfold according to the anticipated scenario, but strategies for responding to one kind of shock may prove useful when a different kind of shock occurs. For example, evacuation procedures that Morgan Stanley established after the bombing of the World Trade Center in 1993 enabled the firm to safeguard all of their employees in the much more severe terrorist attack on September 11, 2001." (Diebold et al., 2010: 26).

12. Strengths and Weaknesses of Scenario Planning as a Risk Management Tool

There could be good reasons for believing that forecasts of any kind and importance are inherently fallible (Wack, 1985a: 73), given dynamic complexity (a specific reason) and given that the future is invariably a combination of the known and the *unknown* or *unknowable* (Diebold et al., 2010) and the proportion of the latter tends to rise as the time-scale extends (a general reason, etc.). A more limited aspiration, of identifying *a range* of versions of what *might* happen, could be, however, a tenable and supportable basis for (qualitative) risk and planning analysis. Precisely, the aim of problem structuring methods like scenario planning is both more modest and more ambitious than that of the previous generation of exact probability-based risk measurement methods (Part I), branding efficiency seeking management of risks in financial systems. More modest, "because they do not set out to capture a single truth [noting that literature also discusses *imprecise* probabilities; C.H.] about the situation from which the one best answer can be derived" (Rosenhead & Mingers, 2009: 2). More ambitious, "because their aim is rather to provide useful assistance to those processes of dialogue and debate which prepare the way for decisions that significantly affect future prospects" (ibid.).

The scenario development and analysis may need a lot of resources and it is difficult to evaluate the effectiveness of the method tout court (Johnston et al., 2008). Moreover, the following more concrete features (Table 7) are seen as key advantages and disadvantages of scenario planning, underscoring that it can be an adequate informative aid to dealing with uncertainty, but is, at the same time, in need of revision for the purposes here (see Part III for a constructive answer).

Table 7: Strengths and weaknesses of scenarios and scenario analysis.

Strengths	Weaknesses
General	
- Scenarios nurture *innovative thinking* about possible future behavioral paths of the systems (Probst & Bassi, 2014: 157); - "better *quality thinking* about the future" (Van der Heijden, 2009: 6).	- The success of the scenario analysis is *contingent on many conditions*: e.g., the plausibility and relevance of scenarios, their coherence, a challenging narrative description of scenarios, etc. - Scenarios require *continuous revision, refinement and control* by a specialized team (Probst & Bassi, 2014: 157).
- Scenarios are an important tool in a larger *learning process* (Van der Heijden, 2009: 118).	- The *interface* of scenarios and decision makers might be ignored or neglected (Wack, 1985b). - Scenarios are *ineffective* if not integrated into the decision-making process (Probst & Bassi, 2014: 157).
- Scenario planning *accepts uncertainty, unpredictability, and vagueness*, and aims to offer *orientation* only (Rosenhead & Mingers, 2009: 11).	- Scenario planning is afflicted with *vagueness, impreciseness,* and a *vulnerability to multiple interpretations* or *concretizations,* and offers at best some *orientation* only.
- People are conceptualized as *active subjects* (Rosenhead & Mingers, 2009: 11)	- In general, *tools*, including scenario planning *and* probabilistic risk models, are *only as good as the people that develop or use them.*
- *Diminished* data demands, achieved by greater *integration* of hard and soft data with social judgments (Rosenhead & Mingers, 2009: 11)	- *Inadequate for short-term planning*: The continuous repetition of the exercise may simply add confusion, as the methodology does not apply well to technical decisions that have to be implemented in the short term (Probst & Bassi, 2014: 157).
- Scenarios abet the *monitoring and identification* of potential future *challenges* resulting from implemented actions (Probst & Bassi, 2014: 157)	- Scenarios require a *disciplined* monitoring, analysis and communication process (Probst & Bassi, 2014: 157).
- To the extent that scenario development stimulates creative thinking and controversial debate (Ringland, 2006), it is supposed to *avoid common errors and biases* like overconfidence, misjudgment of likelihoods and tunnel vision (Comes et al., 2011; Schoemaker, 1995; Eisenhardt, 1989).	- *Cognitive biases*: For example, a design that includes three scenarios describing alternative outcomes along a single dimension is dangerous because many managers cannot resist the temptation to spot the middle scenario as a baseline. A scheme based on two scenarios raises a similar risk if one is easily seen as optimistic and the other pessimistic. Etc. Wack, 1985b.
- Companies find themselves testing a wide *range of hypotheses*, imagining (some/many?) *alternative futures*, involving changes in all sorts of underlying drivers (Roxburgh, 2009)	- Scenarios can induce "a sense of *complacency*, of having all your bets covered" (Roxburgh, 2009). It is *not* possible that scenarios cover the *full range of (future) possibilities*, they "leave you exposed exactly when scenarios provide most comfort. […] We are typically too optimistic going into a downturn and too pessimistic on the way out. No one is immune to this trap, including professional builders of scenarios and the companies that use them." (Ibid.).

	- Likewise, the future is multivariate, and there are elements users will miss when they create scenarios that fall on a single spectrum ("very good", "good", "not so good", "very bad").
Looking at the scenario planning function from the systems approach	
- There is both benefit in the *product* and the *process* (Brummell & Macgillivray, 2008), as the very process of developing scenarios breeds a lot of *insights and understanding* (Meristö, 1989; Roxburgh, 2009) by finding *structure* in the events in the environment (Van der Heijden, 2009: 102).	- Scenarios attempt to give the *whole cause-and-effect story*, leading to a *comprehension* of why things happen. But for this reason they are also *less efficient* as input to yes/no type decision-making. It is *less straightforward* to make a decision on the basis of a set of scenarios than a forecast. (Van der Heijden, 2009: 110).
- Scenarios help decision-makers behold elements of *uncertainty* (Probst & Bassi, 2014: 158).	- Scenarios are too *passive* (Ackoff, in Schoemaker, 2002: 169) and *broad* (Roxburgh, 2009): Emphasizing the search for *external* scenarios leads to a paralysis or passivity about controlling the future. The *endogenous* point of view is the *sine qua non* of systems approaches (Richardson, 2011). - Tools are required that capture not only uncertainties, but that are able to deal with dynamic *complexity* (because complexity is a source of uncertainty; Proposition 2)
- Scenarios do *not* normally produce conclusions in a *mechanistic* way (Probst & Bassi, 2014: 157; Van der Heijden, 2009).	- Scenario planning relies on a *broad notion of scenarios* and can be spelled out very differently in *different contexts*. In particular, developing, analyzing and employing scenarios as a veritable expression of *systems thinking* is by no way certain or compulsory.
- Scenario planning is *non-optimizing*; it seeks alternative solutions which are acceptable on *separate dimensions*, without trade-offs (Rosenhead & Mingers, 2009: 11)	- Grasping scenario planning as a form of *analysis* compromises its potential as a systems tool since systems thinking would require both analysis *as well as synthesis* – systems thinking is *circular* (Schwaninger, 2005: 32, 37) - The call to incorporate systems thinking in the tool of scenario planning (Senge, 2006) is somehow vague, abstract and obscure.
	- There is nothing that is obviously beneficial about a scenario planning activity, simply because some group of people will be the planners and we have *no special reason to trust them* (Churchman, 1968: 149).
	- *VUCA conditions* render useless any efforts to spot the future and to plan responses. Bennett & Lemoine (2014) demonstrate that by overlooking important differences in the conditions that volatility, uncertainty, complexity, and ambiguity describe, we have *disempowered* leaders.

Specific evaluation in a risk management context

Advantages

With regard to the plea by the critical finance community that risk management ought to be characterized more by learning and experiment rather than by rule-based processes, scenario planning should be appreciated as it depends essentially on human capacities to "imagine *alternative futures* to the present rather than quantitative ambitions to predict *the* future" (Power, 2004b: 61). Scenario planning places emphasis on the decision level, on decision-making competence and *effective* decision-making and learning. Another benefit of using a scenario analysis for risk management is that "stress tests can be incorporated as scenarios that a simulation engine can evaluate, thereby bridging stress testing analysis and analysis of more continuous deviations from current state under one roof" (Braswell & Mark, 2014: 263; Rebonato, 2010). Stress tests can help in deciding in advance the actions to take in response to large market moves and they are sometimes used as a way to allocate capital (Mark & Krishna, 2014: 54). Scenarios improve *multi-stakeholder, cross-sectoral* risk management (Probst & Bassi, 2014: 157). Moreover, stress tests can be *easily communicated* to senior management since "the loss outcome(s) being described can be attributed to concrete stress scenarios. For example, a board or executive committee can easily understand a scenario calling for a 20% decline in home prices but would have much greater difficulty understanding what a 99% event looks like." (Rossi, 2014: 92).

Disadvantages

A major issue for scenario planning in combination with stress testing in banking is that the *ignorance towards the upper bound* of possible losses invites *faulty stress testing*. Stress testing resembles a probability-free approach to simulate a single, fixed, large deviation – as if it were the known payoff from a lottery ticket –, ensconced in a protective bubble of parables, otherwise known as scenario descriptions (Taleb, 2008: 2). Against the background of the oil crisis of 1973, Wack (1985b), for example, presents a so-called boom & bust scenario as a series of surprises and their probability of occurrence is not given, nor how severe the bust can turn out to be (e.g., how much money can a bank lose in this scenario?), which might scare banks' risk managers because the information they receive from the model appears to be far too unspecific and, thus, inappropriate for their needs. Considering, for instance, that it is onerous to debate the merits of intuitive (versus a quantitative) criteria or schemes for assessing uncertainties or certain parameters (Shrader-Frechette, 1985: Chapter 6),[251] the matter of defining risk in terms of numbers is crucial. How can managers and investors decide how much risk to take unless they can ascribe some order of magnitude to the risks they face? (Bernstein, 1996b: 259). Taking this exemplary question as prior work into account, we contend the following drastic thesis:

Conjecture 9:

Even though risk managers have been confronted with drawbacks when extreme risks are managed 'by the numbers', they appear to be not willing to embrace unmeasurable uncertainty as long as business is ruled 'by numbers' (which is perhaps even a necessity inherent in financial and economic systems)[252].

But also the choice of a 'maximum (likely)' jump of the loss function would be problematic, as it pre- supposes knowledge of the structure of the distribution in the tails (Taleb, 2008: 2).[253] Stress testing thus suffers from the same limitation as VaR or probabilistic analyses: Even extreme historical events may not be a reliable indicator for future turmoils, they may not be sufficiently stressful (Rossi, 2014: 93).

Moreover, "[h]ypothetical (i.e., non-historical) scenarios can be arbitrarily extreme but, whether hypothetical or historical, scenarios must be credible and achieve buy-in from management. It is difficult to imagine management teams before the crisis placing much credence in stress test results based on a nationwide collapse in home prices as experienced in the years after the boom." (Ibid.).

251 Even if such a criterion could be formulated clearly (a big if), "participants in the debate are likely to approach it in terms of radically different assumptions" (Shrader-Frechette, 1985: 166).

252 Quantifications cannot be avoided when it comes to economic activities, such as the allocation and distribu-tion of goods (Wieland, 1996: 34, 36f.). The form of a numerical representation improves the practicality of business processes and might also be a prerequisite for them to take place in the first place (Boysen, 2002).

253 One illustration of how stress testing can be deemed dangerous is provided by Taleb (2008): "Many firms, such as Morgan Stanley, lost large sums of their capital in the 2007 subprime crisis because their stress test underestimated the outcome – yet was compatible with historical deviations". Traditional stress testing assumes, for example, "that whenever one has seen in the past a large move of, say, 10%, one can conclude that a fluctuation of this magnitude would be the worst one can expect for the future" (Mandelbrot & Taleb, 2010: 52). "Before the crash of 1987 […], stress testing would not have included a 22% drop in share prices within a single day. They [Mandelbrot & Taleb] note that just ten trading days account for 63% of the returns on the stock market over the past 50 years." (Diebold et al., 2010: 26).

Similarly, Mandelbrot & Taleb (2010) caution that traditional stress testing, which relies on selecting a number of worst-case scenarios from the past history and past data, "may be seriously misleading because it implicitly assumes that a fluctuation of this magnitude would be the worst that should be expected. They note that crashes happen without antecedents." (Diebold et al., 2010: 26).[254]

Goodhart (2010) sheds light on a different concern regarding stress testing and scenario planning: "What may matter most in crises are interactive effects that occur when many institutions attempt to adjust their portfolios in the same way at the same time. These are decisive to understanding an institution's vulnerability in a crisis, but are omitted from most scenarios." (Diebold et al., 2010: 26; see 5.1.).

In conclusion, it seems uncontroversial that conventional stress testing (scenario planning), despite its possible inclusion of systems thinking to some extent, (still) rests on the principle that *better risk assessment* (at least in some major part) means *better data* (and not sufficient systems-, complexity- or structure-orientation). Data can be very valuable if tomorrow's world will be much like today's. Under this assumption, which is delicate (see Chapter 7), scenario analysis benefits from better data and data can get better in several ways. One way is new data about phenomena that previously did not exist.

"For example, exchange-traded house price futures contracts have recently begun trading. Many now collect and examine those futures prices, which contain valuable clues regarding the market's view on the likely evolution of house prices. But such data could not have been collected before – they simply did not exist." (Diebold et al., 2010: 5). Due to new data new scenarios could be concocted.

Perhaps most importantly, better financial data and modeling can come out of new insights regarding the determinants of risks and returns (ibid.: 6); see also Chapter 6, where randomness (direct) and complexity (indirect) were identified as determinants of risks, and see Part III. Thus far, literature in both the quantitative (Part I) and qualitative (Part II) camp has, however, treated better risk assessment as mainly better data or progresses in risk measurement due to better data, but what of better tools with which to summarize and ultimately discern complex financial systems where the risks emerge; i.e., really structure-oriented, rather than data-driven models? That is, what of a better *class of models*?

254 In Mandelbrot & Taleb's (2010) view, by contrast, stress test analysis should be complemented with fractal mathematical methods (see also Chapter 2.5.).

13. Deriving Lessons for Rethinking the Approach to Assessing Extreme and Systemic Risks

Faced with the ruins of the house of risk management, we now recognize that the first way to managing extreme and systemic risks effectively (Part I) turned out to be not promising or ineffective (*Propositions 6* and *8*) and that the same holds for the second way in this Part II, which dealt with not quantitative, but qualitative approaches (*Conjecture 9*). Yet, criticizing something is always considerably easier than proposing a constructive alternative. The call for a Third Way, for alternative risk models and measures, better: an alternative class of risk models for complex financial systems thus becomes unmistakable.

In line with the results of Part I and in differentiation to the theses put forward by the critical finance society (Chapter 10), 'trust in numbers' and risk management 'by the numbers' can still be upheld. The Central Argument of Part I of this thesis only passed sentence on *probabilistic* approaches to evaluating extreme and systemic risks (see *Propositions 5* and *6*, but also *8*). The, in some regard, more critical view advanced by the critical finance community, which accuses the 'quantificational spirit' of our age right away, does *not* follow from it (or from Part I altogether). In terms of how risk assessment should work, i.e., become more effective, we share some of the postulates with the critical finance society, including:

- calculative pragmatism in lieu of idealism,
- no gullible efficiency seeking,
- no reduction of risks or uncertainties to measurable silos,
- placing importance on scenario-thinking (especially when linked to systems thinking);

but quarrel with their conclusion: embrace (Knightian) uncertainty and quantitative skepticism. Rather, this study purports

- that our *toolkit* for quantitative risk assessment not only contains probabilistic models, but can be enriched by formal logic and modern computer science based techniques – thereby, we follow the call for a more abstract, less data-centric skill set in risk management (Härle et al., 2016: 5; Brose et al., 2014a: 332):
  - fuzzy logic & non-classical logics for handling uncertainty (see 15.2.),
  - theory of formal (i.e., programming) languages for describing portfolio valuations, etc.;
- that both quantitative and qualitative risk assessment approaches have their strengths which should be unified and augmented:
  - advantages of quantitative approaches: risks can be managed 'by the numbers' (which is crucial, see Conjecture 9), preciseness, rigor, etc.;
  - advantages of qualitative approaches (scenario-thinking): curtailed data demands, modesty (when accepting barely measurable uncertainty), focus on effectiveness and the pursuit of satisficing, non-optimal solutions only, etc.;
- and that our risk modeling endeavors ought to focus on the known,
  - banks' assets and liabilities,
  - structural composition of financial products and instruments (derivatives) through,
  - financial contracts;

  not the unknown,
  - future behavior of the financial system,
  - composition of the financial system,
  - minimum or expected losses, etc.;

and accepts *deep uncertainty*, a subcategory of *Risk I*, emerging from highly organized complexity, (see Chapter 6 and Appendix A) as a fact, not as a problem.

- This study does not state that uncertainty in general would be a given fact (where we could do nothing about it) rather than a problem (which can be solved) because risk is defined in terms of uncertainty (Risk I) and management is about "decision making and decision making involves problem solving" (Ackoff, 1974: 20). Therefore, if we contended that uncertainty would simply be a fact, not a problem, it would not make any sense to become concerned with risk management at all.

- However, concentration on the uncertainty of future outcomes in dynamic and complex financial systems, which pervades both scenario-thinking and quantitative risk management as outlined in Part II and I, respectively, eventually goes hand in hand with problems of induction that, in turn, become fatal in the wake of factual complexity.

To this end, the knowledge dimension needs to be highlighted, and much more than what is typically seen today in risk assessment applications. Our disruptive risk management approach, propounded in the subsequent Part III, is strongly guided by a firm belief that the inclusion of methods from logic and computer science to model the complex factors and structures that determine risk (see the 'iceberg model' in Figure 15) are essential for the establishment of best-practice risk management in banking and beyond. Neither data nor information alone will improve risk management (decisions, see Part IV) "unless the analysis fits the problem" (Brose et al., 2014a: 333). This in turn requires "detailed *structural* data" (ibid.). Part III presents a symbolic approach to risk modeling. It relies on a *quasi* probability theory that is not grounded in analysis, but in algebra, and employs formal languages from functional programming for specifying financial contracts, which allow, for example, to predict the impact of changing correlations on a credit portfolio. We will see and understand that a key benefit of this technique is that a risk model can be derived automatically from a formal description of the individual positions (Jones et al., 2001).

Since this counter-proposal in Part III thus makes use of a formal language as well (like approaches criticized in Part I do), it is important to highlight that we do not seek to radically replace a *risk model* based approach to systemic and extreme risk management by something else (e.g., by qualitative risk analysis tools as Part II suggests). Again, our criticism (Chapter 7) was not of formal methods in general, but of the type of formal method that is used conventionally. In other words, this study *assumes* that formal languages in economics or in risk management contexts, in particular, serve to keep the logic straight, to guarantee that the 'then' does follow the 'if',[255] which it so frequently does not if we just write/use prose (when designing scenarios) because natural languages are basically systems to describe perceptions (Zadeh) and perceptions are imprecise. Further, we *hope* that we are able to uphold that assumption while paying tribute to the critical finance movement, to the finding, for instance, that simply selecting 'ifs' for reasons of conventionality or elegance can be a recipe for great mischief. We further hope to uncover that the following proposal contributes to a truly effective risk management in banking, compared to standard quantitative approaches, on the one hand – insofar, we hope to make use of a *more adequate* formal language –, and compared to qualitative risk and scenario analysis techniques, on the other – insofar, we hope to demonstrate that *our* formal language is *more powerful* than tools referring to common parlance. This valiant goal will be reached by combining the best of both worlds (so to speak) to create an exact, algebraic and explanatory as well as a complexity/systems theory-inspired scenario planning method and, hence, by unveiling a Third Way apart from the ones taken by quantitative enthusiasts and quantitative skepticists.

255 "Mathematics is nothing but a language, with its own grammar and syntax – arguably the simplest, clearest, and most concise language of all" (Sornette, 2003: 135). The mathematical notation used for describing models is unambiguous. It is a language that "is clearer, simpler, and more precise than" such spoken languages as English and its advantage is in the "clarity of meaning and simplicity of language syntax" (Forrester, 1971).

Part III:
In Search of a New Paradigm: The Third Way as a Road to Logic-Based Risk Modeling (LBR)

14. Introduction to Part III

It is high time, however, that we take our ignorance more seriously.
(Friedrich August von Hayek, 1967)

Risk assessment can never fully capture black swans,
but improvements can and should be made compared to the probabilistic approach
that dominates the present quantitative risk assessment practice. […]
The knowledge dimension needs to be highlighted much more strongly […].
(Terje Aven, 2013)

Reconciling right-wing and left-wing politics by advocating a varying synthesis
can be well-captured in The Lord Giddens' metaphor of the Third Way.
In risk management, we find a wing of quantitative idealism and
quantitative scepticism. As an alternative to both, however, we should rely
on precise, rather than non-formal, modelling of what is known
(one's own assets and liabilities) rather than on spuriously precise models of
what is not known (the future behaviour of the financial system).
(Jann Fridolin Müller, 2015)

Every financial crisis is a wake-up call for risk managers: Extreme and systemic risks need to be measured better, they say we must pay more attention to the fat tail of a loss distribution, and so on. But after the models have been tuned and 'improved', the next crisis happens, and the same calls are heard again. The cycle of systemic crisis followed by 'better' risk modeling followed by systemic crisis does not seem to stop – unremitting cycles of 'innovation' in measurement, crisis, and revision, pushing metrics into spheres where the results are "at best ambivalent and at worst dysfunctional" (Power, 2004a: 771).

To this author, this signifies that it is not the parameters of the models which need to be improved (in contrast to so-called quantitative enthusiasts, see Chapter 2 (Part I)), but the models themselves, without throwing out the baby with the bathwater (in contrast to so-called quantitative skepticists, see Chapter 10 (Part II)). Despite the lip service that is often paid to *holistic* risk management (Nario et al., 2016: 24; McNish et al., 2013; Pergler & Lamarre, 2009), a new approach to risk modeling is required, a *hybrid* of scenario-thinking and quantitative ambitions, in order to get a better grasp on just how exposed our (banks') positions are to sudden high-impact, low-probability changes in the environment we operate in. Building better models of extreme and systemic risks is challenging and worthwhile: in this Part III, we will combine the qualitative and the quantitative, imagination and precisiation (which presupposes understanding), art and science, all in the service of achieving truly effective risk management by finding approximate patterns underlying the behavior of financial systems (scenarios) and known/knowable structures of financial instruments or products (via a language for contracts).

As Popper (1963/2002: 38) and after him others have pointed out, "the more we learn about the world and the deeper our learning, the more conscious, specific, and articulate will be our knowledge of what we do not know, our knowledge of our ignorance". A corollary drawn by this study is that we ought to learn enough to know that we cannot know all that we would have to know for a full explanation and prediction as well as an exact assessment of (extreme or systemic) risk phenomena. However, we may partly pierce the boundary and expand the realm of the known by deliberately cultivating a technique which aims at more limited objectives (von Hayek, 1967: 40) – the explanation not of individual *events*, but merely of the appearance of certain *patterns* in the behavior of financial systems as well as the emphasis on fixed *structures* of their subsystems. The focus on engendering insights into the patterns provoked by the systems under study is a consequence of putting emphasis on system understanding (Schwaninger, 2011: 758), which in turn characterizes explanatory models, which this study purports to implant into banks' in-house risk management (see Chapter 8). The service of this approach that does neither tell us what particular events to expect, nor how accurately quantifiable expectations would look like, but only what kinds of more or less likely scenarios we are to expect within a certain range of magnitude (their impact) would perhaps be better described by the terms "systemic explanation" and "orientation"[256] than by speaking of prediction (von Hayek, 1967: 18). Albeit such a modeling technique is limited, "it will make the world around us a more familiar world in which we can move with greater confidence that we shall not be disappointed because we can at least exclude certain eventualities" (ibid.).

256 Note that a function of orientation was also evaluated as a strength (and weakness) of scenario planning in Chapter 12. Here, "orientation" has a more positive connotation because, for example, we will see that the proposal in this Part III does not suffer from vagueness, or a vulnerability to multiple interpretations. See Chapter 19.

The restriction is that the statements from our novel logic-based approach may be less specific (contrasted with those earned on the first way, see Part I), while the extension lies in the fact that we can thereby penetrate into the realm of complex phenomena (Malik, 1996: 205). In this environment, we do not afford to measure uncertainty a priori (which is not possible), nor a posteriori (which gives poor results), but manage uncertainty by focusing on the system structure, which comprises reasoning a priori as well as a posteriori. Another extension is based on a re-examination of the foundations of the modern axiomatic approach to risk measures: Here, we strive for allowing a myriad of new and alternative risk measures, that do not rely on accurate probabilities anymore (which are impossible to obtain) or model outputs in form of a single number (at the expense of analyzing scenarios), but that, instead, come equipped with weaker and less farfetched assumptions and that are open to a variety of formalisms for representing uncertainty. Our framework thus encourages risk modelers to choose whichever representation is best suited to the task; a plea for heterogeneity and diversity which is in line with viewing risk from different angles (e.g., Risk I, Risk II, systemic or extreme risks, deep uncertainty, etc.; see also Condition 1 in 4.1.).

A third main extension of the innovative approach this study is proposing springs from the roots of the Austrian School of Economics[257] and "its unique methodology that is grounded in deduction, [and] *a priorism*" (Spitznagel, 2013: 76). It is the already mentioned shift of focus, from the unknown to the known, which is spelled out hereafter. In the Austrian tradition, we acknowledge that "[o]ne cannot learn from history, *a posteriori*, because causal [and other; C.H.] relationships are deceptively veiled from our perception" (ibid.: 75). "Rather, in many cases the foreseen emerges through the logical rigor of deduction, based on what one knows (and, to some degree, what one observes and experiences) as a sentient human being" (ibid.). Specifically, in our context, banks' assets and liabilities, financial contracts or instruments and their composition as well as other things are known. We ought to utilize this knowledge to measure risks because the past history of an object for risk management, although it should not be ignored, is just to be accepted as *highly insufficient*.

In some sense, it is slightly unrealistic to single out 'logic-based models' as a distinct class within the spectrum of modeling approaches that is paid special

257 Cf. Schulak & Unterköfler (2011) for an overview.

attention to.[258] Nevertheless, there are types of (risk) models "in which representation of the logical structure is the dominant feature" (Flood & Carson, 1993: 188): LBR grasps the structure of financial instruments in a programming language and makes use of fuzzy & non-classical logics for measuring risk (instead of glorifying probability theory as a gold standard). In principle, the employment of such (specifically) logic-based modeling approaches is apt because "[t]hey can provide a clear picture of logical connections and, as such, aid in the understanding of complexity" (ibid.: 189).

Research questions

Pursuing the overarching research question **RQ2** (see also Chapter 3) properly

> **RQ2:**
> How can the measurement and management of systemic or extreme risk be improved to compensate for the shortcomings of conventional quantitative approaches and to account for the financial system's dynamic complexity?

requires to raise certain more specific or sub-questions that guide our research activities in the remaining chapters of this Part III, in order to introduce alternative risk models for complex financial systems and to close the research gap *IV*, respectively.

Sub- or Specific Guiding Questions:

RQ2.1: In what sense is our plea for explanatory risk modeling in banking implemented?
➔ Answered in Chapters 15.4. and 15.6.

RQ2.2: How can the axiomatic approach to risk models by Artzner et al. (1999) be generalized to cover non-probabilistic models of risk?
➔ Answered in Chapter 15.1.

258 "Any model should represent the logical structure and connectivity of the processes under investigation. Equally, assessment of logical consistency is an important ingredient of model validation." (Flood & Carson, 1993: 188). We understand "logic" in a classical way: "Typically, a *logic* consists of a formal or informal language together with a deductive system and/or a model-theoretic semantics" (Shapiro, 2013; cf. also Halpern, 2005: 6).

RQ2.3: To what extent should financial risk modeling make use of 'qualitative' probabilities?

➔ Answered in Chapters 15.1. and 18.

RQ2.4: How can non-probabilistic models of uncertainty within one single formal framework serve as a breeding ground for a new generation of risk management tools that are suited for assessing high-impact, low-probability risks in highly complex financial systems?

➔ Answered in Chapter 15.5.

RQ2.5: What are some concrete LBR models of systemic and extreme risk that fit into the axiomatization developed (in the reply to RQ2.2) and that integrate alternative notions of uncertainty?

➔ Answered in Chapter 16.

RQ2.6: What lessons can be drawn from LBR for actual risk managers and practitioners?

➔ Answered in Chapter 17.

RQ2.7: How are LBR models evaluated against competing probabilistic risk models?

➔ Answered in Chapter 19.

The task ahead is to first delineate the theoretical foundations of our disruptive formalism (Chapter 15). We then test an exemplary LBR risk model, and illustrate our plea for symbolic and logic-based risk modeling with the LTCM example of a liquidity and counterparty risk crisis,[259] followed by an outline of the queries our model will be able to answer (16). We close by ventilating the topic of scales of measurement (18), so-called qualitative probabilities (18), and model validation (19) as well as by detailing lessons for the economic practice (17).

---

259 We are developing a symbolic model of counterparty and liquidity risk, but basically our approach can be generalized to other 'types of risk'. See also Chapter 15.6. and 22.

15. Theoretical Foundations of a Logic-Based Risk Modeling (LBR) Approach

The fact that simple mathematical structures can simulate complex, dynamic systems is well-known and exemplified by, for instance, the “Game of Life” (Berlekamp et al., 2001). Our symbolic models of risk are designed in the tradition of such devices and embedded in a novel LBR approach which consists of three components:

I) A formal framework for risk models, including an axiomatic apparatus (15.1.), and non-probabilistic, but formal representations of uncertainty (15.2.), specifically Spohn’s ranking theory (15.3.);

II) A vocabulary for describing correlations (15.4.), the central and main pillar in Figure 21;

III) An interpretation of this formal language of Jones et al. (2001) for financial contracts in models of extreme and systemic risk (15.5.), as well as of LBR models in total as an exact, explanatory scenario planning method from complexity principles (15.6.).

Parts (I) and (II) are the mathematical underpinnings of part (III), the actual risk models, which is depicted in the following figure. We will now describe the three parts very briefly.

15.1. A less Restrictive Axiomatization

The objective in this subchapter is to generalize the axiomatic approach to risk models by Artzner et al. (1999) to cover non-probabilistic models of risk mainly for two interwoven reasons: On the one hand, we would like to evaluate our risk models in respect to the coherence laws established in their work (see also Chpt. 19), which are widely considered as having achieved the status of a de-facto standard (Riedel, 2004: 186), and, on the other hand, probabilistic models are ineffective for extreme and systemic risks (7.3.).

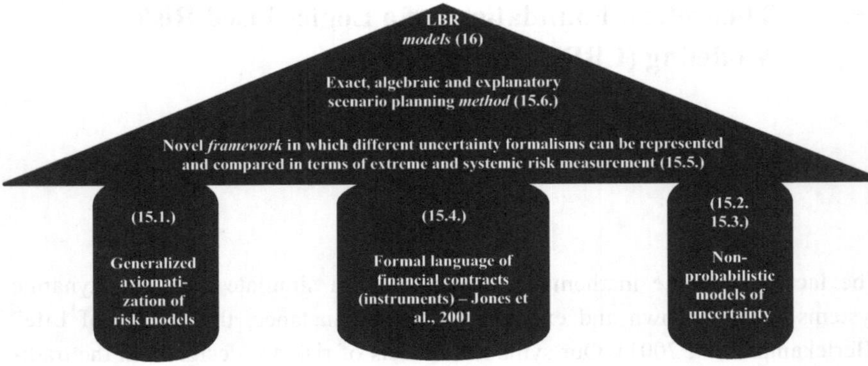

Figure 21: The solid house of LBR: The pillars are well-established in the literature – the right one in the field of formal epistemology, the major load-bearing one in the middle in connection to financial engineering and the left pillar is actually partly new due to the extension of Artzner et al.'s (1999) path-breaking work on risk measurement to non-probabilistic cases. The construction standing on this foundation reflects our principal contribution to research on the constructive side and must be seen as novel in a threefold way: On the broadest scale, LBR represents a whole conceptual framework, on a lower level of abstraction, we refer to LBR as a method which encompasses specific risk models in the most concrete sense of LBR.

Artzner et al. invoke the term "risk" in the tradition of Risk II. The authors assume a probability space $(\Omega, \mathbf{F}, P)$ where, as introduced in 7.2., $\mathbf{F}$ is a σ-field over Ω and P is a probability measure on the measurable space $(\Omega, \mathbf{F})$. Let X be a random variable over the probability space representing the future value of a bank's investments. The key idea now is to introduce the notion of *risk capital*,[260] denoted by m, which is the amount of money that one should invest into a risk-free asset in order to keep the probability of losing X below or equal to a given threshold $1-\alpha$: $P\,(X + m < 0) \leq (1-\alpha)$ (⋮). If we take the smallest value for m that still makes statement ⋮ true, we obtain the well-known VaR measure (2.2.2.): $VaR_\alpha(X) = \inf\{m \in \mathbb{R} \mid P\,(X + m < 0) \leq (1-\alpha)\}$.[261] Other risk measures can be defined in a similar way using the probability space $(\Omega, \mathbf{F}, P)$ and the no-

260 Strictly speaking, Artzner et al. (1999) do not make use of the term "risk capital". They operate with "minimum extra capital" which means that, if invested in the reference instrument, it makes the future value of the modified position become acceptable (ibid.: 204). This, however, is captured by our notion of risk capital.

261 Both definitions (the one in 2.2.2. and the one here in 15.1.) are equivalent, which is evident if we take into account that F is a *loss* distribution and P, in the formulation of Artzner et al., stands for a *value* distribution.

tion of risk capital. In order to respond to RQ2.2, i.e., to generalize the axioms by Artzner et al. (1999), *translation invariance*, *sub-additivity*, *positive homogeneity*, and *monotonicity*,[262] we have to start with the initial definition of a probability space.

Probability space vs. uncertainty space

The construction of a probability space is accompanied by making a bunch of structural assumptions and its full generalization would demand the problematization of every constituent part by heuristically describing and classifying uncertainty (uncertainty mining by means of addressing questions such as: What data is important? What is the quality of the data, the uncertainty about the data? Are sets of data independent? etc.; see also Part IV).[263] We, however, confine ourselves here to generalizing the probability measure P only because this already requires some additional theory which is exposed below in 15.5.[264] For now, where we focus on a generalization of Artzner et al.'s axioms rather than of Kolmogorov's (1933), we sketch the approach in reference to Chapter 7.2., i.e., purged of introducing any further background knowledge, and recall that $P\colon \mathbf{F} \to [0,1]$ such that $P(\Omega) = 1$ and $P(\bigcup A_i) = \Sigma\, P(A_i)$ for all sets $\{A_i\}$ of pairwise disjoint events.

Probability measure vs. uncertainty measure

P will be surrogated by a new measure called $\mathbb{Q}$. The range of $\mathbb{Q}$ does not have to be $[0,1] \subseteq \mathbb{R}$ – instead it is an arbitrary set S, so the signature of $\mathbb{Q}$ is $\mathbb{Q}\colon \mathbf{F} \to S$. Of course, S should not be *completely* arbitrary, it ought to have a certain structure. This structure *can* be inferred from the three invariants that must hold for the original probability measure P (that were not questioned in Chapter 7). As stated in 7.2., the second invariant mandates that the probability of the entire event space Ω equals 1, the max. element of $[0,1]$. For the time being, we accept

262 We go on without reproducing Artzner et al.'s formal definition of coherent probabilistic (!) risk models. Föllmer & Schied's book (2016: Chapter 4) contains an excellent summary.

263 This task is *non*-formal and might be analogous to the procedure of studying and classifying plants in botany (from the general to the specific, bottom-up, and so on). That purely technical answers are incomplete and unsatisfying has been named the *fallacy of unfinished business* (Shrader-Frechette, 1985: Chapter 4).

264 We use *uncertain sequences*, and *uncertainty monads* (see 15.5.3.), concepts from category theory, to integrate the notion of an uncertainty space (15.1.–3.) with the algebra for financial products (15.4.). Cf. also Adachi (2014).

this convention for measurement in terms of S and state that S should be equipped with a preorder $\leq_S$ and a maximum element $\mathbf{1} \in S$. Then $\mathbb{Q}(\Omega) = \mathbf{1}$.[265] However, the third invariant says that the probability of the union of some disjoint events must be equal to the sum of the probabilities of the events. This is genuinely conflict-laden and a much more delicate matter considering the fact that there exist forms of uncertainty which escape a cardinal measurement (see Proposition 17). Therefore, it is really in need of revision (as announced in 7.2.) and to express the third Kolmogorovian requirement in a general way for S, we need to have a binary operation that resembles, but is weaker than, the + operator. Since there is already a partial order on S with a maximum element **1**, the 'natural' next step is to stipulate that S be a semilattice (i.e., a partially ordered set with a binary *join* operation $\vee$).[266]

More precisely, we require that S be a bounded join-semilattice. Then we obtain $\mathbb{Q}(\cup A_i) = \bigvee \mathbb{Q}(A_i)$ for all sets $\{A_i\}$ of pairwise disjoint events. Two short remarks are in order to clarify to what extent we have left the Kolmogorovian home. Firstly, even if we copied all three of his axioms, the crucial point is that we do not automatically end up with classical probabilities – or the unpleasant assumptions of probability-based risk models to that stake, see IIIc) – because there are, in fact, various quantities which do satisfy those postulates (normalized mass, length, area, volume, etc.), and obviously, they have nothing to do with probability as they do not play the right role in our conceptual apparatus (Hájek, 2011). And secondly, the following examples elucidate that our third invariant is, and not only appears to be, less restrictive than Kolmogorov's version since *countable additivity* does not hold in **Example 15.3.**, for instance.

Example 15.1.

An obvious candidate for S is the range $[0, 1]$ with $+$ as the join operation and 1 as the maximum element. This results exactly in the original definition of the probability measure P.

---

265 Kolmogorov's first postulate does not need an explicit appreciation here since we are postponing a specification to **Definition 15.6.** where it is important to be included as we'll assume the existence of a zero element when we introduce uncertainty monads while we wish to keep the definition of an uncertainty model (**Definition 15.1.**) broad and general also in order to remain attractive to accounts in favor of negative 'probabilities', for example.

266 A *lattice* is a set with two binary operations meet and join that are required to be distributive. The V operator ("Big V") takes a set $\{a, b, c, d, e, ...\}$ as an argument and applies v (the binary operator) to all elements: $V(\{a, b, c, d, e, ...\}) = a \vee b \vee c \vee d \vee ...$ v is associative.

Example 15.2.
Another candidate for S is the set $\{T, F\}$ of truth values, with logical OR as the join operation and T as the maximum. This removes any gradual degrees of uncertainty, leaving us only with the two extremes *truth* (complete certainty) and *falsity* (complete uncertainty or impossibility)[267].

Example 15.3.
Consider $S = \{impossible, unlikely, plausible, likely, certain\}$ as an example of a discrete set, with the partial order given by "degree of likelihood" in the meanings of the terms. The **1** element is $certain$, and the binary operation $\vee$ is given by choosing the term with the higher likelihood (for example, $unlikely \vee plausible = plausible$). This is a simple example of how linguistic (and vague, Zadeh) terms can be translated directly into a framework of so-called 'qualitative probabilities'.[268]

Risk capital 2.0 and qualitative models of uncertainty

Now that probability spaces have been replaced with triples $(\Omega, \mathbf{F}, \mathbb{Q})$ for some semilattice S, let us take another look at the definition of *risk capital* which is at the heart of the axiomatization of risk measures. We still assume a 'random'[269] variable X denoting the future value of the investment, though it will be named a measurable function[270] on **F**. First, *nota bene* that risk capital is originally defined in relation to some probability threshold $1-\alpha$. In the original definition, $\alpha \in [0, 1]$ holds, so we now have to require that $\alpha \in S$. With this change we are again able to determine the truth of the proposition $\mathbb{Q}\,(X + m < 0) \leq \alpha$.[271] At this point, we could actually define a less restrictive or qualitative version of VaR (see 15.5.5.) – doing so would be a distraction however, as we are not even

267 Hájek (2010) investigates the difference between a zero probability event and an event that is impossible.
268 cf. Halpern & Rabin, 1987; Segerberg, 1971; Rescher, 1968: Chapter IV; and see also Chapter 18.
269 Note that „random“ can have different meanings (see Chapter 6.2.2.) and that random variables do not need to be described by *probability* functions (in the strict sense, see also Figure 35).
270 Recall that a function $f: X \to Y$ over two sets X and Y equipped with σ-algebras Σ and T, respectively, is *measurable* if and only if for all $t \in \mathrm{T}$, $f^{-1}(t) \in \Sigma$. Random variables are by definition measurable functions.
271 Obviously, we cannot write "$1-\alpha$" here since S can be composed of non-numerical values (see **Example 15.3.**).

half-way towards our final goal: We have reached a definition of risk capital that rests on a *qualitative measure* (Def. 15.1. with respect to RQ2.3), but we have not yet covered the algebraic aspect of our risk models (15.4.), nor their concretization (15.5.4.). Prior to this, we will offer two working definitions[272] to capture what has just been presented and proceed with both restating the laws of coherent risk measures in a general form (15.1.) and enriching the ossature by installing specific theories of uncertainty apart from probability theory (15.2. and 15.3.).

Definition 15.1.
A (qualitative) *uncertainty model* is a triple $(\Omega, \mathbf{F}, \mathbb{Q})$ where Ω is the set of possible states of the world, $\mathbf{F}$ is a σ-field over Ω and $\mathbb{Q}: \mathbf{F} \to S$ for a bounded join-semilattice $(S, \vee, \mathbf{1})$ such that $\mathbb{Q}(\Omega) = \mathbf{1}$ and $\mathbb{Q}(\bigcup A_i) = \bigvee \mathbb{Q}(A_i)$ for all sets $\{A_i\}$ of pairwise disjoint events.

This definition is in harmony with the Definition 2.1. of a risk model (as a sufficiently accurate description of (extreme or systemic) risk given in a formal language) and of "risk" in 4.1., respectively (where the relationship between risk and uncertainty has been established, see Figure 4). In the remainder of this exposition, we will use the term "*valuation*" for a measurable function $X: \mathbf{F} \to \mathbb{R}$. The intuitive meaning is that X represents the possible values of a position (or a portfolio, a trade, etc.), and $X(s)$ is the value of the position for a specific state of the world $s \in \mathbf{F}$.

Coherent risk measures and models in a LBR framework

The second definition, more precisely the amendment of Definition 2.2., we need in this section is that of a *coherent risk measure*. As Definition 2.2. mandates, a risk measure is a function f that assigns a monetary value $r \in \mathbb{R}$ to each valuation X. Risk measures are, or ought to be, characterized by several laws which ultimately brings us to the four axioms put forward by Artzner et al. (1999):

Translation invariance:
If we increase X by a constant amount, say $X' = X + c$, then $f(X')$ should be equal to $f(X) + c$. Consult Riedel (2004: 188) to see why

272 **Definition 15.1.** is provisional only, for instance, because this thesis is not the right place to raise another fun-damental question, the delicate and complex matter of discussing alternatives to a Sigma-algebra, a classical set-theoretic structure, as the incorporation of non-classical logics into LBR would require another foundation. Cf. Weatherson, 2003 for a possible starting point.

we think that this property is reasonable for measuring risks.[273] It has a straightforward equivalent in LBR, since we can add the sequence $\mu\,(\alpha, 1)$ to an uncertain sequence (15.5.3.), increasing the sum of transactions in all branches by α.

Sub-additivity:
The combined risk of two positions is not greater than the sum of the two risks separately: $f\,(X_1 + X_2) \leq f(X_1) + f\,(X_2)$. We believe that this property, which could be stated in the brisk form "a merger does not create extra risk", is a natural requirement as it implies that diversification is beneficial (for an example, cf. Riedel, 2004). This axiom also holds in LBR, because the $\odot_+$ operator over uncertain sequences of transactions (see 15.5.4.) is homomorphic with the + operator over risk measures.

Monotonicity:
If there are two valuations (two positions) X_1 and X_2, and the value of X_2 is greater than or equal to that of X_1 for all states of the world, then the risk of X_2 is higher than or equal to that of X_1. Monotonicity is certainly a reasonable requirement (Riedel, 2004: 188). It is a consequence of the convexity requirement that Artzner et al. impose on acceptance sets, and translates to LBR in a similar way.

Positive homogeneity:
If we multiply the value of a position by a factor $\lambda \geq 0$, then the risk f increases by the same factor, that is, $f(\lambda X) = \lambda f(X)$. Interpretation: Loosely speaking, if the agent doubles her position or portfolio, then she doubles her risk. Positive homogeneity entails that the risk of a risk object is proportional to its size. This postulate holds for LBR models too, because multiplication of all elements of an uncertain sequence by a factor λ commutes with the $fold$ operation in **Definition 15.13**.

---

273 At first sight, Artzner et al. (1999) seem to state something else by the axiom of translation invariance because their factor α appears with positive sign on the left and with negative sign on the right. This is because in their methodology, ρ denotes the *additional capital* that needs to be invested in the risk-free asset to make the position acceptable. Since $\rho\,(X + \alpha * r)$ represents the position X modified by investing α in the risk-free asset, the amount of risk captial required is exactly α smaller than that for the original position X.

These axioms have been extended in numerous ways. An obvious further postulate is that of *normalization*: the risk of the empty position (whose value is always 0) is zero. An important non-trivial addition to Artzner et al.'s coherency axioms is the introduction of *temporality*, of a *dynamic* setting or of an axiom of dynamic consistency by Riedel (2004). Temporality considers how risk measures behave on a time dimension. We will capture the motivation for his major contribution – 'no contradiction in one's risk assessments over time' – by treating uncertain sequences as expression of a temporal sequence of events (15.5.3.); so it seems natural to transfer Riedel's idea into our formalism (Müller & Hoffmann, 2017a: 5.2.).

Definition 15.2.
A *coherent LBR risk measure* or *model* over an uncertainty model $(\Omega, \mathbf{F}, \mathbb{Q})$ is a function $f\colon (\mathbf{F} \to \mathbb{R}) \to \mathbb{R}$ such that f is measurable and has the following properties:

1) For all valuations X and every $c \in \mathbb{R}$, $f(X + c) = f(X) + c$ (*Translation invariance*)
2) For all X_1, $X_2 \in X$, $f(X_1 + X_2) \leq f(X_1) + f(X_2)$ (*Subadditivity*)
3) For all $X_1, X_2 \in X$, $X_1 \leq X_2 \Rightarrow f(X_1) \leq f(X_2)$ (*Monotonicity*)
4) For all X and every $\lambda \geq 0$, we have $f(\lambda X) = \lambda f(X)$ (*Positive homogeneity*).
5) $f(0) = 0$ (*Normalization*).

Definitions 15.1., 15.2. are close enough to the originals in probabilistic terms that the axioms formulated by Artzner et al. can be applied without much ado or many changes to the generalized (LBR) risk models (to be developed in the following). The reproduction of the coherence axioms in the *concretized* language of LBR (where probabilities are going to be replaced by ranks) is expounded elsewhere (Müller & Hoffmann, 2017a: Section 5). In the direction of RQ2.2, which by contrast refers to the general (i.e. not the probabilistic or ranking-theoretic) case (of stating the postulates), we thus conclude that:

Proposition 10:
Laws of coherence for risk models, in the sense of Artzner et al. (1999) and Riedel (2004), can be conferred to non-probabilistic frameworks.

Consequently, we can now move on to the second pillar of our risk modeling approach (out of three): As we showed that reasonable laws of coherent risk models do not necessitate a probabilistic signature, the floor is opened for debating non-probabilistic alternatives to risk or uncertainty modeling.

15.2. Non-Probabilistic Models of Uncertainty

Satisfying the need for reasoning about uncertainty and likelihood in financial risk management is thwarted by the fact that there is sometimes no sound probabilistic basis for doing so (Chapter 7). However, probability theory is perhaps only the earliest, but certainly not the only existing formal modeling approach for coping with uncertainty. This branch of mathematics has grown from its beginnings in the 17th and 18th century to a wide range of procedures and methods. The field was dominated by few homogeneous quantitative methods until the 1970s when the quest for Artificial Intelligence (AI) sparked a great research interest in logical, symbolic, and partly non-numerical models of uncertainty.[274] Apart from qualitative alternatives, several quantitative, but non-probabilistic methods have emerged, which retain high standards of rigor, but often relax, modify or drop some of the usual axioms of, and assumptions behind probability theory. Therefore, they are of special interest to us when we focus on extreme and systemic financial risks in systems that possess the characteristics of organized complexity, i.e., which are too complex or too ill-defined to admit of precise probabilistic analysis (Zadeh, 1969a: 1; Seising, 2010: 4475). In this connection, we should name Zadeh's *principle of incompatibility* (1973). Termed informally, the essence of this principle is that "as the complexity of a system increases, our ability to make precise and yet significant statements about its behavior diminishes until a threshold is reached beyond which precision and significance (or relevance) become almost mutually exclusive characteristics" (Dubois & Prade, 1980: 189; see also Chapter 6.1.3.). Some of the approaches which thrive in such a difficult environment of (organized) complexity are briefly displayed below.

While they all permit us to grasp uncertainty as being measurable, but not necessarily as being composed of different degrees, distinct directions can be distinguished: We find quantitative generalizations of probability theory, (e.g.,

274 Unfortunately, the so-called Golden Age of AI ended without a breakthrough, and modern AI, having been awoken from hibernation by the arrival of *Big Data*, again relies heavily on homogeneous, unimaginative methods.

Dempster-Shafer Theory)[275], substitutions of probabilities *simpliciter* (e.g., Ranking Theory)[276] or new qualitative and quantitative foundations (e.g., modal logics in opposition to classical two-valued propositional logic that underlies probability theory, Adams, 1998: 22; Hájek & Hall, 2002). Some are guided by the old question of *how likely* it is that some statement is true, and others, more deductive directions, turn to new questions of what additional information we can *infer*, based on the knowledge we have. At first sight, the former strategy seems to be more suited for risk assessment (where inductive uncertainty measurement still occupies a prominent position), but one of our findings is that logic-based modeling can also be employed for risk management and should indeed be incorporated into endeavors of describing extreme and systemic risks (which is then rather about the opposite and counterpart, i.e., knowledge, not the the lack thereof)[277].

We scrutinize the following schemes which are normally embedded in rather inductive methods.

Dempster-Shafer Theory

Dempster and Shafer's theory on belief functions (Dempster, 1967; Shafer, 1976) also deals with quantified uncertainties. It attempts to attach numbers to the likelihood of various events and outcomes, just as probability theory does, but it addresses yet another problem. This branch of research is also called "information fusion", and the name hints at the application: With Dempster-Shafer theory we can fuse information from various sources, and account for any discrepancies between those sources. While it is traditionally applied to sensor information, we employ DST in a more deductive style and to reason about financial (macroeconomic) indicators (Müller & Hoffmann, 2017b; http://www.lbrm.de/).

Ranking Theory

is outlined in greater detail below (15.3.).

275 Whereas probabilities are *additive* (see 7.2., Kolmogorov's third axiom), Dempster-Shafer belief functions are only *super-additive*. Therefore, DST is more inclusive.

276 Spohn (2012) introduces *ranks* in place of working with probabilities.

277 As Spohn (2009: 214) once phrased it: "Traditional epistemology is interested in knowledge, a category entirely foreign to probability theory" and its siblings.

On the other hand, symbolic and classically deductive alternatives to numerical probability theory abound in the mathematical areas of logic and algebra. Standard Boolean logic, which at the same time underlies probabilistic reasoning (Chapter 18), can only express two states, namely truth and falsity. There is, however, a wide range of non-standard logics in which it is possible to articulate finer nuances of truth values. Again, we differentiate between several accounts.

Fuzzy Logic or Fuzzy Set Theory

A way of dealing with highly complex systems is to allow imprecision in describing properly aggregated data. The imprecision is not of a statistical nature (although the possibility of imprecise statistical descriptions is included as well), but rather of a more general modality (Klir, 1985: 138). The mathematical apparatus for this new modality is recognized under the name "fuzzy logic". It is a logic where the truth values range from 0 to 1, instead of being exactly one of 0 or 1.[278] The meaning of these truth values is the *extent* to which a statement is true, and not the probability with which it is true. Because fuzzy logic describes graduality and degrees, which are *fuzzy themselves*, it can be used to consider subjective, qualitative and obscure terms in risk modeling, which opens up the possibility to integrate a new type of dependencies between classical key figures and uncertain estimations (Borgonovo & Peccati, 2006).

Non-Monotonic Logic

Non-monotonic logic is an umbrella term for a variety of different logics that can express conflicting information and are able to handle inconsistencies, such as $a \wedge \neg a$ (Besnard & Hunter, 2001). To see why that is useful, consider this example in classical (i.e., monotonic) logic: If we are able to infer a from a set of formulae, then we can infer a from any superset, regardless of what additional information may be available. In non-monotonic logic, this property does not hold, and as a result, we can invalidate prior inferences by adding knowledge. We can use non-monotonic logic to deal with conflicting information which we (most probably) come across when we strive to model financial risks.

278 Accordingly in the parlance of the underlying fuzzy set theory (Zadeh, 1978), we say that an element need not belong to a given set either completely or not at all, but may be a member of the set to a certain degree. In terms of uncertainty modeling, this emphasizes the idea that the degree of confidence in an event is not totally determined by the confidence in the opposite event, as assumed in probability theory (where $(P(A) = 1) \Rightarrow (P(\bar{A}) = 0)$ holds).

Modal logics

Halpern & Rabin (1987) have expressed discomfort with the use of numerical probabilities and quantitative approaches to uncertainty. Instead, they present a modal logic which they call *LL*, the logic of likelihood, where an additional unary operator *L* is used to express modalities such as probability or possibility and that allows to speak about the likelihood of events – something that is clearly a concern for risk models (cf. also Fagin et al., 1990 and Darwiche & Ginsberg, 1992). Notwithstanding the fact that likelihood is not assigned quantitative values through probabilities or ranks etc., Halpern & Rabin (1987: 380) can capture many properties of likelihood in an intuitively appealing way (cf. their paper).

Quo vadis?

We have listed several different kinds of uncertainty models, all of which appear to be useful for financial modeling as they entitle us to describe uncertainty with fewer constraints than classical probabilities that, in turn, have proved fallacious (Chapter 7). And even if the Central Argument was not persuasive, there is no reason (especially, from a systemic viewpoint) why risk models should only rely on one particular representation of uncertainty. Hence, in contrast to much of the stream of the literature which has also recognized the demand for reformation in favor of non-probabilistic approaches (e.g., Dutta, 2015; Katagiri et al., 2013; Liu et al., 2011; Huang et al., 2009b; Lin et al., 2008; Horgby, 1999), but lags behind when it comes to moving beyond compartmentalization towards a holistic view,[279] we aspire to avoid writing models that are tied to a specific uncertainty model. Considering that there is a multitude of risk model purposes to serve, it is entirely implausible that one account could serve all.

If we are able to identify a "common language" in which to express the future behavior of our risk object (e.g., a portfolio) without committing to a single representation of uncertainty, we will be able to write a model once and evaluate it with different uncertainty formalisms, or combinations thereof. Prior to specifying such a formal language, so-called monadic representations of uncertainty (15.5.), which we use to extend a modular and algebraic approach for describing financial contracts (going back to Jones et al., 2001; see Chapter 15.4.), and which is then, when

279 There are attempts of unification like Halpern (2005) and huge handbooks like Gabbay et al. (1994), which, however, leaves us with the impression that one hardly sees the wood for trees.

applied to the context of financial risk management, the actual core of our constructive proposal, we delve into ranking theory (pioneered by Professor Spohn).

15.3. Ranking Theory

We endorse ranking theory as a suitable (but only exemplary) alternative to a probabilistic foundation while strongly encouraging future work to take into account other models of uncertainty (as well as combinations of them) *within* our framework we are establishing in sections 15.5.

Like adherents of probability (DS and possibility) theory, Spohn (2012) uses a quantitative notion of belief that admits of degrees. However, in contrast to proper probabilities, he invokes *ranks* which obey laws of thought and belief that are not identical with the laws of probability (see below). This basic notion of ranking theory is simple, defined by Spohn (2009: 188) and illuminated by an example (in 15.5.4.):

Definition 15.3.:

Let $\mathcal{A}$ be a Boolean algebra over *W*, a non-empty set of mutually exclusive and jointly exhaustive possible worlds or possibilities.[280] Then κ is a *negative ranking function* for $\mathcal{A}$ if, and only if, $\kappa : \mathcal{A} \rightarrow \mathbb{R}^*$, i.e., κ is a function from $\mathcal{A}$ into $\mathbb{R}^* = \mathbb{R}^+ \cup \{\infty\}$ (i.e., into the set of non-negative reals plus infinity) such that for all $A, B \in \mathcal{A}$:

1) $\kappa(W) = 0$ and $\kappa(\emptyset) = \infty$,
2) $\kappa(A \cup B) = \min \{\kappa(A), \kappa(B)\}$
[*the law of disjunction (for negative ranks)*].

$\kappa(A)$ is called the *(negative) rank* of A.

It immediately follows for each $A \in \mathcal{A}$ where $\bar{A}$ denotes the complement of a set *A* (or, when interpreting the set operators as a Boolean algebra, the negation of a term *A*):

3) either $\kappa(A) = 0$ or $\kappa(\bar{A}) = 0$ or both (in which case κ is neutral on A)
[*the law of negation*].

280 Following Artzner et al. (1999: 206), a possibility or a state of the world might be described by a list of the prices of all securities and all exchange rates, when we deal, for example, with market risk.

Admittedly, we might just as well phrase things in positive terms (cf. definition 4 in Spohn, 2009: 191). Yet, although positive ranking functions seem distinctly more natural, Spohn shows that negative ranks behave very much like probabilities (and this parallel would remain concealed if we were thinking in positive terms). According to the standard *interpretation*, a negative ranking function κ expresses a *grading of disbelief*.[281] This reading suggests to regard ranking functions as being designed for the *representation of belief* and, as a matter of fact, Spohn (2009: 192) contends that the study of belief *is* the study of the formal structure of ranks. Intriguingly, however, ranking theory does not deal with degrees right away, but with *ungraded* belief, from which the ranking structure arises. Additionally, Spohn is especially interested in the representation of *the dynamics* of (ungraded) belief. In terms of this second aim, everything stands and falls with Spohn's (2009: 193) notion of *conditional ranks* (cf. his Def. 6 and see our **Definition 15.11.**). Ranking theory then admits a single well-defined conditionalization of ranks, unlike DS belief theory, for which several divergent and competing methods of conditionalization have been proposed (ibid.: 220f.), wherefore we continue with a number of brief comparative remarks.

Delimitation of areas in the realm of uncertainty modeling

A large and natural field of comparison for ranking theory is *nonmonotonic reasoning* due to the joint focus on the revisability of beliefs, which is meticulously investigated by Rott (2001) who proved far-reaching equivalences between many variants on both sides (Spohn, 2009: 221). Ranking theory and *possibility theory* (Dubois & Prade, 1988a), the latter in turn stems from *fuzzy logic or set theory* (Zadeh, 1978), are formally alike,[282] but that does not mean that their interpretations are the same. The same holds true when using the example of (*Dempster-Shafer*) DS belief functions. While negative ranking functions, just like possibility measures, turn out to be formally a special case of DS belief functions, it is to be expected that they are interpretationally at cross-purposes (Spohn, 2009: 223). He (ibid.: 224) therefore concludes that ranking theory is a strong independent pillar

281 For example, if $\kappa(A) = 0$, A is not disbelieved at all; if $\kappa(A) > 0$, A is disbelieved to some positive degree. Belief in A is the same as disbelief in $\bar{A}$; hence, A is *believed* in κ if, and only if, $\kappa(\bar{A}) > 0$. This entails (via the law of negation), but is not equivalent to $\kappa(A) = 0$. Cf. Spohn, 2009: 188.

282 In fact, one can render possibility theory isomorphic to a real-valued version of ranking theory (Huber, 2016).

in that confusingly rich variety of theories found in the uncertainty literature (see the extract in 15.2.). In contrast to those other members of the non-classical probability family, Spohn explains, particularly, that many essential virtues of the probabilistic standard (with its enormous powers, rich details and ramifications) can be duplicated in ranking theory (e.g., an equivalent of Bayes' rule for conditional probabilities). Still, one might suspect then that Spohn can claim these successes only by turning ranks into fake probabilities. He has never left the Bayesian home, it may seem. May we, hence, prompt the question of whether Spohn's (and the other) alternative formal structures eventually reduce to probabilism?

Ranks and Probabilities

The relation between the two is intricate: Does Spohn present his ranks as an independent alternative to (classical) probability or simply probability itself in a different disguise? The latter suspicion is aroused since Spohn (2012: 202f.) first fuels speculation that any probabilistic theorem can be translated into a ranking theorem as the translation of products and quotients of probabilities suggests that negative ranks would simply prove to be the logarithm of probabilities (with respect to a base taken to be some infinitesimal *i*). Yet, at *secunda facie*, the translation is not fool-proof.[283] Spohn then (2012: 205) identifies algebraic incoherencies as well as further disanalogies that are not resolved. An elaboration of his findings would reveal the slight failures of a translation program which turns the sum of probabilities into the minimum of ranks, the product of probabilities into the sum of ranks, and the quotient of probabilities into the difference of ranks – thereby, the probabilistic law of additivity transforms into the law of disjunction, the probabilistic law of multiplication into the law of conjunction,[284] and the definition of conditional probabilities into the definition of conditional ranks (**Definition 15.11.**) etc. Moreover, if at all feasible, an analogy could only be in existence for ranks and *nonstandard* probabilities. All in all, this suggests that ranks really are non-standard counterparts to conventional probabilities even in terms of a formal comparison, let alone utter interpretational differences (and albeit we must point to Spohn's work for the actual comparison due to space constraints here).

283 Cf. Spohn (2005) for slight deviations concerning positive and non-negative instantial relevance; and Spohn (1994) for slight divergences concerning conditional independence.

284 Spohn (2009) enforces the law of conjunction (for negative ranks) as follows: $\kappa(A \cap B) = \kappa(A) + \kappa(B|A)$.

Brief evaluation

We can spot several advantages of ranking theory over its competitors like probability theory. Whereas Spohn (2009) provides evidence in terms of epistemology, we seek to tailor the evaluation more to risk management purposes. In this light, ranking theory, for instance, enables a unified treatment of measured or directly measurable uncertainty *and* qualitative assertions in the same framework, just as fuzzy logic does (Liu et al., 2011). We find a bunch of merits of *such* approaches (cf. Katagiri et al., 2013; Borgonovo & Peccati, 2006), which, however, do not authorize us to single out one specific promising formalism (let's say ranking theory over fuzzy logic). The ultimate reason here for the recourse to ranking theory in preference to other alternative accounts subsumable under the label of 15.2. is, at least at this stage, rather technical than substantial. Recall that in our framework (15.5.) we will use ranking theory (or, in principle, any of its siblings) to model uncertainties as *functions* of the structure of financial products (15.4.), and *not* directly to cope with risks and uncertainties. Now, while the contestation over probability theory has indeed been substantial (Part I), the rather technical argument in favor of ranking theory is twofold: First, while we could appeal to ranking theory or DST to define that function (which will map each 'scenario' to a 'qualitative probability'), monadic representations of uncertainty, it would be more difficult to insert formal logics to this end (which have another structure, provable statements). Second, in contrast to DST (see also footnote 298), ranking theory is particularly well positioned to model beliefs that change over time, and thus integrates well with both Riedel's (2004) call for a dynamic setting for risk measurement (15.1.) and our interpretation of contracts as uncertain sequences (15.5.). Hence, ranking theory.

15.4. Syntax of a Language for Describing Contracts and Correlations

Il n'est pas certain que tout soit incertain.
(Blaise Pascal, 1623 – 1662)

Considering non-probabilistic alternatives to uncertainty modeling (see 15.2. and 15.3.) can be brought to another level of investigation. In lieu of glorifying probability theory that is grounded in *analysis* (Stroock, 2010), we give preference to an *algebraic* approach to measure extreme and systemic risks. Specifically, our proposal is rooted in *abstract algebra*,[285] which is a branch of mathematics that studies the composition and decomposition of structures (Pratt, 2007).

An algebra is a formal language and saying that our approach is algebraic is the same as saying that it is language-based or an interpretation of a formal language, which is outspokenly attached to our definition 2.1 of a risk model. Algebra is appealing to us as risk modelers because it abstracts away from the numerical foundations of probability theory (troublesome according to IIIa) – IIIc) and the succeeding chapters) while retaining many of the features of the original account. In what follows, we outline the algebraic approach by Jones et al. (2001), which we develop further to model risks associated with financial products and instruments. We invite the reader to refer to the original paper for a more detailed exposition of their combinator library and its completeness or essentiality while our own independent contribution in this territory begins in the sections of 15.5., where we propound a novel interpretation, a new semantics of their language (syntax).

Risk Measurement and Contract Specification

In line with what Chapter 8.2. prescribes, we intend to model extreme risks from banks' (not regulators') point of view, which we now decode and specify through focusing on *their* affairs or operations and on evaluating risks of *their* financial products/instruments, derivatives in particular, represented by a bundle of financial contracts. A spotlight on financial contracts is worthwhile as banks can basically be viewed as giant ledgers of *contracts* that have future positive and negative cash flows (Ross, 2016: 170). This entitles us to spell out the desired shift for risk modeling and management as an answer to RQ2.1, RQ1.9.

Proposition 11:

Explanatory risk modeling for banks, which should explain the impact of systemic or extreme risk events on their own exposures, can be operationalized by measuring the risks affiliated with their positions in financial or derivatives trading under extreme scenarios, which can be described structurally (as defined by the composition of derivatives themselves) and systemically (as defined by their behavior in the face of extreme system changes).

285 Not to be confused with elementary algebra.

In financial trading, a position is a binding commitment to buy or sell a given amount of financial products or instruments,[286] such as derivatives that, in turn, are based on other, 'underlying' financial products (as opposed to, say, stocks or basic loans; see the glossary in Appendix A and cf. also Jacque, 2015: Chapter 1). Their name derives from the fact that the prices of derivatives are *derived* from their underlying instruments, via precise mathematical formulas. Derivatives can be used for a number of purposes, for risk management or reduction (e.g., through insuring against price movements) among others (J.P. Morgan, 2013). At the same time, they particularly carry, in classical bankers' jargon, market and counterparty credit risk (e.g., due to events unspecified by the derivative contract; see also Table 2).[287] The risk models of derivatives (such as VaR), however, are not derived from the risk models of their underlying instruments. Instead, they are designed from scratch, exactly like those of their underlying entities (such as an asset, index, or interest rate)[288] or, simply, *underlyings*. Apart from the principal short-comings elucidated in Part I, those conventional risk models for derivatives thus suffer from the problem that they do not make use of detailed structural data that is readily available in the specification of the derivatives themselves. We describe dynamic derivatives in a programming language for financial contracts with the aim of modeling the risk of derivatives as a combination of the risk of their underlyings (analysis) and expounding the function of basal models in more encompassing risk models (synthesis). With that in mind, we pursue, at the end of the day, the overall aim of capturing, explaining, and hedging against the impact of extreme and systemic risk events on banks' own exposures (Proposition 7). Our concern does not relate to the financial system

286 In a static sense, "position" also depicts the amount of financial products, securities or commodities and so forth held by a person, firm, or institution. Then, the boundary between "position" and "portfolio" is fairly fluid – in the language of Jones et al., there is, for example, the "AND" operator, which can be used to merge two positions, so that in an extreme case the whole portfolio could be described by a single position. At the end of the day, we are interested in the portfolio though, which is the sum of all positions, and, therefore, the exact delineation between positions does not matter much.

287 It is clear that different types of derivatives are exposed to counterparty risk to different degrees. For example, while swaps (and others even more) count as relatively risky, standardized stock options by law require the party at risk to have a certain amount deposited with the exchange.

288 Apart from derivatives whose underlyings are that simple, there exist derivatives such as CDO^2 (a CDO whose underlying assets are CDOs) or CDO^3 (the underlying assets are CDO^2) and so on that are much more complex –so that one person's derivative has become another person's underlyer.

and its changes, but rather to market participants' own positions and their propensity to react to radical system changes (Proposition 11).

Even though the number of different (and, indeed, increasingly complex) instruments that banks trade on a daily basis is vast and ever-increasing, it is indeed possible to specify a small set of primitive or atomic contracts that are all we need to comprehend more *complex* ones (cf. Jones et al., 2001). As a consequence, we reason in a systemic manner (which respects analysis as well as synthesis) as follows:

Proposition 12:
Financial products and instruments (particularly, derivatives), that are composed of other financial contracts or underlyings, exhibit structural complexity, which is reducible. Therefore, their risks can be meaningfully analyzed and integrated, i.e., such risks can be taken apart into their components and reassembled from those components.

Proposition 12 justifies us in our modular risk measurement procedure, i.e., of dismantling and unfragmenting financial contracts, the latter also being the approach chosen by Jones et al. (2001). They are, however, interested in financial engineering/pricing (not risk), and the authors do not question probability distributions of prices. Our choice of language elements does not differ from theirs, but albeit the price of a contract and the risk in a position are obviously related, they refer to different research programs, and thus, we pursue a different objective with the interpretation of their language (which we give in 15.5.).

In the following, object level terms in the language of contracts are set in tele type and their interpretations are set in italics. When type annotations are required, they will be separated from their terms by a double colon ::. Some contracts depend on external quantities such as interest rates or stock prices, and some involve not monetary amounts, but other contracts (the underlyings), for example as collateral to a loan (see Appendix A). A contract between two parties defines rights and obligations for each party. Each contract also has an acquisition date and an expiry date (horizon) – it can only be acquired within those two dates.

The language consists of primitives and combinators that describe the relationship between rights, obligations, underlyings, and so forth. $zero :: Contract$ is the first primitive – a contract with no rights, no obligations, and an infinite horizon.[289] The logical next step is $one :: Currency \rightarrow Contract$, mapping a currency to a contract that pays the holder one unit of that currency immediately upon acquisition. $give :: Contract \rightarrow Contract$ reverses the rights and obligations of a contract: All of the original contract's holder's rights become the counterparty's rights and vice versa. With $and :: Contract \rightarrow Contract \rightarrow Contract$ we combine the rights and obligations of two contracts, whereas with $or :: Contract \rightarrow Contract \rightarrow Contract$ we express a choice of one of two contracts (not both).

The combinator $truncate :: Date \rightarrow Contract \rightarrow Contract$ changes or truncates the expiry date of a contract (after this date, it may not be acquired, but may well have rights and obligations). With $at :: Date \rightarrow Contract \rightarrow Contract$ we can acquire a contract at a given date, and $then :: Contract \rightarrow Contract \rightarrow Contract$ lets us replace a contract with another one after the expiry date of the first.

Contracts may depend on observable quantities such as interest rates. Such quantities have the type $Observable$. The Libor (London Interbank Offered Rate, see our glossary), for example, is represented as $libor :: Observable$, a function that returns the interest rate at each day.[290] A number of primitives have been defined for observables: $constant :: Number \rightarrow Observable$ produces an observable with a constant value, $time :: Date \rightarrow Observable$ gives the number of days between the date of the observation and the parameter, and $scale :: Observable \rightarrow Contract \rightarrow Contract$ multiplies the value of a contract by a quantity observed at its acquisition date. The following example shows how to bring the language developed by Jones et al. (2001) into operation to describe a simple contract.

Example 15.4.

A simple, unsecured loan consists of a principal p (paid out at the beginning), interest i and a time span t, in a currency c. At the beginning

---

289 It is common to have a zero element in such programming languages for formal reasons (because this is demanded in definitions such as "monoid", "monad", etc., see 15.5.) as well as for practical reasons (e.g., by "*c or zero*", we can express that there is the option to acquire the contract *c* or not – and "non-acquiring" is just expressed by the contract *zero*).

290 There are primitive observables such as *Libor*, but also combinators that work with observables, such as e.g., *truncate*. In this respect, they do not represent a third category apart from primitives and combinators. They provide a way to access external data.

of the life time of a loan, we (the lender) hand out the principal. The principal can be expressed as a constant observable principal = scale (constant p) (one c), *and the interest is*

interest = scale (constant (i ∗ p)) (one c). *After t days have passed, we receive the principal and interest (assuming only a single interest payment). Such a loan can be expressed as*

```
loan :: Number → Number → Days → Contract
loan p i t = and paid received where
        paid      = give principal
        received  = at t (principal 'and' interest)
        principal = scale (constant p) (one CHF)
        interest  = scale (constant (i ∗ p)) (one CHF)
```

In this definition of *loan*, we assumed Swiss Francs (CHF) as the default currency. The notation *'and'* means that *and* is used as an infix operator, between its arguments, instead of its usual prefix position.[291] Following the convention of the programming language Haskell, a standard language whose syntax is very similar to the mathematical notation, we use indentation to denote locally defined expressions (within the scope of *loan*).[292] Yet, this formulation of loan does neither cover the modularity of our approach, nor mention the possibility of default and assumes that the principal and interest are always paid back at *t*. The latter makes sense, since a default essentially constitutes a violation of the contract, and should thus not be modeled as part of the contract itself. We do, however, have to consider potential defaults in our interpretation of the language as well as more complex examples / financial instruments (15.5.). For now, Table 8 contains a summary of our language constructs borrowed from Jones et al. (2001).

291 The notation usually used in arithmetical and logical formulae and statements is called *infix* and it denotes the placement of operators between operands, i.e.,"infixed operators" – such as the plus sign in "2 + 2".

292 In the examples, we use the programming language Haskell (as did Peyton Jones et al. in their paper). Haskell is a functional programming language well-established in PL research, and the main advantage of using it in this thesis is that it gives us a clean, easy-to-read syntax. For our purposes, Haskell is an implementation of the typed lambda calculus, with one significant syntactic change: Function application is not denoted by braces (), but by a space. So the expression "and paid received" means "and(paid, received)", and "at t (principal 'and' interest)" means "at(t, and(principal, interest))" in prefix notation.

Table 8: Summary of the vocabulary for financial contracts.

Name	*Intuitive Meaning*
$zero :: Contract$	Empty contract
$one :: Currency \rightarrow Contract$	Contract that pays one unit of currency (CHF) upon acquisition
$give :: Contract \rightarrow Contract$	Reverses the rights and obligations of a contract
$and :: Contract \rightarrow Contract \rightarrow Contract$	Combines the rights and obligations of two contracts
$or :: Contract \rightarrow Contract \rightarrow Contract$	Immediately choose one of two contracts
$anytime :: Contract \rightarrow Contract$	Acquire the underlying contract at any time before it expires
$at :: Date \rightarrow Contract \rightarrow Contract$	Acquire the underlying contract at a date
$truncate :: Date \rightarrow Contract \rightarrow Contract$	Changes the horizon of a contract
$then :: Contract \rightarrow Contract \rightarrow Contract$	Replaces a contract with another one after the expiration of the first
$constant :: Number \rightarrow Observable$	Observable with a constant value
$scale :: Observable \rightarrow Contract \rightarrow Contract$	Multiplies the value of a contract by a quantity observed at its acquisition date
$time :: Date \rightarrow Observable$	Get the number of days between the date of the observation and the parameter

In what follows, we will define the semantics of contracts, by translating each part of the object-level syntax into the meta-level language of mathematics.

15.5. Semantics: Financial Contracts as Uncertain Sequences in a Non-Probabilistic Risk Model Context

We now have a vocabulary for describing contracts at hand, but we have not specified the meaning of those contracts. Apart from grasping the valuation of a structurally complex contract as only depending on the valuations of the simpler contracts it consists of, our risk modeling ambitions are indeed based on another key idea: namely, that financial contracts (instruments) in our language are interpreted as *uncertain sequences of transactions* rather than as single values (or probability distributions).[293] In the next sections (15.5.1. and 15.5.2.), we will shape the notion of uncertain sequences intuitively, by developing an example. The formal definition of uncertain sequences will be given thereafter (15.5.3.) before they are instantiated by means of ranking theory (15.5.4.). Ultimately, we introduce another layer of interpretation, namely when we interpret uncertain sequences in turn as scenarios (15.5.5.).

15.5.1. Uncertain sequences by example

Consider the unsecured loan from **Example 15.4.** It involves two transactions: First, in t_1, we transfer the principal p to the borrower, and later in the second transaction t_2 we receive the principal plus interest i in return. We are using the following graphical notation to describe sequences of transactions:

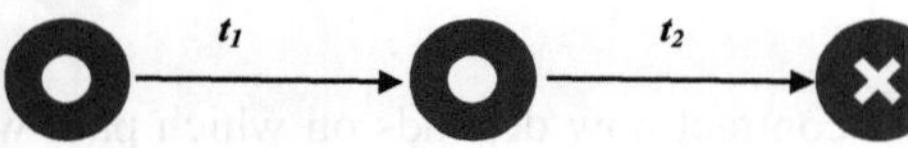

Edges between nodes are annotated with transactions, and their direction indicates chronological order. ⊗ nodes mark the end of a sequence, and ○ nodes are used for non-empty sequences. The value of the first transaction is $t_1 = -p$ (the principal) and the value of the second transaction is $t_2 = p + i$ (return of loan plus interest), resulting in the total value of this contract: $t_1 + t_2 = -p + p + i = i$ – exactly the interest paid by the borrower. Each node in the sequence represents the transactions on a single day, starting from the beginning of the contract. For our example, this means that t_1 occurs on the first day and t_2 on the second day, so the loan is paid back on the very next day. Longer durations, for instance three instead of two days (and so on), will result in a number of edges with the empty transaction e:

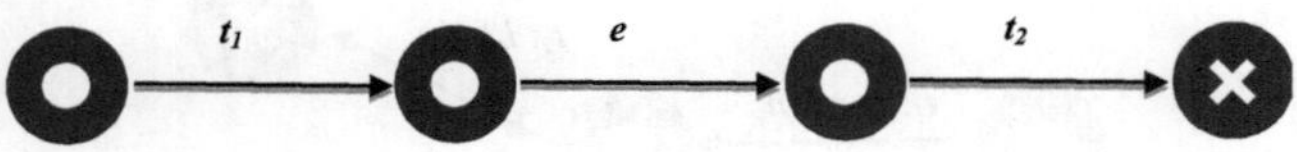

293 "Transaction" is the key concept in double-entry bookkeeping, where it describes the movement of some commodity (money or other) from at least one debit account to at least one credit account. And in fact, to be able to properly work with the assumptions that our price valuations are based on, we use the concept of double-entry bookkeeping, which has been applied in the accounting world for hundreds of years – but only for past data. We extend it so that it can be used for future data as well (cf. Müller & Hoffmann, 2017b).

In the examples, we will mostly elide sequences of empty transactions, but they are useful for modeling real-world contracts where there may be long periods of inactivity. Let us now turn to the uncertainty contained in contracts. We have not considered the alternate outcome, that the borrower defaults and we do not get back the principal. In this case, t_1 would be followed not by t_2, but by a third transaction $t_3 = 0$. To show that there are two potential outcomes of loan, we will display sequences of transactions as directed acyclic graphs (DAG):

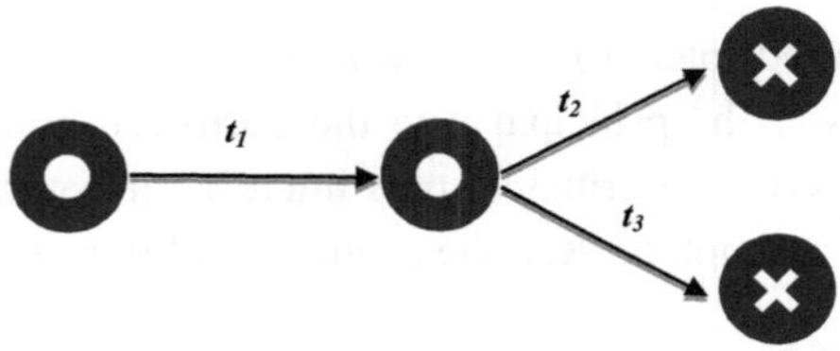

The total value of the contract now depends on which path we take through the graph – it is either $t_1 + t_2$, or $t_1 + t_3$. If we have some knowledge of the likelihood of each outcome, we can annotate the edges of the graph with an uncertainty value to obtain a distribution of all possible outcomes for this contract. For now, we are drawing on a scale of likelihood with values $\{impossible, unlikely, plausible, likely, certain\}$ (see **Example 15.3.**). The positive path (loan is paid back) ending in t_2 consists of a $certain$ step and a $likely$ step, and the negative path ending in t_3 has a $certain$ step followed by an $unlikely$ step. To get the likelihood for an entire path based on the likelihoods of its steps, we apply the min[294] operator succesively. We thus end up with the following mapping of likelihoods to contract values: $\{likely \mapsto i, unlikely \mapsto -p\}$.

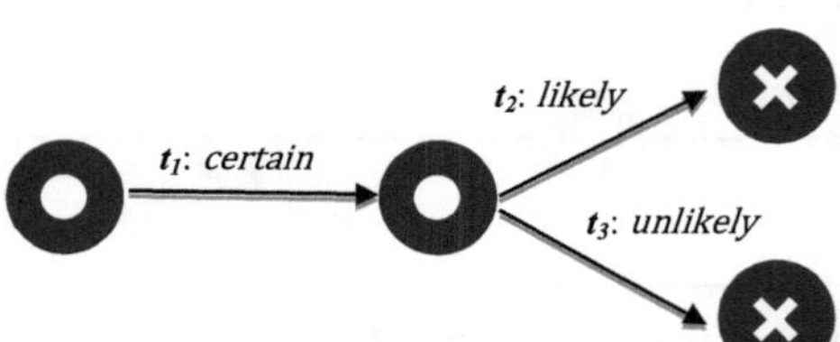

Figure 22: Transactions of an unsecured loan annotated with uncertain values.

294 Assuming an ordering from $impossible$ to $certain$.

In other words, we will gain the interest payment in the likely outcome, and lose the principal in the unlikely outcome. If we had tied in numerical probabilities instead of qualitative likelihoods, we would have multiplied the edge probabilities to arrive at the path probability, and we could also compute derived measures such as the expected value of the contract. However, as stated earlier (15.2.), we wish to remain flexible in the choice of uncertainty formalism(s), so we do not commit to a specific model here. For this reason, we stick with {*impossible*, ... , *certain*} in this example and will make only a small number of assumptions about the uncertainty model when we formalize our approach in the following.

Modularity and Structural Complexity

In the paragraphs above, we have translated contracts to uncertain sequences, which are DAGs whose nodes mark the beginning or end of a sequence and whose edges are branches annotated with likelihoods or some measure of uncertainty. In 15.4. (Proposition 12), we pleaded for the language of financial contracts to be modular, so that its interpretations can be modular, too. For a graphical demonstration of this modularity we need to introduce a more complex contract than *loan*.

Example 15.5.
Loans in financial markets are usually backed by a collateral, an asset or security that is provided by the borrower in exchange for the principal. If the borrower fails to make payments on the loan, the lender keeps the principal to compensate for the default. Mortgages and car loans are familiar examples (backed by the property or car, respectively), but in principle any kind of asset or security can function as collateral. In our parlance of financial contracts, we can define a function coLoan *(co is short for collateralized) with the following signature:*

coLoan :: Contract → Number → Number → Days → Contract

Compared to loan from **Example 15.4.**, *coLoan takes an additional argument, the collateral. The type of this argument is* Contract, *which demonstrates the modularity of our approach: It could be any kind of financial contract, and we could even process the result of* coLoan *to construct yet more complex contracts (which would lead us to Collat-*

eralized Debt Obligations, CDOs, which are packages of loans sold in tranches staggered by credit ratings; see the glossary). In any case, knowing that we (the lender) take the collateral at the beginning of the loan, and return it at the end of the loan, we can define coLoan *as follows:*

```
coLoan :: Contract → Number → Number → Days → Contract
coLoan coll p i t    =  (loan p i t)
                        'and' (get coll)
                        'and' (truncate t (give coll))
```

In this definition, we can see that coLoan *consists of the* loan *function we defined earlier, and two additional transactions:* get coll *at the beginning of the contract, and* give coll *after a period of t days.*

How does coLoan look in the graphical notation? For this example, we first need to specify a collateral. Let us assume the loan is backed up with a corporate bond (yet another loan!) which results in a series of five interest payments, c_1 to c_5. At each step, there is a possibility that the bank defaults, in which case the sequence of transactions ends with *e* and there are no additional payments.

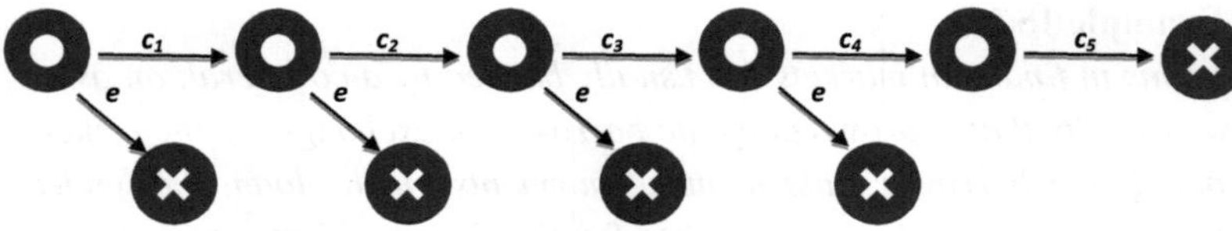

Figure 23: Transactions in a bond brought forward as collateral for a loan.

Figure 23 shows that there are five possible outcomes for the payments received from the bond: The successful outcome (all five transactions from c_1 to c_5), and the four unsuccessful options with an opportunity for default between each payment and the next. Combined with the transactions for the loan, we get the following graph, in which the loan is due after two payments have been made on the bond (Figure 24):

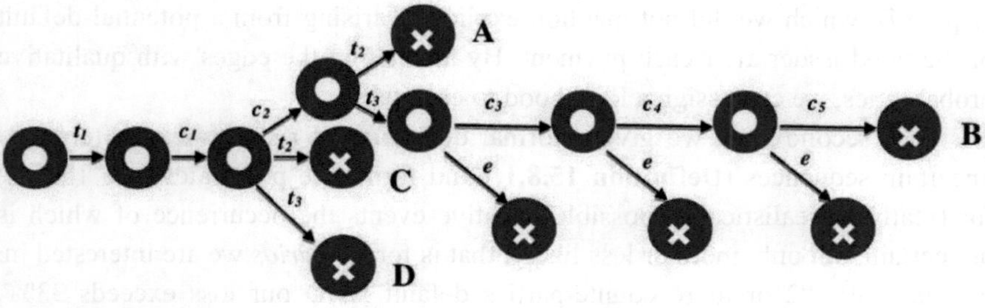

Figure 24: Transactions in a collateralized loan.

This graph has a number of paths and we marked four of them with the letters A to D. Path A is the most positive outcome (from our / the lender's point of view): We hand out the principal of the loan (t_1), receive the collateral (which results in payments c_1 and c_2) and get the principal and interest back, in exchange for the collateral (so there is only one more transaction t_2). Path B is the scenario where the borrower defaults: Instead of getting back the principal and interest, we are left with an empty transaction t_3 when the loan expires, but we keep the collateral and thus receive payments c_3, c_4 and c_5. Note that after each of the collateral's payments c_i it is possible that the bond issuer defaults, rendering our collateral worthless and resulting in a termination of the sequence of payments. In path C, the loan is paid back but the company issuing the collateral defaults after the first payment, c_1. In this case, we still make a profit from the loan, but we miss out on c_2, the second interest payment on the bond. Path D is the worst case: Both the borrower and the bond issuer default.

15.5.2. From contract value to risk

The examples should have made clear how we intend to benefit from the introduction of uncertain sequences. But one question still has to be scrutinized before we can turn to a formal definition of our LBR models: How do uncertain sequences relate to risk?

Consider the scenarios A to D in Figure 24. Each of them corresponds to the default status of the two counterparties involved in the transaction (borrower and bond issuer): In path A, there is no default, in path B the borrower defaults, in path C the bond issuer defaults after one payment and in path D both counterparties default after the first payment on the bond. There are also several variations of path B, which we did not mention explicitly, arising from a potential default of the bond issuer after each payment. By annotating the edges with qualitative probabilities, we can assign a likelihood to each path.

In a second step, we give a formal definition of risk models in terms of uncertain sequences (**Definition 15.8.1.**) and formulate predicates (see 15.5.5.) for (really or realistically) possible negative events the occurrence of which is not certain, but only more or less likely, that is for *scenarios* we are interested in. For example, "2 or more counterparties default AND our loss exceeds 33%" would be such a risk event or scenario. We can then compute the likelihood (which does not have to be the same as a numerical probability, see Chapter 18) that a predicate holds for a specific uncertain sequence.

15.5.3. Formalization of the approach

Having gained an intuition for uncertain sequences we will now define them formally. Figure 24 shows that even a standard contract such as *coLoan* can result in a complex uncertain sequence with many different possible paths. The structural complexity of the model grows fast when contracts are combined. With *coLoan* we have only touched the surface of what is possible in financial trading (Célérier & Vallée, 2014; Jacque, 2015). For example, a number of collateralized loans can be bundled up into a collateralized debt obligation and sold to investors at different 'tranches' (seniority for payments). While such a CDO (glossary) containing multiple *coLoans* would be impossible to visualize graphically in this format, it is straightforward to describe them as a composition of uncertain sequences using the definitions below as well as the vocabulary of contracts from Section 15.4.

To avoid having to draw out each contract individually, as we did with *coLoan* in the example above, we will now give an interpretation of *all* contracts as uncertain sequences. The syntax of the language for contracts by Jones et al. (2001) was defined using principles from programming language research, and in the original paper, an interpretation is provided by means of *denotational semantics* (which is also essential for the modularity of the approach).[295] In the same spirit, we are proposing our risk-based interpretation of the language em-

295 Denotational semantics is a way of describing the meaning of programming languages, by assigning a meaning (the "denotation") to each primitive expression of the language. The meaning of an entire program is then derived from the meanings of its expressions.

ploying denotational semantics. We first establish the formal model of *uncertainty monads*, a concept from category theory, as the cornerstone of our LBR risk modeling framework. In doing so, we follow the tradition established by Moggi (1991) and others, namely of viewing computations as monads in a given category, which is rooted in abstract algebra, underscoring that monads have been employed to solve related problems. As a consequence, we will then proceed with a definition of *uncertain sequences* as an algebraic data type using uncertainty monads.

Uncertainty monads

We will briefly review the relevant definitions and notation from category theory. This section is kept very terse due to space constraints, but we ensured that it is well compatible with the scheme established in MacLane (1971), so we refer the reader to his book for a thorough exposition. A category $\boldsymbol{C}$ consists of a set of objects A, B, C, … and a set of arrows f, g, ... Each arrow points from a 'domain' object to a 'range' object, written as $f : A \to B$. Each object A has an identity arrow 1_A, and there is an associative operation 'o' on arrows, that for every two arrows $f : A \to B$, $g : B \to C$ returns an arrow $g \circ f : A \to C$.

For our purposes, we can think of the objects as sets and of the arrows as functions between those sets. A category has *products* if for any two objects A and B, there is an object $A \times B$ with unique arrows $\pi_A : A \times B \to A$ and $\pi_B : A \times B \to B$. All categories together form a category whose objects are categories and whose arrows are called *functors*. A functor $F : \boldsymbol{C} \times \boldsymbol{C} \to \boldsymbol{C}$ from the product category of **C** to **C** is a *bifunctor*. Functors themselves also form a category, the arrows of which are called *natural transformations* (arrows between functors). An object 1 is called the *terminal object* of a category $\boldsymbol{C}$ if for every object A in $\boldsymbol{C}$ there is a unique arrow $A \to 1$.

Monoidal categories are categories with a binary operation that resembles the properties of monoids – associative and equipped with a unit. We need monoidal categories in order to define uncertainty monads. A *strict monoidal category* $(C, \square, e)$ is a category $\boldsymbol{C}$ with a bifunctor $\square$: $C \times C \to C$ which is associative, $\square\,(\square \times 1) = \square\,(1 \times \square) : C \times C \times C \to C$ and an object e which is a left and right unit for $\square$: $\square(e \times 1) = id_C = \square(1 \times e)$. In order to reduce notation overhead, we will only work with strict monoidal categories in this thesis, even though our definitions can be generalized to all monoidal categories. Any category with finite products is monoidal, including the category of sets, and the category of endofunctors. The latter is monoidal in a second sense, with composition o as the binary operation and *Idc* (the identity functor) as unit: $(\boldsymbol{C}^{\boldsymbol{C}},\ \mathrm{o},\ Id_{\boldsymbol{C}})$. Monoidal categories are important for LBR because we will formulate risk models as a special class of objects in monoidal categories.

A *monad* over a category $\boldsymbol{C}$ is a triple (M, η, μ) where $M : \boldsymbol{C} \to \boldsymbol{C}$ is an *endofunctor* and $\eta : 1_C \to M$ and $\mu : M^2 \to M$ are natural transformations for which the equalities $\mu \circ M\mu = \mu \circ \mu M$ and $\mu \circ M\eta = \mu \circ \eta M = 1_M$ hold. η is called the unit of *M* and μ is called multiplication.

Common Monads. We will now define two specific instances of a monad that are well-known in functional programming. First the *annotation monad*, also known as the "writer monad", based on a monoid: For every monoid (R, ·, 1) the *annotation monad* of *R*, short $Annot_R$, is given by $Annot_R : A \to R \times A$ (tuples of *R* and *A*) with $\eta\ (x) = (\epsilon, x)$ as its unit and $\mu\ \big((r_1,\ (r_2, x))\big) = (r_1 \cdot r_2, x)$ as its multiplication. It annotates values *a* with annotations $r \in \mathbb{R}$ and is presented as a tuple (r, a). Second is the *list monad* (indeterminism monad). The empty list will be denoted with [], and $[x_1, x_2, \ldots, x_n]$ is a list with *n* elements x_1 to x_n. The concatenation of two lists is defined as $[x_1, \ldots, x_n] \lozenge [y_1, \ldots, y_l] = [x_1, \ldots, x_n, y_1, \ldots, y_l]$. The list monad consists of lists of values, and its multiplication is list concatenation. The *list monad* is denoted by $Lst : A \to A^*$ (*lists of A*), with $\eta\ (x) = [x]$ (*a list with one element*) and $\mu\ ([l_1, \ldots, l_n]) = l_1 \lozenge \ldots \lozenge l_n$.

In LBR, we want to describe trades and other objects of risk analysis as uncertain sequences. Sequences traditionally consist of a head and a tail, and in uncertain sequences the tail is given as a value in some uncertainty monad *M*. We will make precise the notion of uncertainty monads prior to formalizing the notion of uncertain sequences thereafter. We start by introducing another way of looking at monads.

Definition 15.4. (*Monoid in Category*).
Let $(\boldsymbol{C}, \square, e)$ be a monoidal category. Then a monoid in $\boldsymbol{C}$ is a triple $(c, \mu : c \square c \to c,\ \eta : e \to c)$ such that *c* is an object of $\boldsymbol{C}$ and the following diagrams *commute*:

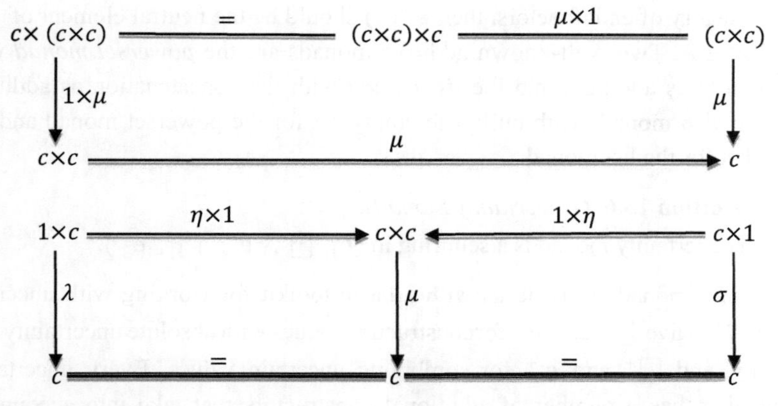

Figure 25: Two commutative diagrams of objects (vertices) and morphisms (arrows or edges) such that all directed paths in the diagrams with the same start and endpoints lead to the same result by composition.[296]

Every monad over $\boldsymbol{C}$ is a monoid in $\boldsymbol{C}^{\boldsymbol{C}}$. *Uncertainty monads* now are not only monoids, but *semirings* in $\boldsymbol{C}^{\boldsymbol{C}}$, as defined below:

Definition 15.5. (*Semiring in Category*).
Let $\boldsymbol{C}$ be a category such that $\boldsymbol{C}$ is monoidal in two products $\square^*$, $\square^+$ with units e^*, e^+ respectively. Then $(\boldsymbol{C}, \square^*, e^*, \square^+, e^+)$ form a semiring if, and only if,

1) $\square^*$ left distributes over $\square^+$: $c\square^*(c\square^+ c) = (c\square^* c)\square^+(c\square^* c)$ and
2) Multiplication with e^+ annihilates c : $c\square^* e^+ = e^+ = e^+\square^* c$.

Intuitively, in the context of uncertainty monads, e^+ maps a value (of *A*) to an element in *MA* with 'zero certainty' (for example, a probability of 0, or the knowledge that a logical proposition is false; see 15.2.). From the same perspective, e^* can be seen as the certain map, expressing absolute certainty – for example, a probability of 1. $\square^+$ fulfills the role of a logical 'or' operator as it is used to combine the uncertainty of its two components additively. If *M* is a semiring

296 Commutative diagrams play the role in category theory that equations play in algebra. Cf. MacLane (1971) and Barr & Wells (2013: Chapter 1.7) for more information, also on how to read such diagrams.

in the category of endofunctors, then $e^+(x)$ should be the neutral element of $\square^+$ for all $x \in A$. Two well-known additive monads are the *powerset monad* with set union ∪ as addition, and the *list monad* with list concatenation as addition. Both are also monads with null: The empty set for the powerset monad and the empty list for the list monad.

Definition 15.6. (*Uncertainty Monad*).

An uncertainty monad is a semiring in $(\boldsymbol{C},\ \square^*,\ e^*,\ \square^+,\ e^+)$.

Uncertainty monads provide us with a basic toolkit for working with uncertain values: We have $\square^*$ and e^* forconstructing values with absolute uncertainty and certainty, and $\square^+$ and e^+ for combining uncertain values. Every uncertainty monad then has a number of additional constructors that take into account its specific structure. The list monad is an uncertainty monad as the list $[a, b, c]$ can be seen as representing three possibilities a, b and c, all with the same likelihood. $\square^*$ is the empty list, and $\square^+$ is the list concatenation. Annotation monads on their own are not uncertainty monads, as they lack the $\square^*$ and $\square^+$ operations, although they allow for a more fine-grained representation of uncertainty (through the annotation value rather than lists). However, we can construct an uncertainty monad over any monoid through composition with the list monad. The composition $M_1 \circ M_2$ of two monads does not yield a new monad automatically, but only in specific cases. Luckily, $Lst \circ Annot_R$ is a monad for any monoid (R, •, 1).

Proposition 13:

Let (R, •, 1) be a monoid. Then $Lst \circ Annot_R$ is an uncertainty monad.[297]

Example 15.6.

Consider the following example, with the monoid $(\mathbb{R}_{\geq 0}, *, 1)$ *(multiplication of real numbers).* [(0.5, a), (0.3, b) (0.2, c)] *means that the probability of* a *is 0.5 and so on. The unit* η *maps an element* x *to the certainty* $[(1, x)]$, and μ $([(p1, [(p1_1, v1_1), (p1_2, v1_2)]), (p2, [(p2_1, v2_1), (p2_2, v2_2)])])$ *is obtained by multiplying the probability of each inner*

297 The proof of this proposition can be found in Appendix F.

element p_{ik} *with that of its outer element* p_i: [(p1 * $p1_1$, $v1_1$), (p1 * $p1_2$, $v1_2$), (p2 * $p2_1$, $v2_1$), (p2 * $p2_2$, $v2_2$)] *and so forth.*

The Giry monad (Giry, 1982) is an uncertainty monad that gives rise to a classical, probabilistic interpretation of uncertainty with continuous distributions. However, we saw that standard probability theory comes at a cost which is not only comparatively high, but really unbearable. The new and interesting twist now is that there are many other monads besides the classical probability monad that are apt for modeling uncertainty. For example, the set of belief assignments forms a monoid under the fusion operation defined in Dubois & Prade (1988b), giving rise to a model of uncertainty that is still quantitative, but not probabilistic (see 15.2., "fuzzy logic or fuzzy set theory").[298] Ergo, in the cadre of different uncertainty monads, the performance of LBR models rooting in ranking theory, for example (see 15.5.4.), or any other non-standard approach to measure uncertainty (15.2.), can in principle be *benchmarked* against standard probabilistic strategies (manifested in the Giry monad, see also 15.5.5.). On top of that, we are also planning to investigate a monad based on formal methods of argumentation (cf. Besnard & Hunter, 2001), which allows for a more principled handling of inconsistencies than our current approach (see also 15.2. "non-monotonic logic").

Uncertain sequences

Monads can be interpreted as models of computation (Moggi, 1989). In that sense, uncertainty monads are models of uncertain computations. In order to be able to reason about sequences of transactions, we now elaborate on *uncertain sequences*. Uncertain sequences have a structure that is not linear (like that of "certain" sequences), but is determined by an uncertainty monad. In **Definition 15.7.**, we grasp uncertain sequences S_M over a monad M as a union of $\star$ (the empty sequence) and $M\ (1_C \times S_M)$ (a pair of a value and the rest of the sequence).

Definition 15.7. (*Uncertain Sequences*).
Every uncertainty monad *M* over a category ***C*** gives rise to a functor $S_M : C \to C$, the uncertain sequences over *M*. S_M is defined as:

$$S_M = 1 + M\ (1_C \times S_M)$$

298 The better-known *Dempster fusion operator* (in DST, see also 15.2) is not associative, because of its normalization factor. Therefore, it cannot be used as the multiplication operator in a monoid.

S_M resembles the typical head-tail structure of lists in functional programming. The head is the first element in the tuple, 1_C – a concrete value. The tail is the rest of the list, again of type S_M. What makes this an *uncertain* list is the fact that it is wrapped in an uncertainty monad *M*. Uncertain sequences S_M are functors, but generally not monads – except for some specific cases of *M*. The empty sequence will be denoted with ⋆.

Example 15.7.
The transactions of the loan from the previous example (see also Figure 22) can be conveyed to the following uncertain sequence. The monad in this case is Lst o Annot$_R$*, a combination of the list monad and the annotation monad.*

$$s_{loan} = [(certain, (t_1, [\\ (likely, (t_2, \star)),\\ (unlikely, (t_3, \star))\\ ]))]$$

This example shows how the graphical notation maps to values of *Lst* o *Annot*$_R$, and from now on, we will only use the graphical notation.

As specification of **Definition 2.1.** and **Definition 2.2.**, we call here a risk model an uncertain sequence whose elements form a semigroup (to enable analysis of different scenarios).

Definition 15.8.1. (*Specification of Risk Models*).
If *M* is an uncertainty monad and (R, $*$) a semigroup, then we use the term "*risk model*" to refer to uncertain sequences $s \in S_M\ (R)$.

Given two risk models $s_1, s_2 \in S_M\ (R)$ and semigroup (R, $*$), we can combine them into a single risk model $s_1 \odot_* s_2$ by adding the elements at each step, effectively taking the cross product of the two sequences.

Definition 15.8.2. (*Combination of Risk Models*).
Let *M* be an uncertainty monad, (R, $*$) a semigroup, and $s_1, s_2 \in S_M\ (R)$ be two uncertain sequences. The combination of s_1 and s_2, short $s_1 \odot_* s_2$ is defined as

$$s_1 \odot_* s_2 = \begin{cases} s_1 & if\ s_2 = \star \\ s_2 & if\ s_1 = \star \\ s_1 >>= (h_1, t_1) \rightarrow (s_2 >>= (h_2, t_2) \rightarrow \mu\,(h_1 * h_2,\ t_1 \odot_* t_2)) & otherwise \end{cases}$$

The empty sequence $\star$ is a neutral element *wrt.* $\odot_*$, giving rise to a monoid of risk models $(S_M(R), \odot_*, 1)$ provided that $(R, *)$ is itself a semigroup. The $\odot_*$ operation is an important part of the toolkit for building risk models with LBR, because it allows us to fuse a number of risk models (e.g., different trades) to form a single, combined risk model. Being able to 'add' multiple risk models is of great theoretical and practical importance, and we will get back to this topic in Chapter 16.2.

Finally, we will need to be able to compute the prefix of length n of an uncertain sequence, in the same way we could compute the prefix of a regular (certain) sequence.

Definition 15.9. (*Prefix of Uncertain Sequence*).
Let M be an uncertainty monad, $(R, *)$ a semigroup, $s \in S_M(R)$ an uncertain sequence and $n \in \mathbb{N}$. The prefix of length n of s is defined as

$$prefix\,(s,n) = \begin{cases} \star & if\ n = 0\ or\ s = \star \\ s >>= (h,t) \rightarrow \mu(h, prefix(t, n-1)) & otherwise \end{cases}$$

Example 15.8.
The sequence s_{loan} *from* **Example 15.7.** *only has a maximum length of two, so we can compute prefixes between 0 and 2 in length:*

$$\begin{aligned} prefix\,(s_{loan}, 0) &= \star \\ prefix\,(s_{loan}, 1) &= [(certain, (t_1, \star))] \\ prefix\,(s_{loan}, 2) &= s_{loan} \end{aligned}$$

The operations $\odot_*$ and $prefix$ are defined independently of the underlying uncertainty monad and can be used with any risk model.

15.5.4. Concrete instantiations of uncertainty monads: ranking functions

Uncertainty monads can be instantiated in many ways, and it is our objective to explore a number of instantiations in future work (cf. also Müller & Hoffmann, 2017a, 2017b). This section serves two purposes: To demonstrate how uncertainty monads can be instantiated for a given model, and to establish the foundation for our case study in Chapter 16. At this point, we would like to recall that we have an ambitious aim which we pursue by conceptualizing LBR as a non-standard scheme for measuring risks in complex systems: namely fundamentally, to offer an alternative to classical probability theory as the foundation of risk modeling. We achieve this by making our framework, uncertain sequences (15.5.3.), parametric in the choice of uncertainty representation. Different possibilities of representing uncertainty are subsumed under the label of 15.2. and ranking theory stands out (15.3.).

As stated earlier, ranking functions (Sphon, 2009: 188) are based on the idea of ranking propositions by disbelief, or *degree of surprise* (Halpern, 2005). Propositions that are more plausible (believed) are assigned lower ranks than less plausible ones. The lowest possible rank is 0, denoting certainty, and the highest is ∞, denoting impossibility. Building on **Definition 15.3.** (Ranking Function), we illustrate the employment of ranking functions by an example.

Example 15.9.

For our LBR risk models, we are interested in the behavior of counterparties, specifically in their ability to meet their contractual obligations. We will assume three counterparties, A, B and C and denote their default events with d_A, d_B and d_C. Table 9 shows the ranking function κ_d. The most likely case is that none of the three counterparties default, and the least likely case (rank 30) is that all three default. The case of one default is much more likely (rank 10) and the case of two defaults is ranked 25.

Table 9: Ranking function κ_d, showing the likelihood of default (d_i) for three counterparties A, B and C. The most likely case is $\overline{d_A} \wedge \overline{d_B} \wedge \overline{d_C}$, meaning no defaults.

κ	$d_A \wedge d_B$	$d_A \wedge \overline{d_B}$	$\overline{d_A} \wedge d_B$	$\overline{d_A} \wedge \overline{d_B}$
d_C	30	25	25	10
$\overline{d_C}$	25	10	10	0

But how do we get from a given ranking function κ to an uncertainty monad M_κ? In order to be able to utilize our earlier definition of an *Lst* ο *Annot*, the combination of list and annotation monad, we need an associative operation on ranking functions with a unit.

Definition 15.10. (*Combination of Ranking Functions*).
Let κ, λ be two ranking functions over $\mathcal{A}$. The combined ranking function $\kappa \oplus \lambda$ is defined as

$$(\kappa \oplus \lambda)(A) = \min \{\kappa(A), \lambda(A)\}.$$

This operation is clearly associative, but it does not have a unit (i.e., there is no κ_1 such that $\kappa_1 \oplus \kappa = \kappa = \kappa \oplus \kappa_1$). The reason is that stipulating $\kappa_1(x) = \infty$ for all x would violate the conditions of **Definition 15.3.**, but any other definition would violate the property that κ_1 is a unit under $\oplus$. We solve this problem by considering *conditional ranking functions* instead, compliant with the approach by Halpern (2005). Intuitively, a conditional ranking function $\kappa(V|U)$ tells us the rank of V under the condition that U is true (that is, under the condition that U has rank 0). This means for example that $\kappa(U|U) = 0$ for all $U \neq \emptyset$. Formally, conditional ranking functions are introduced as follows:

Definition 15.11. (*Conditional Ranking Function*).
A conditional ranking function κ is a function mapping a *Popper algebra*[299] $2^W \times \mathcal{A}'$ *to* $\mathbb{N}^*$ satisfying the following properties:

1) $\kappa(\emptyset|U) = \infty \; if \; U \in \mathcal{A}'$
2) $\kappa(U|U) = 0 \; if \; U \in \mathcal{A}'$
3) $\kappa(V_1 \cup V_2 \,|\, U) = \min\{\kappa(V_1|U), \kappa(V_2|U)\} \; if \; V_1 \cap V_2 = \emptyset,$ $V_1, V_2 \in \mathcal{A}, and \; U \in \mathcal{A}'$
4) $\kappa(U_1 \cap U_2 \,|\, U_3) = \kappa(U_1 \,|\, U_2 \cap U_3) + \kappa(U_2 \,|\, U_3) \; if \; U_2 \cap U_3 \in \mathcal{A}' \; and \; U_1 \in \mathcal{A}$

From now on, we will only consider conditional ranking functions. A non-conditional ranking function κ can be turned into a conditional one by setting

$$\kappa(V|U) = \kappa(V \cap U) - \kappa(U)$$

Conversely, given a conditional ranking function κ and a formula f, we can compute the unconditional rank of f by computing $\kappa(f|\top)$ (where $\top$ symbol-

299 Formally, a *Popper algebra* over W is a set $\mathcal{A} \times \mathcal{A}'$ of subsets of $W \times W$ such that (a) $\mathcal{A}$ is an algebra over W, (b) $\mathcal{A}'$ is a nonempty subset of $\mathcal{A}$, and (c) $\mathcal{A}'$ is closed under supersets in $\mathcal{A}$; i.e., if $V \in \mathcal{A}'$, $V \subseteq V'$, and $V' \in \mathcal{A}$, then $V' \in \mathcal{A}'$. (Popper algebras are named after Karl Popper, who was the first to consider formally conditional probability as the basic notion.) Cf. Halpern (2005: 74f.).

izes *verum* or a tautology as it is custom in formal logics). The $\oplus$ operator (**Definition 15.10.**) naturally extends to conditional ranking functions. In addition, we can define a unit κ_1:

$$\kappa_1 (V|U) = \begin{cases} 0 & if\ U = V \neq \emptyset \\ \infty & otherwise \end{cases}$$

Proposition 14:

Conditional ranking functions form a monoid $\mathfrak{R}$ *with* $(\oplus, \kappa_1)$.[300]

By composing the annotation monad of ranking functions, $Annot_{\mathfrak{R}}$, with the list monad we directly obtain an uncertainty monad (see Proposition 13 in 15.5.3.).

Let us go back to the sequence in Figure 24 (in 15.5.1.) and assume that we had annotated it with a ranking function such as κ_d. Whenever the sequence splits into multiple branches, we gain additional information on each branch. For example, if we follow path A (consisting of transactions t_1, c_1, c_2 and t_2), we know that at no point in the sequence was there a default event for either of the two counterparties. In path C on the other hand, the counterparty of the bond defaulted after one payment, whereas the other counterparty remained liquid throughout. We can annotate the sequence with this information (assuming the bond was issued by counterparty A, and the loan taken by B). The result is shown in Figure 26, ommitting most of path B to save space. If there is a branch in which no additional assumptions are made, we could annotate it with $\top$ (truth) since $\kappa_{\top} = \kappa$.

Comparing Figure 26 to the sequence in Figure 22, we can see that the former is annotated with elements of the algebra on which the ranking function is established, and the latter is annotated with uncertainty values themselves. The disparity is that elements of the algebra do not tell us the likelihood of a branch, and we cannot combine them in a straightforward way to obtain the likelihood of a whole path, for example path A. We, therefore, ought to translate the knowledge available at each step into a new conditional ranking function that is transformed to an annotation of this step. This process is called *conditionalization*, and equivalent methods exist for other representations of uncertainty, such as probability distributions, belief functions, etc. (cf. Halpern, 2005).

300 The proof of this proposition can be found in Appendix F.

Definition 15.12. (*Conditionalization of Ranking Functions*).
Let κ be a ranking function for $\mathcal{A}$, let $U \in \mathcal{A}$ such that $\kappa(U) \neq \infty$. Then the conditional rank of $V \in \mathcal{A}$ given U is defined as $\kappa(V|U) = \kappa(U \cap V) - \kappa(U)$. The function $\kappa_U : V \mapsto \kappa(V|U)$ is a ranking function, called the conditionalization of κ by U.

We are now equipped to model branches in uncertain sequences, by conditioning each branch with the desired information and then combining the branches deploying + of the uncertainty monad. If we wish to model a branch where no information has been gained, we can condition it with $\top$.

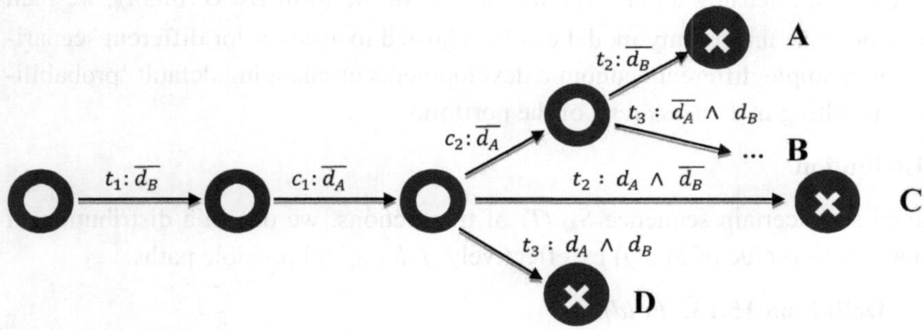

Figure 26: Transactions in a collateralized loan, annotated with default information.

Table 10: κ'_d obtained by conditioning κ_d ***with*** $d_A \vee d_B$. (Table 10 is obtained by applying Def. 15.11. to the ranking function in Table 9.)

κ	$d_A \wedge d_B$	$d_A \wedge \overline{d_B}$	$\overline{d_A} \wedge d_B$	$\overline{d_A} \wedge \overline{d_B}$
d_C	20	15	15	∞
$\overline{d_C}$	15	0	0	∞

Example 15.10.
If we condition κ_d with $d_A \vee d_B$ (meaning that at least one of A and B has defaulted), we receive the function κ'_d as shown in Table 10. The rankings of cases where neither A nor B have defaulted evaluate to ∞. The rankings of the remaining cases are all lower than before (in Table 9).

Note that κ_U is a ranking function, but we annotate uncertain values with conditional ranking functions. We can turn κ_U into a conditional ranking function as described in the previous sections, resulting in κ'_U with $\kappa'_U (V|U) = \kappa_U (V \cap U) - \kappa (U)$. While **Definition 15.12.** specifically applies to ranking functions, similar definitions can be found for other models, including belief functions, possibility measures, and probability measures (see also 15.2.). An overview of the technique is given by Halpern (2005: Chapter 3).

15.5.5. Evaluating risk models

In this section, we will evaluate uncertain sequences of transactions by formulating queries. Focusing on uncertainty monads of the form $Lst \circ Annot_R$, we then show how the uncertainty model can be adjusted to account for different scenarios, for example different economic developments or changing default 'probabilities', resulting in a '*stress test*' of the portfolio.

Distribution

Given an uncertain sequence $S_M (T)$ of transactions, we obtain a distribution of transactions (value of $M (T)$) by effectively '*folding*' all possible paths:

Definition 15.13. (*Fold*).
Let T be a *monoid* and let $S_M (T)$ be an *uncertain sequence* of R. The operation *fold*: $S_M (T) \rightarrow M (T)$ is defined as

$$fold\ (x) = \begin{cases} \eta\ (\epsilon) & if\ x = \star \\ x >>= (h, t)\ \rightarrow fold\ (t) >>= y\ \rightarrow \eta\ (h\ \cdot y) & otherwise \end{cases}$$

Example 15.11.
Let l be the unsecured loan annotated with , unlikely, likely, certain *from Figure 22 (in 15.5.1.). Using* min *and* certain *as the multiplication and unit of the monoid, we get*

$$fold\ (l) = [(likely, t_1 + t_2), (unlikely,\ t_1 + t_3)]$$

For the collateralized loan cl from Figure 26, we get

$$fold\ (cl) = [(\kappa_I, t_1 + c_1 + c_2 + t_2), (\kappa_{II}, t_1 + c_1 + c_2 + t_3), (\kappa_{III}, t_1 + c_1 + t_2), (\kappa_{IV}, t_1 + c_1 + t_3)]$$

The ranking functions κ_i are detailed below, but only for values where they differ from ∞.

$$\begin{aligned} \kappa_I &= \{d_c \mapsto 10, \quad \overline{d_c} \mapsto 0\} \\ \kappa_{II} &= \{d_c \mapsto 15, \quad \overline{d_c} \mapsto 0\} \\ \kappa_{III} &= \{d_c \mapsto 15, \quad \overline{d_c} \mapsto 0\} \\ \kappa_{IV} &= \{d_c \mapsto 5, \quad \overline{d_c} \mapsto 0\} \end{aligned}$$

Each κ_i corresponds to one of the paths A to D in Figure 26, and is defined for d_c and $\overline{d_c}$. The reason for this result is that each of the paths specifies the truth values of d_A and d_B, and therefore only the value of d_c is unknown. For example, path A evaluates to $\overline{d_A} \wedge \overline{d_B}$.

Assuming that the uncertainty monad is $Lst \circ Annot_R$ for a monoid R, and there exists an order $\leq_R$, we can already readdress a prominent question in risk modeling: "What is the minimum loss incurred with a (qualitative) 'probability' of α or smaller?" for an $\alpha \in \mathbb{R}$. This is, as we know, also known as the guiding question behind the *value at risk* (VaR) risk measure (see 2.2.2.).[301] In reference to RQ2.4, which puts forward the quest for novel risk management approaches in finance, we are thus in the position to not only point to the previous subchapter where we exemplified the integration of non-probabilistic models of uncertainty (by means of ranking theory) into one single formal framework, but also to expound that we can thereby enter the realm of risk assessment in financial systems (illustrated in 16.3.).

Predicates

With $fold$ from **Definition 15.13.** we can obtain a distribution of outcomes in the chosen uncertainty model, considering all possible paths. There is another type of analysis we can perform: Instead of applying $fold$ to an entire uncertain sequence, we might want to compute a distribution of only those paths that meet a given condition. Such conditions can be described with *predicates*. For example, we could be keen to test the likelihood that our liquidity drops below a cer-

301 We saw that VaR is not the 'holy grail' of risk measures. We make the comparison with VaR at this place because the definition can be applied to non-probabilistic models in a straightforward way (as announced in 15.1.). As also remarked there (footnote 271), we now write "α" in lieu of "$1-\alpha$" (2.2.2.).

tain threshold during the trade (even if it rises above that threshold again before the end of the trade). By describing this condition as a predicate, we get a distribution in the underlying uncertainty monad of the two truth values $True$ and $False$. The evaluation is straightforward: Given a predicate p and uncertain sequence s, we apply p to s by exploiting the fact that Boolean values form a monoid under disjunction ($\vee$) and $False$.

Definition 15.14. (*Evaluation of predicates*).
Let $s : S_M(T)$ be an uncertain sequence and let $p : T \rightarrow \{True, False\}$ be a predicate on its values. The evaluation of p on s, short $\mathcal{I}(p, s)$ is given by

$$\mathcal{I}(p, s) = fold\left(S_M(p)(s)\right)$$

In **Definition 15.14.** we use the functoriality of uncertain sequences to transform the predicate p into a morphism $S_M(T) \rightarrow S_M(B)$.

Example 15.12.
In the running example of a collateralized loan involving two counterparties (see Figure 26), we are interested in the likelihood that we have to make payment t_2. This can be expressed as the mapping $p_{t2} : x \mapsto x = t_2$, which returns $True$ if a transaction equals t_2 and $False$ otherwise. Applying the predicate to cl, the collateralizsed loan, we get

$$\mathcal{I}(p_{t2}, cl) = [(K_V, True), (K_{V\,I}, False)]$$

with the following ranking functions, again shown only in places where they differ from ∞:

$$\begin{aligned} \kappa_V &= \{d_A \wedge d_C \mapsto 25, \quad d_A \wedge \overline{d_c} \mapsto 10, \quad \overline{d_A} \wedge d_C \mapsto 10, \quad \overline{d_A} \wedge \overline{d_c} \mapsto 0\} \\ \kappa_{V\,I} &= \{d_A \wedge d_C \mapsto 20, \quad d_A \wedge \overline{d_c} \mapsto 15, \quad \overline{d_A} \wedge d_C \mapsto 15, \quad \overline{d_A} \wedge \overline{d_c} \mapsto 0\} \end{aligned}$$

Scenarios

By conditioning the initial ranking function κ we can adjust our model to different scenarios. We introduced this technique in **Example 15.10.**, where we conditioned κ_d with the information that at least one of the counterparties A and B has defaulted. However, by conditioning the initial κ that is used to evaluate an uncertain sequence of transactions $_{\Bbbk}(T)$, we can only change the *a priori* rankings that hold at the beginning of the sequence. If we are inclined to express, for example, that at least one bank defaults within five units of time, we need to change the uncertain sequence itself.

As we already have a means to modify uncertain sequences (in the form of $\odot_*$, **Definition 15.8.2.**), it makes sense to define scenarios in terms of it, avoiding the addition of a new primitive. We will therefore say that a scenario *sc* is a kind of uncertain sequence, and apply it to a risk model *m* by computing $m \odot_* sc$. Scenarios should only change the probabilities of the outcomes in a risk model, not the values of individual transactions (because those are determined by the underlying financial contracts, independently of any uncertainties). This condition ensures that every scenario can be applied to many different risk models, because it is defined without reference to a specific contract. For this reason, scenarios are uncertain sequences over the monoid over the one-element set, $(\{\star\}, \cdot_\star, \star)$.

Definition 15.15. (*Scenario*).
A scenario is an *uncertain sequence* $s \in S_M(\{\star\})$.

Example 15.13.
The case that counterparty A defaults after the second payment is modeled in the following scenario, short sc_1:

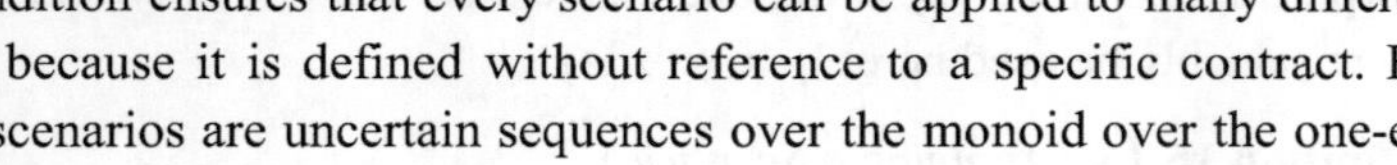

In scenarios, the ⋆ symbol is the only value allowed for transactions (because scenarios are uncertain sequences over the one-element set, and the only element of that set is ⋆). Therefore, every edge on the graph of a scenario is annotated with ⋆. Further, some edges are annotated with the event ⊤, or "any event". Because ⊤ is always true, a branch with the probability ⊤ will always be taken, and conditioning a ranking function $\Bbbk$ with ⊤ has no effect. We can therefore use ⊤ in scenarios whenever we do not want to constrain the set of events under consideration at a particular point.

As shown in **Example 15.13.** and in analogy to the literature review in Chapter 11, scenarios describe sequences of events or expectations of possible future events, relevant to potential business responses, thus constraining the space of possibilities in which a risk model is evaluated. When designing a scenario, one is free to choose how strict this constraint is – for example, we can specify exactly one sequence of events that we want to evaluate (as we have done in the example), or we can more vaguely state that some events are excluded, without changing the probabilities of the remaining events.

To apply a scenario S_M ($\{\star\}$) to a risk model $S_M(T)$, we first need a mapping from $\{\star\}$ to T, so that we can turn the scenario into an uncertain sequence $S_M(T)$ and apply the multiplication operation $\odot_*$. This mapping should be a monoid homomorphism, and since $\{\star\}$ is the one-element set there is only one mapping that may reasonably be used here: $!_T \ : \star \mapsto \epsilon_T$.

Definition 15.16. (*Applying a Scenario*).

Let M be an uncertainty monad, $(T, \cdot, e)$ be a monoid, $r \in S_M\ (T)$ a risk model and $s \in S_M\ (\{\star\})$ be a scenario. The application of s to r is defined as

$$r \odot_{\mathrm{T}} S_M\ (!_T)(r).$$

Example 15.14.

To apply sc_1*, the scenario introduced in* **Example 15.13.**, *to the risk model of the collateralized loan, we first need to compute* $!_T\ (sc_1)$ *– in other words, we need to map* $\star$ *to the null transaction e, resulting in the following sequence* $sc_1' = \ !_T\ (sc_1)$: *Note that* sc_1' *is not a scenario anymore, because its*

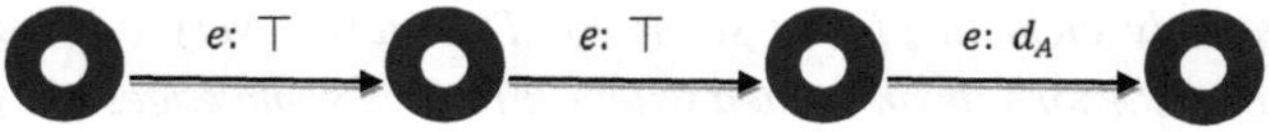

values are transactions instead of $\star$. *Instead,* sc_1' *is a risk model, a value of* S_M (T)*, similar to the model of the collateralized loan cl. We can therefore compute* $cl \odot_{\mathrm{T}} sc_1'$*, resulting in the sequence shown in Figure 27.*

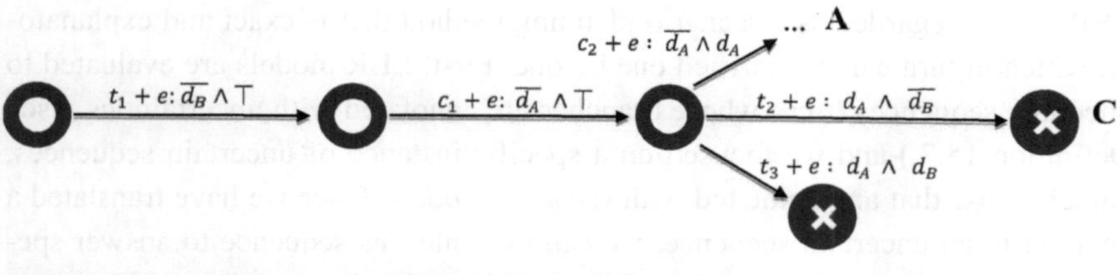

Figure 27: Risk model *cl'*, showing the collateralized loan after applying the scenario from **Example 15.14.** A comparison with Figure 26 points to two important differences. The path after node A has been ommitted, because it will never be reached – its condition is $\overline{d_A} \wedge d_A = \bot$. And each of the first three transactions in the sequence has been augmented by *e* – the empty transaction. This change is only shown for illustrative purposes as it does not alter the value of the uncertain sequence.

In this example, we showed each of the two steps involved in the application of a scenario separately. In an application, the user would only be shown the end result, as the intermediate uncertain sequence (with the empty element *e* substituted for ⋆) is of no relevance to the analysis and interpretation process.

Scenarios can be combined with $\odot_\wedge$, multiplication of uncertain sequences under ∧. $sc_1 \odot_\wedge sc_2$ for two scenarios sc_1 and sc_2 and a semigroup *R* intuitively corresponds to sc_1 *and* sc_2. An important aspect of the practicality of LBR models is what kind of questions they answer, that is, the output of our models, which is thus what the next subchapter deals with.

15.6. Model Interpretation and Output: An Exact, Explanatory Scenario Planning Method

Our models, taking into account the structure of the assets (derivatives), that have been posted as security for loans for example, are intended to be utilized in preparation for and hedging against the impact of systemic and extreme risk events. The latter can be grouped into two themes:

1) *Market Scenarios*: What kind of scenarios may *cause* a rapid change in prices or correlations between prices? Are there any hidden correlations between positions in our portfolio?
2) *Exposure Scenarios*: Are there counterparties to which we have a high indirect exposure? Etc.

LBR can be regarded as a scenario planning method that is exact and explanatory, which in turn can be clarified one by one. First, LBR models are evaluated to uncertain sequences (trees whose branches are annotated with uncertainties – see Definition 15.7.) and we focused on a specific instance of uncertain sequences, namely those that are annotated with *scenario models*. Once we have translated a contract to an uncertain sequence, we can evaluate this sequence to answer specific queries (such as in 1) and 2) above). This evaluation constitutes the output of LBR and elucidates that LBR model outcomes can be tested and simulated. For example, as we are going to do in the case study (see Chapter 16), we can assess the effect of changing the likelihood of default of one counterparty. In this way, LBR is a scenario planning method.

Second, LBR is *exact* since formal, numerical and symbolic, representations of uncertainty (15.2., 15.3.), functional programming (15.4.), as well as their combination respectively (15.5.) really are at its nexus. Put differently, our language-based approach rests on a precise mapping of contracts and their constitutent parts to uncertain sequences. If we apply this mapping not to an entire complex contract, but only to the more basic contracts it consists of, we get a number of uncertain sequences (rather than one all-encompassing sequence). Each of those uncertain sequences itself can be queried and investigated as we suggested above. We can process these partial interpretations and appeal to their role or function in more encompassing risk models, i.e., to assess how the risk model of the more complex contracts is determined by the risk models of their components. When applied in this more *synthesis*-oriented manner, the risk models proposed in this thesis can thus, third, be employed to *explain* in detail how its output is traced back to its input.[302]

Moreover, LBR is *explanatory* in a fundamental sense because explanatory models, in general, focus on, and inquire into, interrelationships, interactions and dependencies in systems at hand (see 8.2.), which holds true for LBR as well. On the one hand, LBR is steered by a question on causal links (see the first one above, in 1)). On the other hand, LBR models themselves, however, foreground rather logical than causal relationships, which does not disqualify them since

302 This feature is much stronger than the truism that the output can always be derived from its input in correct for-mal modeling as the latter does not distinguish explanatory models and systemic modeling, respectively, which res-pects analysis *and* synthesis. The approach of partially evaluating contracts needs to be investigated in future work.

explanatory models generally capture the structures of a system which are constituted by the relations between parts of the system and between parts and the whole (see 8.2.) and these relations can be causal or logical. Logical connections are appreciated in our LBR framework through the integration of both formal logics (see 15.2.) and the vocabulary from Jones et al. (2001).

Caution is required when speaking of "model output" in connection with LBR as it would not do justice to our overall proposal if we simply grasped LBR as a single risk model. Even though we will concretize LBR in Chapter 16 for illustration purposes and to answer RQ2.5, respectively, we usually refer, on the one hand, to model*s*, the plural not the singular. Because, on the other hand, it is more proper to say that it is a novel risk modeling approach, a new framework or class of models, which recalls the three-tier model of LBR (see Figure 21), differentiating between model*s*, method and framework. On the top scale, LBR is conceived of as concrete risk models and their output is a distribution of returns (or losses) over different scenarios, which possess different qualitative probabilities of materialization (Chapter 18) and serve as an anchor around which falsifiable hypotheses can be put up. On the middle layer, we gain certain precise as well as explanatory scenarios, testable and appraised with respect to specific queries, where the appraisal or analysis through *predicates* embodies the output of LBR; and in the broadest sense, it does not make much sense to examine its output, or it is at least underdetermined, namely when we think of LBR as a loosely defined framework or paradigm. (In some regard, we could maybe maintain that a narrative is the output, which is not to neglect in the overall risk management process, see Part IV.) We wish LBR to be understood in this threefold way and for whose scope we achieve the following preliminary result (also with regard to RQ2.1).

Proposition 15:

Structure-oriented and explanatory risk modeling warrants the focus on objects that exhibit much structure. The more complex financial instruments are, the more structure they possess, and the more the modeler can derive from that structure to measure risks.

As a consequence, LBR thrives when we deal with (structurally) complex instruments. This is the hallmark of LBR which faces a trend marked by an exploding number of different financial products that also become more and more complex (Célérier & Vallée, 2014; Admati & Hellwig, 2013).[303] Therefore, its potential as well as the number of its possible application areas is huge (Chapter 17). On the one hand, further evidence for the usefulness of modularity can be found in the realm of CDOs. Before the global financial crisis (and ever since)[304], it has not only been regular CDOs that enjoyed great popularity, but also more exotic products such as CDOs-squared (see footnote 288; cf. Brunnermeier & Oehmke, 2009; Nomura, 2005) – CDOs whose collateral are other CDOs (as opposed to more traditional debts such as mortgages), and CDOs-cubed – CDOs whose collateral are CDOs-squared.

These instruments can be represented in LBR in a straightforward way, because our models for CDOs do not distinguish different types of collateral. Any uncertain sequence of transactions can be employed to represent the collateral, and so our methodology is able to handle CDO-squared, CDO-cubed and, more generally, CDO^n for any n. On the other hand, our approach to risk modeling is by no way even restricted to *financial contracts*: If we have a domain-specific language for, say, *commodity* shipments, we can still apply our proposal for scenarios, as long as that language has an interpretation as uncertain sequences.

Unfortunately, it is currently a not yet settled question where the demarcation line between sufficiently complex and simple financial products runs. This classification is, in fact, much less clear cut than one may suspect (Brunnermeier & Oehmke, 2009: 4; Becker et al., 2012: 5). However, it is clear that if we, for example, invest all our capital in *non-complex* products, such as shares, then LBR cannot say anything about portfolio risk, except for "it can go up or down" – we would simply be at the mercy of deep uncertainty.

303 Célérier & Vallée (2014: 4, 21) also provide evidence for this trend: The more complex a product is, the more profitable it becomes for the bank structuring it.

304 The 2008 fallout gave a few credit products a bad reputation, like CDOs or CDS. But now, a marriage of the two terms (using leverage, of course) is making a comeback – it just comes under a different name: "*bespoke tranche opportunity*". (Bloomberg, 2015).

16. Case Study: LTCM and Extreme Risk

In this inquiry, we envision the behavior of LBR by taking up the case of LTCM from Chapter 5.2. The LTCM case is a predestined application example of LBR since its fall counts as one of the most impressive instances of massive losses in derivative markets. This chapter is structured as follows. We start by reconstructing its dynamic trading and so-called 'fixed income' strategy with an example trade (16.1.), before elaborating on how the portfolio is described in a concrete LBR model (16.2.). The out-come of our exemplary risk model for the portfolio will be discussed at the end, in the remaining two sections, 16.3. based on the three steps of visual data mining (overview – zoom/filter – details); and 16.4. as an overall bottom line.

Derivatives are often subject to the following criticism of hidden tail risk. According to Raghuram Rajan (2006), a former chief economist of the International Monetary Fund (IMF),

> ... it may well be that the managers of these firms [investment funds] have figured out the correlations between the various instruments they hold and believe they are hedged. Yet as Chan and others (2005) point out, the lessons of summer 1998 following the default on Russian government debt is that correlations that are zero or negative in normal times can turn overnight to one, a phenomenon they term "phase lock-in". A hedged position can become unhedged at the worst times, inflicting substantial losses on those who mistakenly believe they are protected.

Furthermore, (credit) derivatives "can be difficult to price due to their complexity and due to some CDOs being based on OTC and assets that are lightly traded or not traded" (Tapiero & Totoum-Tangho, 2012). One of our aims for this case study is therefore to show how the idea that correlations rise in times of crisis can be represented in our LBR models (see also 1) Market Scenarios in 15.6.). More generally, we seek to depict how to describe a realistic trade in LBR, by building a complex model from smaller pieces, and how to extract answers to typical questions in risk management from this model. This chapter thus serves both as pattern for a manual for practitioners and as evidence for the relevance of our approach.

16.1. Example Trade

Generally, LTCM can be classified as a more highly leveraged version[305] of market neutral funds that actively seek to avoid major risk factors, but take bets on relative price movements utilizing investment strategies such as fixed income arbitrage among others (Fung & Hsieh, 1999: 319, 329).[306] LTCM's basic fixed income arbitrage strategy consisted in 'convergence' and 'relative-value' arbitrage: the exploitation of price differences that either must be temporary or have a (ostensibly) high *probability* of being temporary (MacKenzie, 2003: 354). Prototypical in turn were its many trades involving 'swaps', wherefore the following is a description of a swap-spread arbitrage trade. It is based on MacKenzie (2003).

In this trade, LTCM would buy US Treasury bonds with a maturity of twenty years and a yield of 6.77%. At the same time, a swap of a fixed interest rate (in USD) of 6.94% vs. the Libor could be entered into, meaning that LTCM pays 6.94% and receives whatever the Libor rate is. The swap spread is therefore (6.94 - 6.77 = 0.17) %. The trade is profitable for LTCM if it can borrow money at a rate at least 17 basis points (0.17%) *cheaper* than the Libor. At the time, an interest rate of about 20 basis points below the Libor was available to LTCM (the *repo rate*)[307], resulting in a net annual cash flow of 0.03%:

$$
\begin{aligned}
&(Libor\ rate - repo\ rate) + 6.77\% - 6.94\% \\
&= (Libor\ rate - repo\ rate) - swap\ spread \\
&= 0.20\% - 0.17\% \\
&= 0.03\%
\end{aligned}
$$

305 "Hedge funds typically leverage their bets by margining their positions and through the use of short sales" (Fung & Hsieh, 1999: 314).

306 Specifically, LTCM can be viewed as a fixed income arbitrage fund (which are themselves only a small segment in the entire hedge fund and commodity trading advisors fund industry). In contrast to related strategies such as long–short equity, stock index arbitrage, convertible bond arbitrage, fixed income arbitrage generally refers to the trading of price or yield along the yield curve, between corporate bonds and government bonds of comparable characteristics, or more generally, between two baskets of similar bonds that trade at a price spread (Fung & Hsieh, 1999: 320).

307 The discount stems from the bonds being posted as a collateral and a 'haircut' (additional cash from LTCM) to protect against default.

Table 11: Rates for LTCM trade.

Quantity	Symbol	Value
Principal	*P*	100 000 USD
Haircut	*Hc*	500 USD
Swap rate	*Swp*	6.940 %

This trade involves two counterparties, *A* and *B*. One lends money to LTCM and, in return, receives US Treasuries as collateral and the haircut (glossary) from LTCM. The other one pays interest at the Libor rate to LTCM while receiving interest at the fixed rate of 6.94%. In LTCM's case, the two counterparties were usually different in order to obscure the fund's trades (MacKenzie, 2003; Lowenstein, 2002).

16.2. A Fixed Income Portfolio in LBR

We will first incorporate the two parts of the trade separately into LBR and then combine them using the $\odot_+$ operator defined in section 15.5.3.[308] We are going to use the monoid of conditional ranking functions with $\oplus$ and $\mathcal{k}_1$ (see 15.5.4.) in an uncertainty monad *Lst* o $Annot_{\mathfrak{R}}$.

The first part of the trade is essentially the collateralized loan from Figure 26. The collateral in this case are US Treasuries, and the interest rate depends on Libor. We borrow money at an interest rate of 5.425%, and provide US Treasuries and an additional 'haircut' as collateral to secure the loan. Since the loan is used to buy the bonds, the only cashflows involved are the haircut (*hc*), paid by us at the beginning of the transaction, and the interest payments. The variable *p*

308 An alternative approach would be to start with transferring the example to the programming language by Jones et al. (2001), see 15.4., i.e., to combine the two separate parts of the trade by using the *and* operator. The first part is essentially *coLoan*, the collateralized loan from **Example 15.5.** (see 15.5.1.). The collateral in this case are US Treasuries, and the interest rate depends on Libor. By means of the two auxiliary definitions, *repo* for the interest at which LTCM can borrow, and *treasuries* to model US Treasuries we can arrive at the following representation:

```
treasuries :: Double → Double → Days → Contract
treasuries coll p i t  =  (loan p i t)
                          'and' (get coll)
                                'and' (truncate t (give coll))
```

This translation is provided for illustration purposes only. Due to the lack of space we skip a lengthy continuation of this procedure and refer the reader to Müller & Hoffmann (2017b).

stands for the principal, i.e. how much money we borrow. The total length of this transaction is one week. Table 11 shows the fixed quantities involved in the trade. The variable quantities (interest rates) are modeled as uncertain sequences and will be explained next.

Since the profitability of the trade directly depends on the difference between the swap rate and the variable rates, we will model the latter as uncertain sequences. The relevant rates will be abbreviated with *lbr* (Libor), *rp* (repo rate) and *ust* (US Treasury bonds). The repo rate, *rp*, is shown in Figure 28.

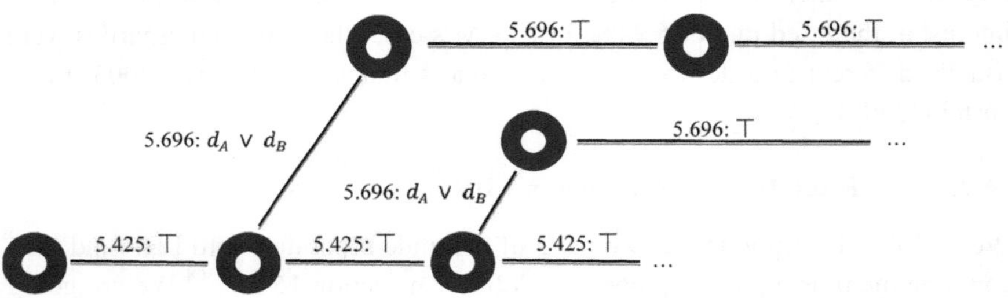

Figure 28: Repo rate *rp* expressed as an uncertain sequence. At each stage the rate either stays the same (condition ⊤) or increases, if one of the counterparties defaults (condition $d_A \vee d_B$).

Note that, in contrast to the uncertain sequences we have shown previously, *rp* does not depict transactions that happen at a point in time. Instead, it shows the interest rate on that day. In order to use *rp* as part of the model of the LTCM trade, we can use $\odot_*$ from **Definition 15.8.2.**, but with multiplication as the semigroup operation. This way, we can multiply a quantity such as the principal *p* with the interest rate at a given day. The libor rate follows a similar structure and is shown in the following Figure 29.

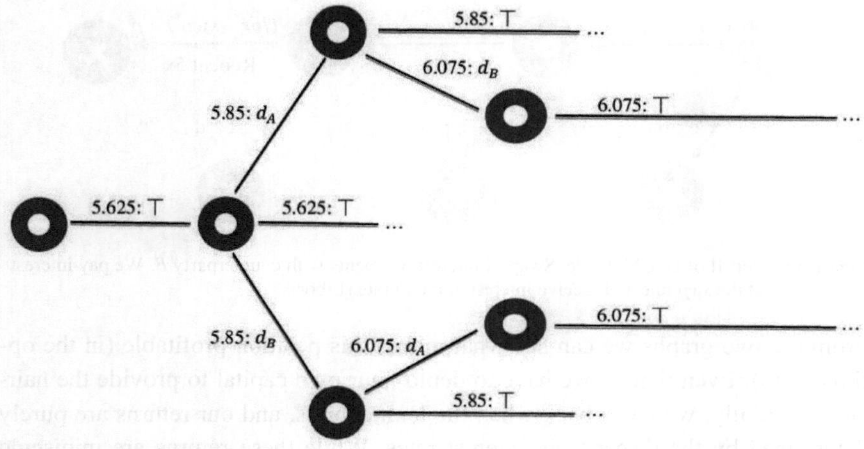

Figure 29: Libor rate *lbr* expressed as an uncertain sequence (values in percent). The rate increases if one counterparty defaults (conditions d_A and d_B), and increases sharply if two counterparties default ($d_A \wedge d_B$). Note that this graph contains a number of similar subsequences, annotated with the condition $\top$ – this information could be compressed by displaying it as a directed acyclic graph instead of a tree.

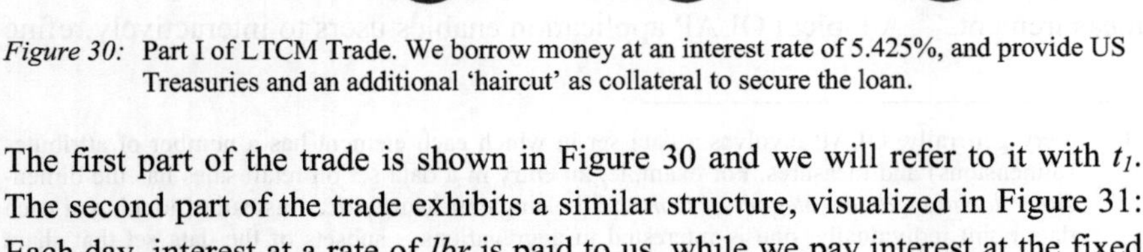

Figure 30: Part I of LTCM Trade. We borrow money at an interest rate of 5.425%, and provide US Treasuries and an additional 'haircut' as collateral to secure the loan.

The first part of the trade is shown in Figure 30 and we will refer to it with t_1. The second part of the trade exhibits a similar structure, visualized in Figure 31: Each day, interest at a rate of *lbr* is paid to us, while we pay interest at the fixed rate *swp*. We refer to this part with t_2.

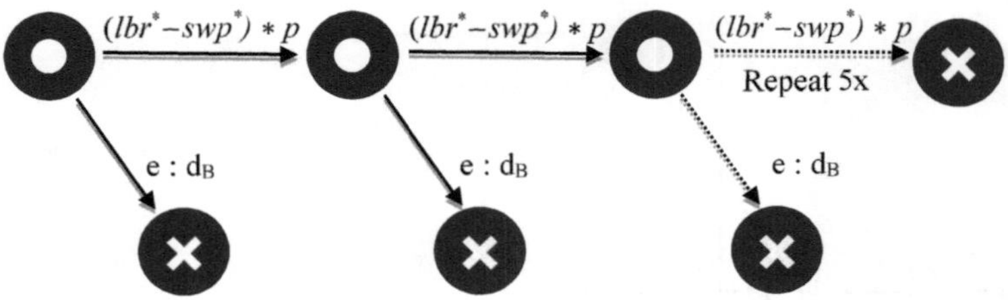

Figure 31: Part II of LTCM Trade. Swap of interest payments with counterparty *B*. We pay interest at the *swp* rate and receive interest at the *lb* rate (Libor).

From the two graphs we can see what makes this position profitable (in the optimal path): Even though we have to deploy our own capital to provide the haircut *hc* initially, we get it back when the loan expires, and our returns are purely determined by the disparity in interest rates. While these returns are miniscule compared to *p*, they are more significant in relation to *hc*, so the return on our capital is higher than the net cash flow of 0.03%. The uncertain sequence representing the overall trade is given by $t_{LTCM} = t_1 \odot_+ t_2$.

16.3. Analysis

The analysis of LBR risk models is an *iterative* and *interactive* process in which small, step-wise transformations are applied to the data. The transformations are intended to highlight interesting patterns, and resemble the workflows of interactive data mining techniques (Keim et al., 2008) used in On-Line Analytical Processing, OLAP (Han & Kamber, 2000), software across business functions including sales and marketing analysis, budgeting, planning, and performance measurement.[309] A typical OLAP application enables users to interactively refine

309 Very generally, OLAP involves a data set in which each element has a number of attributes (dimensions) and measures. For example, an entry in a data set on retail sales has the dimensions: *location, date, category of item* and the single measure *price*. Instead of looking at each data point individually, one is interested in aggregations – subsets of the data set that share some dimensions (e.g., all sales in a location on the same day) and are aggregated on their measures (e.g., average price).
Of most interest to us is the structure of dimensions. Their values are arranged in a lattice, and the "drill-down" and "roll-up" operations correspond to the two binary lattice operations (Kuijpers & Vaisman, 2016). In LBR, we can impose a similar structure on the uncertainty annotations (*Uncertainty Monad*) and on sequences, enabling an analysis workflow similar to that in typical OLAP products.

the aggregated data set by applying filters and other operations (Ravat et al., 2008) to it, commonly following a three-step process: overview, zoom and filter, and details-on-demand (Shneiderman, 1996).

The following paragraphs describe how each of these steps is accomplished in LBR. Since the example trade t_{LTCM} is a bet on the difference between two interest rates (spread), the question that steers this analysis will be, "what could cause the spread to shrink below the threshold of profitability, and how exposed are we to liquidity risk in such a scenario?"

16.3.1. Overview

The first step is to gain an overview of the possible developments of t_{LTCM}. We start by inspecting the graph in Figure 39 (see Appendix G) – however, it is evident that the raw graph of the entire tree is not an appropriate tool for risk analysis, because it contains all possible developments and its size increases in proportion with the number of times the $\odot_*$ is used to combine underlying sequences. Further, this kind of display (rendering the uncertain sequence as a tree) is only possible because we use $Lst \circ Annot_{\mathfrak{R}}$ as the uncertainty monad. Showing the 'raw' data for an uncertain sequence is only possible if the underlying monad lends itself to this kind of visualization – in particular, the probability distribution has to be discrete, so that each value can be shown as a branch. If it was continuous, extracting a tree structure would require a discretization step such as splitting the distribution into percentiles.

We, therefore, need to find a better way to show the possible developments over time, as a high-level starting point for the analysis. One approach is to show the range of possible values at each point in time, resulting in a more traditional graph. To obtain the graph shown in Figure 32, we first compute the prefix at each step using $prefix$ from **Definition 15.9.** For example, $prefix\ (t_{LTCM}, 3)$ gives an uncertain sequence representing the trade after three days. We then compute the distribution of values on that day: $fold(prefix\ (t_{LTCM}, 3))$, and plot the values.

For the case study, we inspect the graph in Figure 32 and decide next to focus the view on days one to eight (Figure 33), in order to get a better idea of the interest-rate based transactions that occur in this time.

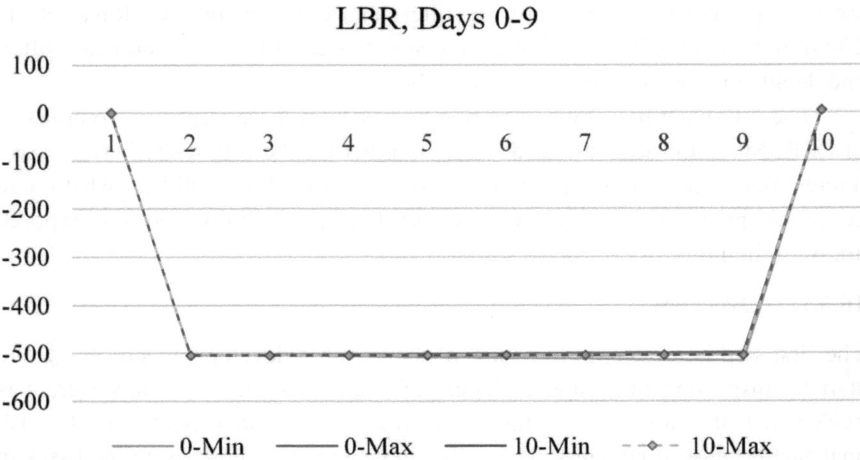

Figure 32: Range of values in the period from zero to nine days, computed with ***prefix*** (**Definition 15.9.**). This technique works independently of the underlying uncertainty monad *M*. Each rank in $\boldsymbol{k}_1$ is represented by two lines, one for the low end of the range (e.g., 10-Min) and one for the high end of the range (10-Max). The graph is dominated by the initial outlay of 500. We restrict the time range to days 1 to 8, as shown next in Figure 33.

16.3.2. Zoom and filter

The overview of the whole trade t_{LTCM} in Figure 32 clearly showed the cash outlay at the beginning, and the recurrency of profitability at the end. However, for the purposes of risk analysis we are more keen to learn about the transactions that occur in between, because they represent the actual fixed-income part of the trade.

The next step in our analysis is, therefore, to restrict the value graph to the period between one and eight days, resulting in Figure 33. Here, the most likely development (rank zero), marks both the high end and the low end of the value graph, as indicated by the (dark and light) green lines. This is due to the dependence on interest rates. The possible developments appear to split after day two.

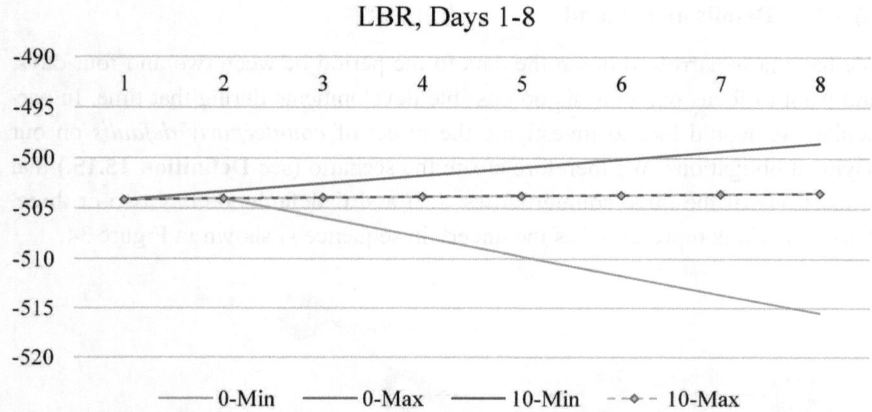

Figure 33: Range of values in the time period from one to eight days. The most likely development, rank zero, marks both the high end and the low end of the value graph, as indicated by the (dark and light) green lines.

Once we have narrowed down the time frame for analysis even further, we can show the subsequence in more detail. One approach is to bring some order into the graph, and reduce the amount of nodes that are visible. In risk models based on $Lst \circ Annot_{\mathbb{k}}$, sequences can be shortened by applying $fold$ to a number of nodes that should be hidden from view. This method is shown in Appendix H (Figure 40, 41).

In Figure 40 in Appendix H, an uncertain sequence is visualized similar to previous graphs, showing the nodes and edges annotated with transactions. However, compared to earlier figures there are two improvements. First, the branches are ordered by transaction value on the y-axis, making it easier to spot cases where unexpected losses are occurring. Second, the initial three nodes have been reduced to two in order to hide the details of this linear subsequence.

A common workflow in interactive OLAP analysis is to isolate an interesting subset of the data and then switch to a different visualization for that subset, so that previously unseen patterns may be revealed. In LBR, we can achieve a similar effect by plotting the values of a sub-sequence as shown in Figure 41.

16.3.3. Details on demand

We have now narrowed down the data to the period between two and four days, and want to focus our analysis on possible developments during that time. In particular, we would like to investigate the effect of *counterparty defaults* on our payment obligations. We therefore create the scenario (see **Definition 15.15.**) that at least one of the three counterparties A, B and C defaults on day two or three. This scenario is represented as the uncertain sequence s_1 shown in Figure 34.

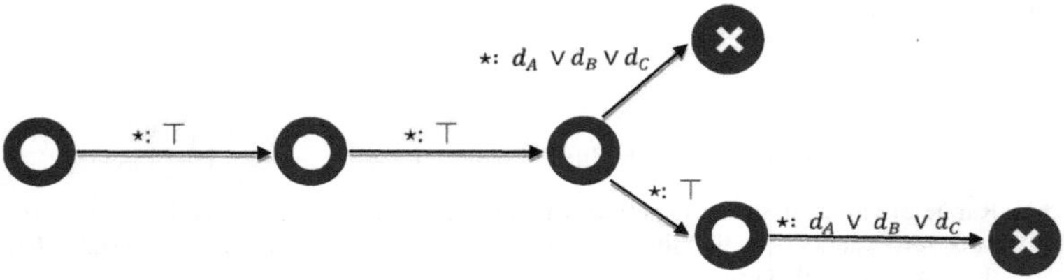

Figure 34: Scenario s_1 modeling the default of A, B or C on day two or three.

By combining s_1 and t_{LTCM}, we get an uncertain sequence showing only the possible transactions for the case that at least one default occurs in the period of interest: $t'_{LTCM} = s_1 \odot_* t_{LTCM}$. This sequence, t'_{LTCM} can then be analyzed again using the approach described in Sections 16.3.1. and 16.3.2.

16.4. Discussion and Conclusion

This case study showed how to model a single trade of the kind favored by LTCM in our approach (in form of t_{LTCM}), and how to evaluate its counterparty and liquidity risks iteratively to answer RQ2.5 on the concretization of LBR models. We were able to perform this analysis without relying on statistical data about interest rates, by utilizing primarily structural information about the rights and obligations towards counterparties. In Chapter 5.2., we were looking at the emergence and development of LTCM's downfall. The trade we analyzed above is a typical example of LTCM's strategy that led to the hedge fund's demise. So, we could generalize our analysis to a large part of LTCM's portfolio, provided it is formalized as an uncertain sequence of transactions. Our model would then have been able to predict some of the consequences of the events in 1998, without having to make difficult assumptions such as pinpointing a probability for a default of the Russian government. However, knowing about the possible consequences of extreme risks is not enough, because one also has to *act* on that knowledge (see Part IV), and as also seen in 5.2., it appears that LTCM's belief in its own invincibility, and consequent refusal to make preparations for an abrupt and thorough worsening of market conditions, also played a role in its failure. LBR of course cannot prevent such errors of judgment (see Chapter 21). But it can be an important addition to the *toolkit* of risks analysts (Chapter 13), because it requires such few assumptions and because of the low cost (time and effort) incurred by analyzing another scenario or formulating another query.

In critical view of our procedure here in this frame, i.e., of having investigated risks by categorization (counterparty vs. liquidity) even though we reject the silo-treatment of risks (see 5.1.), *nota bene* that we do not stipulate any sharp boundaries between risk classes. For example, the transition from counterparty to liquidity was organic: Counterparty and liquidity risk are captured by the same model (splitted in two parts) – more precisely, counterparty risk is a result of repeated transactions with liquidity risk.[310] The specific LBR risk model was labeled by the variable "t_{LTCM}".

One of the challenges in displaying the information was that we cannot compute an expected value from a distribution with ranking functions. We addressed this issue by providing the range of values for each scenario. While the example trade is typical of the type of trades that some hedge funds engage in, our uncertainty model was constricted to the minimum amount necessary for the two use cases. For example, we could have considered more general macroeconomic indicators than just the default events of three counterparties, making the logic available for expressing conditions much more fine-grained. A more detailed version of this case study is explored elsewhere (Müller & Hoffmann, 2017b).

The case study introduced a number of general patterns for risk modeling with LBR, such as using the $\odot_*$, $fold$ and $prefix$ operations to first assemble a model from its components and then reduce it to answer specific questions, for example by applying a scenario (see Figure 34). Even in its basic form, the model presented here is still able to compute not just a general distribution of the expected outcomes, but also the loss given the default of one or more counterpar-

310 Other 'risk silos' could easily enter the stage. For instance, market risk manifests itself because contracts involve market data (like interest rates) and are thus subject to market risk also.

ties. It becomes vividly visible in this case study that there does not exist a single LBR risk analysis outcome, which is in line with what the systems movement propagates (e.g., investigate objects from different angles, in larger and smaller systems): Both Figure 32, 33 and 40, 41 constitute concrete LBR model outputs (the latter, however, with comparative advantages as argued in 16.3.2.), that, in general, hinge on which guiding question is pursued.

By evaluating prefixes of an uncertain sequence we gave a prediction of the liquidity requirements during the trade. Several advantages of our approach stand out and will be presented more comprehensively in Chapter 19. First, LBR models are based on structural descriptions of the trade (specific rights and obligations with counterparties), and not on statistical estimations of the price of the trade. Because of this, we can evaluate the same model in multiple ways, by transforming it and applying the relevant $fold$. Second, LBR models are modular, because a complex model can be assembled from simpler parts (for example, by defining $t_{LTCM} = t_1 \odot_+ t_2$). A practical consequence of modularity, which leads us to the subsequent Chapter 17, is that firms can establish a vocabulary of common trades and so reduce the amount of time needed to create a new model.

17. Managerial Implications

LBR must prove itself not only in relation to the scientific quest for knowledge, but first and foremost as an aid to the people responsibly active in practice (see Part IV). LBR thrives in complex environments and, accordingly, there is a whole myriad of real-world application contexts where LBR models can flourish. One of its primary and predestined employments is *financial investment planning, wealth and portfolio management*. Portfolios are traditionally structured to cope with 'normal' levels of volatility, but in the wake of the abnormal the time-honored principle of reducing and controlling risk by diversification falls short.[311] A solution for wealth and portfolio management can be tail hedging, which allows portfolios to be positioned more offensively in a world of turmoil caused by recurring financial bubbles.

The basic idea of active and dynamic *tail risk hedging* is that severe system crises (as in 2008) create exploitable opportunities for investors since an increase in risk exposures (via risky assets) during those stressful times may improve the return distribution of most investment portfolios ("simply because valuations are cheap and risk premiums are high"; Davis & Page, 2013: 302). Put differently, a tail-hedging strategy is not only risk-reducing but also return-enhancing and it should be thought of "not as a high-frequency trade or even passive buy-and hold but rather as an asset-allocation decision" (Bhansali, 2014: 73). In general, there are many ways to approach tail hedging, ranging from a simple purchase of 'insurance' or the holding of cash, via put options to a portfolio of volatility-focused strategies that spans multiple asset classes and financial instruments

311 Historical relationships between many asset classes broke down and correlations rose in the financial crisis which crescendoed in 2008, so that even carefully diversified portfolios suffered. For example, the average 60 (stocks) / 40 (bonds) portfolio lost more than 29% in the year ending February 28, 2009. Source: Barclays Capital, S&P and AllianceBernstein (McKoan & Ning, 2011). However, diversification could indeed have its resurgence, namely on a meta level; then higher order diversification would mean that "guarding against the tails is best achieved by a mix of approaches rather than blind adherence to one" (Bhansali, 2014: 46).

which can be described in our formal language of LBR. In this area of wealth and portfolio management, LBR can be applied in two different ways. First, it complements risk management tools and systems which are currently used. By comparing the different approaches and their performance through case studies and simulations, risk managers will be able to spot divergences which may hint at risk factors that are genuinely not picked up by one of the methods, but that are clearly of crucial importance to tail risk hedging.[312] Second, LBR can become part of a tail risk management toolkit for drafting new investment strategies. In this application, risk measured by LBR is, for instance, one of a number of indicators that influence the allocation of funds in a portfolio. The first use case benefits from requiring very little change to existing processes for modeling and managing risk, and is, therefore, a suitable starting point for the introduction of LBR to wealth management firms.

The second use case requires the application of the theoretical principles behind LBR to an entire investment business, so there is a bigger hurdle to implementing it in practice. We believe though that the latter is the more promising application in the long term, because it would not only improve awareness of risks from extreme or tail events to our portfolio, but also decrease cost by applying automated reasoning techniques and yield new insights on investment strategies to the desired end that returns are increased by diminishing the downside of present investment strategies. The second use case further clarifies that LBR has the potential to transcend the narrow framework of risk measurement (and enter the investment side), which is remarkable since its intrinsic performance value for practitioners might then really be unimpaired despite that ineffective risk assessment (which we aspire to overcome in this thesis) is not always the most pressing *practical* issue. There exist others which are predominantly culpable for

312 Such a case study could be steered by the following question: What is the performance of a LBR-based tail hedging strategy compared to a more traditional one? Due to the scarce data on extreme or systemic risk events, the case study would not be able to conclusively judge the quality of the predictions of both models (see also Chapter 19 on model validation). However, the case study would shed some light on the behavior of both models for recent specific events, depending on the period that is selected (e.g., the global financial crisis, the Asian crisis). Perhaps more importantly, it would also allow us to compare the cost of different approaches.

past risk management failures in real systems and/or which are easier to surmount (Wiggins & Metrick, 2014).[313]

In connection with the subject of the previous chapter, other territories of LBR application enclose the assessment of liquidity and counterparty risk. Many organizations engaged in financial or physical trading activities, such as *brokers*, *banks* or *commodity trading houses*, face the challenge to manage substantial counterparty risks. In this realm, LBR could also help break through these obstacles. Nonetheless, a thorough evaluation and identification of possible LBR implications for management must be postponed due to the radical novelty of LBR (specifically, in terms of risk management *practices*). For now, we synthesize with regard to RQ2.6 about the practical value of LBR on a not yet solid basis:

Conjecture 16:

A logic-based risk modeling approach (LBR) is, prima facie, suitable for the economic practice and can be employed for not only direct and narrow risk assessment, but also financial investment planning, portfolio, wealth and tail risk management, by asset managers, brokers, banks or commodity trading houses among others.

To strengthen the potential of LBR further, it can be demarcated from established, used and concrete alternatives in academia as well as of the economic practice. Three rival approaches are singled out.

"Finance without Probability": Shafer & Vovk (2001) propose a game-theoretic framework as a mathematical foundation for probability where all its classical interpretations (Hájek, 2011) fit into it and which can dispense with the partly troublesome stochastic assumptions currently accepted in finance theory (see e.g., IIIc) in 2.4.). Instead of employing a stochastic mod-

313 For example, the demise of Lehman Brothers, which is willingly treated as a model case of (glaring) risk management failure, was preceded by the operation of "a very respectable risk management system" (ibid.: 1). The collapse of the investment bank can namely be fully explained by the fact that Lehman actively began dismantling its carefully crafted risk management framework as it pursued a new high-leverage growth strategy. "[I]t exceeded many risk limits, aggressively increased a number of risk metrics, disregarded its risk procedures, and excluded risk management personnel from key decisions. In October 2007, it replaced its well-regarded chief risk officer with a seasoned deal maker who lacked professional risk management experience." (Ibid.).

el, their game-theoretic approach can use the market to price volatility, to test for market efficiency, etc. From the angle of LBR, Shafer & Vovk's (2001) ideas to handle various practical and theoretical complications associated with conventional probability-based models are thus similar to what we are trying to achieve by introducing ranking theory (and other non-standard non-probabilistic models of uncertainty). However, since the authors are more concerned with efficiency (like the efficient-market hypothesis) in lieu of addressing effectivity in the first place and as they do not expand on the complexity and structures of financial instruments altogether – indeed their attention is restricted to European and American options –, we would be reluctant to call their proposal a true competitor of LBR. This holds for the next two alternatives to a much lesser degree.

ACTUS (Algorithmic Contract Types Unified Standards). The goals of project ACTUS, put forward by Deloitte Consulting LLP and the Brammertz Consulting GmbH among others, are similar to ours in that it, "the ACTUS project aims to establish a global standard that allows a consistent mapping of financial instruments by means of unambiguously defined and standardized contract types" (Brammertz Consulting, 2014), using the obligations of counterparties and external risk factors as the most basic data for analysis (Mendelowitz et al., 2013). However, the approach differs from LBR in mainly three aspects. First, ACTUS defines a collection of around thirty standard contracts, while we only define a small collection of building blocks from which a large variety of contracts can be derived. A drawback of their catalogue approach is that it only covers contracts that are currently in use, whereas ours can be employed to describe contracts that are completely novel.[314] Our case study in the previous chapter illustrated the difference very well. The trade described in Section 16.1. consists of an interest rate swap and a collateralized loan. Each of those can be modeled with ACTUS contract types, but their combination (the actual trade) cannot. In LBR on the other hand, we can simply use the $\oplus$ operator to obtain a combined model of the two. The combined model takes into account inter-

314 Cf. Jones et al. (2001): "The finance industry has an enormous vocabulary of jargon for typical combinations of financial contracts […]. Treating each of these individually is like having a large catalogue of prefabricated components. The trouble is that someone will soon want a contract that is not in the catalogue."

dependencies between risk events. For example, the default of one counterparty leads to an increased default risk of all other counterparties.

Further, when modeling trades with ACTUS one has to specify a set of default events, including dates, as input to the model. In LBR we use uncertain sequences to describe all possible combinations of default events. Because of this structure, we are able to automatically identify the most relevant default scenarios. A final disparity between ACTUS and LBR is that our modeling approach allows for a variety of representations of uncertainty, including ranking functions as we have shown in examples throughout Part III. ACTUS does not address the question of uncertainty representation directly, but it does make use of common techniques for calculating the price of financial instruments, and so implicitly assumes classical probability throughout.

Fault Tree Analysis. The way we visualized uncertain sequences as trees, for example in Figure 26 and Figure 29, is visually similar to fault tree analysis (FTA), a failure analysis technique used primarily in safety and reliability engineering (Tapiero, 2013: 208) but also in finance and credit risk analysis (e.g., Gatfaoui, 2008). However, FTA is fundamentally different from LBR. First, traditional FTA does not have a notion of time and therefore cannot express the temporal sequence of transactions that our LBR models are based on. A fault tree in FTA is essentially a term in Boolean algebra that is interpreted in classical probability theory. The trees that LBR deals with represent sequences of events, and while terms in a Boolean algebra do appear in our models, they act as conditioners of the underlying uncertainty models. In FTA the terms stand for actual events (in the probability-theoretic sense of the word) and are ultimately combined into a single event whose probability can be computed.

Second, FTA is a top-down analysis method, because the first step in fault-tree analysis is to pick a critical event. The analysis then focuses on potential causes for that specific event. LBR, by contrast, is both analytical and synthetic (see 15.6. and 15.4.), it is a bottom-up method because it starts by describing the individual components of a trade. An LBR risk model for a firm is assembled from a number of risk models for its branches, departments, and so forth. Only after the LBR model has been defined we may pick one, or a number of, critical events to study, by describing them as scenarios

(15.5.5.). While LBR can be used to predict the consequences of individual critical events, it also has explanatory power and supports other analyses (see 15.5.5. on evaluating risk models, and the case study). Our approach thus avoids having to focus on a single event appointed beforehand and *ex ante*, and encourages a dynamic, interactive way of analyzing and synthesizing risks. A general appraisal of LBR on a larger scale follows in Chpt. 19.

18. Scales of Measurement and Qualitative Probabilities

It is a commonplace that we must not undertake impermissible transformations on the data we wish to analyze, nor must we make interval statements on ordinal data, in particular (Flood & Carson, 1993: 41f.).[315] In this thesis, we differentiated between different forms of risk and uncertainty (see Chapter 4) and investigated their relationship with different forms of complexity (see Chapter 6.1.4. and 6.2.2.). Based on the characterization of *deep uncertainty* which emerges from highly organized and dynamic complexity and which is not measurable in probability terms (see Table 5; cf. also Stulz, 2008; Kuritzkes & Schürmann, 2010; Kwakkel et al., 2010; Pruyt & Kwakkel, 2014), we hypothesize that when we as risk modelers are in a state of deep uncertainty about some future data or events (see our understanding of "risk" proposed in Chapter 4.1.), then we can perform, not a cardinal, but an ordinal 'measurement' of that risks only.[316] In other words freely adapted from the logician and philosopher W.V.O. Quine, cardinalists' overpopulated universe offends the aesthetic sense of us who have a taste for desert landscapes. Their aspiration after pedantic preciseness abets a breeding ground for disorderly mathematical operations on data and risks that necessitate modesty.

---

315 We differentiate among four types of scales: *nominal*, *ordinal*, *interval* and *ratio*. According to Tal (2015: 3.2), "[n]ominal scales represent objects as belonging to classes that have no particular order, e.g., male and female. Ordinal scales represent order but no further algebraic structure" and admit of any transformation function as long as it is monotonic and increasing. Celsius is an example of interval scales: "they represent equality or inequality among intervals of temperature, but not ratios of temperature, because their zero points are arbitrary. The Kelvin scale, by contrast, is a ratio scale, as are the familiar scales representing mass in kilograms, length in meters and duration in seconds." This classification was further refined to distinguish between linear and logarithmic interval scales and between ratio scales with and without a natural unit (ibid.). "Ratio scales with a natural unit, such as those used for counting discrete objects and for representing probabilities, were named 'absolute' scales" (ibid.).

316 It is an open issue whether the representation of magnitudes on ordinal scales should count as measurement at all (Tal, 2015).

Proposition 17:
Deep uncertainty does not admit of degrees, but is a merely comparative notion.

Proposition 17 complements the qualification of the term "deep uncertainty" which was introduced in 6.1.4. It clarifies that some uncertainties or risks have to be measured on an ordinal scale, from which it does not follow that we would always be bound to the constraints of ordinal schemes (which represent order but no further algebraic structure) when we model risks because not all of them are laden with deep uncertainty. However, on the one hand, Wang (1996: 3), for example, claims that "the main function of a risk measure is to properly rank risks", which points to the centrality of ordinality. On the other, given Proposition 17 and the significance of deep uncertainty for risk assessment in dynamically complex financial systems, we must employ a formal apparatus for modeling that approves both a common cardinal as well as an ordinal theory where degrees of uncertainty have no arithmetical meaning.

While classical probabilities are represented on more demanding cardinal (precisely, absolute) scales, LBR makes room for evaluating ordinal risks. In the context of this work, we confined ourselves to ranking theory (15.3.), which allows for more generality than probability theory and (at least in its early version) assumes an arbitrary set of ordinal numbers as the range of a ranking function (Spohn, 1983, 1988). (If we intend to calculate with ranks though, this meant to engage into *ordinal arithmetic*, which is awkward; Spohn, 2009.)[317] However, it is interesting to see that Spohn's (2009) law of disjunction (see definition 15.3.) can be conferred to ordinal scales.

In the broader context of LBR, it is very valuable that it comprises models and theories that are explicitly skeptical about degrees of, or quantitative approaches to, uncertainty. In an environment where deep uncertainty predominates, LBR could thus tie in, for instance, modal logics or the proposal of Halpern & Rabin (1987), in particular, where more than an ordinal assignment is not strived for as likelihood is not assigned quantitative values through numerical probabilities or ranks etc. (see the meaning of qualitative probabilities below instead). The following Figure 35 integrates the new dimensions around *deep uncertainty* and scales of measurement in the known, but slightly altered frame-

317 Spohn (2009), therefore, confines himself to complete ranking functions.

work about the disassembly of the complexity notion and a characterization of its different subtypes.

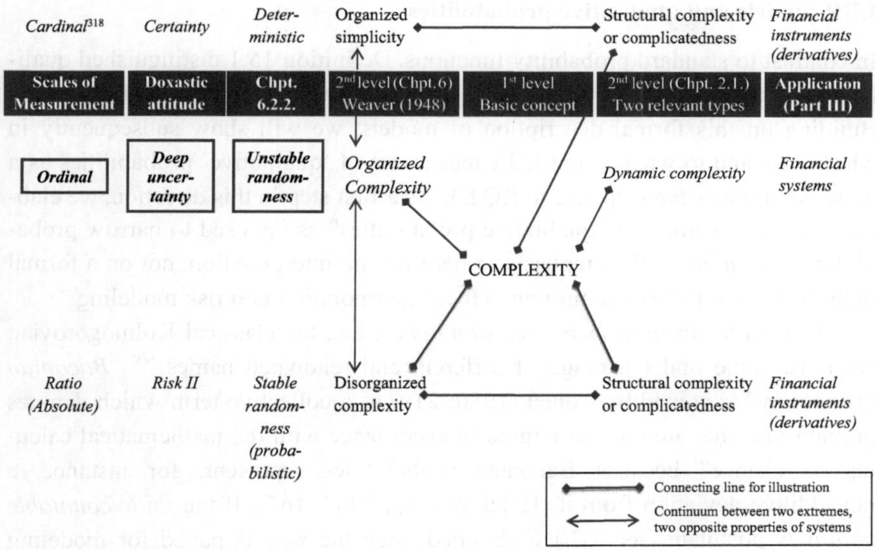

Figure 35: The disassembly of complexity III: The unifying framework.

Figure 35 consolidates new and previous insights about traits of complexity and extends former schemes (e.g., the Weaverian). It not only illustrates that organized or dynamic complexity produces unstable randomness (see also Figure 16), which in turn is responsible for a magnitude of uncertainty that can only be captured on an ordinal scale, but also, on the right-hand side, that LBR might be driven by the challenge of dynamic complexity in financial systems; however, it nonetheless exploits the opportunities of structural complexity as related to financial instruments. *Nota bene* that furthermore dynamic complexity and structural complexity, at least in this example, are entangled: A major source of the increased interconnectedness and complexity of modern financial systems are the new products like CDSs and CDOs, which leads to the fact that more and more

318 The condition of *summativity* holds (see 6.1.1.).

financial institutions interact over time (Admati & Hellwig, 2013: 161, 66-69, 181; Boot, 2011: 1; Brunnermeier & Oehmke, 2009: 2).

LBR models and qualitative probabilities

In contrast to standard probability functions, Definition 15.1 distinguished qualitative or, as we may now add, partially[319] *ordinal* measures of uncertainty. Building on this formal description of models, we will show subsequently in what sense and to what extent LBR makes use of 'qualitative' probabilities as a more comprehensive response to RQ2.3. As a first step in this direction, we elaborate on the meaning of "qualitative probabilities" as opposed to narrow probabilities *simpliciter* – the emphasis is here on the interpretation, not on a formal definition (15.1.) – prior to turning to their incorporation into risk modeling.

Departures from probabilities *simpliciter*, i.e., the classical Kolmogorovian calculus, come under a range of different and renowned names.[320] "*Baconian probability*" is coined by Cohen (1980: 219) as a collective term which denotes probabilities that are not "structured in accordance with the mathematical calculus of chance" because Baconian probabilities represent, for instance, a nonadditive deviation from it (Hájek & Hall, 2002: 167). If the *finite/countable additivity* postulate (see 7.2.) is dropped, then the way is paved for modeling ordinal risks properly. In this tradition (cf. also Fine, 1973), we conceive of qualitative probabilities as probabilities where we *dispute the requirement that they have to have numerical values*. Put differently, LBR is compatible with both, it favors a *cardinal* measurement (be it conventionally probabilistic or embedded in (forms of) ranking theory, DST, etc.), depending on the quality of the data, i.e., if deep uncertainty is not an overwhelming issue in the environment we operate in; but, at the same time, it countenances theories of *comparative probability*, exemplified by statements of the form "A is at least as probable as B", which exactly corresponds to an *ordinal* measurement.

In terms of another major disparity between classical and qualitative probabilities, we woud like to stress that probabilistic reasoning presupposes classical two-valued logic, in the sense that the definition of probability functions requires

319 Compare, for instance, example 15.1 (cardinal) and example 15.3 (ordinal) in Chapter 15.1.

320 For example, there are advocates of *indeterminate, imprecise* or *vague probabilities*, who represent probabilities not as single numbers, but as intervals, or more generally sets of numbers (e.g., Bradley & Steele, 2014; van Fraassen 1990). Skyrms (1980) allows probabilities to be *infinitesimal*. Some physicists have flirted with *complex-valued probabilities* and so forth.

notions from classical logic (Adams, 1998: 22; Weatherson, 2003: 111; footnote 278). On the other hand, LBR is amenable to non-classical and modal logics (see 15.2.), which can bear fruits in attempts to remove difficulties with two-valued logic, particularly in fuzzy sets, and complex systems (Jaynes, 2003: 18). In this further explored respect, qualitative probabilities under the guise of different models of uncertainty find their concrete way into LBR, ensuing from LBR models that are designed in accordance with definition 15.1 (ad RQ2.3). The Euler diagram hereinafter sums up and depicts the extension of "qualitative probability" in terms of its relationship to some other similar concepts.

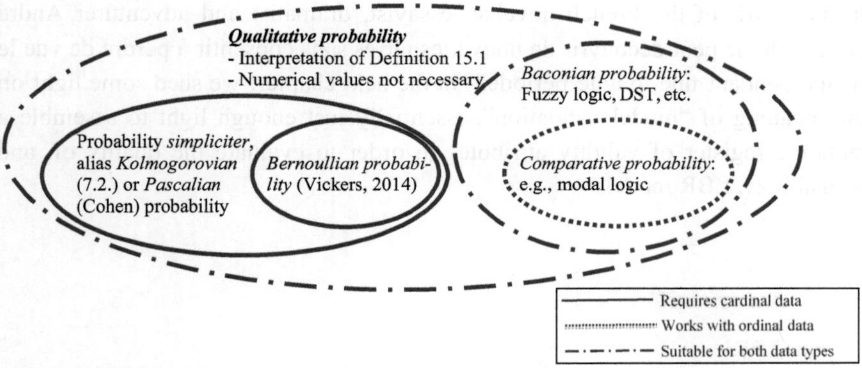

Figure 36: The notion of qualitative probability as head of a cluster.

The transition from classical to qualitative or Baconian probabilities does not involve a loss of relevant information and, therefore, seems tenable or even reasonable for risk modelers. First, we comply with the highest measurement standards permissible – cardinal risks permit a cardinal measurement of risks and ordinal risks reclaim ordinal measurement techniques. Second, the actual origin of risk measurement is the actual *decison* about taking a risk or allowing one to take it, which is fundamentally *binary* (i.e., of the "yes or no" type), with the result that ordinal information often suffices (Artzner et al., 1999: 208; and see also Part IV). Third, risk managers (i.e., decision-makers) are mostly concerned about the *cost* or *the severity of tail events*, rather than their probability of occurrence or other statistical properties (Bhansali, 2014: 14). The *strategic* question one must ask is not, how likely is the extreme risk event? The questions must be:

What is the situation and its impact if that crisis strikes, no matter how small the probability? What makes the difference between survival and almost certain ruin? Etc. (Malik, 2007: 112f.; Bhansali, 2014: 15). We should prioritize *resilience* and persistent *effectivity* over efficiency and alleged 'optimization' because success relates to the former in the light of (deeply) unforeseen events (Bhattacharya et al., 2015: 933; Probst & Bassi, 2014: 124; Sheffi, 2005).

Having both the right conceptual vocabulary (interpretation as qualitative probabilities) and the right underlying mathematics (uncertainty models) is essential for being able to understand and explain organized complex systems as well as their manifestations (in banking) and implications (for risk management). In the words of the French novelist, essayist, dramatist and adventurer André Gide: "On ne peut découvrir de nouvelles terres sans consentir à perdre de vue le rivage pendant une longue période." In the next chapter, we shed some light on the meaning of "model validation", essentially just enough light to assemble a tentative register of validity attributes in order to evaluate the quality of, and plausibilize, LBR models.

19. Model Validation

The assurance of model validity is a prominent challenge in the social sciences (Grösser & Schwaninger, 2012: 157; Schwaninger, 2010: 1422). Surely, it is an uncontroversial and unambiguous matter in *pure* mathematics – namely, a matter of formal accuracy rather than practical use. *Such* mathematical models or pure analytic statements "do not make any assertion about the empirical world, but simply record our determination to use symbols in a certain fashion" (Ayer, 1952: 31) and, therefore, they can be shown to be either true or false. In this study (and the social sciences tout court), however, we have to rest content with imperfect models.[321] (Numerical or mental) models with *empirical* content, such as LBR and other models of financial systems, are by their very nature abridged and restricted representations of the real world and thus "wrong" (Sterman, 2000: 846).[322] As they never comprehensively capture the complexity of the social system of interest, their absolute validation, verification is impossible (Sornette, 2003: 134f.; Sterman, 2002; Zeigler et al., 2000; Forrester, 1961: 123).[323] This means that validity cannot reveal itself mechanically in our realm. It is not sufficient to point to an entirely theoretical validation in the form of (sound) mathematical propositions, theorems, formal algorithms, etc.

---

321 In addition, House & McLeod (1977) reject the desirability of perfect models, even as an ideal concept.

322 This is consistent with our definition 2.1. and even if risks are conceived of as subjective constructions, in lieu of real-world, objective phenomena, they would eventually be representations of the real world. The tension between 'objective' representation and 'subjective' construction is resolvable, e.g. if the modeler is regarded as creating "a new world" (von Foerster, 1984) by the act of either observing or modeling (cf. also Watzlawick, 1980).

323 "The word 'verify' derives from the Latin *verus* – truth; Webster's defines 'verify' as 'to establish the truth, accuracy, or reality of.' 'Valid' is defined as 'having a conclusion correctly derived from premises… Valid implies being supported by objective truth.' By these definitions, no model [with empirical content; C.H.] can ever be verified or validated. Why? Because all models are wrong." (Sterman, 2000: 846). See also footnote 214.

A second overrestriction of the notion of model validity, and thus a second major problem with so-called early logical empiricism (or logical positivism),[324] lies in the insistence on predictive ability as the *only* criterion for model justification (cf. also Milton Friedman's appeal for *positive finance*; McGoun & Zielonka, 2006: 49; Scherer & Marti, 2008: 263)[325]. As Barlas & Carpenter (1990: 154) have outlined:

> Since, according to logical positivism, the content of a scientific theory [or model; C.H.] is irrelevant to the philosophical problem of verification, explanatory power is not a criterion. According to the principle of verifiability (or falsifiability), the only criterion for justification is whether the observations match with the predictions (implications) of the theory. According to this view, explanation may be quite important in other activities, such as the construction of new theories, but has nothing to do with justification.

Yet, relying merely on predictions for model validation resembles an absurdity.[326] Indeed, apart from the accuracy of predictions as an admittedly important aspect of the *quality* or *usefulness* or *validity* of a model, i.e., how adequately the inferences from the model match reality, other criteria (see below), and specifically the plausibility of the model assumptions, need to be taken into account. Explanation must be esteemed as evidence of knowledge (Barlas & Carpenter, 1990: 154) and a model ought to generate the "right output for the right reasons" (Barlas, 1996: 186; Forrester, 1968) since model validity cannot be controverted without reference to a specific (modeling) purpose (Forrester, 1961). In other words, it is a relative concept.

Hence, in contrast to validation in the sense of preserving truth, on the one hand, and reliability of predictions, on the other hand, the validity of a model should be defined broadly and loosely as "usefulness with respect to some purpose" (Barlas, 1996: 84), as "the property a model has of adequately reflecting the system being modeled, contingent on the model's purpose" (Kleindorfer &

324 Cf. Barlas & Carpenter (1990: 154), and Creath (2011).

325 *Positive finance* purports that a model or hypothesis "is true if it corresponds to what people are doing" (McGoun & Zielonka, 2006: 49). Positive finance is the most widespread variant of *positivistic finance*, which in turn predominates within the finance discipline (Scherer & Marti, 2008: 263) and which "considers phenomena as ontologically given to the observer (i.e., the researcher) and suggests a structural similarity (or even identity) between financial models and hypotheses and the financial markets that they describe" (ibid.). Positivistic finance not only deals with the misguided question of under what conditions a model or hypothesis is *true*, but also provides inadequate answers (cf. Scherer & Marti, 2008, who, however, seem to overlook the former).

326 Toulmin (1977), by reviewing the last 25 years of philosophy of science, finds that we would then consider horse race tipsters scientists and evolutionary biology nonscientists.

Geneshan, 1993; cf. also Grösser & Schwaninger, 2012: 157). Put differently, "[a] model is valid if it represents what it is supposed or claimed to represent" (Schwaninger, 2010: 1422). Conceptually, the validation process is an iterative learning cycle, embedded throughout the model-building operation (Richardson & Pugh, 1981: 311; see Figure 19). It becomes a semiformal, conversational process in which validation efforts gradually establish (more but not completeness achieving) trust and confidence in a model (Barlas, 1996; Klir, 1991: 119; Forrester & Senge, 1980) and where understanding is enhanced through the interaction of a formal model (e.g., a risk model) with a mental model (i.e., of individuals or groups) (Morecroft, 2007: 375). As a consequence, we can summarize in the words of Barlas & Carpenter (1990: 157) that

> [a] valid model is assumed to be only one of many possible [or admissible; Dubois & Prade, 1980: 189] ways of describing a real situation. No particular representation is superior to all others in any absolute sense, although one could prove to be more effective. No model can claim absolute objectivity, for every model carries in it the modeler's world view. Models are not true or false but lie on a continuum of usefulness.

In this respect and steered by the prior work of Rossi (2014: 79ff.), Stern & Feldman (2013), Schwaninger & Grösser (2008: 451), Holton & Lowe (2007), McNeil et al. (2005: 41) and Bacharach (1989: 500), we elicit a set of criteria that aids to evaluate the validity, usefulness or quality of a model, in general, and of LBR risk models, in juxtaposition to primarily probabilistic rivals (Table 3), in particular. Further, we organize model validity features under the latter rubric by grouping them as rather theoretical or more practical. This collection is meant to be illustrative rather than exhaustive; overlappings are avoided.

Table 12 gives an overview of the different dimensions of model validity which this study proposes based on the aforenamed prior work in the literature. They are spelled out, delineated, and discussed in the context of LBR thereafter, which also functions as a résumé of this Part III.

Table 12: Validating LBR risk models along a collective of reasonable criteria.

Dimensions / criteria	*Logic-Based Risk Modeling (LBR)*	*Competing models*
(1) Falsifiability	In several regards	Not discussed
(2) Comparability	In several regards	Not discussed
(3) Parsimony and simplicity	Prima facie - better than - better than	Due to (**): Non-feasibility of absolute validation - Probabilistic risk models - Explanatory risk models
(4) Reduction of costs	In many regards better than, in some regards worse than (e.g., due to increased computational complexity)	Probabilistic risk models (due to **)
(5) Fruitfulness	Only time and feedback from the economic practice can tell	Other risk (specifically probabilistic) models (due to **)
(6) Reliability and precision	Prima facie - better (reliability) and worse (precision) than - better than	Due to (**) - Probabilistic risk models - Qualitative risk analysis
(7) Comprehensiveness and clarity	Prima facie better than	Other risk (specifically probabilistic) models (due to **)
(8) Coherence	Prima facie better than	Probabilistic risk models (due to **)
(9) Aggregate and (unit) specific	No significant differentiation	
(10) Forward looking	Prima facie better (explanatory power yielding orientation or clear and reliable predictions) and worse (when accounting for costs of liquidation on prospective losses) than	Probabilistic risk models (due to **)
(11) International, financial institutions broadly	No significant differentiation	

General attributes of model validity:

1) *Falsifiability or refutability*: The ability of a model (theory or hypothesis or conjecture etc.) to be falsified (refuted) or supported.[327]
LBR models ensure falsifiability in more than one sense:
   - Each interrelationship can be tested, both *logically* (through representation of relationships in formal logics (Chapter 15.2.) and functional programming (15.4.)) and *empirically* (through resorting to existing financial contracts (Chapter 15.4. and 15.5.) and case studies (16.)).
   - LBR models make the underlying (e.g., structural) assumptions *explicit and transparent* – 'white boxes instead of black boxes' –, they are *formalized*, thus, *testable and falsifiable* (Chapter 15).
   - Popper's *critical rationalism* (1959a, 1963/2002) praises deductive relations and LBR, in an Austrian tradition, also puts emphasis on a *deductive* procedure (Chapter 15 and Proposition 12), which is explicit and rigorous, whereas probabilistic risk modeling approaches are much less skeptical about empirics and hinge on inductive procedures (see Chapter 7). And the more explicit and rigorous a solution is, the more easily it is criticizable (Floridi, 2013: 29).
   - LBR model outcomes can be *tested / simulated* (Chapters 15.6. and 16); the models' performance can be *benchmark*ed against e.g., standard probabilistic strategies (reference modes, see 15.5.).[328] The basic value of a model or simulation outcome consists in it embodying hypotheses (to be developed) that can be refuted and serve as an

327 In general, theories, models, hypotheses, and any other claims to knowledge are specified, they can and should be rationally criticized, and (if they have empirical content) be submitted to tests. These tests are essentially endeavors of refutation, as established in Popper's critical rationalism (Popper, 1959a, 1963/2002; see footnote 208). The test object cannot be confirmed or proven (see above, the first flaw of logical empiricism), it can only be falsified. "If, however, the attempt of falsification is not successful, then it can be temporarily maintained" (Schwaninger & Grösser, 2008: 450). Accordingly, "[t]he most important question about any financial model is how wrong it is likely to be, and how useful it is despite its assumptions" (Derman & Wilmott, 2009).

328 The performance of a method "is characterized by the degree of its success in dealing with the class of problems to which it is applicable. It can be expressed in various ways, typically by the percentage of cases in which the desirable solution is reached, by the average closeness to the desirable solution, or by a characterization of the worst case solution." (Klir, 1991: 88f.).

anchor around which arguments can be built (Schwaninger & Grösser, 2008: 450).[329] For more details, see comparability.

2) *Comparability*: If absolute model validation is not feasible, the evaluation of models in comparison to other models becomes crucial. The focal risk model, modeling approach or paradigm should thus allow for a clear comparison to rival models, measures, methods, methodologies or procedures.

   Application of the criterion to LBR:

   - LBR not only nominates concrete risk models, but also embeds the measurement of extreme and systemic risks in a *larger framework*, where the choice of uncertainty formalisms becomes a parameter of the model, so it can be adapted to the particular application (15.5.), and it is not constrained to classical probabilities (15.2.; proof of *commensurability*). In particular, it contains, as opposed to narrow probabilistic frameworks (Chapter 7), the equipment to construct models tailored to the object of our interest, namely extreme and systemic risks (Proposition 11).
   - The path-breaking work by Artzner et al. (1999), which can and ought to be extended to a multi-period or dynamic framework (Riedel, 2004), sets the 'gold standard' for *coherent* risk measures (15.1.). We recast and incorporate their findings into the LBR system (see Proposition 10), which enables us to compare different risk measures in terms of their obedience or non-obedience to those postulates (proof of *commensurability*).
   - Since LBR focuses on risk posed by rare, high-impact events, it naturally *complements* conventional risk models which are better suited for evaluating more regular market swings or less significant credit risks etc. Through *case studies and simulations*, we compare standard and our non-standard risk models over time to spot areas of interest, where the approaches diverge. They are intended to answer many questions, such as the following in a portfolio manage-

329 Simulation methods are among the most adequate in environments of (high) dynamic and organized complexity because they enable us to trace, capture, manipulate, and study the elements of dynamic complexity (e.g., multiple, delayed, nonlinear effects) *in vitro* (Harrison et al., 2007; Axelrod, 2005; Zeigler et al., 2000).

ment context: Do LBR risk models lead to a change in the risk-reward ratio of a certain portfolio? That is, does the performance of the portfolio (beta measure) change when using LBR? Are the differences in measured risk correlated to changes of the portfolio value? Etc. There are at least two major problems with case studies and simulations that we need to be aware of: Historic data is no good indicator of future performance (Chapter 7). The outcome (successful/unsuccessful) may be due to some parameters of the study, for example the chosen time period or the selected portfolio, and cannot necessarily be seen as an indicator of the quality of our model.

- The established *Monte Carlo simulation* method can be applied in principle, which would require us though to adopt the classic probabilistic interpretation of our uncertainty models.[330] Yet, the flipside would be an augmentation of comparability of our models to orthodox models.
- LBR is not only compared abstractly to probability-based risk models, but its merits are briefly highlighted in contrast to the concrete alternatives *ACTUS* and *Fault tree analysis* (Chapter 17).
- Any bank that has a conventional (e.g., a VaR-based) risk management system could switch to LBR with negligibly additional computational effort. Insofar, the systems are *compatible.*

3) *Parsimony and simplicity*: This characteristic of model validity, in essence, advocates the avoidance of multifariousness (as opposed to the capability for absorbing complexity, which has to be fostered as Ashby's law postulates)[331]. The parsimony of the model refers to its limited size and its simplicity "lies in the small set of components it consists of, which is fully transparent and focused on the essentials" (Schwaninger & Grösser, 2008: 458).

- In general, models and theories should be as simple as possible, but not simpler than that (attributed to Einstein and at least partially rooting in *Occam's razor*).

---

330 We would need to generate random data which necessitates a probability distribution, so all information we could get out of the simulation would be a function of those distributions.

331 Ashby's law of requisite variety can be quoted as: "Only variety can destroy [absorb, C.H.] variety". Cf. Ashby (1956) and Schwaninger (2009: 14).

The users of a model (e.g., risk managers) ought to understand the model. Given that "[c]omplexity is linked to a lack of understanding" (Schwaninger, 2009: 11), it should only be added to the degree it favors another desired attribute.

- Application of the criterion to LBR as opposed to other explanatory risk models: Instead of succumbing to temptations towards capturing the combinatorial richness of real financial systems, the complications of structural or disorganized complexity at the expense of tackling *dynamic or organized complexity*, LBR is driven by a specific problem or issue to "explain the impact of systemic risk events on [banks'] own exposures" (see Proposition 7 and Proposition 11) and not by ambitions to reflect a whole (financial) system with all its details. This marks a vital disparity between LBR and many *explanatory* risk models primarily designed for regulators (see Chapter 8.2. and Appendix E).
- Application of the criterion to LBR as opposed to probabilistic models: LBR is *modest.* No complicated procedures (like in EVT) are needed when accepting *deep uncertainty* as barely measurable (Definition 15.1 and Proposition 17), whereas capabilities of probabilistic approaches are overestimated if applied to the assessment of extreme and systemic risks in financial systems, which should be considered outside the scope of the Kolmogorov system (Chapter 7, 8, 10).

4) *Reduction of costs* emanating from the limitations of techniques applied to risk measurement;
The pressure for cost savings will continue (Härle et al., 2016: 7). Application of the criterion to LBR as opposed to probabilistic models:
   - The wealth of statistical techniques available for dealing with disorganized complexity is contrasted with the (absolute) paucity of such techniques for coping with unstable and wild randomness (Chapter 6) – "[a] popular fix [by standard theorists] is censorship, hypocritically termed 'rejection of outliers'" (Mandelbrot, 1983). LBR, however, is capable of capturing extreme risks, which are accompanied by unstable randomness and organized complexity, respectively, and thereby cuts down *costs through* abolishing *censorship.*

- Probabilistic predictions are not useless, not ineffective in an *absolute* sense, because, even though uncertainty in predictions is inherent in the complexity of the task, they "are better than pure chance once users know their shortcomings and take those into consideration" (Sornette, 2003: 322).[332] Yet, while acknowledging that the application of (working) models to particular areas of experience (i.e., phenomena that have a reasonable degree of complexity) is almost always schematic and highly approximate in character (Suppes, 1984: 115), we allege that probability theory and its application in financial risk management is *less effective*[333] (ergo, more costly) than LBR. This is basically the main outcome of the reasoning in the preceding chapters (e.g., LBR comes with lower model risk) as the overall title of this work presages.
- *Increased automatization* and, thus, e.g., decreased *overhead costs*, result from LBR due to its algebraic underpinnings and an automatic translation of any material financial contract, that can be incorporated in the language of Jones et al. (2001), into our risk model (Chapter 15.4., 15.5.; cf. also Härle et al., 2016: 5). While logic-based approaches are burdened with *computational complexity* or *algorithmic / Kolmogorov complexity* (see 2.1. and Appendix C)[334] which is directly correlated to their expressiveness, they make it possible to automatically prove new sentences, which is exactly what is required to discover previously unknown correlations.
- *Knowledge reusability* is accomplished through inferring the risk profile of complex derivatives from their structure alone. As derivatives are composed from simpler parts and ultimately from primitives, their risk models are also composed from simpler

332 Moreover, even if a model were maladaptive when used for quantitative prediction, it "can be an informative aid to understanding phenomena and processes" (Frigg et al., 2014: 20).

333 A comprehensive overview of validation of econometric models is provided by Dhrymes et al. (1972).

334 "*Computational complexity* is a characterization of the time or space (memory) requirements for solving a problem by a particular method" (Klir, 1991: 88). The problem size can be viewed as being represented by the required time or memory space. As a consequence, *computational complexity* or *algorithmic complexity* (see also Chapter 2, footnote 40) entails *costs* which must be overcompensated.

parts. In other words, we reuse risk information on their underlyings in lieu of designing ad-hoc risk models from scratch for each derivative. This reduces the cost of developing risk models (see Proposition 12 and Chapter 15.4.).

5) *Fruitfulness*: The question here is whether the theory-building process has led to important insights and ultimately to the development of new knowledge.
   Application of the criterion to LBR as opposed to other risk (specifically probabilistic) models:
   - In theoretical terms, LBR is *novel* on several accounts. It focuses on the knowledge rather than the speculation dimension and, essentially, constitutes a plea for symbolic and logic-based risk modeling. We think outside the box when we describe risks by means of decomposing risk objects, singling out their known structures by analyzing financial contracts, resulting in a novel (risk-focused) interpretation of an established programming language for derivatives, and when we make use of interactive visualizations to present our results. LBR expands the toolset for determining extreme risks (Chapter 13, 15, 16). Etc. See also the list of propositions (Appendix B).
   - In practical terms, i.e., LBR models provide a conceptual framework for practice (see also the criteria 9-11 below): At the end of the day, it is actual risk managers, i.e., practitioners as the target group for which the models have been eventually created, who should, first and foremost, assess the worth, significance and practicality of a model (Schwaninger & Grösser, 2008: 451). In this regard, the thrust of our initial action plan is twofold: To persuade professionals of the superiority of LBR, we conducted a first *case study* of measuring systemic risk in a business situation (Chapter 16), on the one hand, and launched a *webpage* (http://www.lbrm-labs.net/), on the other (and beyond this dissertation project), where we provide an interactive tool which our *stakeholders*, our partnering firms, in particular, may use to run *simulations* and compare the performance of LBR with benchmarks under different circumstances and market conditions. Overall, the fruitfulness

of LBR could be striking (see Conjecture 16) considering the fact that we live in a world overpopulated by complex financial instruments (Chapter 15.6.). Yet, given the demanding goals of the LBR program, research and applications beyond the boundaries of current endeavors are indicated (see Chapter 22).

Theoretical attributes of (risk) model validity:

6) *Reliability and precision*: Model reliability can be understood as the extent to which the employment of a method is free of measurement errors (e.g., the consequences of a model test remain constant, if repeated under 'identical' (if possible) conditions; Schwaninger & Grösser, 2008: 459). In a general reply to the problem of *model risk*, any model needs to have its own error taken into account (Chapter 21).
   - Application of the criterion to LBR as opposed to probabilistic models: LBR often only countenances an *ordinal* or *imprecise measurement* of extreme and systemic risks in banking. However, albeit a probabilistic approach would be more precise, a more expressive language in terms of measurement in this field (see Chapter 18), it turns out wrong after all (see Chapter 7 and 8), which can be rephrased as subscribing to the myth of pedantic and "infinite precision" (Rebonato, 2007: 257). Put another way, the latter *implies errors* (more precise, but also more erroneous) while the former proves to be more *robust and reliable* and, thus, less afflicted by measurement errors (less precise, but also less prone to error). See also the trade-off between relevance and precision described by Zadeh's *principle of incompatibility* (Zadeh, 1973 and Chapter 15.2.) for discerning the superiority of LBR which does not make a fetish of rigor and mathematical formalism, but is tolerant of imprecision and partial truths.
   - Moreover, statements on an ordinal scale of measurement *suffice* since we "often need only a ranking of relative riskiness to make

the decision" (Granger, 2010: 36).[335] Specifically, the likelihood of extreme losses or systemic events is much less important than their *severity* (Bhansali, 2014: 14) wherefore *comparative* (as a subclass of *qualitative*) *in lieu of classical probabilities* are all we need to assess their rarity (see Chapter 18 and Definition 15.1).

- As contrasted with qualitative scenario and stress testing analysis, LBR does not suffer from vagueness, impreciseness, and a vulnerability to multiple interpretations or concretizations, but entitles us to manage risks 'by the numbers' (which is key, see Conjecture 9). LBR mainly proceeds deductively, in favor of *rigor* as opposed to impreciseness. For instance, we agitated the subject of modern financial systems and their structures (Chapter 6) and *derived* modeling demands for handling extreme and systemic risks effectively (Chapter 8.2. and 15, Proposition 12).

7) *Comprehensiveness and clarity*: This criterion establishes whether the risk model is sufficiently broad to cover the substantive issues of risk management interests (e.g., what-if-questions rather than if-ones), as well as sufficiently clear so that propositions and lessons can easily be drawn from it.

Application of the criterion to LBR:

- LBR facilitates the description or modeling of risks from *different angles*; e.g., appreciating different risk notions (Chapter 4), measurement techniques (where probability theory is only one example, 15.2.), which manifests *systemic and holistic and, therefore, comprehensive thinking.*
- The LBR modeling approach differentiates between *different and important logical and epistemological steps and levels*, which should not be confounded: e.g., what risk is and how risk is measured, described or managed (see Chapter 4).
- We have paid close attention to the consistent and accurate use of the terms, constructs and concepts which appear in, or are ger-

335 Cf. also Renn (2008: 4) who reinforces this statement: "In managing risks one is forced to distinguish between what is likely to be expected when selecting option X rather than option Y, on the one hand, and what is more desirable or tolerable: the consequences of option X or option Y, on the other."

mane to, the emerging LBR modeling approach. They were explained, also in terms of their relationships (e.g., see Table 5), and documented in a glossary (Appendix A) to furnish an exact and coherent *conceptual apparatus*. As opposed to probabilistic approaches (Chapter 7), LBR is *conceptually appropriate* (Chapter 15).

- o By harnessing the work of Jones et al. (2001) on a language for describing contracts (15.4.), we ensure that LBR can describe a wide range of financial contracts. Due to the constructive nature of our approach, we do not constrain ourselves to a fixed number of common contracts (cf. ACTUS), and make it possible to apply our models to novel kinds of contracts that are as of yet unknown. Therefore, LBR is *comprehensive in the number of derivatives* that can be expressed in it.
- o LBR is further holistic and systemic, respectively, in terms of pooling resources of both analytical and synthetical thinking (see 15.4., 15.6., 16.3. and Proposition 12).

8) *Coherence*: Risk models ought to be coherent which implies that they must satisfy, in the view of most risk experts/scholars, the first four (Artzner et al., 1999) of the following axioms (15.1.). The fifth (cf. Riedel, 2004; and see "uncertain sequences" in 15.5.3. as the temporal component of LBR) was added as a requisite in the wake of the dynamic perspective which is adopted in this study.

- o Translation invariance
- o Sub-additivity
- o Positive homogeneity
- o Monotonicity
- o Dynamic consistency

Application of the criterion to LBR:

- o LBR models obey these postulates if the modeler wishes to specify them accordingly (see **Definition 15.2.**; Müller & Hoffmann, 2017a) whereas common risk models (VaR, Chpt. 2) are *incompatible* with some axioms (sub-additivity), showing that LBR is well-behaved in a formal sense.
- o In terms of the coherence between the model and real systems, LBR model assumptions are *weaker and more realistic* than what

is commonly assumed in probability-based models. Specifically, the messy imperfection of the real world, which is not only black and white and which does not allow us to work with perfect models, is reflected in the choice of our formal apparatus: *ranking theory* (Chapter 15.3.) and its siblings (15.2.) in lieu of (pure) probabilistic reasoning which in turn presupposes classical two-valued logic (Chapter 18; Weatherson, 2003).

Specific attributes designating risk models as particularly useful and valuable to risk managers and practitioners (Stern & Feldman, 2013: 746f.). This sublist is rather practice-oriented and it is supposed to be derived from needs, pain points in the economic practice. In real settings, by real examples, we will be able to find out where the real virtues and limitations within risk management lie (Embrechts, 2000).

9) *Aggregate and (unit) specific*: The risk model should be clearly linked to the overall level of risk. Managers also wish to know how to apportion that aggregate total across units (markets, positions, etc.).
Application of the criterion to LBR:
   - Like VaR or ES, LBR is *universal*: *within its scope*, we encounter any instrument and any underlying source of risk (e.g., market turbulences, credit crises, etc., see 5.1./2.). On the highest level, for example, the allocation of funds in a portfolio describes the ratio of long to short positions, but the LBR approach permits us to elaborate on strategies in any level of detail (specific industries, markets, derivatives, etc.). Because risk measures defined in LBR use the same mathematical language as investment rules in a strategy, there is no need to translate between different scales, which would only reduce the fidelity of the data (Chapter 15 and 17).
   - It is currently a not yet settled question if LBR is *less universal* than its competitors as it appears at least to be predestined for tail risks in the realm of liquidity and counterparty, on the one hand, and for sufficiently complex financial instruments (whatever that means, most probably excluding basic loans, stocks etc.), on the other. Future research is indicated to determine the *scope* of LBR (in continuation of Proposition 15).

- o LBR models are designed in the spirit of the interplay between *aggregate and unit specific views*.
- o The analysis of LBR risk models is an *iterative* and *interactive* process (Chapter 16.3.) where zoom and filters are applied, which is in line with what systemics propagates (e.g., see Figure 20 and 19). LBR lends itself to sophisticated, appealing data visualization programs – e.g., the award-winning Tableau Software™. In contrast to many existing tools, LBR is not static and inflexible, and it not only supports 'traditional' applications of risk models, such as sensitivity / liquidity analysis. LBR and uncertain sequences really offer abundant opportunities to get integrated in practice.
- o Harboring sub-additive measures of risk (as posited in 15.1.), LBR values, e.g., of different trading desks, can be *aggregated* to the firm-level in a way that respects portfolio diversification.

10) *Forward looking* (cf. also *diachronic sensibility*, which has been discussed in connexion with Dutch Book arguments; van Fraassen, 1989): The risk model ought to possess sensible and distinctly desirable time series properties. The model should increase (long) before a financial crisis or another risk event impacts the bank's positions, for example, and be able to maintain *consistency over time*, as well as to *examine emerging trends or patterns* in a risk object's (e.g., a portfolio's) risk profile.
Application of the criterion to LBR:

- o In contrast to many standard approaches, LBR is an *explanatory modeling technique* (see Chapter 8.2., 15.6. and Table 3) and, thus, elucidates why the system behaves as it does and not differently by capturing structural determinants (the network of contracts or of assets and liabilities). Specifically, it explains the impact of systemic and extreme risk events on banks' own exposures and draws attention not to the symptoms of difficulty (certain possible and very uncertain events), but rather to the underlying drivers (dynamic and organized complexity as well as their antecedents in terms of the high, increasing but exploitable structural complexity of financial products). Predictions can be inferred from LBR's explanatory power (Chapter 2.2.1. and Figure 19).

- o With regard to Riedel's requirement of temporality for the axiomatic framework of Artzner et al. (1999), we treat *uncertain sequences* as expression of a temporal sequence of events (see 15.5.).
- o In contrast to traditional and prevailing risk models, LBR does *not* hinge mainly on *hindsight* due to curtailed data demands and a structure- or pattern- (not event-)oriented alignment.
- o *Foresight* requires *system understanding* which, in turn, is facilitated by focusing not on a variety of systems, but dynamic complexity (Chapter 6 and Figure 15). In such complex environments, LBR does not offer meticulous predictions, but *orientation in lieu of* pushing *predictive power* (Chapter 14), thereby acknowledging that the behavior of the financial system and minimum or expected losses are *deeply* unknown (Table 5). Hence, it eschews the trap of endless specification. The downside is that LBR is limited in, e.g., taking into account the exact costs of liquidation on prospective losses ((see 16.4.) because this would fall under the heading of "deep uncertainty", which is circumnavigated). And "illiquidity of markets is nowadays regarded by many risk managers as the most important source of model risk" (McNeil et al., 2005: 41).[336]

11) *International* (if relevant) and *financial institutions broadly*: Global systems and markets necessitate a global approach to risk, also given that the network of financial activities is international (see Appendix E) and not just performed by banks (in the proper sense), but by a myriad of other financial institutions (including shadow banking etc.).
Application of the criterion to LBR:
    - o LBR is a *systemic* approach and, while systems in their entirety can be large or small (recall that "system" is a *formal* concept, see 2.1.), an emphasis on *global* financial systems was placed.
    - o A plea against the compartmentalization of risks and for *global and holistic thinking* was put forward (see 5.1.).

336 Assume that the measurement of a certain risk leads to the decision of liquidating a certain position. While some measures like VaR recommend that no more than an amount l would be lost in liquidating the position (for a VaR estimate at a certain confidence level, e.g., $\alpha = 0.95$) (Lawrence & Robinson, 1995), the act of liquidation would in fact have the effect of "moving the price against the trader disposing of a long position or closing out a short position. For large positions and illiquid instruments the costs of liquidation can be significant […]." (Ibid.).

- *Heterogeneity* of financial systems is acknowledged and "banks" has been used in a very broad sense, i.e., in place of "financial institutions" at large (see Introduction).

In a nutshell, we gain the following intermediate result on the validation of LBR models (ad RQ2.7); intermediate since the foregoing catalogue of criteria a) does not claim to be comprehensive, and b) its application to LBR models reflects a gradual learning and conversational process, which can be iterated and then possibly lead to different (e.g., more nuanced or diverging) outcomes.

Proposition 18:

A logic-based risk modeling approach (LBR) is more valid or useful or of higher quality, respectively, than conventional probabilistic approaches to assessing extreme and systemic risks in a modern financial system, emanating from its dynamic and organized complexity.

All things considered, the question, which guides us, is not how existing models of systemic or extreme risk should be improved in the proper sense, because this would be tantamount to blind efficiency seeking, but, in a more disruptive sense, they should be replaced for particular applications to extreme and systemic financial risks and,[337] generally speaking, be complemented by logic-based risk models (LBR). LBR turns out to be more effective than rival models in the face of dynamically complex financial systems and, hence, constitutes the core of our proposal for approaching the overarching RQ2.

Others have suggested what is now reserved for future discussion, namely that a *good* systematic risk model should encourage companies to hedge and reward companies that do not play with the system to increase their benefits – "detect and punish *speculation*" (Bernard et al., 2013: 178; Riedel, 2013). Thereby, we enter the broader territory of decision-making *competency* where we always need what we may refer to as "managerial review and judgment", where the decision-maker sees beyond the formal decision support (Aven, 2013b: 48). Indeed, decision-making and risk management are inseparable.

337 As stated earlier, the scope of LBR is not yet defined. At least, it bears fruits in the realm of liquidity and counterparty risks, as well as in connection with complex financial instruments.

Part IV:
Meta Level: Thinking about Thinking and Practices – What it Means to Reach Effective Risk Management Decisions

Part IV

Meta Level: Thinking about Thinking and Practices - What it Means to Reach Effective Risk Management Decisions

20. Introduction to Part IV as Overall Conclusion

There is an art of which every human being should be a master, the art of reflection.[338] Very pertinent is the question which the English poet Samuel Taylor Coleridge puts, – "If you are not a thinking man, to what purpose are you a man at all?" (Coleridge, 2015). Daniel Kahneman differentiates between "Thinking, Fast and Slow". Yet, both instinctive and emotional thinking (what he calls fast thinking) and more deliberative, more logical or analytical thinking (what he calls slow thinking) can be superficial and quick, as well as premature and insufficient. In our time where analytical *and quick* thinking (skills) is (are) often praised, rewarded and overrated, it (they) might really go (lead) astray or might only be indispensable because people have begun too late to think about an issue (Ulrich & Probst, 1990: 299). Thus, *deep thinking* – and, as special cases, creative or disruptive (Schumpeter) and holistic or systems thinking –, which takes time, ought to be honored. From time to time, we must step out of the stream of direct experience and our immediate responses to it. Otherwise, there is the veritable risk that one might just end up being quick on the avoidable road to doom and disaster.[339]

By profound thinking or reflection, we are able to unmask the illusion that all financial market participants can eradicate their risk or hedge them all away at the same time. Moreover, it helps us identify a "trap for logicians" that we as logicians (see Part III) would like to escape. "Life is 'a trap for logicians' because it is almost reasonable but not quite; it is usually sensible but occasionally otherwise" (Lowenstein, 2002: 69). "It looks just a little more mathematical and regular than it is, its exactitude is obvious, but its inexactitude is hidden; its wildness lies in wait"

338 Wilhelm von Humboldt jotted down a few aphorisms which, posthumously, his editors put under the heading "About Thinking and Speaking". The first three aphorisms deal with reflection, "the essence of thinking", and the second stands out: "In order to reflect, the mind must stand still for a moment in its progressive activity, must grasp as a unit what was just presented, and thus posit it as object against itself" (cited in von Glaserfeld, 1995: 90).

339 In the less drastic and sharp words of Zaleznik (2004): Managers "instinctively try to resolve problems quickly – sometimes before they fully understand a problem's significance".

(Bernstein, 1996b: 331). Beyond doubt, logics and mathematics in economics and finance serve to keep the reasoning straight, to make sure that one step of an argument leads in an orderly way to the next, which is frequently not the case when we condemn formal methods. Thus, formal methods have been embraced to assess and manage risks (see Part III). But even though "[c]rystal-clear logical connections[340] between the 'if' and the 'then' are, of course, desirable, […] we cannot neglect the choice of the 'ifs'" (Bhidé, 2010: 84; see also Part II and III). Picking 'ifs' just because they are best suited to some special (e.g., a specifically elegant or convenient) form of mathematical or formal risk modeling can open the door to great mischief (ibid.). This logician's trap would be to use, in other words, a standard risk model (Part I) for past data from an imperfect world, constituting an elusive and random sequence of events rather than a set of independent or normally distributed etc. observations, which is what many standard, i.e., probabilistic risk models demand or assume (see IIIc) in 2.4.), because many economic and financial variables and quantities look like they would possess such idealized properties. Yet once again, "resemblance to truth is not the same as truth. It is in those outliers and imperfections that the wildness lurks." (Bernstein, 1996b: 335).

Finally, risk management not only struggles with those problems for (especially some) 'logicians' (who neglect whether the assumptions, they need to establish if a certain modeling approach is selected and applied, are satisfied), but also with many more, partly pressing issues. For example, risk management sometimes creates new risks even as it brings old risks under regulation and control to some extent. "Our faith in risk management encourages us to take risks we would not otherwise take" (ibid.).

Against this background of lurking traps on the terrain of risk management, the call for an avoidance strategy cannot be ignored. The fourth part of this dissertation functions as a concluding paragraph. It does not launch another in-depth discussion, rather it offers an overarching conclusion and embeds the preceding study and analysis in the larger context of decision-making competency in the risk field. This manifests a synthesis, essential for systems thinking (Appendix A), where we envision the focal object, risk measurement, as being part of the overall process of risk management in banking and beyond.

340 Of course, to avoid a misinterpretation of his words, logicians are only interested in the form, not the content of an argument (the latter including assertions about causal relationships between events).

21. Escaping the Traps for Logicians: Towards Decision-Making Competency in Risk Management

Follow effective action with quiet reflection.
From the quiet reflection will come even more effective action.
(Peter Ferdinand Drucker)[341]

"The financial markets, seen by many as the most efficient and farsighted,[342] should rapidly evolve to near-optimality due to the huge stakes and enormous talent brought to bear. Yet even the highly sophisticated hedge funds [like LTCM, C.H.] bear the scars of self-inflicted wounds from open-loop thinking [see 5.1.; because their risk models have missed to consider that other actors might pursue the same or a similar strategy as an input to the models; C.H.]." (Sterman, 2000: 697). At best, the result is *inefficiency*; at worst, it is *ineffectivity* which hurts the organization, the people in it, and not too rarely third parties or even the larger society. In the densely connected, complex and turbulent world of ours, optimization or efficiency may still be desiderata, but ensuring effectivity, often taken for granted or underappreciated as a minimum accomplishment, would be a respectable primary goal; worth striving for when tackling an issue like evaluating systemic and extreme risks within complex financial systems. Good and effective risk management, in turn, ultimately comes down to making good decisions. "Risk assessment has a decision-guiding purpose" (Hansson, 2007: 23; cf. also Taleb, 2013: 7). The output of the risk management process, where evaluating risks is the crucial step (see 2.2. and cf. Stulz, 2008: 59), is, as stated earlier, "an array of concrete decisions, such as whether to make or to refuse a loan, whether to add capital to the firm, or how to hedge a position" (Brose et al., 2014a: 369). What can good, adequate or effective risk management

341 As quoted in Edersheim (2006: x).

342 "The chief problem is the absence of an obvious counterfactual: how well is the financial sector allocating our economy's capital *compared to what*? If we did not rely on our banks, other private lenders, and stock and bond markets to allocate our capital, with all the cost that they entail, how else would we perform this function?" (Friedman, 2010: 17).

achieve? In the following, we are committed to determine effective risk management in the sense of characterizing decision-making competency in a risk management context of banking and by taking the results from Part I–III explicitly into account. We begin with a negative answer to the foregoing question.

Every approach to risk management can be maladaptive

Effective risk management does *not* provide a guarantee against failure (Stulz, 2008: 60). The employment of any, even of an entirely effective decision-supportive tool for quantitative or qualitative risk assessment and management can neither eliminate *model risk* (McNeil et al., 2005: 3), nor compulsorily entail good risk management decision outcomes. Risks are inevitably cohesive with undeniable uncertainty (be it measurable or not, see our definition in 4.1.), which implies that taking and managing risks is connected with uncertain decision outcomes. The decisive point for grasping the quality of a risk management decision is then not represented by the still uncertain amount of actual profit or loss induced by that action because, at the point of decision-making, a certain chance of loss could be more than offset by a certain chance of rewards, but still failure could occur at the end. We should therefore not base our judgment on the effectiveness of risk management tools on the *ex ante* unknowable (values), which is, unfortunately, not sufficiently acknowledged in the literature and practice.[343] For example, the mere fact that the risk management function of many banks "played an essential role in the recent financial crisis does not necessarily mean that it was at fault in any way. Some risks are worth taking, and even great risks may be rationally chosen if the [expected] returns are sufficiently high." (Boatright, 2011: 11).[344]

---

343 For example, Williams (2010: 107) writes naively: "Lehman traders took on risk with each trade every day. At day's end, these bets showed up on the firm's profit and loss (P&L) statement as either profit or loss. This provided immediate feedback on whether risk was appropriately managed or not."

344 "Do not treat risk management as distinct from profit making and as an afterthought; treat them as profit-generating activities" (Taleb et al., 2009: 80). Even though this imperative sounds plausible and compelling, it might be problematic and in conflict with our mindset because "as profits swell, risk management is viewed as a constraint on profit – a dangerous sentiment" (Williams, 2010: 105). "If you save people in the process of drowning you are considered a hero. If you prevent people from drowning by averting a flood you are considered to have done nothing for them. Such asymmetry is apparent: you do not get bonus points for telling agents to *avoid* investing. They want 'something tangible'." (Taleb, 2005: 55).

Effective risk management is ascribed to well-informed decision-making where the risks are known[345] and understood by decision-makers

Nevertheless, it is evident in the recent financial crisis, "that the leaders of financial institutions of all kinds did not understand the risk they were taking and made decisions that not only turned out badly but were objectively unwarranted at the time" (ibid.). In other words, risk management should enable *well-informed decision-making*, which is not a trivial matter to describe. The decisive point for grasping the quality of a risk management decision is thus represented by the degree of which decision-makers *know and understand* the risks "associated with possible outcomes of the firm's strategy before they make decisions to commit the firm's capital" (Stulz, 2008: 60). The purpose of risk management is "to ensure that top management knows and understands the risks and the potential gains and makes prudent trade-offs" (Boatright, 2011: 11).

Understanding risks does not culminate in risk control, but creates room for more cybernetic regulation

This study discerns this risk management goal of comprehending risks not as *controlling risks* (in contrast to Bessis (2010: 37), for example) since control is not feasible (in consonance with the critical finance society, see Chapter 10). Systems science, including cybernetics (Wiener, 1961; Ashby, 1956; Ulrich & Probst, 1990: 19), sheds more light on *regulation*, less on *controlling* when dealing with dynamic and organized, complex and open systems (Ulrich & Probst, 1990: 256).[346] Accordingly, seen from the theoretical perspective adopted here in this thesis, risk management in banking should result in more regulation and less control. And as Professor Paul Embrechts added,[347] cybernetic regulation, in more than one sense, may indeed be important in a financial world more and more engulfed by algorithmic trading, blockchain technology, machine learning, Fintech etc.

---

345 We follow Kuritzkes & Schürmann (2010) in calling a risk *known* if it can be identified and quantified *ex ante*.

346 The central theme of cybernetics is regulation and control which are intimately related (Ashby, 1956: 195, 213). For a discussion of "steering", "control" and "regulation", cf. Ashby, 1956: Part III; Ulrich & Probst, 1990: 78-89.

347 Interview, 13th October 2016.

Following Ulrich & Probst (1990: 256), control presupposes a high degree of knowledge of possible future disturbances in the system and requires a very rapid and prescient intervention, i.e., before the disturbance actually occurs. However, this requirement may hardly be met by banks or organizations as (far as) they are open systems, which are incorporated in an extremely dynamic, organized and complex environment (ibid.). Furthermore, isolating the firm from the outside to ward off disturbances is also only possible to a very limited extent because, otherwise, it loses its integrability into the environment and, therefore, its viability (Beer, 1959). Thus, the more complex the environment, the less promising is a risk management approach that sees its role in the direct control of the individual system elements. Often this provokes a vicious circle (Ulrich & Probst, 1990: 256): the less it is feasible for a risk manager to really steer and determine what is happening, the more he intervenes in the system in a commanding and after control striving way, in the vain attempt to finally transfer the situation into a manageable one for all times. What is needed is a change in perspective: "[A] social system is not primarily subject to exogenous control but [...] it regulates and steers itself to a great extent" (Schwaninger, 2009: 16). And not the individual activities of elements, but the structure of systems ought to be put at the center of attention; a transition from control (attempts) to regulation is a *sine qua non* for absorbing and coping with complexity, which is to create a play of complexity reduction and complexity increase (Ulrich & Probst, 1990: 63f.). In other words, "most of the complexity absorption takes place within the systems, not between them. These forces of self-organization must be purposefully leveraged." (Schwaninger, 2009: 16).

Amidst philosophy of science

Part I to IV predicate on methodological thinking; the systematic study of methods that have been and predominantly are, but should in fact not be applied within the discipline of risk management (Part I), methods that should at least be complemented (Part II) or rendered more precise by a novel, formal logic-based approach to extreme and systemic risk modeling (Part III), which should be evaluated against the larger framework of the actual task and purpose of risk management (Part IV).

True decision-making competency involves modesty: insights into the limits and limitations of methods

Intellectual modesty follows from personal reflectiveness, which has, for example, the following facets:

- using numerical *and* symbolic models of risk boldly to estimate values without being overly impressed by mathematics (Derman & Wilmott, 2009);
- opening the black boxes of risk modeling and global finance (MacKenzie, 2005) in order to fully understand the premises and conclusions of mathematical theorems (Das et al., 2013: 702);
- not expecting more from risk management than it can deliver (Stulz, 2008: 58; in particular, manageable knowable unknowns vs. unmanageable unknowable unknowns, see the next sections);
- questioning not only alleged solutions to (the seemingly right) problems, but also whether we deal with the right problems at all (Ackoff, 1974: 8).

Part I and II gave an insight into the limits and limitations of conventional quantitative risk models and qualitative risk management instruments. While the literature discusses extensively three types of theoretical risk management failures in connection with risk models' shortcomings (see Chapter 2 and cf. also Stulz, 2008 for an overview and the classification scheme)[348], this study foregrounded a more fundamental issue. We saw that both kinds of approaches – quantitative and qualitative – suffer from a fundamental and disastrous problem of induction emerging from real-world complexity, that is, exactly not a problem of opacity, which could be cleared up by more information. With regard to the quantitative camp, the Central Argument (Chapter 7) demonstrated that any choice of a particular probability distribution, from which conventional risk measures or models are derived, is arbitrary in nowadays world and cannot be vindicated. Due to modern financial systems' complexity (6.3.), the accuracy and suitability of a probability distribution for future observations cannot be determined with any reliable certainty from past data. This is essentially the problem

348 As stated earlier, Stulz (2008) introduces the following three classes: 1) Failure to use suitable risk metrics (e.g., a risk model is more complicated than necessary); 2) Mismeasurement of known risks (e.g., a risk model assumes the wrong loss distribution); and 3) Mismeasurement stemming from overlooked risks (e.g., a model is unable to incorporate new risks).

of induction which together with some other uncontroversial premises leads to the conclusion that there is especially no point in retreating into the cosy closed space of probability theory for systemic and/or extreme risk management purposes and that such blinkered assessment approaches ought to be abandoned due to conceptual inappropriateness.

With regard to the qualitative camp, jumping from the pan of probabilistic reasoning into the fire of measurement refusal, a morass of induction manifests itself in a less narrow sense. But basically by the same token, stress testing and scenario analysis must be viewed critically. They rely on selecting a number of scenarios from the *past* history to describe possible *future* situations, which may be seriously leading astray since they implicitly suppose "that a fluctuation of this magnitude would be the worst that should be expected" (Diebold et al., 2010: 26). And even though there is the significant difference that quantitative enthusiasts try to measure (partially un- or at least barely measurable) uncertainty while quantitative skepticists accept or even embrace unmeasurable risks, both camps have in common that they focus on the uncertainty of future outcomes, which is eventually a recipe for problems of induction, which, in turn, become acute and impetuous in light of factual complexity. The complexity of (financial) systems evokes events and unstable random behavior of systems which can be characterized as *deeply* uncertain (as far as the systems are of high dynamic and organized complexity, and not merely complicated; see also Table 5 in Chapter 6).

Deep uncertainty signifies that meaningful classical probabilities cannot be obtained and, following Stulz (2008) and Kuritzkes & Schürmann (2010), that we are unable to assess such risks (concerning deeply uncertain events) meaningfully at present (see also Chapter 18). Yet, the bottom line is *not* that we should throw our hands in the air, putting the case for extreme views (as e.g. exposed in Taleb, 2007a) by conceding that the limitations are overwhelming and that no value can be given to a scientific/rational approach to finance and to assessing extreme and systemic risks, in particular. Rather, the proposed solution was to accept deep uncertainty as a fact (instead of regarding it as the central problem to be solved), but to not let our risk modeling endeavors be fully dictated by this fact; the goal is rather to spot the system's structures and its complexity which both yields risks (see Figure 15) and delivers an important aspect of risk measurement (in terms of complex derivatives, see Proposition 11). Thereby, we place, in the tradition of Austrian economics, emphasis on the known in lieu of the unknown.

Decision-making competency comprises the use of good and effective risk management methods: Part III aimed at enhancing our risk management methods by expanding the realm of known risks and, thus, facilitates effective risk management

As stated earlier, decision-making competency and, as a consequence, effective risk management require that risks are known and understood by decision-makers. In this light, LBR is a better, a more valid and effective tool (compared to conventional quantitative and qualitative methods of risk management, see also Chapter 19) as it enlarges the realm of known risks. Hitherto unknown risks can be transformed into the known, which clarifies that such unknowns really were knowable unknowns (instead of unknowable unknowns, where, by definition, little can be done to learn about or manage the situation).

Specifically, we modeled extreme and systemic risks that banks are exposed to by measuring risks of their financial products and instruments (derivatives such as options, swaps, futures, etc.; see Appendix A) which we describe in a programming language for financial contracts (15.4.). This vocabulary determines a small collective of primitive or atomic contracts that are sufficient to describe many of them through composition. Programs in this language are then interpreted as uncertain sequences – sequences that have a structure similar to lists in functional programming (consisting of a head element and the tail of the sequence), except that a given sequence may have more than one tail, and the different tails are annotated with expressions of belief (15.5.). Uncertain sequences are parametric in the choice of uncertainty representation, and so can be instantiated with probability distributions, DS belief or ranking functions, and others. In this work, we argued for, and made use of ranking theory. The elements of uncertain sequences in our case have been transactions between us and various counterparties. By aggregating all transactions in a sequence, we were able to compute the total value of the position that the sequence represents, within a novel model of uncertainty. Hence, Part III looked at risks, in general, from a different angle, namely no longer, from a crude event-oriented worldview, as an accurately measurable quantity that can be ultimately concluded from historical data, but rather as an abstract entity – the 'uncertainty', for which various mathematical models exist (15.2.). While domain-specific languages have been well-researched within functional programming, as have uncertainty models within formal epistemology, the potential of a combination of the two for a pathbreaking approach to risk management has not been realized so far. Our work was committed to close this important gap and to expand the toolset for assessing extreme and systemic financial risks effectively.

Our focus has been on the question of how the exposure to risks varies with a bank's activities and trading positions, and not on classical probabilities – be it in the form of whole distributions or their tails (Part I) or in form of worst-case assumptions (Part II). Put differently, we heed the ancient wisdom that decision-makers are mostly concerned about the cost of mistakes, rather than an exact, but futile conjecture about some statistical properties as we live in a payoff space, not a probability space (Taleb, 2013: 41; cf. also Braswell & Mark, 2014: 188; Rebonato, 2007: 254; and see Chapter 18). More comprehensively, the quality of LBR risk models in differentiation to mainly common probabilistic approaches has been ascertained by a bunch of aspects (Chapter 19). However, at the end of the day, holistic or systems *thinking*, even in its sophisticated form of LBR, tackling unresolved problems of risk management and society, is only a necessary antecedent of holistic *action*.

A latent paradox: Effective risk management and mitigation deteriorates risks

Effective risk management is not only incapable of providing a guarantee against failure, but, counter-intuitively, effective quantitative or technical risk assessments like LBR might even be a source of new risk as soon as it is perceived as advantageous by (sufficiently many) risk managers or experts.

In general, "stability is destabilizing" (Minsky, 1986/2008), relative tranquility encourages more risk-taking; notably technical risk evaluations "constitute legitimization strategies for justifying the creation of ubiquitous risks and lure people into accepting threats to their lives and livelihoods that they would not accept on the basis of their intuitive feelings" (Renn, 2008: xiv; see also Chapter 10).[349] Tools of risk measurement cater to our tendency to understate uncertainty and complexity in order to offer an illusion of understanding the world (Mandelbrot & Taleb, 2010: 47; cf. also Cassidy, 2010; The Economist,

349 Economists are well-aware of such 'unintended' effects. For example, Peltzman (1975) authored a controversial paper (which was picked up by Gary S. Becker and others) where he argued that mandatory safety devices such as seatbelts decrease the likelihood that drivers are harmed if they crash, but also encourage drivers to be more reckless. 'Holding other factors constant', he found that mandating seatbelt use caused more accidents.

1999). It is an unpleasant but inevitable fact that theoretically beneficial model properties (model level) do not necessarily lead to practical enhancements in larger concrete systems.

In particular, if LBR became the new gold standard, this might have implications (in a dynamic and complex system) which are unforeseeable at the moment. For instance, risk managers could overestimate the power of LBR (e.g., by trying to transform the unknowable into the known) or if they adopted LBR – especially if it was applied by a high number of users/banks;[350] and in the extreme, a new *cult* of modeling would result –, new feedback (loops) would emerge that affects the functioning and the constitution of the system as well as the effectiveness of risk management approaches (Billioa et al., 2012: 555). More drastically, one might even provide the pessimistic outlook, to which we would agree if "right" meant "efficient", "optimal", or "a single best" but not if it meant "an effective": "Many academics imagine that one beautiful day we will find the 'right' model. But there is no right model, because the world changes in response to the ones we use." (Derman & Wilmott, 2009).

The conclusion here is fourfold:

First, tackling *open-loop thinking* is an enduring task along the different steps in an iterative risk management process.

Second, *empirical evaluations* are unavoidable for model validation (see Chapter 19 and 22).

Third, we conjecture that, in the economic practice, *prudence* is a virtue, prudence in acting is a dominant strategy and that most successful risk managers excel since, in the face of fallible models combined with possibly harmful dynamics, they manage to keep *exposure* very low (Sheffi, 2005). "Instead of trying to anticipate low-probability, high-impact events, we should lower our vulnerability to them. Risk management, we believe, should be about lessening the impact of what we don't understand." (Taleb et al., 2009: 78; see also Chapter 18). When we recognize that designing and employing risk models has enormous effects on banks, other users, and the economy in toto, many of them beyond our comprehension, we ought to "make sure that a given strategy, however good it may look *ex ante*, will not bring about unacceptable losses if events do not unfold according to plan A (or B)" (Rebonato, 2007: 145). Likewise, we ought to

350 In a competitive world a recipe followed by everyone cannot possibly be a formula for success.

pay attention to possible warning signs of financial turmoil (e.g., excess leverage, lack of transparency, hubris, funding mismatches, …) and adopt a complexity worldview to not see single causes, but many insignificant inputs, e.g., for a financial crisis, "that may be amplified and may accumulate over time to reach a tipping point and cause a catastrophic event; or cancel each other out" (Rzevski & Skobelev, 2014: 21). Etc.

Finally, no single model output can capture (extreme and systemic) risks comprehensively, but we can still have a handle on them so long as we use a variety of decisional tools and risk indicators and so long as we can have an *open mind*.

Practical Wisdom is trump for determining decision-making competency: Formal modeling does not substitute for human judgment in evaluating risks

While risk models and their technical sophistication might sometimes overwhelm the human capability to comprehend them (Jagadish, 2013), they also satisfy our ingrained human desire to simplify by squeezing into one single model output matters that are too rich to be described by it (Mandelbrot & Taleb, 2010: 47). We like simplicity, but we like to recall that it is our models that are complicated or (in better cases) simple (i.e., not more complicated than necessary) and their result which can (but should not) be simplistic, not the world, which is complex.

What would there be to do if some factors just *cannot* be reasonably considered in a risk model? Where should we draw the demarcation line between a legitimate reduction, a reasonable abstraction and a naïve reductionism, a blind oversimplification (Hohwy & Kallestrup, 2008; Knox, 2015; also von Mises, 1949/1998: 214f.; Dreyfus, 1972/1999: 55f.)? Metaphorically speaking, do mathematical models "[strip] actual events to the bones or [cut] away vital parts of their anatomy" (von Bertalanffy, 1968/2013: 113)? It appears that such questions have been disregarded too much for too long and, instead, it has been pointed to the practicality of sacrificing reality for elegance. On the other hand, a critical question is also whether it is more arbitrary to quantify imperfectly (but have the qualitative risk factors counted) or not to quantify such items at all (and have them possibly ignored; Shrader-Frechette, 1985: 190).

Albeit fuzzy logic, for example (see 15.2.), addresses this latter dilemma of how to deal with vague and qualitative assessments in favor of quantification (which is in line with Conjecture 9), the high degree of abstraction which is implied by formal risk modeling, in general, is tantamount to an immense risk of a *reductionism*. Purely technical answers are incomplete and unsatisfying. Reductionisms should not be accepted readily and sustainably though as they are guilty of imposing untenable a priori metaphysics on the world and on science (Brandon, 1996: 189). The knowledge of the own 'pragmatic reduction' alone is not enough to tackle the resulting deficits. Rather, there should be thorough reflection on the once excluded, seemingly captured contents, and a proper disclosure of the abstraction process in its full extent or manifestation. It would be requisite to fathom ways of how to extinguish the deficits encountered. The latter is unfortunately all too often reserved for philosophy, theology, sociology and other disciplines.

In a risk management context, the decision-maker thus needs to know not just the output of a formal risk model, which is only an intermediate result in a risk assessment process, but also an appropriate amount of information surrounding it. Because what is (apparently) not measurable and cannot be expressed in mathematical form could disappear from sight, and a dominant pursuit of accuracy would entail that small parts were taken out of larger contexts in order to capture a simplified picture and single relationships accurately (Ulrich & Probst, 1990: 15f.). Different endeavors, as Aristotle wrote, necessitate different degrees of precision and finance or risk management is not among the natural sciences (where less 'extra' and soft information is needed). On the decision level, risk managers should profit from their experience in the financial arena, not in the sense of involving an obscurantist intuitionism or a mechanical and uncritical application of habits of thought to fields different from those in which they have been formed (von Hayek); but experience that sensitizes them for what should be formally modeled, and how (e.g., problematize the construction of an *uncertainty space*, see Chapter 15.1.), as well as experience that has taught them to be very humble in applying mathematics to real systems, and to be extremely wary of ambitious theories, which are in the end trying to model human behavior (Derman & Wilmott, 2009). Rather than simply navigating the rules and incentives established by others (Schwartz & Sharpe, 2010), risk managers are encouraged to identify and cultivate their practical wisdom. Our technical risk evaluations eventually face the tribunal of reflectivity and such practical wisdom. In other, context-related words, risk professionals should focus on

- disclosing the abstraction and reduction (or reductionism?) process of risk modeling in its comprehensive extent and manifestation;
- qualitative managerial judgments about investment or risk strategies, market conditions etc. which are valuable inputs into risk management processes (at best, integrated in a systematic, consistent fashion with quantitative tools; Getmansky et al., 2015: 88); because not everything that is germane to risk assessment might be captured in formal models and, in particular, risk measurement should succeed a non-formal heuristic reasoning to facilitate a clear, transparent and steered formalization of risks;
- disciplining or challenging, at the same time, intuition because the quality of an intuitive judgment requires an assessment of the regularity in the domain and the predictability of the environment (Kahneman & Klein, 2009);
- reaching a so-called *reflective equilibrium*, in the most general sense "the end-point of a deliberative process in which we reflect on and revise our beliefs about an area of inquiry" (Daniels, 2011; cf. also Goodman, 1955: 65-68); the inquiry might be the broad question, "how to manage extreme and systemic risks effectively?" or it might be much more specific;
- bringing holistic and systems thinking in line with holistic and systemic action, which requires us to treat the tackling of open-loop thinking as a permanent and perennial task;
- …[351]

Practical wisdom helps raise awareness of how to interpret the results gained by means of risk models and how to embed them in the larger risk management process (cf. also Derman & Wilmott, 2009; Bäcker, 2008; Rebonato, 2007).

351 Scordis (2011: 10) objects that such guides or handbooks for competent behavior are of limited practical value because "judgments are emergent rather than static, vague rather than clear, particular rather than universal". We would disagree that this list is of limited practical value since it is attached to central and relevant research results of this study.

Bottom line

Beyond doubt, it is still a long way from here to a sustainable solution to both theoretical and practical risk management issues and failures. Much remains to be done but the path forward to new horizons continues: "No matter how efficient school training may be, it would only produce stagnation, orthodoxy, and rigid pedantry if there were no uncommon men pushing forward beyond the wisdom of their tutors" (von Mises, 1957/2005: 175). For now, the subsequent proposition summarizes our tentative insights on effective risk management and decision-making competency.

Proposition 19:

Effective risk management can be characterized in the sense of decision-making competency. In demarcation to ineffective risk management, decision-making competency and effective risk management have the following features (among others):

- *realizing that every approach to risk management can be inappropriate*
- *understanding and knowing risks*
- *creating room for more cybernetic regulation in lieu of risk control*
- *being intellectually modest and perceiving limits and limitations of methods*
- *using effective risk modeling approaches that enlarge the realm of known risks*
- *cultivating prudence as a successful strategy in risk management*
- *fostering practical wisdom.*

22. Final Remarks and a Path for Future Research

Crisis, a serious or decisive state of things, or the point of time when an affair must soon terminate or suffer a material change, a turning point, a critical juncture.

Revolution, a total or radical change of circumstances or of system.

(Webster's Universal Dictionary, 1936)

The presence, if not prevalence, of crises is not unusual in many systems. Current risk management and financial systems are not an exception. It does not follow, however, that they must decline and face doom. "Decline and doom are not inevitable; they can be avoided, but they may not be. Survival is not inevitable either." (Ackoff, 1974: 3). This dissertation paved the ground for an intellectual revolution in financial risk management, particularly of extreme and systemic events, in four regards: It highlighted I) fundamental drawbacks of classical quantitative risk measurement and II) qualitative risk assessment (in reference to the first main research question, Chapter 3)[352], hence deriving the ineptness of much admired methods in a more concise and cogent way than in the existing literature on risk management. It showed III) a way of overcoming these shortcomings (to respond to the second main RQ, Chapter 14) in the shape of an elaborated program, ready to be fitted for practical use. Finally, by its systemic point of view and by stressing and advancing the 'starting from the known' approach, it offered IV) a concluding synthesis and new impulses for the general reflection on risk management methods. In the face of the valiant and heterogeneous goals of this dissertation, it is clear that some of its pieces merely set out a program and outline an agenda for future research. In other words, not all of the research questions stated earlier could have been answered comprehensively. Many ex-

352 Recall: RQ1: Are the taken-for-granted quantitative risk assessment/management approaches, including VaR, CoVaR, ES, etc., effective; if not, under what conditions are they useless and do become themselves a risk object for banks? RQ2: How can the measurement/management of systemic or extreme risk be improved to compensate for the shortcomings of the approaches from I and to account for the financial system's dynamic complexity? For a detailed answer to RQ1, see the résumé in 8.1. whereas Part IV accounts for a global, synthesizing view.

planations can be offered for this limitation. For instance, risk management "is an enormous and enormously intricate topic" (Brose et al., 2014a: 370). At the same time, the whole range of topics touched upon here is merely the tip of an iceberg. We hope the references in the text will serve as useful pointers to more rigorous investigations.

Clearly, the passages on logic-based risk modeling (LBR) might leave the reader with more questions than answers today, and that should be no surprise. In consonance with the message of Chapter 21, it might be a good thing, on the one hand, when the output of any sophisticated risk model raises more questions than it answers because "new questions will have advanced the thinking" (Pergler & Freeman, 2008: 13). On the other hand, the conventional or standard methods of modern financial risk analysis have benefited from more than a half-century of study and development, by thousands of mathematicians, economists and financial analysts. Given this discrepancy, it is high time that work on LBR finds its continuation. For example, up to now LBR has only been illustrated by, and applied to, the example of the fall of LTCM as a liquidity and counterparty risk crisis. Other (larger) case studies, e.g., in cooperation with an existing financial institution and for other contexts – both within banking (e.g., 'other risk categories' as the literature would put it) and beyond (e.g., physical trading via commodity trading houses or maybe even ostensibly remote territories like risks in political systems)[353] –, or the derivation of possible implications for related fields like Modern Portfolio Theory etc. would be desirable as those extensions might, for example, aid to determine the scope of LBR.

The discussion in this work rests on, and is shaped by, selected theoretical perspectives, our interpretations and evaluations, and it is obvious that our underlying subversive views on what is the 'best' way of defining risk and grasping or enhancing risk management affects our analysis. (Nick Watkins from the LSE once put it like this: One of the terrible dangers in complexity science is that it is at its peak of arrogance.)

What is essential in the thesis and decisive for its possible impact are the arguments propounded, their objective validity and quality. However, other lines

353 At least, systemic risks are virulent in political systems. For instance, the 'systemic' metaphor (from the Introduction) "for it is your business, when the wall next door catches fire" (Horace 65–8 BC, Epistles) unfolds its dramatic and explosive force (e.g., from a Western perspective) in the wake of global attacks by the so-called IS or ISIS or Daesh that recruits so-called jihadists from all over the world. Cf. Bar-Yam, 2015.

of productive future inquiry would be necessary to remove the limitations of current work. For example, *financial* systems or risk management in *banking* were only the context in many ways. In concrete terms, this means, among others, that since statistics or probability theory is relied upon in almost all empirical scientific research, serving to obtain, support and communicate scientific findings, the Central Argument (of Part I) could help initiate paradigm changes in many other fields that deal with dynamically and organizationally (not disorganizationally)[354] complex systems as well. Insights also ought to acquire part of their potential force from empirical observations about such systems' attributes and their behavior (which are partially available already).[355]

Apart from that, possible future avenues of research might include a transfer and advancement of our ideas and research output to/for *regulatory* risk management contexts as opposed to *internal* risk management purposes;[356] or empirical work to test our propositions or corresponding hypotheses. In this connection, it would also be very interesting to compare the kind of explanatory systemic risk modeling for market participants introduced here in Part III to the classical, and perhaps weak, explanatory systemic risk models for regulators which are already out there (e.g., King et al., 2014) in a systematic manner. Moreover, understanding the nature of systemic risk, reaching its systems part, and conceptualizing curative and management tools necessitates further well-funded multi-disciplinary research (Fouque & Langsam, 2013: xxviii). If this study stimulates further controversy of how to conceive risk and approach risk management, as such debate is considered very important for the development of the risk fields (Aven, 2012: 34), it will have served a useful purpose.

The task ahead would furthermore also be to construct, in a very practical sense, risk management and financial systems that better serve economic welfare by insisting on more robustness and effectiveness (Kohn, 2010: 303). In terms of a unification of analysis and synthesis, we should do both, focusing on and learning about individual items (e.g., underlyings of derivatives) as well as looking at the system as a whole (e.g., complex derivatives; see 15.4.), the interactions among risks (see 16), markets and participants that might unveil a vulnerability

354 Again, the merits of probability theory are undeniable (see also Chapter 6.1.2. and Figure 13).
355 Cf., e.g., Richardson (1999); Forrester (1969).
356 For example, a novel and good risk measure could be used to levy a speculation or risk tax (Riedel, 2013: 181).

which could be missed otherwise (see 5.1.). In response to the quest for "a better way for the financial system to deal with the unknowns and the unknowables that are the inevitable consequence of an innovative and adaptable market-based financial system and economy" (ibid.), this thesis showed in the end one (among many more possible) starting point(s) for how to develop a more stable and humane[357] financial economy. We need change. The public reclaims it. But first we expect a serious, open debate about what kind of financial and risk management systems will be truly *effective*, that is for example "sustain real, inclusive dynamism that enriches the lives of all" (Bhidé, 2010: 297). First impetus has been initiated in this frame when Part III presented an effectively effective system for systemic risk assessment instead of trying (and failing) to render an ultimately ineffective approach more efficient by tuning probabilistic models and improving their parameters while not preventing risk management failure.

This work is finally foundational in that it could form part of a new 'science of complexity' (Casti, 1992). Much more can be done in this regard, including the integration of this piece into other work in the field of 'complex systems', especially with regard to examining not only possible sources of risk and randomness, but also of complexity (Hoffmann, 2016). Perhaps a very promising way this work could be extended by complexity explorers is towards a model of the process of risk modeling itself. "The future depends greatly on what problems we decide to work on and how well we use Systems Age technology to solve them" (Ackoff, 1974: 18).

The use of modern (Part I) as well as postmodern (Part III) quantitative risk management methods for decision support is invariably limited but powerful if properly employed – in fact, quantitative but quasi postmodern risk management was endorsed in Part III. Yet, the role of judgment (Bhidé, 2010) and practical wisdom (Aristotle; Schwartz & Sharpe, 2010) in applying those methods will continue to be of central importance (Part II, IV). "The tension between calculation, qualitatively justified procedures, and judgment will not disappear" (Suppes, 1984: 221). Nor will its reflective and meta-theoretical analysis. Appealing to more intellectual modesty in academia and risk management in the

357 For example, no blind faith in numbers and risk models (see the previous chapter). Yet, this plea for a more humane financial economy does not pre-determine the validity of the so-called argument from dehumanization, namely that a hitherto uninvaded sphere of human activity and phenomena (e.g., the value of life, well-being, feelings etc.) ought not to be subjected to "the dehumanization of quasi-economic rationalization" (cf. e.g. Shrader-Frechette, 1985: 172).

sense of Sir Karl Popper, we would like to close with a bon mot by the French author and laureate of the Nobel Prize in Literature in 1947, André Gide: "*Croyez ceux qui cherchent la vérité, doutez de ceux qui la trouvent.*"

References

Aaronson, S. 2014. The Quest for Randomness. American Scientist, 102: 170–173.

Abberger, K., & Nierhaus, W. 2008. How to define a recession?. CESifo Forum, 4: 74–76.

Abdellaoui, M., Baillon, A., Placido, L., & Wakker, P.P. 2011. The Rich Domain of Uncertainty: Source Functions and Their Experimental Implementation. American Economic Review, 101: 695–723.

Acharya, V., & Steffen, S. 2013. Analyzing Systemic Risk of the European Banking Sector. In. J.-P. Fouque, & J.A. Langsam (Eds.). Handbook on Systemic Risk. Cambridge: Cambridge University Press: 247–282.

Acharya, V., Brownless, C., Engle, R., Farazmand, F., & Richardson, M. 2013. Measuring Systemic Risk. In. J.-P. Fouque, & J.A. Langsam (Eds.). Handbook on Systemic Risk. Cambridge: Cambridge University Press: 196–225.

Acharya, V., Pedersen, T., Philippon, T., & Richardson, M. 2010. Measuring systemic risk. AFA 2011 Denver Meetings Paper. Available at: http://dx.doi.org/10.2139/ssrn.1573171.

Ackoff, R.L. 1974. Redesigning the Future: Systems Approach to Societal Problems. London: John Wiley & Sons.

Ackoff, R.L. 1971. Towards a system of system concepts. Management Science, 17: 661–671.

Ackoff, R.L. 1960. Systems, organizations and interdisciplinary research. General Systems Yearbook, 5: 1–8.

Adachi, T. 2014. Toward Categorical Risk Measure Theory. Theory and Applications of Categories, 29: 389–405.

Adams, J. 1995. Risk. London: UCL Press.

Adams, E.W. 1998. A Primer of Probability Logic, Stanford, CA: CSLI Publications.

Adams, H. 1918. The Education of Henry Adams. Boston: Houghton-Mifflin.

Adrian, T., & Brunnermeier, M. 2011. CoVaR. FRB of New York Staff Report No. 348. Available at: http://ssrn.com/abstract=1269446 (19/11/15).

Adrian, T. 2007. Measuring Risk in the Hedge Fund Sector. Current Issues in Economics and Finance, 13: 1–7.

Admati, A., & Hellwig, M.F. 2013. The Bankers' New Clothes: What's Wrong with Banking and What to Do about It. Princeton: Princeton University Press.

Albeverio, S., Jentsch, V., & Kantz, H. (Eds.). 2010. Extreme Events in Nature and Society. Berlin: Springer.

Alderson, D.L., & Doyle, J.C. 2010. Contrasting Views of Complexity and Their Implications For Network-Centric Infrastructures. IEEE Transactions on Systems, Man, And Cybernetics – Part A: Systems and Humans, 40: 839-852.

Allen, F., & Gale, D. 2009. Understanding Financial Crises. Oxford: Oxford University Press.

Allen, F., & Gale, D. 2000. Financial contagion. Journal of Political Economy, 108: 1–33.

Amini, H., Cont, R., & Minca, A. 2012. Stress-testing the resilience of financial networks. International Journal of Theoretical and Applied Finance, 15: 1–20.

Anand, A.I. 2010. Is Systemic Risk Relevant to Securities Regulation? University of Toronto Law Journal, 60: 941–981.

Anderson, P.W. 1999. Complexity Theory and Organization Science. Organization Science, 10: 216–232.

Anderson, P.W. 1972. More Is Different. Science, New Series, 177: 393–396.

Angius, S., Frati, C., Gerken, A., Härle, P., Piccitto, M., & Stegemann, U. 2011. Risk modeling in a new paradigm: developing new insight and foresight on structural risk. McKinsey Working Papers on Risk, 13: 1–12.

Angyal, A. 1969. A Logic of Systems. In. F.E. Emery (Ed.). Systems thinking. Harmondsworth: Penguin Books: 17–29.

Argandoña, A. 2012. Three Ethical Dimensions of the Financial Crisis. IESE Business School Working Paper, 944: 1–16.

Arnoldi, J. 2009. Alles Geld verdampft. Finanzkrise und Weltrisikogesellschaft. Frankfurt a.M.: Suhrkamp.

Artzner, P., Delbaen, F., Eber, J.-M., & Heath, D. 1999. Coherent measures of risk. Mathematical Finance, 9: 203–228.

Arvind, V. 2014. Normal numbers and algorithmic randomness: a historical sketch. Current Science, 106: 1687–1692.

Ashby, W.R. 1973. Some peculiarities of complex systems. Cybernetic Medicine, 9: 1–6.

Ashby, W.R. 1956. An Introduction to Cybernetics. London: John Wiley & Sons.

Aven, T., & Krohn, B.S. 2014. A new perspective on how to understand, assess and manage risk and the unforeseen. Reliability Engineering and System Safety, 121: 1–10.

Aven, T. 2013a. Practical implications of the new risk perspectives. Reliability Engineering and System Safety, 115: 136–145.

Aven, T. 2013b. On the meaning of the black swan concept in a risk context. Safety Science, 57: 44–51.

Aven, T. 2012. The risk concept – historical and recent development trends. Reliability Engineering and System Safety, 99: 33–44.

Aven, T., & Renn, O. 2009. On risk defined as an event where the outcome is uncertain. Journal of Risk Research, 12: 1–11.

Axelrod, R. 2005. Advancing the art of simulation in the social sciences. In J.-P. Rennard (Ed.). Handbook of research on nature inspired computing for economy and management. Hershey, PA: Idea Group.

Ayer, A. 1952. Language, Truth, and Logic. New York: Dover.

Bacharach, S.B. 1989. Organizational theories: some criteria for evaluation. Academy of Management Review, 14: 496–515.

Bachelier, L. 1900. Théorie de la spéculation. Annales Scientifiques de l'Ecole Normale Supérieure, 17: 21–86.

Bäcker, D. 2008. Womit handeln Banken? Eine Untersuchung zur Risikoverarbeitung in der Wirtschaft. Frankfurt a.M.: Suhrkamp.

Bailey, R.E. 2005. The Economics of Financial Markets. Cambridge / New York / Melbourne: Cambridge University Press.

Bak, P. 1996. How Nature Works: The Science of Self-Organized Criticality. New York: Copernicus.

Baldwin, J.S., Rose-Anderssen, C., Ridgway, K., Allen, P.M., Lopez, A., Strathern, M., & Varga, L. 2006. Management Decision-Making: Risk Reduction through Simulation. Risk Management (Special Issue: Complexity, Risk and Emergence), 8: 310–328.

Bandte, H. 2007. Komplexität in Organisationen. Organisationstheoretische Betrachtungen und agentenbasierte Simulation. Wiesbaden: Deutscher Universitäts-Verlag.

Bank for International Settlements (BIS). 1994. 64th Annual Report. Basel: BIS.

Bank of England Systemic Risk Survey, Table A1: Key Risks to the UK Financial System. July 2008 & May 2009: 231. Available at: http://www.bankofengland.co.uk/publications/quarterlybulletin/qb090305.pdf (12/5/2014).

Bank of England. 2005. Financial Stability Review, 18: June 2005. Available at: http://www.bankofengland.co.uk/publications/Documents/fsr/2005/fsrfull0506.pdf (12/5/2014).

Banks, E. 2009. Risk and Financial Catastrophe. New York: Palgrave Macmillan.

Banks, E. 2005. Catastrophic Risk. Analysis and Management. Chichester: John Wiley & Sons.

Barabási, A.-L. 2002. Linked: The New Science of Networks. Cambridge, MA: Perseus.

Barlas, Y. 1996. Formal Aspects of Model Validity and Validation in System Dynamics. System Dynamics Review, 12: 183–210.

Barlas, Y., & Carpenter, S. 1990. Philosophical roots of model validation: two paradigms. System Dynamics Review, 6: 148–166.

Barr, M., & Wells, C. 2013. Toposes, Triples and Theories. Berlin: Springer.

Bartholomew, P., & Whalen, G. 1995. Fundamentals of Systemic Risk. In. G.G. Kaufman (Ed.). Research in Financial Services: Banking, Financial Markets, and Systemic Risk. Vol. 7, Greenwich, CT: JAI Press Inc.: 3–17.

Bartram, S.M., Brown, G.W., & Hund, J.E. 2007. Estimating systemic risk in the international financial system. Journal of Financial Economics, 86: 835–869.

Bar-Yam, Y. 2015. Peace for Syria. Presentation at the Tufts Fletcher School of Law and Diplomacy (September 21, 2015). Available at: http://www.necsi.edu/research/ethnicviolence/peaceforsyria.html (10/12/15).

Basel Committee on Banking Supervision (BCBS). 2015. Operational risk – Revisions to the simpler approaches. Available at: http://www.bis.org/publ/bcbs291.pdf (09/11/16).

Basel Committee on Banking Supervision (BCBS). 2011. Messages from the Academic Literature on Risk Management for the Trading Book, Working Paper, 19. Basel: Bank for International Settlements (BIS), January.

Basel Committee on Banking Supervision (BCBS). 1996. Amendment to the Capital Accord to Incorporate Market Risks. Basel: Bank for International Settlements (BIS).

Battiston, S., Farmer, J.D., Flache, A., Garlaschelli, D., Haldane, A.G., Heesterbeek, H., Hommes, C., Jaeger, C., May, R., & Scheffer, M. 2016. Complexity theory and financial regulation. Economic policy needs interdisciplinary network analysis and behavioral modeling. Science, (19 February 2016).

Battiston, S., Delli Gatti, D., Gallegati, M., Greenwald, B.C., & Stiglitz, J.E. 2012. Liaisons dangereuses: Increasing connectivity, risk sharing, and systemic risk. Journal of Economic Dynamics & Control, 36: 1121–1141.

Beck, U. 1992. Risk Society. London: Sage Publications.

Becker, M., Döhrer, B., & Johanning, L. 2012. Überlegungen zur Verbesserung des Anlegerschutzes: Transparenz versus Komplexität von Finanzprodukten. Diskussionspapier. WHU – Otto Beisheim School of Management.

Beer, S. 1959. Kybernetik und Management. Translated by I. Grubrich. Frankfurt a. M.: S. Fischer Verlag.

Bennett, N. & Lemoine, G.J. 2014. What a difference a word makes: Understanding threats to performance in a VUCA world. Business Horizons, 57: 311–317.

Benthem van, J. 1983. The Logic of Time. Dordrecht: Kluwer.

Berkovitz, J., Frigg, R., & Kronz, F. 2006. The Ergodic Hierarchy, Randomness and Chaos. Studies in History and Philosophy of Modern Physics, 37: 661–91.

Berlekamp, E.R., Conway, J.H., & Guy, R.K. 2001. Winning Ways for your Mathematical Plays, Wellesley, MA: A.K. Peters Ltd.

Bernanke, B.S., & James, H. 1991. The Gold Standard, Deflation, and Financial Crisis in the Great Depression: An International Comparison. In. R.G. Hubbard (Ed.). Financial Markets and Financial Crises. Chicago: University of Chicago Press.

Bernard, C., Brechmann, E.C., & Czado, C. 2013. Statistical Assessments of Systemic Risk Measures. In. J.-P. Fouque, & J.A. Langsam (Eds.). Handbook on Systemic Risk. Cambridge: Cambridge University Press: 165–179.

Bernoulli, J. 1713/1988. Ars conjectandi. In. I. Schneider (Ed.). Die Entwicklung der Wahrscheinlichkeitstheorie von den Anfängen bis 1933. Darmstadt, 1988: Wissenschaftliche Buchgesellschaft: 62–68.

Bernoulli, J. 1713. Ars conjectandi, opus posthumum. Accedit Tractatus de seriebus infinitis, et epistola gallicé scripta de ludo pilae reticularis, Basel: Thurneysen Brothers.

Bernstein, P.L. 1996a. The New Religion of Risk Management. Harvard Business Review, 74: 47–51.

Bernstein, P.L. 1996b. Against the Gods: The Remarkable Story of Risk. New York: Wiley.

Bertsimas, D., Lauprete, G.J., & Samarov, A. 2000. Shortfall as a risk measure: properties, optimization and applications. Working paper, Sloan School of Management, MIT, Cambridge.

Bervas, A. 2006. Market Liquidity and its incorporation into Risk Management. Financial Stability Review, 8: 63–79.

Besio, C. 2014. Transforming Risks into Moral Issues in Organizations. In. C. Luetge, & J. Jauernig (Eds.). Business Ethics and Risk Management. Dordrecht: Springer: 71–84.

Besnard, P., & Hunter, A. 2001. A logic-based theory of deductive arguments. Artificial Intelligence, 129: 203–235.

Bessis, J. 2010. Risk Management in Banking. New York: Wiley.

Bhansali, V. 2014. Tail risk hedging creating robust portfolios for volatile markets. New York: Mcgraw-Hill Education.

Bhansali, V., & Wise, M. 2001. Forecasting Portfolio Risk in Normal and Stressed Markets. Journal of Risk, 4: 91–106.

Bhattacharya, S., Goodhart, C.A.E., Tsomocos, D.P., Vardoulakis, A.P. 2015. A Reconsideration of Minsky's Financial Instability Hypothesis. Journal of Money, Credit and Banking, 47: 931–973.

Bhidé, A. 2010. A Call for Judgment: Sensible Finance for a Dynamic Economy. New York: Oxford University Press.

Billio, M., Getmansky, M., Lo, A.W., & Pelizzon, L. 2012. Econometric measures of connectedness and systemic risk in the Finance and insurance sectors. Journal of Financial Economics, 104: 535–559.

Bisias, D., Flood, M., Lo, A., & Valavanis, S. 2012. A Survey of Systemic Risk Analytics. Annual Review of Financial Economics, 4: 255–296.

Black, F., & Scholes, M. 1973. The pricing of options and corporate liabilities. Journal of Political Economy, 81: 673.

Blankfein, L. 2009. Do not destroy the essential catalyst of risk, Financial Times, 8 February.

Bloomberg, 2015. Goldman Sachs Hawks CDOs Tainted by Credit Crisis Under New Name. Available at: http://www.bloomberg.com/news/articles/2015-02-04/goldman-sachs-hawks-cdos-tainted-by-credit-crisis-under-new-name (15/11/16).

Bloomfield, B. 1982. Cosmology, knowledge and social structure: the case of Forrester and system dynamics. Journal of Applied Systems Analysis, 9: 3–15.

Blyth, M. 2010. Coping with the black swan: The unsettling world of Nassim Taleb. Critical Review, 21: 447–465.

Board of Governors of the Federal Reserve System. 2001. Policy Statement on Payments System Risk. Washington, D.C., May 30: Docket No. R-1107: 1–13.

Boatright, J.R. 2011. The Ethics of Risk Management: A Post-Crisis Perspective. In. BBVA (Eds.). Ethics and Values for the 21st Century. Madrid: BBVA.

Boatright, J.R. 2008. Ethics in Finance. Oxford: Blackwell Publishing.

Bonabeau, E. 2007. Understanding and Managing Complexity Risk. MIT Sloan Management Review, 48: 62–68.

Bookstaber, R., Glasserman, P., Iyengar, G., Luo, Y., Venkatasubramanian, V., & Zhang, Z. 2015. Process Systems Engineering as a Modeling Paradigm for Analyzing Systemic Risk in Financial Networks. The Journal of Investing, 24: 147–162.

Bookstaber, R. 2009. Testimony of Richard Bookstaber Submitted to the U.S. House of Representatives, Committee on Science and Technology, Subcommittee on Investigations and Oversight, For the Hearing: "The Risks of Financial Modeling: VaR and the Economic Meltdown". Congressional Testimony, September 10, 2009. Available at: http://bookstaber.com/rick/Testimony_of_Richard_Bookstaber_to_House_20090910.pdf (06/11/14).
Boot, A.W.A. 2011. Banking at the Cross Roads: How to deal with Marketability and Complexity?. Amsterdam Center for Law & Economics Working Paper No. 2011-07: 1–42.
Borel, E. 1909. Les probabilités dénombrables et leurs applications artithmétiques. Rendiconti del Circolo Matematico di Palermo, 27: 247–271.
Borgonovo, E., & Peccati, L. 2006. Uncertainty and global sensitivity analysis in the evaluation of investment projects. International Journal of Production Economics, 104: 62–73.
Bougen, P. 2003. Catastrophe risk. Economy and Society, 32: 253–274.
Boulton, J., & Allen, P. 2007. The Complexity Perspective, In. M. Jenkins & V. Ambrosini (Eds.). Advanced Strategic Management: A Multi-perspective Approach. New York: Palgrave Macmillan.
Boyle, D. 2001. The tyranny of numbers: Why counting can't make us happy. London: Harper-Collins.
Boysen, T. 2002. Transversale Wirtschaftsethik. Ökonomische Vernunft zwischen Lebens- und Arbeitswelt", URL: http://www1.unisg.ch/www/edis.nsf/SysLkpByIdentifier/2644/$FILE/dis2644.pdf. (07/06/14).
Bradley, S., & Steele, K. 2014. Should subjective probabilities be sharp? Episteme, 11: 277–289.
Bradley, R., & Drechsler, M. 2014. Types of Uncertainty. Erkenntnis, 79: 1225–1248.
Bradley, R. 2010. Ten Rationality Theses. Unpublished. Available at: http://personal.lse.ac.uk/bradLEYR/pdf/Chapter3.pdf (24/03/15).
Brammertz Consulting, 2014. ACTUS: A unified standard for the representation of financial data. Available at: http://www.brammertz-consulting.ch/wp-content/uploads/2011/02/ACTUS_Standardized_contracts.pdf (14/11/16).
Brandon, R.N. 1996. Concepts and Methods in Evolutionary Biology. Cambridge: Cambridge University Press.
Braswell, J., & Mark, R. 2014. Banking and financial activities in the real economy. In. M.S. Brose, M.D. Flood, D. Krishna, & B. Nichols (Eds.). Handbook of Financial Data and Risk Information I: Principles and Context. Cambridge: Cambridge University Press: 179–270.
Brose, M.S., Flood, M.D., & Rowe, D.M. 2014a. Risk management data and information for improved insight. In. M.S. Brose, M.D. Flood, D. Krishna, & B. Nichols (Eds.). Handbook of Financial Data and Risk Information I: Principles and Context. Cambridge: Cambridge University Press: 328–380.
Brose, M.S., Flood, M.D., Krishna, D., & Nichols, B. (Eds.). 2014b. Handbook of Financial Data and Risk Information II: Software and Data. Cambridge: Cambridge University Press.
Brose, M.S., & Flood, M.D. 2014. Editors' introduction to Part I. In. M.S. Brose, M.D. Flood, D. Krishna, & B. Nichols (Eds.). Handbook of Financial Data and Risk Information I: Principles and Context. Cambridge: Cambridge University Press: 5–7.
Brown, G.S. 1957. Probability and Scientific Inference. New York: Longmans, Green & Co.
Brownless, C., & Engle, R. 2011. Volatility, correlation and tails for systemic risk measurement. Working paper. Available at: http://faculty.washington.edu/ezivot/econ589/VolatilityBrownlees.pdf.
Brummell, A., & Macgillivray, G. 2008. Scenario Planning: A Tool to Navigate Strategic Risks. Available at: http://scenarios2strategy.com/pdf/Scenario%20Planning%20-%20A%20Tool%20for%20Navigating%20Strategic%20Risk.pdf. (29/05/14).
Brunnermeier, M.K., Crockett, A., & Goodhart, C. 2009a. Nature of System is Risk. In. M. Brunnermeier, A. Crocket, C. Goodhart, A. Perssaud, & H. Shin (Eds.). The Fundamental Principles of Financial Regulation. Geneva: International Center for Monetary and Banking Studies: 13–24.

Brunnermeier, M.K., Crocket, A., Goodhart, C., Perssaud, A., & Shin, H.S. 2009b. The Fundamental Principles of Financial Regulation. Geneva: International Center for Monetary and Banking Studies. Available at: https://www.princeton.edu/~markus/research/papers/Geneva11.pdf (15/12/14).

Brunnermeier, M.K. 2009. Deciphering the Liquidity and Credit Crunch 2007- 08. Journal of Economic Perspectives, 23: 77–100.

Brunnermeier, M.K., & Oehmke, M. 2009. Complexity in financial markets. Working paper. http://dl4a.org/uploads/pdf/Complexity.pdf.

Buchanan, M. 2013. Power laws and the new science of complexity management. In. B. McKelvey (Ed.). 2013. Complexity. Critical Concepts. Vol. 5. London / New York: Routledge: 435–446.

Bulmer, M.G. 1979. Principles of Statistics. New York: Dover Publications.

Burchell, S., Clubb, C., Hopwood, A., & Hughes, J. 1980. The roles of accounting in organizations and society. Accounting, Organizations and Society, 5: 5–27.

Burt, G., Wright, G, Bradfield, R., Cairns, G., & van der Heijden, K. 2006. The Role of Scenario Planning in Exploring the Environment in View of the Limitations of PEST and Its Derivatives. International Studies of Management and Organization, 36: 50–76.

Byrne, D., & Callaghan, G. 2014. Complexity Theory and the Social Sciences. London / New York: Routledge.

Caballero, R.J., & Simsek, A. 2009. Complexity and Financial Panics. Working Paper. Available at: http://www.nber.org/papers/w14997 (29/09/15).

Caldwell, R. 2012. Systems Thinking, Organizational Change and Agency: A Practice Theory Critique of Senge's Learning Organization. Journal of Change Management, 12: 145–164.

Capponi, A. 2013. Pricing and Mitigation of Counterparty Credit Exposures. In. J.-P. Fouque, & J.A. Langsam (Eds.). Handbook on Systemic Risk. Cambridge: Cambridge University Press: 485–511.

Cartwright, N. 1983. How the Laws of Physics Lie. Oxford: Oxford University Press.

Casati, R., & Varzi, A. 2014. Events. In. E.N. Zalta (Ed.). Stanford Encyclopedia of Philosophy, http://plato.stanford.edu/entries/events/ (27/10/2014).

Cassidy, J. 2010. What's Wrong with Risk Models?. The New Yorker. http://www.newyorker.com/news/john-cassidy/whats-wrong-with-risk-models (28/03/2014).

Casti, J.L. 1992. The simply complex: trendy buzzword or emerging new science? Bulletin of the Santa Fe Institute, 7: 10–13.

Cecchetti, S.G. 2008. Money, Banking and Financial Markets. New York: McGraw-Hill Higher Education.

Célérier, C., & Vallée, B. 2014. What Drives Financial Complexity? A Look into the Retail Market for Structured Products. HEC Paris Research No. Fin-2013-1013. Available at: http://www.hbs.edu/faculty/conferences/2013-household-behavior-risky-asset-mkts/Documents/What-Drives-Financial-Complexity_Celerier-Vallee.pdf (06/05/16).

Chaitin, G. 1969. On the length of programs for computing finite binary sequences. Journal of the Association of Computing Machinery, 16: 145–159.

Choi, Y. & Douady, R. 2013. Financial Crisis and Contagion: A Dynamical Systems Approach. In. J.-P. Fouque, & J.A. Langsam (Eds.). Handbook on Systemic Risk. Cambridge: Cambridge University Press: 453–479.

Christoffersen, P.F., Diebold, F.X., & Schürmann, T. 2003. Horizon Problems and Extreme Events in Financial Risk Management. In. B. Warwick (Ed.). The Handbook of Risk. Hoboken, NJ: John Wiley & Sons: 155–170.

Churchman, C.W. 1968. The Systems Approach. New York: Dell Publishing.

Churchman, C.W. 1961. Prediction and Optimal Decision. Philosophical Issues of a Science of Values. Englewood Cliffs, NJ: Prentice-Hall.

Cilliers, P. 1998. Complexity and postmodernism. Understanding complex systems. London/New York: Routledge.

Clauset, A., Shalizi, C.R., & Newman, M.E.J. 2009. Power-law distributions in empirical data. Society for Industrial and Applied Mathematics Review, 51: 661–703.

Cohen, L.J. 1980. Some Historical Remarks on the Baconian Conception of Probability. Journal of the History of Ideas, 41: 219–231.

Coleridge, S.T. 2015. The Complete Works of Samuel Taylor Coleridge: Poetry, Plays, Literary Essays, Lectures, Autobiography and Letters. G. Doré (Ed.). E-artnow.

Collier, S.J. 2008. Enacting catastrophe: preparedness, insurance, budgetary rationalization. Economy and Society, 37: 224–250.

Comes, T., Hiete, M., Wijngaards, N. & Schultmann, F. 2011. Decision Maps: A Framework for Multi-Criteria Decision Support under Severe Uncertainty. Decision Support Systems, 52: 108–118.

Committee of Sponsoring Organizations of the Treadway Commission (COSO). 2004. Enterprise Risk Management – Integrated Framework: Executive Summary, Technical Report. September. Available at: http://www.coso.org/documents/COSO_ERM_ExecutiveSummary.pdf. (09/09/15).

Cont, R., Moussa, A., & Santos, E.B. 2013. Network Structure and Systemic Risk in Banking Systems. In. J.-P. Fouque, & J.A. Langsam (Eds.). Handbook on Systemic Risk. Cambridge: Cambridge University Press: 327–368.

Corley, K.G., & Gioia, D.A. 2011. Building theory about theory building: what constitutes a theoretical contribution? Academy of Management Review: 36: 12–32.

Cristelli, M. 2014. Complexity in Financial Markets. Modeling Psychological Behavior in Agent-Based Models and Order Book Models. Berlin: Springer.

Creath, R. 2011. Logical Empiricism. In. E.N. Zalta (Ed.). Stanford Encyclopedia of Philosophy, http://plato.stanford.edu/search/searcher.py?query=Logical+Empiricism (22/02/2016).

Crotty, J. 2009. Structural causes of the global financial crisis: a critical assessment of the 'new financial architecture'. Cambridge Journal of Economics, 33: 563–580.

Crutchfield, J., & Wiesner, K. 2010. Simplicity and complexity. Physics World. February 2010: 36–38.

Cyert, R.M., & Grunberg, E. 1963. Assumption, Prediction, and Explanation in Economics. In. R.M. Cyert, & J.G. March (Eds.). A Behavioral Theory of the Firm. Englewood Cliffs, NJ: Prentice-Hall: 298–311.

Daft, R. 1992. Organization Theory and Design. St. Paul, MN: West Publishing.

Daniels, N. 2011. Reflective Equilibrium. In. E.N. Zalta (Ed.). Stanford Encyclopedia of Philosophy, http://plato.stanford.edu/entries/reflective-equilibrium/ (10/11/2015).

Daníelsson, J. 2003. On the Feasibility of Risk Based Regulation. CESifo Economic Studies, 49: 157–179.

Daníelsson, J. 2002. The emperor has no clothes: limits to risk modelling. Journal of Banking and Finance, 26: 1273–1296.

Daníelsson, J., Embrechts, P., Goodhart, C., Keating, C., Muennich, F., Renault, O., & Shin, H.S. 2001. An Academic Response to Basel II. LSE Financial Markets Group. Special Paper Series. No. 130. Available at: http://www.bis.org/bcbs/ca/fmg.pdf (16/11/16).

Das, B., Embrechts, P., & Fasen, V. 2013. Four theorems and a financial crisis. International Journal of Approximate Reasoning, 54: 701–716.

Das, S. 2006. Traders Guns and Money: Knowns and Unknowns in the Dazzling World of Derivatives, Harlow: Prentice Hall.

Dasgupta, A. 2011. Mathematical Foundations of Randomness. In. P.S. Bandyopadhyay, & M.R. Forster (Eds.). Philosophy of Statistics. Handbook of the Philosophy of Science. Oxford: North Holland Publishing: 641–712.

Davis, J.M., & Page, S. 2013. Asset Allocation with Downside Risk Management. In. H.K. Baker & G. Filbeck (Eds.). Portfolio Theory and Management. Oxford: Oxford University Press: 293–313.

Davis, J.P., Eisenhardt, K.M., & Bingham, C.B. 2007. Developing theory through simulation methods. Academy of Management Review, 32: 480–499.

De Bandt, O., & Hartmann, P. 2000. Systemic Risk: A Survey. Frankfurt: European Central Bank Working Paper, 35.

De Fontnouvelle, P., Jordan, J., & Rosengren, E. 2006. Implications of alternative operational risk modeling techniques. In. M. Carey, & R. Stulz (Eds.). Risks of Financial Institutions. Chicago: University of Chicago Press: Chapter 10.

De Moivre, A. 1711. De Mensura Sortis. Philosophical Transactions, 27: 213–264.

Dempster, A.P. 1967. Upper and lower probabilities induced by a multivalued mapping. The Annals of Mathematical Statistics, 38: 325–339.

Derman, E., & Wilmott, P. 2009. The financial modelers' manifesto. Available at: http://ssrn.com/abstract=1324878.

Detken, C., & Nymand-Andersen, P. 2013. The New Financial Stability Framework in Europe. In. J.-P. Fouque, & J.A. Langsam (Eds.). Handbook on Systemic Risk. Cambridge: Cambridge University Press: 748–774.

Dhrymes, P.J., et al. 1972. Criteria for Evaluation of Econometric Models. Annals of Economic and Social Measurement, 1: 291–324.

Diebold, F.X., Doherty, N.A., & Herring, R.J. 2010: Introduction. In. F.X. Diebold, N.A. Doherty, & R.J. Herring (Eds.). The Known, the Unknown, and the Unknowable in Financial Risk Management. Measurement and Theory Advancing Practice. Princeton/Oxford: Princeton University Press: 1–30.

Diebold, F.X., Schuermann, T., & Stroughair, J. 1998. Pitfalls and Opportunities in the Use of Extreme Value Theory in Risk Management. In. A.-P. N. Refenes, J.D. Moody, & A.N. Burgess (Eds.). Advances in Computational Finance, 3-12. Amsterdam: Kluwer Academic Publishers.

Donohoe, H.M., & Needham, R.D. 2009. Moving Best Practice Forward: Delphi Characteristics, Advantages, Potential Problems, and Solutions. International Journal of Tourism Research, 11: 415–437.

Downey, R., & Hirschfeldt, D.R. 2010. Algorithmic Randomness and Complexity. Berlin: Springer.

Dreyfus, H.L. 1972/1999: What Computers Still Can't Do. A Critique of Artificial Reason. Cambridge, MA: MIT Press.

Drobny, S. 2006. Inside the House of Money: Top Hedge Fund Traders on Profiting in the Global Markets. Chichester: John Wiley & Sons.

Drucker, P.F. 2006. The Effective Executive: The Definitive Guide to Getting the Right Things Done. New York: Collins.

Dubin, R. 1978. Theory development. New York: Free Press.

Dubois, D. & Prade, H. 1988a. Possibility Theory. An Approach to Computerized Processing of Uncertainty. New York: Plenum.

Dubois, D. & Prade, H. 1988b. Representation and combination of uncertainty with belief functions and possibility measures. Computational Intelligence, 4: 244–264.

Dubois, D., & Prade, H. 1980. Fuzzy Sets and Systems: Theory and Applications. Chestnut Hill, MA: Academic Press.

Duffie, D. 2007. Innovations in Credit Risk Transfer: Implications for Financial Stability mimeo, Stanford University, Stanford, CA: http://www.stanford.edu/~duffie/BIS.pdf.

Dutta, P. 2015. Uncertainty Modeling in Risk Assessment Based on Dempster-Shafer Theory of Evidence with Generalized Fuzzy Focal Elements. Fuzzy Information and Engineering, 7: 15–30.

Drzik, J., Nakada, P., & Schuermann, T. 2004. Risk capital measurement in financial institutions – Part one. Available at: http://www.Erisk.com.

Eagle, A. 2012. Chance versus Randomness. In. E.N. Zalta (Ed.). Stanford Encyclopedia of Philosophy, http://plato.stanford.edu/entries/chance-randomness/ (08/10/2015).

Eagle, A. 2005. Randomness is Unpredictability. British Journal for the Philosophy of Science, 56: 749–90.
Earman, J. 1986. A Primer on Determinism, Dordrecht: D. Reidel Publishing.
ECB, 2010. Has the financial sector grown too big? Speech by Lorenzo Bini Smaghi, Member of the Executive Board of the ECB Nomura Seminar, The paradigm shift after the financial crisis, Kyoto, 15 April 2010. Available at: https://www.ecb.europa.eu/press/key/date/2010/html/sp100415.en.html (10/12/14).
Edersheim, E.H. 2006. The Definitive Drucker: Challenges For Tomorrow's Executives -- Final Advice From the Father of Modern Management. New York: McGraw Hill Professional.
Edmonds, B. 1999. Syntactic Measures of Complexity. A thesis submitted to the University of Manchester for the degree of Doctor of Philosophy in the Faculty of Arts. Available at: http://bruce.edmonds.name/thesis/ (09/05/15).
Eisenhardt, K.M. 1989. Making Fast Strategic Decisions in High-Velocity Environments. Academy of Management Journal, 32: 543–576.
Ellsberg, D. 1961. Risk, Ambiguity, and the Savage Axioms. The Quarterly Journal of Economics, 75: 643–669.
Embrechts, P., Höing, H., & Juri, A. 2003. Using copulae to bound the Value-at-Risk for functions of dependent risks. Finance & Stochastics, 7: 145–167.
Embrechts, P. 2000. Extreme value theory: potential and limitations as an integrated risk management tool. Derivatives Use, Trading & Regulation, 6: 449–456.
Embrechts, P., Resnick, S.I., & Samorodnitsky, G. 1999. Extreme value theory as a risk management tool. North American Actuarial Journal, 26: 30–41.
Embrechts, P., McNeil, A., & Straumann, D. 1998. Correlation and dependency in risk management: properties and pitfalls. Available at: https://people.math.ethz.ch/~embrecht/ftp/pitfalls.pdf (19/07/15).
Embrechts, P., Klüppelberg, C., & Mikosch, T. 1997. Modelling Extremal Events for Insurance and Finance. Berlin: Springer.
Engel, J., & Gizycki, M. 1999. Conservatism, Accuracy and Efficiency: Comparing Value at Risk Models. APRA, wp0002.
Engle, R.F. 1982. Autoregressive conditional Heteroskedasticity with Estimates of the Variance of U.K. Inflation, Econometrica, 50: 987–1008.
Erben, R.F., & Romeike, F. 2006. Abschied von der Glockenkurve. Risikomanager, 11: 20–22.
Esposito, E. 2014. The Present Use of the Future: Management and Production of Risk on Financial Markets. In. C. Luetge, & J. Jauernig (Eds.). Business Ethics and Risk Management. Dordrecht: Springer: 17–26.
Esposito, E. 2011. The Future of Futures. The Time of Money in Financing and Society. Cheltenham, UK / Northampton, MA: Edward Elgar Publishing, Inc.
Ewald, F. 1991. Insurance and Risk. In. G. Burchell, C. Gordon, & P. Miller (Eds.). The Foucault Effect: Studies in Governmentality. London: Harvester Wheatsheaf: 197–210.
Fagin, R. & Halpern, J.Y., & Meciddo, N. 1990. A Logic for Reasoning about Probabilities. Information and Computation, 87: 78–128.
Falconer, K. 2013. Fractals. A Very Short Introduction. Oxford: Oxford University Press.
Fama, E.F. 1970. Efficient Capital Markets: A Review of Theory and Empirical Work. The Journal of Finance, 25: 383–417.
Fama, E.F. 1965. The Behavior of Stock Market Prices. The Journal of Business, 38: 34–105.
Fama, E.F. 1963. Mandelbrot and the Stable Paretian Hypothesis, Journal of Business, 35: 420–429.
FCIC, 2011. The Financial Crisis Inquiry Report. Final Report of the National Commission on the Causes of the Financial and Economic Crisis in the United States. http://fcic-static.law.stanford.edu/cdn_media/fcic-reports/fcic_final_report_full.pdf (28/03/2014).
Fedel, M., Hosni, H., & Montagna, F. 2011. A logical characterization of coherence for imprecise probabilities. International Journal of Approximate Reasoning, 52: 1147–1170.

Ferguson, N. 2008. Wall Street Lays Another Egg. Vanity Fair. Available at: http://www.vanityfair.com/news/2008/12/banks200812 (18/09/15).
Financial Times. 2009a. Useless Finance, Harmful Finance and Useful Finance, 4 April.
Financial Times. 2009b. Seeds of its own destruction, 8 March.
Fine, T. 1973. Theories of Probability. New York: Academic Press.
Fisher, I. 1933. The Debt-Deflation Theory of Great Depression. Econometrica, 1: 337–357.
Flood, M.D. 2014. A brief history of financial risk and information. In. M.S. Brose, M.D. Flood, D. Krishna, & B. Nichols (Eds.). Handbook of Financial Data and Risk Information I: Principles and Context. Cambridge: Cambridge University Press: 8–32.
Flood, R.L., & Carson, E.R. 1993. Dealing with Complexity. An Introduction to the Theory and Application of Systems Science. New York / London: Plenum Press.
Floridi, L. 2013. The Philosophy of Information. Oxford: Oxford University Press.
Föllmer, H., & Schied, A. 2016. Stochastic Finance: An Introduction in Discrete Time. Berlin/Boston: Walter de Gruyter.
Forrester, J.W. 1994. Learning through system dynamics as preparation for the 21st century. Systems Thinking and Dynamic Modeling Conference for K12 Education, Concord, MA.
Forrester, J.W., & Senge, P.M. 1980. Tests for building confidence in system dynamics models. In. A.A. Legasto, J.W. Forrester, & J.M. Lyneis (Eds.). System Dynamics: TIMS Studies in the Management Sciences. Amsterdam: North-Holland: 209–228.
Forrester, J.W. 1975. The Impact of Feedback Control Concepts on the Management Sciences. In. Collected Papers of Jay W. Forrester. Cambridge, MA: Wright-Allen Press.
Forrester, J.W. 1971. Counterintuitive behavior of social systems. Technology Review, 73: 52–68.
Forrester, J.W. 1969. Urban Dynamics. Cambridge, MA: MIT Press.
Forrester, J.W. 1968. A Response to Ansoff and Slevin. Management Science, 14: 601–618.
Forrester, J.W. 1961. Industrial Dynamics. Cambridge, MA: MIT Press.
Forrester, J.W. 1958. Industrial Dynamics: A major breakthrough for decision makers. Harvard Business Review, 36: 37–66.
Fouque, J.-P., & Langsam, J.A. 2013. Introduction. In. J.-P. Fouque, & J.A. Langsam (Eds.). Handbook on Systemic Risk. Cambridge: Cambridge University Press: xx–xxviii.
Freitag, W. 2015. I bet you'll solve Goodman's Riddle. The Philosophical Quarterly, 65: 254–267.
Freixas, X., Parigi, M., & Rochet, J. 2000. Systemic risk, interbank relations and liquidity provision by the central bank. Journal of Money Credit and Banking, 32: 611–638.
French, K.R., Baily, M.N., Campbell, J.Y., Cochrane, J.H., Diamond, D.W. Duffie, D., Kashyap, A.K., Mishkin, F.S., Rajan, R.G., Scharfstein, D.S., Shiller, R.J., Shin, H.S., Slaughter, M.J., Stein, J.C., & Stulz, R.M. 2010. The Squam Lake Report. Fixing the Financial System. Princeton/Oxford: Princeton University Press.
Friedman, B.M. 2010. Is our Financial System Serving Us Well? Dædalus, 139: 9–21.
Friedman, B.M., & Laibson, D.I. 1989. Economic Implications of Extraordinary Movements in Stock Prices. Brookings Papers on Economic Activity, 2: 137–172.
Friedman, M. 1976. Price Theory: A Provisional Text. Chicago: Aldine.
Frigg, R., Smith, L.A., Stainforth, D.A. 2015. An assessment of the foundational assumptions in high-resolution climate projections: the case of UKCP09. Synthese, 192: 3979–4008.
Frigg, R., Bradley, S., Du, H., & Smith, L.A. 2014. Laplace's demon and the adventures of his apprentices. Philosophy of Science, 81: 31–59.
Frigg, R., Bradley, S., Machete, R.L., & Smith. L.A. 2013. Probabilistic Forecasting: Why Model Imperfection Is a Poison Pill. In. H. Anderson, D. Dieks, G. Wheeler, W. Gonzalez, & T. Übel (Eds.): New Challenges to Philosophy of Science. Berlin/New York: Springer: 479–491.
Frigg, R. 2004, In What Sense is the Kolmogorov-Sinai Entropy a Measure for Chaotic Behaviour? – Bridging the Gap Between Dynamical Systems Theory and Communication Theory. British Journal for the Philosophy of Science, 55: 411–434.
Fung, W., & Hsieh, D.A. 1999. A primer on hedge funds. Journal of Empirical Finance, 6: 309–331.

Futuyma, D.J. 2005. Evolution. Cumberland, MA: Sinauer.
Gabbay, D.M., Hogger, C.J., & Robinson, J.A. (Eds.). 1994. Handbook of Logic in Artificial Intelligence and Logic Programming. Vol. 3. Nonmonotonic Reasoning and Uncertainty Reasoning. Oxford: Oxford University Press.
Gaffeo, E., & Tamborini, R. 2011. If the Financial System Is Complex, How Can We Regulate it?. International Journal of Political Economy, 40: 79–97.
Garbolino, E., Chery, J.-P., & Guarnieri, F. 2016. A Simplified Approach to Risk Assessment Based on System Dynamics: An Industrial Case Study. Risk Analysis, 13 January.
Garnier, J., Papanicolaou, G., & Yang, T.-W. 2013: Diversification in Financial Networks may Increase Systemic Risk. In. J.-P. Fouque, & J.A. Langsam (Eds.). Handbook on Systemic Risk. Cambridge: Cambridge University Press: 432–443.
Garsten, C. & Hasselström, A. 2003. Risky business: Discourses of risk and (ir)responsibility in globalizing markets. Ethnos: Journal of Anthropology, 68: 249–270.
Gary, M.S., Kunc, M., Morecroft, J.D.W., Rockart, S.F. 2008. System dynamics and strategy. System Dynamics Review, 24: 407–429.
Gatfaoui, H. 2008. From Fault Tree to Credit Risk Assessment: A Case Study. Post-Print hal-00564963, HAL, March 2008.
Gausemeier, J., Fink, A., & Schlake, O. 1998. Scenario Management: An Approach to Develop Future Potentials. Technological Forecasting & Social Change, 59: 111–130.
Geithner, T.F., & Metrick, A. 2015. The Global Financial Crisis, Lecture at Yale School of Management. Fall 2015. Lecture slides available upon request.
Gell-Mann, M. 1994. The Quark and the Jaguar – adventures in the simple and the complex. London: Little, Brown and Co.
Georgantzas, N.C., & Acar, W. 1995. Scenario-Driven Planning: Learning to Manage Strategic Uncertainty. Westport, CT: Quorum Books.
Gershenson, C. (Ed.). 2008. Complexity. 5 Questions. Copenhagen: Automatic Press.
Getmansky, M., Lee, P.A., & Lo, A.W. 2015. Hedge Funds: A Dynamic Industry In Transition. Working paper. Available at: http://papers.ssrn.com/sol3/papers.cfm?abstract_id=2637007 (03/11/15).
Gibbert, M., & Ruigrok, W. 2010. The "What" and "How" of Case Study Rigor: Three Strategies Based on Published Work. Organizational Research Methods, 13: 710–737.
Gibbert, M., Ruigrok, W., & Wicki, B. 2008. What passes as a rigorous case study?. Strategic Management Journal, 29: 1465–1474.
Giddens, A. 1990. The Consequences of Modernity. Cambridge, UK: Polity Press.
Gilli, M., & Kellezi, E. 2006. An Application of Extreme Value Theory for Measuring Financial Risk. Computational Economics, 27: 1–23.
Giry, M. 1982. A categorical approach to probability theory. In. Categorical
aspects of topology and analysis. Vol. 915 of Lecture Notes in Mathematics: 68–85.
Goldstein, D.G. & Taleb, N.N. 2007. We Don't Quite Know What We Are Talking About When We Talk About Volatility. Available at: http://www-stat.wharton.upenn.edu/~steele/Courses/434/434Context/Volatility/ConfusedVolatility.pdf (15/06/15).
Gomez, P., & Probst, G. 1997. Die Praxis des ganzheitlichen Problemlösens: Vernetzt denken. Unternehmerisch handeln. Persönlich überzeugen. Bern: Haupt.
Gomez, P. 1981. Modelle und Methoden des systemorientierten Managements. Bern: Haupt.
Goodhart, C.A.E. 2010. Domestic Banking Problems. In. F.X. Diebold, N.A. Doherty, & R.J. Herring (Eds.). The Known, the Unknown, and the Unknowable in Financial Risk Management. Measurement and Theory Advancing Practice. Princeton/Oxford: Princeton University Press: 286–295.
Goodman, N. 1955. Fact, Fiction, & Forecast, Cambridge, MA: Harvard University Press.

Gorton, G.B., & Metrick, A. 2012. Getting Up to Speed on the Financial Crisis: a One-Weekend-Reader's Guide. NBER Working Paper No. w17778. Available at: http://papers.ssrn.com/sol3/papers.cfm?abstract_id=1989347 (10/02/16).

Gorton, G.B., & Metrick, A. 2009. Haircuts. Yale Working Paper 15273. Available at: http://www.nber.org/papers/w15273.

Gottman, J.M. 1981. Time-Series Analysis. A comprehensive introduction for social scientists. Cambridge: Cambridge University Press.

Granger, C.W.J. 2010. A Decision Maker's Perspective. In. F.X. Diebold, N.A. Doherty, & R.J. Herring (Eds.). The Known, the Unknown, and the Unknowable in Financial Risk Management. Measurement and Theory Advancing Practice. Princeton/Oxford: Princeton University Press: 31–46.

Granovetter, M. 1985. Economic action and social structure: the problem of embeddedness. American Journal of Sociology, 91: 481–510.

Granovetter, M. 1973. The strength of weak ties. American Journal of Sociology, 78: 1360–1380.

Greenbaum, S.I. 2015. Tail-Risk Perspectives. The Journal of Investing, 24: 164–175.

Greenspan, A. 2007. The Age of Turbulence: Adventures in a New World. New York: Penguin Books.

Gribbin, J. 2005. Deep simplicity. Chaos, complexity and the emergence of life. London: Penguin Books.

Grimmett, G., & Stirzaker, D. 2001. Probability and Random Processes. Oxford: Oxford University Press.

Gronemeyer, M. 2014. Decision-Making as Navigational Art: A Pragmatic Approach to Risk Management. In. C. Luetge, & J. Jauernig (Eds.). Business Ethics and Risk Management. Dordrecht: Springer: 85–96.

Grösser, S.N. 2013. Co-evolution of standards in innovation systems: The dynamics of voluntary and legal building codes. Berlin: Springer.

Grösser, S.N., & Schwaninger, M. 2012. Contributions to model validation: hierarchy, process, and cessation. System Dynamics Review, 28: 157–181.

Group of Ten. 2001. Consolidation in the financial sector. Bank for International Settlements publication, Basel.

Gudonavičius, L., Bartosevičienė, V., & Šaparnis, G. 2009. Imperatives for Enterprise Strategists. Engineering Economics, 1: 75–83.

Gulati, R. 2007. Tent poles, tribalism, and boundary spanners: The rigor-relevance debate in management research. Academy of Management Journal, 50: 775–782.

Gurley, J.G., & Shaw, E.S. 1960. Money in a Theory of Finance. Washington D.C: Brookings Institution.

Gurusamy, S. 2008. Financial Services and Systems. Boston, MA: Irwin/McGraw-Hill.

Gyntelberg, J. & Wooldridge, P. 2008. Interbank Rate Fixings During the Recent Turmoil. Bank for International Settlements Quarterly Review. March 2008: 59–72.

Hacking, I. 2006. The Emergence of Probability: A Philosophical Study of Early Ideas about Probability, Induction and Statistical Inference. Cambridge: Cambridge University Press.

Hagel, J. 2013. The power of power laws. In. B. McKelvey (Ed.). 2013. Complexity. Critical Concepts. Vol. 5. London / New York: Routledge: 460–466.

Hájek, A. 2011. Interpretations of Probability. In. E.N. Zalta (Ed.). Stanford Encyclopedia of Philosophy, http://plato.stanford.edu/entries/probability-interpret/ (17/11/2013).

Hájek, A. 2010. A Plea for the Improbable. Available at: http://ir.lib.uwo.ca/philosophyevents/10/ (15/04/16).

Hájek, A. 2009. Arguments For – Or Against – Probabilism?. In. F. Huber & C. Schmidt-Petri (Eds.). Degrees of Belief. Dordrecht: Springer: 229–251.

Hájek, A., & Hall, N. 2002. Induction and Probability. In. P. Machamer, & M. Silberstein (Eds.). The Blackwell Guide to the Philosophy of Science. Malden, MA: Blackwell Publishing: 149–172.

Haldane, A.G. & May, R.M. 2011. Systemic risk in banking ecosystems. Nature, 469: 351–355.
Halpern, J.Y. 2005. Reasoning About Uncertainty. Cambridge, MA: MIT Press.
Halpern, J.Y., & Rabin, M.O. 1987. A Logic to Reason about Likelihood. Artificial Intelligence, 32: 379–405.
Han, J., & Kamber, M. 2000. Data Mining: Concepts and Techniques. San Francisco, CA: Morgan Kaufmann Publishers.
Hansson, S.O. 2011: Risk. In. E.N. Zalta (Ed.). Stanford Encyclopedia of Philosophy, http://plato.stanford.edu/entries/risk/ (17/11/2013).
Hansson, S.O. 2007. Risk and ethics: three approaches. In. T. Lewens (Ed.). Risk – Philosophical Perspectives. Oxon: Routledge: 21–35.
Härle, P., Havas, A., & Samandari, H. 2016. The future of bank risk management. McKinsey Working Papers on Risk, 1, Summer 2016: 1–9.
Harrison, J.R., Lin, Z., Carroll, G.R., & Carley, K.M. 2007. Simulation modeling in organizational and management research. Academy of Management Review, 32: 1229–1245.
Haynes, J. 1895. Risk as an economic factor. The Quarterly Journal of Economics, 9: 409.
Heidbrink, L. 2003. Kritik der Verantwortung. Zu den Grenzen verantwortlichen Handelns in komplexen Kontexten. Göttingen: Velbrück Wissenschaft.
Heinemann, S. 2014. Ethik der Finanzmarktrisiken am Beispiel des Finanzderivatehandels. Paderborn: Mentis.
Helbing, D. 2013. Globally networked risks and how to respond. Nature, 497: 51–59.
Helbing, D. 2010. Systemic Risks in Society and Economics. IRGC – The Emergence of Risks: Contributing Factors. October: 1–25.
Hellwig, M.F. 2008. Systemic risk in the financial sector: an analysis of the subprime-mortgage financial crisis. Preprints of the Max Planck Institute for Research on Collective Goods Bonn 2008/43: 129–207.
Hellwig, M.F. 1998. Banks, Markets, and the Allocation of Risks. Journal of Institutional and Theoretical Economics, 154: 328–351.
Hellwig, M.F. 1995. Systemic Aspects of Risk Management in Banking and Finance. Schweizerische Zeitschrift für Volkswirtschaft und Statistik / Swiss Journal of Economics and Statistics, 131: 723 – 737; http://www.sjes.ch/papers/1995-IV-9.pdf.
Hellwig, M.F. 1994. Liquidity Provision, Banking, and the Allocation of Interest Rate Risk. European Economic Review, 38: 1363–1389.
Heri, E. & Zimmermann, H. 2001. Grenzen statistischer Messkonzepte für die Risikosteuerung. In: H. Schierenbeck, B. Rolfes, & S. Schüller (Eds.). Handbuch Bankcontrolling. Wiesbaden: Gabler Verlag: 995–1014.
Hieronymi, A. 2013. Understanding Systems Science: A Visual and Integrative Approach. Systems Research and Behavioral Science, 30: 580–595.
Hoffmann, C.H., & Müller, J. 2017. Managing Extreme and Systemic Risks: A Plea in favor of the Known. Under consideration for publication in Journal of Risk.
Hoffmann, C.H. 2016. Structure-based Explanatory Modeling of Risks. Towards Understanding Dynamic Complexity in Financial Systems. Accepted for publication in Systems Research & Behavioral Science.
Hoffmann, C.H., & Grösser, S.N. 2014. Strategic planning in banks, embedded in a dynamically complex financial system. Annual Meeting of the Strategic Management Society, Madrid.
Hoffmann, C.H. 2009. Über den Hauptsatz in der Kunst des Vermutens. Eine kurze Abhandlung. Working paper (unpublished).
Hohwy, J., & Kallestrup, J. 2008. Being Reduced: New Essays on Reduction, Explanation, and Causation. Oxford: Oxford University Press.
Holland, P.R. 1993. The Quantum Theory of Motion: An Account of the de Broglie-Bohm Causal Interpretation of Quantum Mechanics. Cambridge: Cambridge University Press.

Holton, E.F., & Lowe, J.S. 2007. Toward a general research process for using Dubin's theory building model. Human Resource Development Review, 6: 297–320.
Homer, J., & Oliva, R. 2001. Maps and models in system dynamics: a response to Coyle. System Dynamics Review, 17: 347–355.
Horgby, P.-J. 1999. An Introduction to Fuzzy Inference in Economics. Homo Oeconomicus, 15: 543–59.
House, P.W., & McLeod, J. 1977. Large-Scale Models for Policy Evaluation. New York: Wiley.
Hsieh, D.A. 1991. Chaos and nonlinear dynamics: Application to financial markets, Journal of Finance, 46: 1839–1877.
Huang, X., Zhou, H., & Zhu, H. 2009a. A framework for assessing the systemic risk of major financial institutions. Journal of Banking & Finance, 33: 2036–2049.
Huang, T., Zhao, R., & Tang, W. 2009b. Risk Model with Fuzzy Random Individual Claim Amount. European Journal of Operational Research, 192: 879–890.
Hubbard, D. 2009. The Failure of Risk Management: Why It's Broken and How to Fix It. Oxford: Wiley-Blackwell.
Huber, F. 2016. Formal Representations of Belief. In. E.N. Zalta (Ed.). Stanford Encyclopedia of Philosophy, http://plato.stanford.edu/entries/formal-belief/ (26/04/2016).
Huberman, B.A., & Hogg, T. 1986. Complexity and Adaptation. Physica, 22: 376–384.
Hughes, B.D. 1995. Random Walks and Random Environments. Vol. 1. Oxford: Clarendon Press.
Hull, J.C. 2010. Risk Management and Financial Institutions. Boston: Pearson.
Hull, J.C. 2005. Options futures and other derivatives. London: Prentice Hall.
Hume, D. 1739-40/1888. Hume's Treatise of Human Nature. L.A. Selby Bigge (Ed.). Oxford: Clarendon Press.
Illari, P. & Williamson, J. 2012. What is a mechanism? Thinking about mechanisms across the sciences. European Journal for Philosophy of Science, 2: 119–135.
Illing, M., & Liu, Y. 2006. Measuring financial stress in a developed country: An application to Canada. Journal of Financial Stability, 2: 243–265.
Ismael, J. 2015. Quantum Mechanics. In. E.N. Zalta (Ed.). Stanford Encyclopedia of Philosophy, http://plato.stanford.edu/entries/qm/ (24/03/2015).
ISO. 2009. Risk Management – Vocabulary. Guide 2009, 73.
Jackson, M.C. 1993. Beyond the fads: systems thinking for managers. University of Hull Centre for Systems Studies Working Paper, 3: 1–34.
Jacobs, J. 1961. The Death and Life of Great American Cities. New York: Vintage.
Jacque, L.L. 2015. Global Derivative Debacles: From Theory to Malpractice. Singapore: World Scientific Publishing.
Jagadish, H.V. 2013: Data for Systemic Risk. In. J.-P. Fouque, & J.A. Langsam (Eds.). Handbook on Systemic Risk. Cambridge: Cambridge University Press: 3–8.
Jasanoff, S. 1999. The Songlines of Risk. Environmental Values. Special Issue: Risk, 8: 135–152.
Jaynes, E.T. 2003. Probability Theory: The Logic of Science. Cambridge: Cambridge University Press.
Jeffrey, R.C. 1983. The Logic of Decision, Chicago: University of Chicago Press.
Joe, H. 1997. Multivariate Models and Dependence Concepts. London: Chapman & Hall.
Johansen, A., & Sornette, D. 2010. Shocks, Crashes and Bubbles in Financial Markets. Brussels Economic Review, 53: 201–253.
Johansen, A., & Sornette, D. 2001. Large Stock Market Price Drawdowns Are Outliers. Available at: http://arxiv.org/pdf/cond-mat/0010050.pdf.
Johnson, N., Zhao, G., Hunsader, E. Meng, J., Ravindar, A., Carran, S., & Tivnan, B. 2012. Financial black swans driven by ultrafast machine ecology. Working Paper (07/02/2012). Available at: http://arxiv.org/abs/1202.1448 (17/12/14).
Johnson, S., & Kwak, J. 2009. Seduced by a model. New York Times: Economix, October 1. Available at: http://economix.blogs.nytimes.com/2009/10/01seduced-by-a-model/ (07/03/14).

Johnston, M., Gilmore, A., & Carson, D. 2008. Dealing with Environmental Uncertainty: The Value of Scenario Planning for Small to Medium-Sized Entreprises (SMEs). European Journal of Marketing, 42: 1170–1178.

Joint Central Bank Research Conference. 1995. In. McNeil, A., Frey, R., & Embrechts, P. 2005. Quantitative Risk Management. Princeton: Princeton University Press.

Jones, S.P., Eber, J.-M., & Seward, J. 2001. Composing Contracts: An Adventure in Financial Engineering. In. FME (Ed.). Formal Methods for Increasing Software Productivity. International Symposium of Formal Methods Europe. March 12–16, 2001, Proceedings, Berlin: Springer.

Jorion, P. 2000. Risk Management Lessons from Long-Term Capital Management. European Financial Management, 6: 277–300.

Jorion, P. 1997. Value at Risk: The New Benchmark for Controlling Market Risk. Chicago: Irwin.

J.P. Morgan, 2013. Derivatives and Risk Management Made Simple. Available at: https://www.jpmorgan.com/jpmpdf/1320663533358.pdf (27/04/16).

Juri, A., & Wühtrich, M. 2003. Tail dependence from a distributional point of view. Extremes, 3: 213– 246.

Kahneman, D., & Klein, G. 2009. Conditions for intuitive expertise: A failure to disagree. American Psychologist, 64: 515–526.

Kampen, van N.G. 2007. Stochastic Processes in Physics and Chemistry. Amsterdam: North-Holland.

Kaplan, R.S., & Mikes, A. 2012. Managing Risks: A New Framework. Harvard Business Review, June: 48–60.

Kaplan, S., & Garrick, B.J. 1981. On the quantitative definition of risk. Risk Analysis, 1: 11–27.

Katagiri, H., Uno, T., Kato, K., Tsuda, H., & Tsubaki, H. 2013. Random fuzzy multi-objective linear programming: Optimization of possibilistic value at risk. Expert Systems with Applications, 40: 563–574.

Katz, D., & Kahn, R.L. 1969. Common characteristics of open systems. In. F.E. Emery (Ed.). Systems thinking. Harmondsworth: Penguin Books: 86–104.

Kauffman, S.A. 1993. The Origins of Order. Self-Organization and Selection in Evolution. New York: Oxford University Press.

Kaufman, G.G., & Scott, K.E. 2003. What Is Systemic Risk, and Do Bank Regulators Retard or Contribute to It? Independent Review, 7: 371–392.

Kaufman, G.G. 1995. Comment on Systemic Risk. In. G.G. Kaufman (Ed.). Research in Financial Services: Banking, Financial Markets, and Systemic Risk. Greenwich, CT: JAI Press Inc.: 47–52.

Keim, D.A., Andrienko, G.L., Fekete, J.-D., Kohlhammer, C.G.J., & Melançon, G. 2008. Visual analytics: Definition, process, and challenges. In. A. Kerren, J. Stasko, J.-D. Fekete, C. North (Eds.). Information Visualization – Human-Centered Issues and Perspectives. Berlin: Springer: 154–175.

Keller, E.F. 2009. Organisms, Machines, and Thunderstorms: A History of Self-Organization, Part Two. Complexity, Emergence, and Stable Attractors. Historical Studies in the Natural Sciences, 39: 1–31.

Kelly, R. 1995. Derivatives – A Growing Threat to the International Financial System. In. J. Michie, & J.G. Smith (Eds.). Managing the Global Economy. Oxford / New York / Athens: Oxford University Press: 213–231.

Keynes, J.M. 1937. The General Theory. Quarterly Journal of Economics, 51: 209–233.

Kindleberger, C.P. 1978. Manias, panics, and crashes. New York: Basic Books.

King, A., Liechty, J.C., Rossi, C.V., & Taylor, C. 2014. Frameworks for systemic risk monitoring. In. M.S. Brose, M.D. Flood, D. Krishna, & B. Nichols (Eds.). Handbook of Financial Data and Risk Information I: Principles and Context. Cambridge: Cambridge University Press: 105–147.

Kirchhof, R. 2003. Ganzheitliches Komplexitätsmanagement. Grundlagen und Methodik des Umgangs mit Komplexität im Unternehmen. Wiesbaden: Springer Fachmedien.

Klein, R., & Scholl, A. 2004. Planung Und Entscheidung. München: Vahlen.
Kleindorfer, G.B., & Geneshan, R. 1993. The philosophy of science and validation in simulation. Proceedings of the 25th Conference on Winter Simulation, Los Angeles, CA.
Klimek, P., Obersteiner, M., & Thurner, S. 2015. Systemic trade-risk of critical resources. Working paper. Available at: http://arxiv.org/abs/1504.03508 (09/05/15).
Klir, G.J. 1991. Facets of Systems Science. New York / London: Plenum Press.
Klir, G.J. 1985. Complexity: Some General Observations. Systems Research, 2: 131–140.
Knight, F.H. 1921. Risk, uncertainty and profit. Mineola, NY: Dover Publications.
Knox, E. 2015. Abstraction and its Limits: Finding Space For Novel Explanation. Noûs, 49: 1–20.
Kohn, D.L. 2010. Crisis Management: The Known, the Unknown, and the Unknowable. In. F.X. Diebold, N.A. Doherty, & R.J. Herring (Eds.). The Known, the Unknown, and the Unknowable in Financial Risk Management. Measurement and Theory Advancing Practice. Princeton/Oxford: Princeton University Press: 1–30.
Kolmogorov, A.N. 1965. Three Approaches to the Definition of the Concept "Quantity of Information". Problemy Peredachi Informatsii, 1: 3–11.
Kolmogorov, A.N. 1963. On Tables of Random Numbers. Sankhya, 25: 369–376.
Kolmogorov, A.N. 1933. Grundbegriffe der Wahrscheinlichkeitsrechnung. Berlin: Julius Springer.
Kon, S.J. 1984. Models of Stock Returns – A Comparison, Journal of Finance, 39, 147–165.
Kosow, H., & Gaßner, R. 2008. Methoden Der Zukunfts-und Szenarioanalyse: Überblick, Bewertung und Auswahlkriterien". Wertstattbericht Nr. 103 des Instituts für Zukunftsstudien und Technologiebewertung (IZT). Available at: http://www.izt.de/fileadmin/downloads/pdf/IZT_WB103.pdf. (29/05/14).
Koslowski, P. 2012. The Ethics of Banking: Conclusions from the Financial Crisis (Issues in Business Ethics). Heidelberg: Springer.
Kripke, S.A. 1982. Wittgenstein on Rules and Private Language. An Elementary Exposition. Cambridge, MA: Harvard University Press.
Kröger, W., & Zio, E. 2011. Vulnerable Systems. Berlin: Springer.
Kroszner, R.S., Laeven, L., & Klingebiel, D. 2007. Banking crises, financial dependence, and growth. Journal of Financial Economics, 84: 187–228.
Krugman, P. 2009. The Return of Depression Economics. And the Crisis of 2008. New York: Norton.
Kuhn, T. 1970. The Structure of Scientific Revolutions. Chicago: University of Chicago Press.
Kuijpers, B., & Vaisman, A.A. 2016. A formal algebra for OLAP. CoRR, abs/1609.05020.
Kuritzkes, A. & Schürmann, T. 2010. What we Know, Don't Know, and Can't Know about Bank Risk. A View from the Trenches. In. F.X. Diebold, N.A. Doherty, & R.J. Herring (Eds.). The Known, the Unknown, and the Unknowable in Financial Risk Management. Measurement and Theory Advancing Practice. Princeton/Oxford: Princeton University Press: 103–144.
Kwakkel, J.H., Walker, W.E., Marchau, V.A.W.J. 2010. Classifying and communicating uncertainties in model-based policy analysis. International Journal of Technology, Policy and Management, 10: 299–315.
Kyburg, H.E., & Teng, C.M. 2001. Uncertain Inference. Cambridge: Cambridge University Press.
Kyburg, H.E. 1974. The Logical Foundations of Statistical Inference. Dordrecht: D. Reidel Publishing.
Ladley, D. 2011. Contagion and risk-sharing on the inter-bank market. Working paper 11/10, University of Leicester.
Laeven, L., & Valencia, F. 2008. Systemic Bank Crises: A New Database. International Monetary Fund Working Paper WP/08/224 (17/11/2013).
Lai, M. 2015. Giraffe: Using Deep Reinforcement Learning to Play Chess. Available at: https://arxiv.org/abs/1509.01549 (22/11/16).
Lane, D.C. 2000. Should System Dynamics be Described as a 'Hard' or 'Deterministic' Systems Approach. Systems Research and Behavioral Science, 17: 3–22.

Lane, D.C. 1994. With a little help from our friends: how system dynamics and 'soft' OR can learn from each other. System Dynamics Review, 10: 101–134.

Laplace, P.S. 1826/1951. Philosophical Essay on Probabilities, New York: Dover.

La Porte, T.R. 1975a. Chapter I. Organized Social Complexity: Explication of a Concept. In. T.R. La Porte (Ed.). Organized Social Complexity: Challenge to Politics and Policy. Princeton: Princeton University Press: 3–39.

La Porte, T.R. 1975b. Chapter X. Complexity and Uncertainty: Challenge to Action. In. T.R. La Porte (Ed.). Organized Social Complexity: Challenge to Politics and Policy. Princeton: Princeton University Press: 332–357.

Lawrence, C., & Robinson, G. 1995. Liquid measures. Risk, 8: 52–55.

Leamer, E.E. 1983. Let's Take the Con out of Econometrics. American Economic Review, 73: 31–43.

Lee, C., Lee, A., & Lee, J. (Eds.). 2010. Handbook of quantitative finance and risk management. New York: Springer.

Lee, A.M. 1976: Past Futures. Operational Research Quarterly, 27: 147–153.

Leibniz, G.W. 1703/1962. Brief XIII. Leibniz an Jac. Bernoulli. 3/12/1703. In. C.I. Gerhardt (Ed.). Mathematische Schriften. Band III/1. Hildesheim: Georg Olms Verlagsbuchhandlung: 79–84.

Le Monde. 2013. Fabrice Tourre, le Dr Frankenstein de Goldman Sachs En savoir plus sur, 15 July. Available at: http://www.lemonde.fr/economie/article/2013/07/15/fabrice-tourre-le-dr-frankenstein-de-goldman-sachs_3447598_3234.html#WwBzGk2O6KZECJRi.99.

Levy, D. 1994. Chaos theory and strategy: Theory, application, and managerial implications. Strategic Management Journal, 15: 167–178.

Lewis, D.K. 1980. A Subjectivist's Guide to Objective Chance. In. R.C. Jeffrey (Ed.). Studies in Inductive Logic and Probability. Vol. II. Berkeley: University of Berkeley Press: 263–293.

Liechty, J. 2013. Statistics and Systemic Risk. In. J.-P. Fouque, & J.A. Langsam (Eds.). Handbook on Systemic Risk. Cambridge: Cambridge University Press: 163–164.

Lin, C.-S., Khan, H.A., Chang, R.-Y., & Wang, Y.-C. 2008. A New Approach to Modeling Early Warning Systems for Currency Crises: Can a Machine-Learning Fuzzy Expert System Predict the Currency Crises Effectively? Journal of International Money and Finance, 27: 1098–1121.

Linstone, H.A., & Turoff, M. 1975. The Delphi Method: Techniques and Applications. Online source: http://is.njit.edu/pubs/delphibook/delphibook.pdf. (29/05/2014).

LiPuma, E., & Li, B. 2005. Financial Derivatives and the Rise of Circulation. Economy and Society, 34: 404–427.

Litzenberger, R.H., & Modest, D.M. 2010. Crisis and Noncrisis Risk in Financial Markets. In. F.X. Diebold, N.A. Doherty, & R.J. Herring (Eds.). The Known, the Unknown, and the Unknowable in Financial Risk Management. Measurement and Theory Advancing Practice. Princeton/Oxford: Princeton University Press: 74–102.

Liu, P., Zhang, X., & Liu, W. 2011. A risk evaluation method for the high-tech project investment based on uncertain linguistic variables. Technological Forecasting & Social Change, 78: 40–50.

Lloyd, S. 2001. Measures of Complexity: A Nonexhaustive List. IEEE Control Systems Magazine, August 2001. Available at: http://ieeexplore.ieee.org/stamp/stamp.jsp?arnumber=939938 (11/05/15).

Loewer, B. 2001. Determinism and Chance. Studies in History and Philosophy of Modern Physics, 32: 609–620.

Longin, F.M. 2000. From value at risk to stress testing: The extreme value approach. Journal of Business, 96: 383–408.

Longin, F.M. 1996. The asymptotic distribution of extreme stock market returns. Journal of Banking & Finance, 24: 1097–1130.

Lorenz, E.N. 1963. Deterministic Non-periodic Flow. Journal of the Atmospheric Sciences, 20: 130–141.

Lorsch, J.W. 2009. Regaining Lost Relevance. Journal of Management Inquiry, 18: 108–117.
Lowenstein, R. 2002. When Genius Failed: The Rise and Fall of Long-Term Capital Management. New York: Random House.
Lucas, R.E. 1976. Econometric Policy Evaluation: A Critique. In. K. Brunner, & A. Meltzer. The Phillips Curve and Labor Markets. New York: Carnegie-Rochester Conference Series on Public Policy, 1: 19–46.
Luce, R.D., & Raiffa, H. 1957. Games and Decisions. New York: Wiley.
Luhmann, N. 1991. Soziologie des Risikos. Berlin / New York: de Gruyter.
Lux, T. 1998. The socio-economic dynamics of speculative markets: interacting agents, chaos, and the fat tails of return distributions. Journal of Economic Behavior & Organization, 33: 143–165.
MacKenzie, D. 2006. An Engine Not a Camera: How Financial Models Shape Markets. Cambridge, MA: MIT Press.
MacKenzie, D. 2005. Opening the black boxes of global finance. Review of International Political Economy, 12: 555–576.
MacKenzie, D. 2003. Long-Term Capital Management and the sociology of arbitrage. Economy and Society, 32: 349–380.
MacLane, S. 1971. Categories for the Working Mathematician. New York: Springer.
Malevergne, Y., & Sornette, D. 2006. Extreme Financial Risks. From Dependence to Risk Management. Berlin: Springer.
Malik, F. 2008. Unternehmenspolitik und Corporate Governance. Wie sich Organisationen selbst organisieren. Frankfurt a.M.: Campus.
Malik, F. 2007. Gefährliche Managementwörter – Und warum man sie vermeiden sollte. Frankfurt a.M.: Campus.
Malik, F. 1996. Strategie des Managements komplexer Systeme. Ein Beitrag zur Management-Kybernetik evolutionärer Systeme. Bern: Haupt.
Malz, A.M. 2011. Financial Risk Management. New York: Wiley.
Mandelbrot, B., & Taleb, N.N. 2010. Mild vs. Wild Randomness: Focusing on Those Risks That Matter. In. F.X. Diebold, N.A. Doherty, & R.J. Herring (Eds.). The Known, the Unknown, and the Unknowable in Financial Risk Management. Measurement and Theory Advancing Practice. Princeton/Oxford: Princeton University Press: 47–58.
Mandelbrot, B., & Hudson, R.L. 2008. The (Mis)behavior of Markets: A Fractal View of Risk, Ruin and Reward. London: Profile Books.
Mandelbrot, B. 1997a. Fractals and Scaling in Finance: Discontinuity, Concentration, Risk. New York: Springer.
Mandelbrot, B. 1997b. Three Fractal Models in Finance: Discontinuity, Concentration, Risk. Economic Notes by Banca Monte dei Paschi di Siena, 26: 171–212.
Mandelbrot, B. 1983. The fractal geometry of nature. New York: Freeman.
Mandelbrot, B., & van Ness, J.W. 1968. Fractional Brownian motions, fractional noises and applications. Society for Industrial and Applied Mathematics Review, 10: 422–437.
Mandelbrot, B. 1967. How Long Is the Coast of Britain? Statistical Self-Similarity and Fractional Dimension. Science, 156: 636–638.
Mandelbrot, B. 1965. Very long-tailed probability distributions and the empirical 'distribution of city sizes'. In. F. Massarik, & P. Ratoosh (Eds.). Mathematical Explorations in Behavioral Science. Homewood, IL: Clarendon Press: 322–332.
Mandelbrot, B. 1963a. New methods in statistical economics. The Journal of Political Economy, 71: 421–440.
Mandelbrot, B. 1963b. The Variation of Certain Speculative Prices, Journal of Business, 35: 394–419.

Mark, R., & Krishna, D. 2014. Risk management. In. Brose, M., Flood, M., Krishna, D., & Nichols, B. Handbook of financial data and risk information. Principles and context. Cambridge: Cambridge University Press: 33–74.

Markowitz, H.M. 1952. Portfolio Selection. The Journal of Finance, 7: 77–91.

Marron, D. 2007. 'Lending by numbers': credit scoring and the constitution of risk within American consumer credit. Economy and Society, 36: 103–133.

Martin-Löf, P. 1966. The Definition of a Random Sequence. Information and Control, 9: 602–619.

Mayer, C. 2013. Firm Commitment. Why the corporation is failing us and how to restore trust in it. Oxford: Oxford University Press.

McCulloch, J.H. 1996. Financial Applications of Stable Distributions. In. G.S. Maddala, & C.R. Rao (Eds.). Handbook of Statistics, Vol. 14. Amsterdam: North Holland Publishing: 393–425.

McDonald, R.L. 2006. Derivatives markets. Boston: Addison-Wesley.

McDonough, W.J. 1998. Statement before the Committee on Banking and Financial Services, U.S. House of Representatives, October 1. Federal Reserve Bulletin, 84: 1050–1054.

McGoun, E.G., & Zielonka, P. 2006. The Platonic foundations of finance and the interpretation of finance models. Journal of Behavioral Finance, 7: 43–57.

McGoun, E.G. 1995. Machomatics in egonomics. International Review of Financial Analysis, 4: 185–199.

McKelvey, B. (Ed.). 2013. Complexity. Critical Concepts. London / New York: Routledge.

McKoan, JJ., & Ning, M. 2011. Taking the Sting out of the Tail: Hedging Against Extreme Events. AllianceBernstein Research Perspectives. Available at: https://www.abglobal.com/abcom/segment_homepages/defined_benefit/3_emea/content/pdf/taking-sting-out-of-tail.pdf (02/05/16).

McNeil, A., Frey, R., & Embrechts, P. 2005. Quantitative Risk Management. Princeton: Princeton University Press.

McNish, R., Schlosser, A., Selandari, F., Stegemann, U., & Vorholt, J. 2013. Getting to ERM. A road map for banks and other financial institutions. McKinsey Working Papers on Risk, 43: 1–11.

Mehta, A., Neukirchen, M., Pfetsch, S., & Poppensieker, T. 2012. Managing market risk: Today and tomorrow. McKinsey Working Papers on Risk, 32: 1–16.

Meltzer, A. 2012. Why capitalism?. New York: Oxford University Press.

Mendelowitz, A., Brammertz, W., & Khashanah, K. 2013. Improving systemic risk monitoring and financial market transparency: Standardizing the representation of financial instruments. Available at: http://www.brammertz-consulting.ch/wp-content/uploads/2011/02/Actus_OFR_FED_status_report.pdf (14/11/16).

Meredith, J. 1993. Theory Building through Conceptual Methods. International Journal of Operations & Production Management, 13: 3–11.

Meristö, T. 1989. Not Forecasts but Multiple Scenarios When Coping with Uncertainties in the Competitive Environment. European Journal of Operational Research, 38: 350–357.

Mikes, A. 2011. From counting risk to making risk count: Boundary-work in risk management. Accounting, Organizations and Society, 36: 226–245.

Mikes, A. 2010. Measuring and Envisioning Risks: Boundary-Work in Risk Management. Working paper. Available at: http://papers.ssrn.com/sol3/papers.cfm?abstract id=1654254 (30/11/14).

Mikes, A. 2009a. Risk management and calculative cultures. Management Accounting Research, 20: 18–40.

Mikes, A. 2009b. Becoming the lamp bearer: The emerging roles of the chief risk officer. In J. Fraser, & B. Simkins (Eds.). Enterprise risk management: Today's leading research and best practices for tomorrow's executives. New York, NY: John Wiley & Sons.

Mill, J.S. 1843. System of Logic, Ratiocinative and Inductive: Being a Connected View of the Principles of Evidence and the Methods of Scientific Investigation. Vol. 1, London: John W. Parker.

Miller, S.L., & Childers, D. 2012. Probability and Random Processes, New York: Academic Press.

Miller, J.H., & Page, S.E. 2007. Complex Adaptive Systems. An introduction to computational models of social life. Princeton: Princeton University Press.

Millo, Y., & MacKenzie, D. 2009. The usefulness of inaccurate models: Towards an understanding of the emergence of financial risk management. Accounting, Organizations and Society, 34: 638–653.

Minoiua, C., & Reyesb, J.A. 2013. A network analysis of global banking: 1978–2010. Journal of Financial Stability, 9: 168–184.

Minsky, H.P. 1992. The Financial Instability Hypothesis. Working Paper 74, Jerome Levy Economics Institute, Annandale on Hudson, NY.

Minsky, H.P. 1986/2008. Stabilizing an Unstable Economy. Foreword by Henry Kaufman. New York: McGraw-Hill.

Mishkin, F.S. 2007. The Economics of Money, Banking and Financial Institutions. Upper Saddle River, NJ: Pearson Addison Wesley.

Mishkin, F.S. 1995. Comment on Systemic Risk. In. G.G. Kaufman (Ed.). Research in Financial Services: Banking, Financial Markets, and Systemic Risk. Greenwich, CT: JAI Press Inc.: 31–45.

Mistrulli, P.E. 2011. Assessing financial contagion in the interbank market: Maximum entropy versus observed interbank lending patterns. Journal of Banking & Finance, 35: 1114–1127.

Mitchell, M. 2009. Complexity: A Guided Tour. Oxford: Oxford University Press.

Moggi, E. 1991. Notions of Computation and Monads. Information and Computation, 93: 55–92.

Moggi, E. 1989. Computational lambda-calculus and monads. Proceedings of the Fourth Annual Symposium on Logic in computer science: 14–23.

Morecroft, J. 2007. Strategic Modelling and Business Dynamics. A feedback systems approach. Chichester: John Wiley & Sons.

Morin, E. 2008. On Complexity. Cresskill, NJ: Hampton Press.

Morrow, R.A., & Brown, D.D. 1994. Critical Theory and Methodology. London: Sage.

Moss, D.A. 2002. When All Else Fails. Government as the Ultimate Risk Manager. Cambridge, MA: Harvard University Press.

Müller, J., & Hoffmann, C.H. 2017a. Logic-Based Risk Modeling for Derivatives. Under consideration for publication in International Journal of Approximate Reasoning.

Müller, J., & Hoffmann, C.H. 2017b. Symbolic Risk Modeling to Cope with Uncertainty in Risk Measurement. Under consideration for publication in Journal of Risk and Decision Analysis.

Nag, R. Hambrick, D.C., & Chen, M. 2007. What is strategic management, really? Inductive derivation of a consensus definition of the field. Strategic Management Journal, 28: 935–955.

Nario, L., Pfister, T., Poppensieker, T., & Stegemann, U. 2016. The evolving role of credit portfolio management. McKinsey Working Papers on Risk, 1, Summer 2016: 20–29.

Nathanaël, B. 2010. The Basel Committee's December 2009 Proposals on Counterparty Risk. In. Federal Reserve/FSA presentation at the International Workshop on Counterparty Risk Management and Application of CVA, Bank of Japan, June 14, 2010.

Neave, E.H. 2010. Modern Financial Systems: Theory and Applications. Chichester: John Wiley & Sons.

Nelsen, R.B. 2006. An introduction to copulas. Berlin: Springer.

Neumann von, J., & Morgenstern, O. 1944. Theory of Games and Economic Behavior. Princeton: Princeton University Press.

Newman, M.E.J. 2013. Power laws, Pareto distributions and Zipf's Law. In. B. McKelvey (Ed.). 2013. Complexity. Critical Concepts. Vol. 5. London / New York: Routledge: 15–67.

Nida-Rümelin, J. 2002. Ethische Essays. Frankfurt a.M.: Suhrkamp.

Nier, E., Yang, J., Yorulmazer, T., & Alentorn, A. 2007. Network models and financial stability. Journal of Economic Dynamics and Control, 31: 2033–2060.

Nitschke, J.R. 2009. Systems chemistry: Molecular networks come of age. Nature, 462: 736–738.

Nocera, J. 2009. Risk Management: What Led to the Financial Meltdown. The New York Times Magazine, Blog. January 2. Available at: http://www.nytimes.com/2009/01/04/magazine/04risk-t.html (06/11/14).

Nomura, 2005. CDOs-Squared Demystified. Available at: http://www.markadelson.com/pubs/CDOs-Squared_Demystified.pdf (15/11/16).

NZZ, 2016. Falcon Private Bank. Die Finma greift durch. Available at: http://www.nzz.ch/ wirtschaft/unternehmen/falcon-private-bank-die-finma-greift-durch-ld.121385 (21/11/16).

Oet, M.V., Eiben, R., Bianco, T., Gramlich, D., Ong, S.J., & Wang, J. 2013. Systemic Risk Early Warning System: A Micro-Macro Prudential Synthesis. In. J.-P. Fouque, & J.A. Langsam (Eds.). Handbook on Systemic Risk. Cambridge: Cambridge University Press: 791–846.

Papaioannou, M.G., Park, J., Pihlman, J.& van der Hoorn, H. 2015. Institutional Investors' Behavior during the Recent Financial Crisis: Evidence of Procyclicality. The Journal of Investing, 24: 16–30.

Paulson, H.M. 2011. On the Brink. Inside the Race to Stop the Collapse of the Global Financial System. New York / Boston: Business Plus.

Pearson, K. 1905. The Problem of the Random Walk. Nature, 72: 294.

Pedercini, M. 2006. What's behind the blue arrow? The notion of causality in System Dynamics. Proceedings of the 24th International Conference of the System Dynamics Society, Nijmegen: The System Dynamics Society.

Pedersen, L.H. 2015. Efficiently Inefficient: How Smart Money Invests and Market Prices Are Determined. Princeton: Princeton University Press.

Peitgen, H.-O., Jürgens, H., & Saupe, D. 2004. Chaos and fractals: New Frontiers of Science. New York: Springer.

Peltzman, S. 1975. The Effects of Automobile Safety Regulation. Journal of Political Economy, 83: 677–726.

Pergler, M., & Lamarre, E. 2009. Upgrading your risk assessment for uncertain times. McKinsey Working Papers on Risk, 9: 1–10.

Pergler, M., & Freeman, A. 2008. Probabilistic modeling as an exploratory decision-making tool. McKinsey Working Papers on Risk, 6: 1–18.

Perrow, C. 1984. Normal Accidents: Living with High-Risk Technologies. New York: Basic Books.

Peters, O., & Gell-Mann, M. 2016. Evaluating gambles using dynamics. Chaos, 26.

Pflug, G. 2000. Some remarks on the value-at-risk and the conditional value-at-risk. In. S. Uryasev (Ed.). Probabilistic Constrained Optimization: Methodology and Applications. Dordrecht: Kluwer Academic Publishers.

Pina, M. & Rego, A. 2010. Complexity, simplicity, simplexity. European Management Journal, 28: 85–94.

Poledna, S., & Thurner, S. 2016. Elimination of systemic risk in financial networks by means of a systemic risk transaction tax. Quantitative Finance, 11 Apr 2016.

Popper, K.R. 1963/2002. Conjectures and Refutations. The Growth of Scientific Knowledge. London / New York: Routledge.

Popper, K.R. 1959a. The Logic of Scientific Discovery. New York: Basic Books.

Popper, K.R. 1959b. The Propensity Interpretation of Probability. British Journal of the Philosophy of Science, 10: 25–42.

Porter, T. 1995. Trust in Numbers – The Pursuit of Objectivity in Science and Public Life. Princeton: Princeton University Press.

Posner, R.A. 2004. Catastrophe. Risk and Response. Oxford / New York / Auckland: Oxford University Press.

Postma, T.J.B.M., & Liebl, F. 2005. How to Improve Scenario Analysis as a Strategic Management Tool?. Technological Forecasting & Social Change, 72: 161–173.

Power, M.K. 2009. The risk management of nothing. Accounting, Organizations and Society, 34: 849–855.

Power, M.K. 2007. Organized Uncertainty: Designing a World of Risk Management. Oxford: Oxford University Press.

Power, M.K. 2004a. Counting, control and calculation: Reflections on measuring and management. Human Relations, 57: 765–783.

Power, M.K. 2004b. The Risk Management of Everything. London: Demos.

Power, M.K. 2003. The Invention of Operational Risk. London School of Economics and Political Science, ESCR Centre for the Analysis of Risk and Regulation, Discussion Paper, 16.

Pratt, V. 2007. Algebra. In. In. E.N. Zalta (Ed.). Stanford Encyclopedia of Philosophy, http://plato.stanford.edu/entries/algebra/ (12/04/16).

Pritsch, G., Stegemann, U., & Freeman, A. 2008. Turning risk management into a true competitive advantage. Lessons from the recent crisis. McKinsey Working Papers on Risk, 5: 1–10.

Probst, G. & Bassi, A.M. 2014. Tackling Complexity. A Systemic Approach For Decision Makers. Sheffield: Greenleaf Publishing Limited.

Probst, G. 1981. Kybernetische Gesetzeshypothesen als Basis für Gestaltungs- und Lenkungsregeln im Management. Bern: Haupt.

Pruyt, E., & Kwakkel, J.H. 2014. Radicalization under deep uncertainty: a multimodel exploration of activism, extremism, and terrorism. System Dynamics Review, 30: 1–28.

Pryke, M. & Allen, J. 2000. Monetized Time-Space: Derivatives – Money's New Imaginary. Economy and Society, 29: 264–284.

Rajan, R.G. 2006. Has financial development made the world riskier? European Financial Management, 12: 499–533.

Ram, C., Montibeller, G., & Morton, A. 2011. Extending the Use of Scenario Planning and MCDA for the Evaluation of Strategic Options. Journal of the Operational Research Society, 62: 817–829.

RAND Corporation, 1955. A Million Random Digits with 100,000 Normal Deviates. New York: Free Press.

Rapoport, A. 1986. General System Theory: Essential Concepts & Applications. Cambridge, MA: Abacus Press.

Rapoport, A. 1966. Mathematical Aspects of General Systems Theory. General Systems, 11: 3–11.

Rapoport, A. 1953. Operational Philosophy – Integrating Knowledge and Action. New York: Harper & Brothers.

Rasmussen, N. 1975. Reactor Safety Study. WASH-1400, NUREG-75/014. Washington D.C.: US Government Printing Office.

Ravat, F., Teste, O., Tournier, R., & Zurfluh, G. 2008. Algebraic and graphic languages for OLAP manipulations. IJDWM, 4: 17–46.

Rebonato, R. 2010. Coherent Stress Testing: A Bayesian Approach to the Analysis of Financial Stress. Chichester: John Wiley & Sons.

Rebonato, R. 2007. Plight of the Fortune Tellers: Why We Need to Manage Financial Risk Differently. Princeton: Princeton University Press.

Rebonato, R. 2002. Theory and Practice of Model Risk Management. Working Paper. Available at: http://www.quarchome.org/ModelRisk.pdf (05/02/15).

Redak, V. 2011. Europe's Next Model: Zur Bedeutung von Risikomodellen in Finanzmarktlehre, -aufsicht und -industrie. PROKLA, 164/3: 447–458.

Rehmann-Sutter, C. 1998. Involving Others: Towards an Ethical Concept of Risk. Risk: Health, Safety & Environment, 9: 119–136.

Reichenbach, H. 1949. The Theory of Probability. Berkeley: University of California Press.

Reinhart, C.M. & Rogoff, K.S. 2013. Banking crises: An equal opportunity menace. Journal of Banking & Finance, 37: 4557–4573.

Reinhart, C.M. & Rogoff, K.S. 2009. This Time Is Different: Eight Centuries of Financial Folly. Princeton / Oxford: Princeton University Press.

Renn O., & Klinke, A. 2012. Complexity, Uncertainty and Ambiguity in Inclusive Risk Governance. In. T.G. Measham and S. Lockie (Eds.). Risk and Social Theory in Environmental Management. Collingwood, Australia: CSIRO Publishing: 59–76.

Renn, O., & Keil, F. 2009. Was ist das Systemische an systemischen Risiken? GAIA, 18: 97–99.

Renn, O., & Keil, F. 2008. Systemische Risiken: Versuch einer Charakterisierung. GAIA, 17: 349–453.

Renn, O. 2008. Risk Governance. Coping with Uncertainty in a Complex World. London / New York: Earthscan.

Rescher, N. 1968. Topics in Philosophical Logic. Dordrecht: D. Reidel Publishing.

Resnick, S.I. 1998. Why non-linearities can ruin the heavy-tailed modeler's day. In. R. Adler, R. Feldman, & M. Taqqu (Eds.). A Practical Guide to Heavy Tails: Statistical Techniques and Applications. Boston: Birkhäuser: 219–239.

Richardson, G.P. 2011. Reflections on the foundations of system dynamics. System Dynamics Review, 27: 219–243.

Richardson, G.P. 1999. Feedback Thought in Social Science and Systems Theory. Waltham, MA: Pegasus Communications.

Richardson, G.P. 1997. Problems in causal loop diagrams revisited, System Dynamics Review, 13: 247–252.

Richardson, G.P., & Pugh, A.L. 1981. Introduction to System Dynamics Modeling with DYNAMO. Cambridge, MA: Productivity Press.

Riedel, F. 2013. Die Schuld der Ökonomen. Was Ökonomie und Mathematik zur Krise beitrugen. Berlin: Econ.

Riedel, F. 2004. Dynamic Coherent Risk Measures. Stochastic Processes and Applications, 112: 185–200.

Ringland, G. 2006. Scenario Planning: Managing for the Future. Chichester: John Wiley & Sons.

Rootzén, H., & Klüppelberg, C. 1999. A Single Number Can't Hedge Against Economic Catastrophes. Royal Swedish Academy of Sciences, 28: 550–555.

Rosa, E.A. 1998. Metatheoretical foundations for post-normal risk. Journal of Risk Research, 1: 15–44.

Rosen, R. 1987. Some Epistemological Issues in Physics and biology. In. B.J. Hiley, & F.D. Peat (Eds.) Quantum Implications: Essays in Honour of David Bohm. London: Routledge: 314–327.

Rosenhead, J. 1989. Introduction: old and new paradigms of analysis. In. J. Rosenhead (Ed.). Rational Analysis for a Problematic World: Problem Structuring Methods for Complexity, Uncertainty and Conflict. Chichester: Wiley: 1–20.

Ross, A. 2016. The Industries of the Future. How the next 10 years of innovation will transform our lives at work and home. London: Simon & Schuster.

Ross, S.A., Westerfield, R.W., & Jaffe, J.F. 2013. Corporate Finance. New York: McGraw-Hill Irwin.

Rossi, C.V. 2014. Portfolio risk monitoring. In. M.S. Brose, M.D. Flood, D. Krishna, & B. Nichols (Eds.). Handbook of Financial Data and Risk Information I: Principles and Context. Cambridge: Cambridge University Press: 75–104.

Rossi, S. 2011. Can it happen again? International Journal of Political Economy, 40: 61–78.

Rosenhead, J. & Mingers, J. 2009. A New Paradigm of Analysis. In. J. Rosenhead, & J. Mingers (Eds.). Rational Analysis for a Problematic World Revisted. Chichester: John Wiley & Sons: 1–19.

Rothschild, M., & Stiglitz, J.E. 1970. Increasing risk, 1: A definition. Journal of Economic Theory, 2: 225–243.

Rott, H. 2001. Change, Choice and Inference: A Study of Belief Revision and Nonmonotonic Reasoning Oxford: Oxford University Press.

Roubini, N., & Mihm, S. 2011. Crisis Economics. A Crash Course in the Future of Finance. London: Penguin Books.

Rowe, D. 2009. To VaR or not to VaR? Insurance Risk and Capital. Available at: www.dmrra.com/otherarticles.php (06/11/14).

Roxburgh, C. 2009. The Use and Abuse of Scenarios. McKinsey Quarterly, November: 1-10. Available at: http://www.valor-art.net/Publicacoes/26.pdf. (29/05/14).

Ryle, G. 1949. The Concept of Mind. London: Hutchinson.

Rzevski, G., & Skobelev, P. 2014. Managing Complexity. Southampton: WIT Press.

Salmon, M., Earman, J., Glymour, C., Lennox, J.G., Machamer, P., & McGuire, J.E. 1992. Introduction to the philosophy of science. Indianapolis & Cambridge: Hackett.

Saunders, A., & Cornett, M. 2010. Financial institutions management. A risk management approach. New York: McGraw-Hill Irwin.

Sargut, G., & McGrath, R. 2011. Learning to live with complexity. Harvard Business Review, 69: 69–76.

Savage, L.J. 1954. The Foundations of Statistics. New York: Dover Publications.

Sayama, H. 2015. Introduction to the Modeling and Analysis of Complex Systems. New York: Open SUNY Textbooks.

Schaffernicht, M. 2007. Causality and diagrams for system dynamics. Proceedings of the 2007 International Conference of the System Dynamics Society, Boston: The System Dynamics Society.

Scherer, A.G., & Marti, E. 2008. The Normative Foundation of Finance: How Misunderstanding the Role of Financial Theories Distorts the Way We Think About the Responsibility of Financial Economists. In. P. Shrivastava, & M. Statler (Eds.). Learning From The Global Financial Crisis. Creatively, Reliably, and Sustainably. Stanford, CA: Stanford Business Books: 260–290.

Schinasi, G.J. 2004, Defining Financial Stability. International Monetary Fund Working Paper, WP/04/187. Available at: http://core.ac.uk/download/pdf/7187004.pdf (01/03/14).

Schneider, I. (Ed.). 1988. Die Entwicklung der Wahrscheinlichkeitstheorie von den Anfängen bis 1933. Einführungen und Texte. Darmstadt: Wissenschaftliche Buchgesellschaft.

Schoemaker, P.J.H. 2002. Profiting from Uncertainty. Strategies for Succeeding no Matter What the Future Brings. New York: The Free Press.

Schoemaker, P.J.H. 1995. Scenario Planning: A Tool for Strategic Thinking. Sloan Management Review, 36: 25–40.

Schulak, E.G., & Unterköfler, H. 2011. The Austrian School of Economics: A History of Its Ideas, Ambassadors, & Institutions. Auburn, AL: Ludwig von Mises Institute.

Schumpeter, J.A. 1954/1994. History of Economic Analysis (with a new introduction by Mark Perlman). New York: Oxford University Press.

Schwaninger, M. 2011. System Dynamics in the Evolution of the Systems Approach. In. R.A. Meyers (Ed.). Complex Systems in Finance and Econometrics. New York: Springer.

Schwaninger, M. 2010. Model-based management (MBM): a vital prerequisite for organizational viability. Kybernetes, 39: 1419–1428.

Schwaninger, M. 2009. Intelligent Organizations. Powerful Models for Systemic Management. Berlin: Springer.

Schwaninger, M., & Grösser, S.N. 2008. System Dynamics as Model-Based Theory Building. Systems Research and Behavioral Science, 25: 447–465.

Schwaninger, M. 2005. Systemorientiertes Design – ganzheitliche Perspektive in Innovationsprozessen. In. B. Schäppi, M.M. Andreasen, M. Kirchgeorg, & F.-J. Radermacher (Eds.). Handbuch Produktentwicklung. München: Hanser: 29–56.

Schwaninger, M., & Hamann, T. 2005. Theory-building with system dynamics. In. R. Moreno-Díaz, F. Pichler, & A. Quesada-Arencibia (Eds.). Computer Aided Systems Theory – EUROCAST 2005, Berlin: Springer: 56–62.

Schwarcz, S.L. 2008. Systemic Risk. Duke Law School Legal Studies. Research Paper Series, 163: 193–249.

Schwartz, B., & Sharpe, K. 2010. Practical Wisdom: The Right Way to Do the Right Thing. New York: Penguin Books.
Scordis, N.A. 2011. The Morality of Risk Modeling. Journal of Business Ethics, 103: 7–16.
Scott, W.R. 1992. Organizations: Rational, Natural and Open Systems. Englewood Cliffs, NJ: Prentice-Hall.
Segel, L.A. 1995. Grappling with complexity. Complexity, 1: 18–25.
Segerberg, K. 1971. Qualitative probability in a modal setting. In. E. Fenstad (Ed.). Proceedings 2nd Scandinavian Logic Symposium. Amsterdam: North-Holland.
Seising, R. 2012. WarrenWeaver's "Science and complexity" Revisited. In. R. Seising, & V.S. González (Eds.). Soft Computing in Humanities and Social Sciences. Berlin / Heidelberg: Springer: 55–87.
Seising, R. 2010. Cybernetics, system(s) theory, information theory and Fuzzy Sets and Systems in the 1950s and 1960s. Information Sciences, 180: 4459–4476.
Sen, A. 1986. The Right to Take Personal Risks. In. D. MacLean (Ed.): Values at Risk. New Jersey: Rowman & Allanheld: 155–170.
Senge, P.M. 2006. The fifth discipline: The art and practice of the learning organization. New York: Currency & Doubleday.
Senge, P.M. 1992. Creating the learning organization. An interview with Peter M. Senge author of The Fifth Discipline: The Art & Practice of the Learning Organization. By D.E. Meen, & M. Keough. The McKinsey Quarterly, 1: 58–86.
Shafer, G. 1976. A mathematical theory of evidence. Princeton: Princeton University Press.
Shapiro, S. 2013. Classical Logic. In. E.N. Zalta (Ed.). Stanford Encyclopedia of Philosophy, http://plato.stanford.edu/entries/logic-classical/ (11/06/16).
Sharpe, W.F. 1966. Mutual Fund Performance. The Journal of Business, 39: 119–138.
Shafer, G., & Vovk, V. 2001. Probability and Finance: It's Only a Game! Chichester: John Wiley & Sons.
Sheffi, Y. 2005. The Resilient Enterprise: Overcoming Vulnerability for Competitive Advantage. Cambridge, MA: MIT Press.
Shefrin, H. 2013. Assessing the Contribution of Hyman Minsky's Perspective to Our Understanding of Economic Instability. Available at: http://ssrn.com/abstract=2311045 (16/02/2016).
Shiller, R.J. 2012. Finance and the Good Society. Princeton / Oxford: Princeton University Press.
Shiller, R.J. 2005. 'Irrational Exuberance' – Again. CNN Money, January 25. Available at: http://money.cnn.com/2005/01/13/real estate/realestate shiller1 0502/ (04/01/14).
Shneiderman, B. 1996. The eyes have it: A task by data type taxonomy for information visualizations. Proceedings of the 1996 IEEE Symposium on Visual Languages, Boulder, CO. September 3-6: 336–343.
Shrader-Frechette, K.S. 1991. Risk and Rationality. Berkeley / Los Angeles / Oxford: University of California Press.
Shrader-Frechette, K.S. 1985. Science Policy, Ethics, and Economic Methodology: Some Problems of Technology Assessment and Environmental-Impact Analysis. Dordrecht: D. Reidel Publishing.
Siggelkow, N. 2001. Change in the presence of fit: The rise, the fall, and the renaissance of Liz Claiborne. Academy of Management Journal, 44: 838–857.
Silverman, B.W. 1986. Density Estimation for Statistics and Data Analysis. New York: Chapman and Hall.
Simon, H.A. 1962. The Architecture of Complexity. Proceedings of the American Philosophical Society, 106: 467–482.
Simpson, G.W., & Kohers, T. 2002. The Link Between Corporate Social and Financial Performance: Evidence from the Banking Industry. Journal of Business Ethics, 35: 97–109.
Skyrms, B. 1980. Causal Necessity. New Haven: Yale University Press.

Smith, D., & Tombs, S. 2000. Of course it's Safe, Trust Me! Conceptualizing Issues of Risk Management within the Risk Society. In. E. Coles, D. Smith, & S. Tombs (Eds.). Risk Management and Society. London: Kluwer: 1–30.

Snowling, S. 2000. Evaluation of modelling uncertainty and the role of model complexity in risk assessment. Ph.D. Thesis. McMaster University, Canada.

Söderlind, P. 2014. Lecture Notes in Finance (Master in Quantitative Economics & Finance): Risk Measures (Chapter 6). University of St. Gallen, Switzerland.

Solomonov, R. 1964. A formal theory of inductive inference, Part I. Information and Control, 7: 1–22.

Somfai, E. 2013: Statistical mechanics of complex systems. In. R. Ball, V. Kolokoltsov, & R.S. MacKay (Eds.). Complexity Science. London Mathematical Society Lecture Note Series 408. Cambridge: Cambridge University Press: 210–245.

Sornette, D. 2009. Dragon-Kings, Black Swans and the Prediction of Crises. International Journal of Terraspace Science and Engineering, 2: 1–18.

Sornette, D. 2003. Why Stock Markets Crash: Critical Events in Complex Financial Systems. Princeton / Oxford: Princeton University Press.

Soros, G. 2013. Fallibility, reflexivity, and the human uncertainty principle, Journal of Economic Methodology, 20: 309–329.

Soros, G. 2008. The New Paradigm for Financial Markets: The Credit Crisis of 2008 and What It Means. New York: Public Affairs.

Spitznagel, M. 2013. The Dao Capital. Austrian Investing in a Distorted World. Hoboken, NJ: John Wiley & Sons.

Spohn, W. 2012. The Laws of Belief. Ranking Theory and its Philosophical Applications, Oxford: Oxford University Press.

Spohn, W. 2009. A Survey of Ranking Theory. In. F. Huber & C. Schmidt-Petri (Eds.). Degrees of Belief. Dordrecht: Springer: 185–228.

Spohn, W. 2005. Enumerative Induction and Lawlikeness. Philosophy of Science, 72: 164–187.

Spohn, W. 1994. On the Properties of Conditional Independence. In. P. Humphreys (Ed.). Patrick Suppes: Scientific Philosopher. Vol. 1: Probability and Probabilistic Causality. Dordrecht: Kluwer: 173–194.

Spohn, W. 1988. Ordinal Conditional Functions. A Dynamic Theory of Epistemic States. In. W.L. Harper, & B. Skyrms (Eds.). Causation in Decision, Belief Change, and Statistics. Vol. II. Dordrecht: Kluwer: 105–134.

Spohn, W. 1986. The Representation of Popper Measures. Topoi, 5: 69–74.

Spohn, W. 1983. Eine Theorie der Kausalität. Habilitationsschrift, München.

Stacey, R.D. 2010. Complexity and Organizational Reality. Uncertainty and the Need to Rethink Management after the Collapse of Investment Capitalism. London / New York: Routledge.

Staum, J. 2013. Counterparty Contagion in Context: Contributions to Systemic Risk. In. J.-P. Fouque, & J.A. Langsam (Eds.). Handbook on Systemic Risk. Cambridge: Cambridge University Press: 512–544.

Stegemann, U. 2013. International Current Topics in Bank Strategy. Lecture 1, Bank Fundamentals. University of Constance, Germany.

Steigleder, K. 2012. Risk and Rights. Towards a Rights based Risk Ethics. Working paper. Available at: http://www.ruhr-uni-bochum.de/philosophy/angewandte_ethik/papers.html.de (03/06/2014).

Sterman, J.D. 2002. All models are wrong: reflections on becoming a systems scientist. System Dynamics Review, 18: 501–531.

Sterman, J.D. 2000. Business Dynamics. Systems Thinking and Modeling for a Complex World. Boston, MA: Irwin/McGraw-Hill.

Sterman, J.D. 1994. Learning in and about complex systems. System Dynamics Review, 10: 291–330.

Sterman, J.D. 1989. Modeling managerial behavior: Misperceptions of feedback in a dynamic decision making experiment. Management Science, 35: 321–339.
Stern, G., & Feldman, R.J. 2013. Regulation: Introduction. In. J.-P. Fouque, & J.A. Langsam (Eds.). Handbook on Systemic Risk. Cambridge: Cambridge University Press. 745–747.
Stiglitz, J.E. 2002. Globalization and its Discontents. London: Penguin Books.
Stout, L.A. 2012. Uncertainty, Dangerous Optimism, and Speculation: An Inquiry Into Some Limits of Democratic Governance. Cornell Law Faculty Publications. Paper 719. Available at: http://scholarship.law.cornell.edu/facpub/719. (09/09/15).
Stout, L.A. 1995. Betting the Bank: How Derivatives Trading Under Conditions of Uncertainty Can Increase Risks and Erode Returns In Financial Markets. The Journal of Corporate Law, 21: 53–68.
Stroock, D.W. 2010. Probability Theory. An Analytic View. Cambridge: Cambridge University Press.
Stulz, R. 2009. Six Ways Companies Mismanage Risk. Harvard Business Review, March.
Stulz, R. 2008. Risk Management Failures: What Are They and When Do They Happen?. Journal of Banking and Finance, 20: 58–67.
Stulz, R. 2002. Derivatives and risk management. Toronto: Thomson Learning.
Stulz, R. 1996. Rethinking risk management. Journal of Applied Corporate Finance, 9: 8–24.
Stumpf, M.P.H., & Porter, M.A. 2012. Critical Truths About Power Laws. Science, 335: 665–666.
Sullivan, R. 2009. Governance: travel and destinations. Financial Analysts Journal, 65: 6–10.
Sun, W., Rachev, S., & Fabozzi, F.J. 2009. A New Approach of Using Lévy Processes for Determining High-Frequency Value at Risk Predictions. European Financial Management, 15: 340–361.
Suppes, P. 1984. Probabilistic Metaphysics. Oxford: Blackwell.
Suppes, P. 1983. Reductionism, atomism and holism. In. Parts and Wholes. Proceedings of the International Workshop in Lund, Sweden. Vol. 1. Stockholm: 134–140.
Swiss Federal Banking Commission. 2008. Subprime-Krise: Untersuchung der EBK zu den Ursachen der Wertberichtigungen der UBS AG. Available at: https://www.finma.ch/FinmaArchiv/ebk/d/publik/medienmit/20081016/ubs-subprime-bericht-ebk-d.pdf (23/07/15).
Swiss Re, 2016. Liability Risk Drivers. Bringing a forward-looking perspective into liability modelling. Available at: http://www.asiainsurancereview.com/Document/swiss%20re.pdf (27/06/16).
Tal, E. 2015. Measurement in Science. In. E.N. Zalta (Ed.). Stanford Encyclopedia of Philosophy, http://plato.stanford.edu/entries/measurement-science/ (03/03/16).
Talbott, W. 2008. Bayesian Epistemology. In. E.N. Zalta (Ed.). Stanford Encyclopedia of Philosophy, http://plato.stanford.edu/entries/epistemology-bayesian/ (26/10/15).
Taleb, N.N. 2013. Probability and Risk in the real world. A mathematical parallel version of the Incerto: I) Antifragile, II) The Black Swan, III) The Bed of Procrustes, & IV) Fooled by Randomness. Available at: http://www.datascienceassn.org/sites/default/files/Probability%20and%20Risk%20in%20the%20Real%20World.pdf. (18/12/15).
Taleb, N.N. 2012. Antifragile: how to live in a world we don't understand. London: Allen Lane.
Taleb, N.N., Goldstein, D.G., & Spitznagel, M.W. 2009. The Six Mistakes Executives Make in Risk Management. Harvard Business Review, 87: 78–81.
Taleb, N.N. 2008. Finiteness of Variance is Irrelevant in the Practice of Quantitative Finance. Available at: http://papers.ssrn.com/sol3/papers.cfm?abstract id=1142785 (25/09/15).
Taleb, N.N. 2007a. The black swan: The impact of the highly improbable. New York: Random House.
Taleb, N.N. 2007b. Fooled by randomness. The hidden role of chance in life and in the markets. London: Penguin Books.
Taleb, N.N. 2005. Mandelbrot Makes Sense: A Book Review Essay. Wilmott magazine: 50–59.
Taleb, N.N., & Pilpel, A. 2004. On the Unfortunate Problem of the Nonobservability of the Probability Distribution. Working paper (unpublished).

Tapiero, C.S. 2013. Engineering Risk and Finance. International Series in Operations Research & Management. Berlin: Springer.

Tapiero, C.S., & Totoum-Tangho, D. 2012. CDO: A modeling prospective. Risk and Decision Analysis, 3: 75–88.

The Economist. 2014. Combating bad science – Metaphysicians. Available at: http://www.economist.com/news/science-and-technology/21598944-sloppy-researchers-beware-new-institute-has-you-its-sights-metaphysicians (19/07/15).

The Economist. 1999. The price of uncertainty. Available at: http://www.economist.com/node/345991 (19/07/15).

The Royal Swedish Academy of Sciences, 1997. Press Release. 14 October 1997. Available at: http://www.nobelprize.org/nobel_prizes/economic-sciences/laureates/1997/press.html (23/12/14).

The Wall Street Journal, 2000. In. McNeil, A., Frey, R., & Embrechts, P. 2005. Quantitative Risk Management. Princeton: Princeton University Press.

Thiagarajan, S.R., Alankar, A., & Shaikhutdinov, R. 2015. Tail Risk: Challenges, Mitigation, and Research Opportunities. The Journal of Investing, 24: 113–121.

Thom, R. 1975. Structural Stability and Morphogenesis; An Outline Of A General Theory Of Models. Boston, MA: W.A. Benjamin, Reading.

Thomas, R. 2001. Business Value Analysis: Coping with Unruly Uncertainty. Strategy & Leadership, 29: 16–24.

Thompson, D. 1967. Organizations in Action. New York: McGraw-Hill.

Thurner. S., & Poledna, S. 2013. DebtRank-transparency: Controlling systemic risk in financial networks. Scientific Reports, 3: 1888: 1–7.

Thurner, S. 2012. OECD Reviews of Risk Management Policies. Systemic financial risk. OECD publishing.

Thurner, S., Farmer, J.D., & Geanakoplos, J. 2010. Leverage Causes Fat Tails and Clustered Volatility. Cowles Foundation Discussion Paper, 1745. Available at: http://cowles.econ.yale.edu/.

Toulmin, S. 1977. From Form to Function: Philosophy and History of Science in the 1950s and Now. Daedalus, 106: 143–162.

Trieschmann, J., Hoyt, R., & Sommer, D. 2005. Risk Management and Insurance. Mason, OH: Thomson-South Western.

Tsay, R.S. 2010. Analysis of Financial Time Series. New York: Wiley.

Turing, A.M. 1936. On computable numbers with an application to the Entscheidungsproblem. Proceedings of the London Mathematical Society, 42: 230–265.

UBS, 2013. Annual Report 2013. Available at: http://www.ubs.com/global/en/about_ubs/investor_relations/annualreporting/2013.html (19/02/15).

UBS, 2008. Shareholder Report on UBS's Writedowns. Available at: http://www.ubs.com/1/e/investors/shareholderreport/remediation.html (07/02/14).

Ulrich, H., & Probst, G.J.B. 1990. Anleitung zum ganzheitlichen Denken und Handeln. Ein Brevier für Führungskräfte. Bern/Stuttgart: Haupt.

Ulrich, P. 2014. Grundideen und Entwicklungslinien integrativer Wirtschaftsethik. Jubiläumstagung 25 Jahre IWE, Universität St. Gallen. St. Gallen, 6.–7. November 2014.

Ulrich, P. 1993. Transformation der ökonomischen Vernunft. Fortschrittsperspektiven der modernen Industriegesellschaft. Bern/Stuttgart/Wien: Haupt.

Upper, C., & Worms, A. 2004. Estimating bilateral exposures in the German interbank market: Is there a danger of contagion? European Economic Review, 48: 827–849.

Vaihinger, H. 1913/2013. Die Philosophie des Als Ob. Paderborn: Salzwasser-Verlag.

Van der Heijden, K. 2009. Scenarios: The Art of Strategic Conversation. Chichester: John Wiley & Sons.

Van de Kuilen, G., & Wakker, P.P. 2011. The Midweight Method to Measure Attitudes toward Risk and Ambiguity. Management Science, 57: 582–598.

Van de Ven, A.H. 2007. Engaged Scholarship: A Guide for Organizational and Social Research, Oxford: Oxford University Press.
Van Fraassen, B. 1990. Figures in a Probability Landscape. In. J.M. Dunn & A. Gupta (Eds.). Truth or Consequences. Dordrecht: Kluwer: 345–356.
Van Fraassen, B. 1989. Laws and Symmetry, New York: Oxford University Press.
Van Oorschot, K.E., Akkermans, H., Sengupta, K., & Van Wassenhove, L.N. 2013. Anatomy of a Decision Trap in Complex New Product Development Projects. Academy of Management Journal, 56: 285–307.
Varnholt, B. 1995. Systemrisiken auf Finanzmärkten unter besonderer Berücksichtigung der Märkte für Derivate. Dissertation Nr. 1686 der Hochschule St. Gallen (HSG) für Wirtschafts-, Rechts- und Sozialwissenschaften. Stuttgart/Wien: Haupt.
Varum, C.A., & Melo, C. 2010. Directions in Scenario Planning Literature – A Review of the Past Decades. Futures, 42: 355–369.
Vecchiato, R. 2012. Environmental Uncertainty, Foresight and Strategic Decision Making: An Integrated Study. Technological Forecasting & Social Change, 79: 436–447.
Vickers, J. 2014. The Problem of Induction. In. E.N. Zalta (Ed.). Stanford Encyclopedia of Philosophy, http://plato.stanford.edu/entries/induction-problem/ (27/03/2015).
Vitali, S., Glattfelder, J.B., & Battiston, S. 2011: The Network of Global Corporate Control. Available at: http://arxiv.org/abs/1107.5728 (08/12/14).
Von Bertalanffy, L. 1968/2013. General System Theory. Foundations, Development, Applications. New York: George Braziller.
Von Foerster, H. 2003. Understanding Understanding: Essays on Cybernetics and Cognition. New York: Springer.
Von Foerster, H. 1985. Comments on Norbert Wiener's Cybernetics; Cybernetics ; Men, Machines, and the World About. In. P. Masani (Ed.). Norbert Wiener: Collected Works, IV, Cambridge: MIT Press: 800–803.
Von Foerster, H. 1984. Observing Systems. Seaside, CA: Intersystems Publications.
Von Glaserfeld, E. 1995. Radical Constructivism. A way of Knowing and Learning. London: The Falmer Press.
Von Hayek, F.A. 1967. Studies In Philosophy, Politics And Economics. London: Routledge.
Von Hayek, F.A. 1943. Scientism and the Study of Society. Economica, New Series, 10: 34–63.
Von Linné, C. 1751/2012. Philosophia Botanica. Charleston, SC: Nabu Press.
Von Mises, L. 1957/2005. Theory and History. An Interpretation of Social and Economic Evoluion. Indianapolis, IN: Liberty Fund.
Von Mises, L. 1949/1998. Human Action: A Treatise on Economics. The Scholar's Edition. Auburn, AL: Ludwig von Mises Institute.
Von Mises, R. 1957. Probability, Statistics and Truth. New York: Dover.
Von Mises, R. 1919. Grundlagen der Wahrscheinlichkeitsrechnung. Mathematische Zeitschrift, 5: 52–89.
Von Neumann, J., & Morgenstern, O. 1944: The Theory of Games and Economic Behavior, Princeton: Princeton University Press.
Wack, P. 1985a. Scenarios: Unchared Waters Ahead. Harvard Business Review, September-October: 73–89.
Wack, P. 1985b. Scenarios: Shooting the Rapids. Harvard Business Review, November.
Wald, A. 1950. Statistical Decision Functions. New York: John Wiley and Sons.
Waldrop, M.M. 1992. Complexity: The Emerging Science at the Edge of Order & Chaos. New York: Simon and Schuster.
Wallace, R.J. 1994. Responsibility and the Moral Sentiments, Cambridge, MA: Harvard University Press.
Walsh, P.R. 2005. Dealing with the Uncertainties of Environmental Change by Adding Scenario Planning to the Strategy Reformulation Equation. Management Decision, 43: 113–122.

Wang, T. 1996. A Characterisation of Dynamic Risk Measures. Working paper, Faculty of Commerce, University of British Columbia.

Warren, K. 2008. Strategic Management Dynamics. Chichester: John Wiley & Sons.

Warren, K. 2004. Why has feedback thinking struggled to influence strategy and policy formulation? Suggestive evidence, explanations and solutions. Systems Research and Behavioral Science, 21: 331–347.

Watzlawick, P. (Ed.). 1980. Invented Reality: How Do We Know What We Believe We Know? (Contributions to Constructivism). New York: W.W. Norton and Company.

Weatherson, B. 2003. From Classical to Intuitionistic Probability. Notre Dame Journal of Formal Logic, 44: 111–123.

Weaver, W. 1967. Science and Imagination. Selected Papers of Warren Weaver. New York / London: Basic Books.

Weaver, W. 1963. Lady Luck. The Theory of Probability. Harmondsworth: Penguin Books.

Weaver, W. 1948. Science and Complexity. American Scientist, 36: 536–544.

Wehinger, G. 2012. Banking in a challenging environment: Business models, ethics and approaches towards risks. OECD Journal: Financial Market Trends, 2: 79–88.

Weiss, G.H. 1994. Aspects and Applications of the Random Walk. Amsterdam: North-Holland.

Weistroffer, C. 2012. Macroprudential Supervision. In Search of an Appropriate Response to Systemic Risk. Deutsche Bank Research. Current Issues. May 2012.

Werndl, C. 2009. What Are the New Implications of Chaos for Unpredictability? British Journal for the Philosophy of Science, 60: 195–220.

Whetten, D.A. 1989. What constitutes a Theoretical Contribution? Academy of Management Review, 14: 490–495.

Wieland, J. 1996. Ökonomische Organisation, Allokation und Status. Tübingen: Mohr Siebeck.

Wiener, N. 1961. Cybernetics, or Control and Communication in the Animal and the Machine. Cambridge, MA: MIT Press.

Wiggins, R.Z., & Metrick, A. 2014. The Lehman Brothers Bankruptcy B: Risk Limits and Stress Tests. Yale Program on Financial Stability Case Study 2014-3B-V1, October 2014.

Williams, M. 2010. Uncontrolled Risk. The Lessons of Lehman Brothers and How Systemic Risk Can Still Bring Down the World Financial System. New York: McGraw Hill.

Willke, H., Becker, E., & Rostásy, C. 2013. Systemic Risk. The Myth of Rational Finance and the Crisis of Democracy. Frankfurt/New York: Campus.

Willett, A.H. 1901/1951. The Economic Theory of Risk and Insurance. Philadelphia: The University of Pennsylvania Press.

Wilson, D. 2001. Operational Risk. In. L. Borodovsky, & M. Lore (Eds.). The Professional's Handbook of Financial Risk Management. Oxford: Butterworth-Heinemann: 377–413.

Wright, G., & Cairns, G. 2011. Scenario Thinking – Practical Approaches to the Future. New York: Palgrave Macmillan.

Wynne, B. 1992. Risk and Social Learning: Reification to Engagement. In. S. Krimsky, & D. Golding (Eds.). Social Theories of Risk. Westport, CT: Praeger: 275–297.

Yamai, Y., & & Yoshiba, T. 2002. On the validity of value-at-risk: comparative analyses with Expected Shortfall. Discussion paper. Monetary and Economic Studies, Bank of Japan's Institute for Monetary and Economic Studies, January 2002: 57–86.

Zadeh, L.A., & Desoer, C.A. 1979. Linear System Theory. The State Space Approach. Huntington, NY: Robert E. Krieger Publishing.

Zadeh, L.A. 1978. Fuzzy Sets as a Basis for a Theory of Possibility. Fuzzy Sets and Systems, 1: 3–28.

Zadeh, L.A. 1973. A system-theoretic view of behaviour modification. In. H. Wheeler (Ed.). Beyond the Punitive Society. San Francisco: Freeman: 160–169.

Zadeh, L.A. 1969a. Towards a Theory of Fuzzy Systems. Electronic Research Laboratory, University of California, Berkeley. 94720 Report No. ERL-69-2.

Zadeh, L.A. 1969b. Biological Application of the Theory of Fuzzy Sets and Systems. In. L.D. Proctor (Ed.). The Proceedings of an International Symposium on Biocybernetics of the Central Nervous System. London: Little, Brown and Comp: 199–206.

Zadeh, L.A. 1962. From Circuit Theory to System Theory. Proceedings of the IRE, 50: 856– 865.

Zaleznik, A. 2004. Managers and Leaders: Are They Different? Harvard Business Review, January. Available at: https://hbr.org/2004/01/managers-and-leaders-are-they-different (30/12/15).

Zeeman, E.C. (Ed.). 1977. Catastrophe Theory. London: Addison-Wesley.

Zeigler, B.P., Praehofer, H., & Kim, T.G. 2000. Theory of Modeling and Simulation. San Diego, CA: Academic Press.

Zikmund, W.G., Babin, B.J., & Carr, J.C. 2013. Business research methods. Australia: South Western Cengage Learning.

Zimmermann, J. 2014. Foreign/native decision-makers and strategic change: How subjective perceptions cause an organizational liability. Working paper. Presented at: Annual Meeting of the Strategic Management Society, Madrid.

Appendices

To access the book's appendix, please visit www.springer.com and search for the author's name.

MIX
Papier aus verantwortungsvollen Quellen
Paper from responsible sources
FSC® C105338

If you have any concerns about our products,
you can contact us on
ProductSafety@springernature.com

In case Publisher is established outside the EU,
the EU authorized representative is:
Springer Nature Customer Service Center GmbH
Europaplatz 3, 69115 Heidelberg, Germany

Printed by Libri Plureos GmbH
in Hamburg, Germany